CONTENTS

Dave Roberts

CORIOLIS GROUP BOOKS

Publisher	*Keith Weiskamp*
Copy Editor	*Jenni Aloi*
Technical Reviewer	*Phil Kunz*
Proofreader	*Diane Green Cook*
Interior Design	*Bradley Grannis*
Layout Production	*Bradley Grannis*
Technical Illustrations	*Gary Smith*
Publicist	*Shannon Bounds*
Indexer	*Diane Green Cook*

Distributed to the book trade by IDG Books Worldwide, Inc.

Library of Congress Cataloging-in-Publication Data

Roberts, Dave
    PC Game Programming Explorer / Dave Roberts
        p. cm.
    Includes Index
    ISBN 1-883577-07-1 : $34.95

Printed in the United States of America

10 9 8 7 6 5 4 3 2 1

To my wife, Dawn.

ACKNOWLEDGEMENTS

I'd like to acknowledge the help of the following people in making this book happen: my wife Dawn who gave me support and encouragement, Keith Weiskamp who knew a good thing when he saw it, my uncle Fred Burns who interested me in animation at a young age and gave me a lot of background information for the animation chapter, Michael Abrash who documented Mode X and wrote a great series of articles about it, Themie Gouthas who wrote the XLIB Mode X library and released the source code for it, the great folks at The Coriolis Group who put together a super book, and finally my mom and dad who kept telling me that writing was a good thing to know, even if I wanted to be an engineer.

Hooking the System Timer Interrupt   313

Cleaning Up   315

SYNCHRONIZING A TIMER TO VERTICAL RETRACE 318

eXplorer PROJECT   *Demonstration Program*   *322*

Chapter 11   Creating Alien Alley   329

THE MAIN GAME LOOP 331

INTRO SCREENS AND TITLE 334

THE ANIMATION LOOP 336

SETTING UP MODE X 340

Eliminating the Need for Clipping   341
The Status Display   342

GETTING INPUT 345

MOVING SPRITES 347

COLLISION DETECTION 352

ERASING AND DRAWING 355

PREFACE

I was about nine years old when I saw my first video game. I was walking through the San Francisco International airport with my parents, heading to a gate to pick up some relatives. I remember being fascinated with the movement of the objects on the screen—a ball bouncing off two movable paddles.

I became lost in this simple, primitive, electronic world. It was amazing! It was like air-hockey, but without an air table or a puck. "How'd they do that?" I wondered. Suddenly, I wanted to play! I ran to my father to get a quarter, but he said that there wasn't time. The flight was arriving soon and we still had to get to the gate.

The game, of course, was Pong.

Many others followed Pong—Space Invaders, Asteroids, Battlezone. And each time, I'd wonder, "How'd they do that?" The action, the sounds—simply incredible.

When I was 14, my family purchased an Apple][+ computer. I finally had the tools necessary to start building my own games. My friends and I went right to work. Pong was easy to duplicate. We soon had moving paddles and balls bouncing around the screen. We then graduated to more lofty goals, much more lofty than the meager after-school time allotment we had available, and certainly more lofty than the 64 KB of RAM the old Apple][had available. We never did finish much but we sure had a great time experimenting.

THE AUDIENCE FOR THIS BOOK

This book is for those of you out there who ask, "How'd they do that?" whenever you see a new video game. It's for those who are interested in writing their own games for fun and possibly for profit. It's for anybody who likes to program but doesn't like to work on anything practical like databases or network device drivers.

Simply, it's for those of you who have imagination, like to create your own worlds, and want to know how to go about doing it.

A GLANCE INSIDE

This book is about programming fast-action video games. It introduces some of the techniques that professional programmers use to produce quality games. Along the way, it will present a complete game program, *Alien Alley*. The program is presented in a modular form and many of the individual modules can be reused easily in your own game programs.

Although the game focuses on fast-action games, many of the techniques can also be applied to strategy games. For instance, the chapters on the VGA, color, and sound are applicable to most any sort of game.

New game programming techniques are invented continuously by clever programmers seeking to do the impossible. Not only are these new techniques numerous, but they are often guarded as proprietary secrets. The ability to do the impossible is certainly an advantage in the market place, and although these techniques are eventually discovered, they do not start life as well documented tutorials with example code.

The techniques presented here are the basics. After learning them you will be well equipped to explore and discover for yourself the other, more complicated tricks.

Although this text concentrates on the IBM PC compatible platform, many of the general techniques presented here are applicable to other platforms as well. For example, although the code to perform "dirty rectangle" animation is written for a VGA card, the concept of dirty rectangle animation translates to any other platform a reader may be using.

Dave Roberts
Fremont, CA

LET THE GAMES BEGIN

THE GREAT ADVENTURE

CHAPTER 1

To get into the fast lane of game programming, all you need is the right gaming knowledge and the desire to practice and experiment.

So you're interested in game programming, are you? Well, you've come to the right place. In this book we'll examine many of the techniques that professional gamers use to produce the latest products on the shelf today, and we'll turn you into a game programmer before you know it.

Game development is the most challenging and fun form of programming. There are many programmers who started programming because they saw a game in an arcade or on a computer somewhere and they said, "Hey, I can do that." It's an irresistible force that just seems to draw in programmers. Perhaps it's the ability to create your own worlds and have people derive some pleasure in playing with something you brought to life. Perhaps it's the blend of sight and sound, that fusion of graphic art, musical composition, and raw programming. Who knows? Whatever it is, it's fun and certainly rewarding if it's done right.

The problem with game programming is that it often seems so complicated. You can learn to pro-

THE STRUCTURE OF A GAME PROGRAM

Before diving into the details of game programming, let's take a look from 30,000 feet in the air. This will help us identify those things that we'll have to learn before we can put together a full game and will allow us to divide the task into appropriate segments.

All computer programs perform essentially the same tasks—they receive input, process it, and create output. Of course, the details differ wildly whether the program is a word processor, a spreadsheet, a database, or a game. In a game program, receiving input amounts to reading the state of a few input devices like a keyboard or joystick. Processing this input involves moving all the onscreen objects around, computing collisions between them, and deciding whether objects like missiles should be fired or the player's ship destroyed. Finally, creating output equates to drawing all the resulting action on the screen so that the player can react further. If you repeat this cycle hundreds of thousands of times, very quickly, you have a game program.

In C, the code to process input might look something like this:

```
PlayerAlive = TRUE;
PlayerWon = FALSE;
while (PlayerAlive && !PlayerWon) {
    GetUserInput();
    MoveObjects();
    CheckCollisions();
    DrawAnimationFrame();
    SpeedCheck();
}
```

Here, the loop, and hence the game, will continue to run as long as the player is still alive and has not won the game. Each pass through the loop represents one frame of animation. On each pass, the user's input is fetched from one or more input devices. Next, the new positions of all the objects on the screen are calculated, taking the user's input into account. With all the objects moved, collisions between objects are checked. If things do collide, certain actions are taken. For instance, a collision between the player object and something else might start a sequence of animation that shows an explosion where the ship was located, as well as initiate an explosion sound. Given the current positions of objects, and whether they are colliding, the next task is to draw the next frame of animation. Finally, a speed check is made to ensure that the game is not running too fast to be playable. If it is, a delay is added to slow the game down to the standard running speed.

Of course, it's not quite as simple as it appears here. There is a lot of code behind such functions as **DrawAnimationFrame**. Our task throughout the remaining chapters is to fill in the details of such functions as **DrawAnimationFrame**. We'll learn how each of the functions in our example can be implemented and what factors are important in deciding among several different implementation choices.

ASSUMED KNOWLEDGE

Some authors seem to assume readers know almost nothing about anything when they start reading. For instance, a reference book on VGA programming that I own includes two sections about programming in C and assembly language! Imagine walking into a college-level physics class and having the teacher start with long division.

Game programming is just like physics. It's one of those application areas where a whole bunch of disciplines come together at once. And just like a physics text, you won't find this book teaching you all the prerequisites. Rather, this book expects that you've spent a bit of time understanding the basic machine you'll be programming: the IBM PC.

Fast-action video games virtually mandate that the programmer directly access the hardware of the machine. You should understand what interrupts are, the basic architecture of the 80x86 family of processors, and the basic architecture of the IBM PC.

If you don't understand all the prerequisites right now, don't be worried. There are plenty of supplementary reading recommendations at the end of this book. Feel free to grab one of the reference books and read it while you also read this one. In doing this, you'll gain an understanding of the applications that the other material can be used for. Sometimes it's easier and more fun to learn both subjects at one time.

EXAMPLE CODE

The example code in this book is written in C and a little bit of assembly language. Where assembly language is used, however, I've included the equivalent C code in comments. If you have a working knowledge of C, you'll be able to understand the examples. The language choices should not be taken as a recommendation to use any particular language. Although most action games will require *some* routines to be written in assembly language for speed, most game code can be written in a number of high-level languages. I simply used C. Pascal is an equally valid choice.

C++ was not used in the book because it is harder to read than C, and those not familiar with it would have a harder time picking up the basic concepts because of this. Standard, well-written ANSI C has the virtue of being fairly easy to read, even by those who do not program with it regularly.

The example code is compatible with Borland C++ 3.1 and 4.0. In truth, this only reflects testing. The code may work equally well on a number of other compilers, but it has only been tested with Borland's products. In the event that the code is not strictly compatible with your development tools, don't worry; the code is straightforward enough to be easily ported to whatever development environment you happen to have (e.g., Microsoft's toolset). In most cases, the only problems you might have would be with the names of standard macros or DOS library routines. These will be identified immediately during compiling and linking, and a simple search and replace should correct the problem.

Like most source code included in books, the code here probably includes some unintended bugs. Although I have tested as much as time allows, I cannot hope to have gotten rid of them all. I trust that you will excuse any that you find and that they will not impair your understanding of the techniques this book describes.

Asserting Myself

Many of the functions present in the source code contain runtime assertion checking using the ANSI C standard assertion mechanism. If you aren't familiar with assertion checking, you should be. Assertions are one of the best bug-elimination tools available.

Assertions provide a mechanism to check assumptions about the state of a program at runtime. The **assert** function call is really a C preprocessor macro. Normally, the macro expands to a conditional expression that will halt the program during runtime if the argument passed to the **assert** function is logically false. The assertion macro displays the filename and line number of the assertion statement that failed, which precisely identifies which function had the problem. If the **_NDEBUG** symbol is defined when a module is compiled, the macro expands to a null statement, eliminating all traces of itself from the program. This allows for many runtime checks to be included in debugging versions of the code, while not burdening the final release with overhead when it is not needed.

Even though asserts are usually removed from the final version of a program using the **_NDEBUG** compile switch, they remain in the source code and serve to document assumptions made throughout the code. This helps programmers understand the range limits of a function's input parameters or some quirky assumptions, even if another programmer wrote the original source code many years ago.

Suffice to say that it's a very useful debugging technique and an all-around good habit to get into.

Using GAMEDEFS.H

Most of the example code uses a header file named GAMEDEFS.H. This is a general header file that defines some useful types and constants. GAMEDEFS.H is shown in Listing 1.1.

Listing 1.1   GAMEDEFS.H

```
/* File: GAMEDEFS.H
** Description:
**     Contains general type defs.
*/

#ifndef _GAMEDEFS_H

typedef char            INT8;
typedef unsigned char   UINT8;
typedef int             INT16;
typedef unsigned int    UINT16;
typedef long            INT32;
typedef unsigned long   UINT32;

typedef unsigned int    WORD;
typedef unsigned long   LONG;

typedef int             BOOL;

#define TRUE (1)
#define FALSE (0)

#define DIM(x) (sizeof(x)/sizeof(x[0]))

#define LOWBYTE(x) ((x) & 0xFF)
#define HIGHBYTE(x) (((x) >> 8) & 0xFF)

/* just define these in terms of the Borland library macros */
#define MIN(a,b) min(a,b)
#define MAX(a,b) max(a,b)
```

```
/* interrupt acknowledgement stuff */
#define PIC              (0x20)
#define NONSPECIFIC_EOI  (0x20)

typedef struct {
    int Top;
    int Left;
    int Bottom;
    int Right;
} RECT;

#define _GAMEDEFS_H

#endif
```

OTHER MATERIALS

Writing a state-of-the-art fast-action game can require many tools. Some of the things that you may want to acquire include:

- *A code profiler.* If you want your code to go as fast as it can, a profiler will help determine where your program spends its time. This allows you to concentrate your optimizing effort on the functions that are time wasters, not those that aren't. Surprisingly, programmers have a very poor record of identifying which functions in their programs are the most in need of optimization; they frequently optimize the wrong ones. Some of the higher-end programming packages ship with profilers included. To help you optimize your code, you might want to get a copy of Michael Abrash's *Zen of Code Optimization.*

- *A book about IBM PC compatible hardware.* This will be an invaluable reference for programming the various hardware components of a PC.

- *A book of PC interrupts.* Game programmers need to deal with the IBM hardware at the lowest level. Software interrupts are the method used to communicate between applications programs, DOS, and the BIOS. A book documenting all the various PC interrupts can be your map through this web of interactions.

- *A book about 3-D graphics.* If you want to write the next jet-fighter flight simulation, you need to know about 3-D graphics. This book does not cover any of the techniques used in 3-D graphics, so I would recommend that you get one of the many books available on the subject.

With that, off we go . . .

MASTERING THE KEYBOARD

Here's your chance to learn how to program the keyboard for fast game control. You'll even see how to set up the keyboard as if it were a set of buttons.

If you step into an arcade center, you'll find a room full of games with buttons, joysticks, track balls, steering wheels, and a host of other gizmos. Over the years, creative game developers have tried just about everything under the sun to help game players interact with their games. When it comes to your PC, on the other hand, the keyboard is the king of input devices. And if you want to write games that can be played on most PCs, you'll need to wire in the keyboard to your games.

In this chapter we'll take you inside the keyboard and show you how to work with scan codes, keyboard ports, and we'll even explore a handy keyboard interrupt for reading multiple keys pressed at the same time. If you have never programmed the keyboard before, you'll really benefit from the keyboard handling routines that we'll present.

If you've written any C or C++ programs at all, you've probably used a few of the standard library functions to get input from the keyboard and display data on the screen. Let's look at an example. This simple program uses the **getch** and

putch functions to do our input and output work:

```
/*
** File: DOSIO.C
**
** Description: reads characters from the keyboard and echoes
**    them to the screen via DOS.
*/
#include <conio.h>

int main(void)
{
   int c;

   directvideo = 0;    /* tells putch() to use BIOS instead of */
                       /* direct video writes */
   do {
     c = getch();      /* get character from DOS */
     putch(c);         /* print it using BIOS */
     if (c == 13)      /* if CR, add LF to move down a line */
        putch(10);
   } while (c != 3);   /* end if it's Ctrl+C */
   return 0;
}
```

This code demonstrates the simplest way to get input from your keyboard. It reads characters typed at the keyboard and echoes them back to the screen. Nothing tricky here!

What is important to know is what's going on behind the scenes. When your program uses the **getch** function, a low-level DOS I/O function gets called by **getch** to read a character from the keyboard. (In this case, the DOS function is known as DOS INT 21h, function 01h.) The **putch** function is used to print a character to the screen and corresponds to the DOS INT 21h, function 02h. Actually, **putch** has two modes of operation. One mode uses the PC BIOS to write to the screen and the other uses direct video adapter accesses. Using direct accesses is faster but is not compatible with video adapters that aren't IBM compatible. Setting the Borland C++ global variable **directvideo** to zero forces **putch** to use the BIOS rather than direct video access.

So what's wrong with this program? Technically nothing. Although these DOS routines are fine stuff for getting and displaying simple input, they are limited because they are designed to access a single keystroke at a time. When you press a key, DOS serializes the typed character into an *input stream*. (Some folks like to call this the *keyboard buffer*.) By calling DOS repeatedly with a function like **getch**, you can retrieve the sequence of characters the user typed. This approach works well for programs like word processors or spreadsheets where the typed characters correspond to lines of text. In an action game, however, you need much more power to handle those rapid-fire adventure scenes that you're eager to write—and users are eager to play!

 In this chapter we'll develop a set of useful "button-style" **OVERVIEW** keyboard processing functions using the files KEYBOARD.H and KEYBOARD.C. Then, we'll show you how to use these keyboard processing routines in a fun explorer project named KBDEMO.C.

THE SECRET IS BUTTONS

Most action games you write will need to allow the user to press several keys at the same time to perform an action. For example, the player of your game may need to both shoot a gun and turn left at the same time. Your game may also allow multiple players to play at the same time, using the same keyboard. As we've mentioned, the old PC character stream is not appropriate for getting input from multiple keys or both players at the same time. So what now?

We'll use a clever workaround to solve this dilemma. We'll treat the keyboard as if it were a set of buttons. Viewing the keyboard as a set of buttons allows us to test for multiple keys being held down simultaneously.

So how do we make the keyboard look like a set of buttons? The first step is understanding how keystrokes are generated by the internal hardware and passed to "normal" programs through the BIOS and DOS.

INTRODUCING THE KEYBOARD CONTROLLER

Your PC includes a keyboard controller, an Intel 8042 in the original PC/AT. The keyboard controller communicates with the keyboard over a serial line. If you examine Figure 2.1, you'll see that when a key is pressed, the keyboard sends a code to the keyboard controller. The program in the 8042 translates the code given by the keyboard into a system *scan code* that is available to the system. The keyboard controller interrupts the processor whenever a keyboard event occurs, generating INT 9. The *software interrupt service routine* (ISR), usually in the BIOS, reads the code from the keyboard controller to find out what happened.

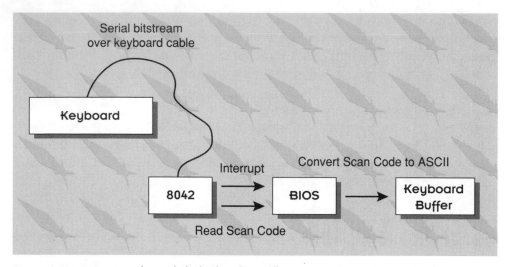

Figure 2.1 *Processing a key with the keyboard controller.*

Using Scan Codes

As I mentioned a moment ago, the code that the BIOS reads from the keyboard controller is called a *scan code*. A scan code is an 8-bit number that indicates which key on the keyboard was involved with the keyboard event. As Figure 2.2 shows, the high bit of the scan code is set to 1 if the event corresponds to a key release. It is reset to 0 if the key was pressed instead of released. The lower seven bits contain the actual scan code of the key. For example, the scan code 1Eh indicates that the "A" key was pressed. The scan code B3h indicates that the period key (".") was released.

Note that the scan code does not correspond to an ASCII value. A scan code is turned into an ASCII character by the BIOS keyboard ISR. A single scan code, in fact, can correspond to multiple characters in the ASCII character set. For instance, the scan code 20h indicates that the "D" key was pressed. This same

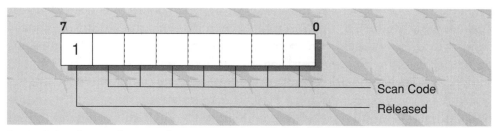

Figure 2.2 *Format of a scan code.*

scan code will be generated whenever the user presses the "d" key. So how are the ASCII characters "D", "d", and Cul+D generated? After all, you need to hit the "D" key to generate each of these. The answer is that it all depends which other keys are being held down at the time. Keys such as Shift, Ctrl, and Alt also have scan codes. Whenever each of these modifier keys is pressed, the BIOS sets flags in memory. When a subsequent key is pressed, the BIOS uses the current state of the modifier keys to map the scan code generated by the keyboard controller to the appropriate ASCII value. That's all there is to it!

Typically, whenever a keystroke is generated and handled by the BIOS, the ASCII value for the key is stored in a small queue. A call to a BIOS or DOS routine to get the next keystroke returns the first character in the queue.

Understanding Keyboard Ports

To communicate with the keyboard controller we use two I/O ports: 60h and 64h. Port 60h is the input and output buffer port. This port inputs scan codes from the keyboard controller and writes data to the 8042 and the keyboard itself. Port 64h is the status and command register. When read, port 64h returns the status of the 8042 and the keyboard interface. When written to, this port operates as a command port. The value written tells the 8042 to perform tasks such as a self-test or to send the next data byte written to port 60h to the keyboard. Table 2.1 summarizes the ports of the 8042.

Reading a scan code from the keyboard is as simple as reading port 60h. The act of reading the port automatically clears the keyboard event and allows the 8042 to send another event. Each event is signaled by the keyboard controller by interrupting the processor on IRQ 1, corresponding to INT 9.

Unless you are doing something fairly complex with the keyboard controller, you typically won't have to manipulate port 64h. We won't be using it for anything in our game programming.

Table 2.1   *8042 Keyboard Controller Port Functions*

Name	Port	Function
Output Buffer	60h	Returns scan codes from keyboard
Input Buffer	60h	Data to 8042
Command Register	64h	Commands to 8042
Status Register	64h	Status of 8042

THE KEYBOARD BUTTON PROJECT

Now that we know how the keyboard works, how do we set it up so that it can be controlled like a set of buttons?

The answer is to intercept the interrupt generated by the keyboard controller. This trick will allow us to directly access the scan codes of the keys that the user has pressed. We'll also be able to store the state of the keyboard so that it can later be tested by a program. The module KEYBOARD.C demonstrates how this is accomplished.

Button-Style Keyboarding

For our first project, we'll create a set of useful "button-style" keyboard processing functions. The files you'll need for this project include KEYBOARD.H and KEYBOARD.C. You can get these files from the companion disk or you can type them.

Starting with KEYBOARD.H

KEYBOARD.H, shown in Listing 2.2, is the include file we need to implement the keyboard routines. It declares the functions that are defined in the main module, KEYBOARD.C. It also defines a bunch of symbolic names for the scan codes of various keys. These symbolic names are easier to work with than cryptic scan code numbers. Here is the complete KEYBOARD.H file:

Listing 2.1   KEYBOARD.H

```
/* File: KEYBOARD.H
** Description:
**    Header file for KEYBOARD.C.  Contains symbolic name
**    definitions for each of the keyboard scancodes and
**    declares each of the public functions in KEYBOARD.C.
*/
#ifndef _KEYBOARD_H

void SetButtonKeysMode(void);
void SetNormalKeysMode(void);
int GetKeyState(int scanCode);
int GetTrueKeyState(int scanCode);

#define KEY_A          (0x1E)
#define KEY_B          (0x30)
#define KEY_C          (0x2E)
#define KEY_D          (0x20)
```

```
#define KEY_E          (0x12)
#define KEY_F          (0x21)
#define KEY_G          (0x22)
#define KEY_H          (0x23)
#define KEY_I          (0x17)
#define KEY_J          (0x24)
#define KEY_K          (0x25)
#define KEY_L          (0x26)
#define KEY_M          (0x32)
#define KEY_N          (0x31)
#define KEY_O          (0x18)
#define KEY_P          (0x19)
#define KEY_Q          (0x10)
#define KEY_R          (0x13)
#define KEY_S          (0x1F)
#define KEY_T          (0x14)
#define KEY_U          (0x16)
#define KEY_V          (0x2F)
#define KEY_W          (0x11)
#define KEY_X          (0x2D)
#define KEY_Y          (0x15)
#define KEY_Z          (0x2C)
#define KEY_1          (0x02)
#define KEY_2          (0x03)
#define KEY_3          (0x04)
#define KEY_4          (0x05)
#define KEY_5          (0x06)
#define KEY_6          (0x07)
#define KEY_7          (0x08)
#define KEY_8          (0x09)
#define KEY_9          (0x0A)
#define KEY_0          (0x0B)
#define KEY_DASH       (0x0C)        /* -_ */
#define KEY_EQUAL      (0x0D)        /* =+ */
#define KEY_LBRACKET   (0x1A)        /* [{ */
#define KEY_RBRACKET   (0x1B)        /* ]} */
#define KEY_SEMICOLON  (0x27)        /* ;: */
#define KEY_RQUOTE     (0x28)        /* '" */
#define KEY_LQUOTE     (0x29)        /* '~ */
#define KEY_PERIOD     (0x33)        /* .> */
#define KEY_COMMA      (0x34)        /* ,< */
#define KEY_SLASH      (0x35)        /* /? */
#define KEY_BACKSLASH  (0x2B)        /* \| */
#define KEY_F1         (0x3B)
#define KEY_F2         (0x3C)
#define KEY_F3         (0x3D)
#define KEY_F4         (0x3E)
#define KEY_F5         (0x3F)
#define KEY_F6         (0x40)
#define KEY_F7         (0x41)
#define KEY_F8         (0x42)
#define KEY_F9         (0x43)
#define KEY_F10        (0x44)
```

```
#define KEY_ESC          (0x01)
#define KEY_BACKSPACE    (0x0E)
#define KEY_TAB          (0x0F)
#define KEY_ENTER        (0x1C)
#define KEY_CONTROL      (0x1D)
#define KEY_LSHIFT       (0x2A)
#define KEY_RSHIFT       (0x36)
#define KEY_PRTSC        (0x37)
#define KEY_ALT          (0x38)
#define KEY_SPACE        (0x39)
#define KEY_CAPSLOCK     (0x3A)
#define KEY_NUMLOCK      (0x45)
#define KEY_SCROLLLOCK   (0x46)
#define KEY_HOME         (0x47)
#define KEY_UP           (0x48)
#define KEY_PGUP         (0x49)
#define KEY_MINUS        (0x4A)
#define KEY_LEFT         (0x4B)
#define KEY_CENTER       (0x4C)
#define KEY_RIGHT        (0x4D)
#define KEY_PLUS         (0x4E)
#define KEY_END          (0x4F)
#define KEY_DOWN         (0x50)
#define KEY_PGDOWN       (0x51)
#define KEY_INS          (0x52)
#define KEY_DEL          (0x53)

#define _KEYBOARD_H
#endif
```

The Main Keyboard Routines

We're now ready to explore the code that contains the main keyboard handling routines. In a nutshell, the file KEYBOARD.C provides a new keyboard ISR as well as routines for installing and removing it. KEYBOARD.C also provides functions for reading the state of the keyboard. Here is the complete file:

Listing 2.2   KEYBOARD.C

```
/* File: KEYBOARD.C
** Description:
**    Defines routines for reading the state of the keyboard as
**    a set of buttons.
** Copyright:
**    Copyright 1994, David G. Roberts
*/

/* header files */
#include <assert.h>
#include <dos.h>
#include "gamedefs.h"
#include "keyboard.h"
```

```
/* constants */
#define MAX_SCANCODES       (128)
#define NEW_HANDLER         (1)
#define OLD_HANDLER         (0)
#define KEYBOARD_INPUT      (0x60)
#define KEYBOARD_XT_CLEAR   (0x61)

/* module variables */
static void far interrupt (*OldInt9Handler)();  /* old keybd int handler */
static int       KeyboardStateFlag = OLD_HANDLER;/* current keybd handler */
static UINT8     KeyStateArray[MAX_SCANCODES];   /* current key state */
static UINT8     WasPressedArray[MAX_SCANCODES]; /* flags set if key hit */

/*
    Function: KeyIntHandler
    Description:
        Replacement for the BIOS Int 9 handler.  Detects when a
        key is pressed and released.  Updates KeyStateArray to
        reflect the state of each key.  Sets KeyStateArray to 1 if key
        is currently being held down, 0 if released.  When a key is
        released, WasPressedArray is set to 1.  This allows a program to
        detect that a key was pressed and then released between
        checks of the array.  WasPressedArray is cleared by the program
        reading the state of a key, not by this routine.  KeyStateArray
        and WasPressedArray are indexed by the keyboard scan code returned
        from the keyboard controller.
*/
static void far interrupt KeyIntHandler(void)
{
    UINT8 ScanCode;
    UINT8 Temp;

    /* read scan code */
    ScanCode = inportb(KEYBOARD_INPUT);

    /* clear keyboard controller on XT machines */
    Temp = inportb(KEYBOARD_XT_CLEAR);
    outportb(KEYBOARD_XT_CLEAR, Temp | 0x80);
    outportb(KEYBOARD_XT_CLEAR, Temp & 0x7F);

    if (ScanCode & 0x80) {
        /* key up */
        ScanCode &= 0x7F;
        KeyStateArray[ScanCode] = 0;
    }
    else {
        /* key down */
        KeyStateArray[ScanCode] = 1;
        WasPressedArray[ScanCode] = 1;
    }

    outportb(PIC, NONSPECIFIC EOI);
}
```

```
/*
    Function: SetButtonKeysMode
    Description:
        Sets up the keyboard as a set of buttons.  To do this,
        SetButtonKeysMode() initializes the key state and was-pressed
        arrays and installs the INT 9 handler, KeyIntHandler().
*/
void SetButtonKeysMode(void)
{
    int i;

    /* If this is not true, the calls to SetButtonKeysMode() and */
    /* SetNormalKeysMode() have not been balanced and trouble */
    /* could result when you quit the program and try to */
    /* restore the original INT 9 handler. */
    assert(KeyboardStateFlag == OLD_HANDLER);

    /* initialize state arrays */
    for (i = 0; i < 128; i++) {
        KeyStateArray[i] = WasPressedArray[i] = 0;
    }

    /* install new handler */
    OldInt9Handler = getvect(9);
    setvect(9, KeyIntHandler);

    /* mark new handler as being installed */
    KeyboardStateFlag = NEW_HANDLER;
}

/*
    Function: SetNormalKeysMode
    Description:
        NormalKeys() sets the INT 9 handler back to the routine
        stored in OldInt9Handler.  This routine should only be called
        after SetButtonKeysMode() has been called.  If this routine is
        called before SetButtonKeysMode() has been called at least once,
        the INT 9 vector will be set to garbage.
*/
void SetNormalKeysMode(void)
{
    /* If this is not true, there could be big problems at */
    /* program termination.   */
    assert(KeyboardStateFlag == NEW_HANDLER);

    /* reinstall original handler */
    setvect(9, OldInt9Handler);

    /* indicate that the old handler is current */
    KeyboardStateFlag = OLD_HANDLER;
}
```

```
/*
    Function: GetKeyState
    Description:
        Returns 1 if the key is currently down or was pressed
        since this function was last called for the key,
        0 otherwise.  The function continues to return 1 as
        long as the key is held down.  This function should only
        be called while in SetButtonKeysMode() mode.
*/
int GetKeyState(int ScanCode)
{
    int result;

    /* scan codes should only be 0-127 */
    assert(ScanCode < 128);
    assert(KeyboardStateFlag == NEW_HANDLER);

    result = KeyStateArray[ScanCode] | WasPressedArray[ScanCode];
    WasPressedArray[ScanCode] = 0;
    return result;
}

/*
    Function: GetTrueKeyState
    Description:
        Returns 1 if the key is currently down.  The function
        continues to return 1 as long as the key is held down.
        This function differs from GetKeyState() in that it does
        not check if the key has been pressed and then released
        before this function was called.  Note that GetKeyState()
        will still indicate if this has happened, even if this
        function is called first.  This function should only
        be called while in SetButtonKeysMode() mode.
*/
int GetTrueKeyState(int ScanCode)
{
    int result;

    /* scan codes should only be 0-127 */
    assert(ScanCode < 128);
    assert(KeyboardStateFlag == NEW_HANDLER);

    result = KeyStateArray[ScanCode];
    return result;
}
```

The functions defined in this file are listed in Table 2.2. Notice that two of the functions are used for setting the state of the keyboard handling routines, and two are used for reading the state of keys. The fifth function is the new keyboard ISR that allows us to examine keyboard scan codes.

Table 2.2 *KEYBOARD.C Function Descriptions*

Function	Description
KeyIntHandler	The new keyboard ISR
SetButtonKeysMode	Installs the new keyboard ISR and initializes the key state array
SetNormalKeysMode	Removes the new keyboard ISR and returns to standard keyboard processing
GetKeyState	Returns the state of a given key, either pressed or released, when in "button keys mode;" this function will indicate that a key is pressed—even if it is currently released—if the key has been pressed since this function was last called for the particular key
GetTrueKeyState	Same as GetKeyState, but the indication reflects the exact state of the key at the time the routine is called

The Secret Ingredient—A New Keyboard Interrupt Service Routine

The key to the KEYBOARD.C module is the routine **KeyIntHandler**. This routine replaces the normal BIOS keyboard ISR and allows our programs to examine the keyboard scan codes as they are generated.

As you can see, the new ISR is actually very simple. It starts by saving some registers that it will use and loading the segment containing the **KeyStateArray** and **WasPressedArray** arrays into register DS. To read the scan code from the keyboard controller, the ISR inputs a byte from port 60h. The ISR then notifies the keyboard controller that it has received the scan code by reading a byte from port 61h, setting the high-order bit of the data value just read, writing the resulting value back to port 61h, resetting the value's high-order bit, and finally writing the value back to port 61h, again.

"Wait a minute!" you are probably thinking. "What's this port 61h stuff? You didn't tell us anything about this mysterious port 61h."

Well, you're right. We slipped that one in there. If you'll remember, we said that getting a scan code was as simple as reading port 60h and that the keyboard controller would clear itself. In fact, this is the case with PC/AT compatible machines. With older XT machines, the program actually has to signal the keyboard controller that it has read the scan code by fiddling with port 61h. The previous piece of code will work on both AT and XT machines. On an AT machine, the manipulation of port 61h is simply ignored. If you know that your program will only be running on AT compatible machines, you can safely omit the port 61h gyrations. But it is better to be safe than sorry.

After reading the scan code, the ISR gives a non-specific end of interrupt (EOI) command to the programmable interrupt controller (PIC). This command tells the PIC that the highest priority interrupt has been serviced and clears the interrupt.

When the ISR finishes fiddling with the hardware, it interprets the scan code. The ISR first checks to see if the high-order bit of the scan code is set or reset. If it's set, the ISR knows that the key has just been released; otherwise, the key has been pressed. The ISR reflects the state of the key in **KeyStateArray**.

KeyStateArray is just a set of flags for each of the keys on the keyboard. If the byte at the scan code index is 01h, the key is currently down. If the byte is 00h, the key is up. Our program will be able to test the state of any key by looking at the **KeyStateArray** flag corresponding to the scan code it is interested in. Note that 128 values are defined for the array but only 101 keys are usually present on an extended keyboard. The extra bytes are just for safety. Because the keyboard controller can potentially generate scan codes with values from 0 to 127, if somebody defines another keyboard with extra keys on it, we're safe.

In addition to reflecting the current state of the key in the **KeyStateArray**, the ISR also sets a flag corresponding to the scan code in **WasPressedArray**. **WasPressedArray** is used to make sure that a program sees a key press if the key is quickly released. Since the ISR no longer queues keystrokes, a program could potentially lose a key press if it did not examine **KeyStateArray** while the key was down. A set value of **WasPressedArray** and a reset value of **KeyStateArray** corresponding to a scan code indicates that a key is not presently pressed but was pressed since the last time the program checked the array.

Finally, the ISR returns. Note that the routine is a true interrupt service routine and must end with an IRET instruction rather than a typical RET. If you simply use a RET, the stack won't be cleaned up correctly and your program will eventually crash.

Setting the Keyboard Mode

SetButtonKeysMode and **SetNormalKeysMode** are used to install and remove the keyboard interrupt handler. **SetButtonKeysMode** initializes the two key state arrays and installs the INT 9 handler. **SetNormalKeysMode** just removes the handler. The variable **KeyboardStateFlag** is used to keep track of the keyboard state and is checked by the assertion statement. Problems will result if **SetButtonKeysMode** is called when the keyboard is already in this mode. In this case, the old keyboard ISR address that is saved by the first call to **SetButtonKeysMode** will be overwritten with the address of our new ISR when the routine is called a second time. Although two consecutive calls to

SetNormalKeysMode won't cause problems, this event is checked for and indicates a potential bug in the program.

A program can use these two routines to control the way the keyboard is handled in different parts of a program. During most game play, the keyboard will be in the "button" state. However, when the high score entry screen is displayed, "normal" keystrokes should be in effect so that the user can enter his or her name.

Testing Key States

GetKeyState and **GetTrueKeyState** are called by a program to determine whether a given key is pressed or released. **GetKeyState** returns 1 if the key either is being pressed, or has been pressed since the routine was called last for the given scan code. **GetTrueKeyState** returns 1 only if the key is currently being held down.

GetKeyState ensures that all keypresses are received by the program, even if the user presses and releases the key between calls to **GetKeyState**. This is typically what we want so that user input isn't dropped. In the event that we really want to see the true current state of a key, **GetTrueKeyState** gives us this capability.

USING THE KEYBOARD ROUTINES

Now that we've explored all of the code we need to create our "button-style" keyboard routines, let's put the code to work. Later in the book we'll use this code to create a fun game, but for now our main interest is to show you how to use the functions.

A Button Keyboard Demo

The program KBDEMO.C, shown in Listing 2.3, shows off our new keyboard routines. The program demonstrates multiple keys being held down at once.

Compiling and Linking

You can compile the KBDDEMO program using the Borland C++ 3.1 IDE by typing "bc kbddemo.prj" and then selecting Compile | Make from the menus. If you would rather use the command line compiler, convert the KBDDEMO.PRJ file to a makefile using the PRJ2MAK program supplied with Borland C++ 3.1. Type "prj2mak kbddemo.prj" to create the KBDDEMO.MAK and KBDDEMO.CFG files.

If you are using Borland C++ 4.0, choose Project | Open Project from the IDE menus. Open the KBDDEMO.PRJ file. Borland C++ will convert the version 3.1 .PRJ file to a version 4.0 .IDE file. Compile and link the program by choosing Project | Make All from the IDE menus.

Listing 2.3   KBDDEMO.C

```c
/* File: KBDDEMO.C
** Description:
**   Demo of the keyboard module.
** Copyright:
**   Copyright 1994, David G. Roberts
*/

#include <stdio.h>
#include "keyboard.h"

/* string names for each of the characters in the numbers row */
char *KeyNameArray[] = {
    "",                /* 0x00 - place holder */
    "Esc",             /* 0x01 - place holder */
    "1",               /* 0x02 */
    "2",               /* 0x03 */
    "3",               /* 0x04 */
    "4",               /* 0x05 */
    "5",               /* 0x06 */
    "6",               /* 0x07 */
    "7",               /* 0x08 */
    "8",               /* 0x09 */
    "9",               /* 0x0A */
    "0",               /* 0x0B */
    "-",               /* 0x0C */
    "=",               /* 0x0D */
    "Backspace"        /* 0x0E */
};


int main(void)
{
    int i;

    SetButtonKeysMode();

    while (!GetKeyState(KEY_ESC)) {

        for (i = 2; i <= 0x0E ; i++) {
            if (GetKeyState(i)) {
                printf("%s ", KeyNameArray[i]);
            }
        }
        printf("\n");
    }
```

```
    SetNormalKeysMode();

    return 0;
}
```

This program simply demonstrates that multiple keys can be held down at one time. When you run the program, try holding down more than one of the number keys along the top of the keyboard. The program sits in a tight loop and prints the name of each key that is currently pressed. It exits when it detects Esc being pressed.

The **KeyNameArray** maps scan codes to a key name string. The scan code number is used to index the array and retrieve the appropriate name. Scan code names must be given in order, with no blank positions.

The program as printed only checks the number keys, the dash key ("-"), the equals key ("="), and the Backspace key. This limitation exists purely to save space. As an exercise, you can use the KEYBOARD.H file to add more scan code names to **KeyNameArray**. Be sure to change the loop limit in the **for** loop to match the last index you add.

What's next? Well, maybe we're ready to go catch a mouse!

CATCHING THE MOUSE

So you want to set a mouse trap, eh? The mouse is in such widespread use that it has become necessary to program games to use it as an input device.

With the rise of Microsoft Windows and OS/2, the mouse has become widespread on the PC platform. Typically, a mouse does not make a very good input device for fast-action games but sometimes it is preferable to a keyboard, and since the mouse is so widely available, most games support a mouse as an input device.

The programming interface to a mouse is done at a slightly higher level than the keyboard. Rather than access the mouse hardware directly, a program interfaces with a mouse driver, typically supplied by the mouse manufacturer. By convention, the driver and the program use INT 33h to communicate. Although the drivers supplied by some manufacturers support additional functionality (support for three buttons, for instance), a basic set of operations is supported by all drivers.

Surprisingly, many other devices also communicate via the mouse driver. For instance, a track-ball is simply an upside-down mouse and uses a mouse-interface driver to communicate with programs. The interfacing program has no knowledge if the actual device is a mouse, a track-ball, a graphics tablet, or some other device, because the mouse driver abstracts the specifics of the hardware and presents a single functional interface.

 In this chapter we'll create a handy mouse interface module using the files MOUSE.H and MOUSE.C. Later, we'll show you how to wire the mouse into your programs by creating an event-driven demo program.

WORKING WITH THE MOUSE

The mouse driver takes care of drawing a cursor on the screen in all the standard video modes (we'll talk about Mode X later). The cursor defaults to an inverse block character in text modes and to an arrow in graphics modes. The shape of the cursor is controllable in both text and graphics modes.

In addition, the mouse cursor can be hidden or made visible by calling driver functions. The mouse cursor should be hidden, when a program draws to the screen beneath it. If the cursor is not hidden the screen will become corrupted when the mouse driver moves the cursor. For simplicity, some programs simply hide the cursor whenever they update the screen, regardless of whether the mouse cursor and the new information overlap. The mouse driver always keeps track of the current location of the cursor, whether it is visible or not. This way, when the cursor is made visible, it will appear at the appropriate location.

To keep track of whether the mouse is visible or not, the driver uses a counter. The counter is initialized to -1. The cursor is made visible when the counter reaches 0. Requests to hide the cursor decrement the counter by 1. Requests to show the cursor increment the counter by 1. Why use a counter rather than a simple boolean flag (visible or not visible)? The answer is that you don't want the cursor to be made visible by a low-level routine before it is supposed to be.

For example, suppose you had a routine A that was responsible for drawing something on the screen. Routine A first hides the cursor, draws something, calls routine B to draw something else, draws a third thing, and then makes the cursor visible again. Now, suppose routine B can also be called by routines other than A. Before routine B can do its drawing, it also must hide the cursor because it doesn't know whether the cursor is already hidden. The problem comes when routine B tries to show the cursor after finishing its drawing. If routine B was called from routine A, you don't want routine B to show the cursor; routine A still has drawing to do. If routine B was called from another routine, however, it may want to restore the cursor. Using a counter allows the show and hide calls to balance one another (sort of like nested parentheses) without using complicated tests. Routines simply hide the cursor when they need to and the cursor will only become visible again when the top level routine finally shows it.

The cursor uses a hot-spot to identify which pixel of the cursor corresponds to the mouse position when the cursor is drawn. For instance, the hot-spot could be set at the tip of an arrow image but might be set in the center of a cross-hair image. The driver uses the hot-spot location to offset the cursor image correctly. Note that a hot-spot is only used for graphics mode cursors. In text mode, the cursor is always one character in size and is drawn at the mouse position.

Tracking Mouse Coordinates

When the mouse driver reports the position of the cursor, the value it returns is measured in mouse coordinates rather than in screen coordinates. The cursor's position on the screen is mapped into mouse coordinates before it is returned. For example, in text modes, the mouse coordinate system runs from (0,0) to (640,200). If the current text mode is 40 columns by 25 lines, the horizontal coordinate numbers returned from the mouse driver will always be a multiple of 16. The vertical coordinates will always be a multiple of 8. If the current text mode is 80 columns by 25 lines, each coordinate, both horizontal and vertical, will be a multiple of 8.

In EGA and VGA graphics modes, with the exception of modes 0Dh and 13h, the mouse coordinate system corresponds directly to the screen coordinate system. In mode 0Dh, the mouse coordinate system is 1,280 columns by 200 rows. In mode 0Dh, horizontal mouse coordinates are always multiples of 4. In Mode 13h the horizontal mouse coordinates range from 0 to 640 while the vertical coordinates range from 0 to 200. The horizontal coordinates must be divisible by 2.

Note that the conversion factors from mouse coordinates to screen coordinates are always powers of 2, so fast shifts rather than slow divides can be done to convert.

Sensitivity and Acceleration

Now that we understand how the mouse coordinate system is related to the screen coordinate system, it's important to understand how the physical motion of the mouse is translated into mouse coordinates.

A mouse reports position changes to the driver in units of *mickeys*. A mickey is the fundamental resolution of the physical mouse hardware. A mouse that has 1/400-inch resolution will define a mickey as 1/400-inch. A mouse that has 1/200-inch resolution will define a mickey as 1/200-inch.

Personal preference determines how the mouse responds to movement. Some people like to have a screen width correspond to a large distance on their desktops. Others like a simple flick of the wrist to shoot their mouse across the screen. To accommodate different tastes, the driver defines a mouse sensitivity factor. This factor is used to convert mickeys into mouse coordinates. Typical drivers use default values of one mickey per horizontal mouse coordinate and two mickeys per vertical coordinate. This sensitivity can, of course, be set by the user.

Finally, the driver defines a mouse acceleration threshold (also called the double-speed threshold). The mouse driver determines how fast the mouse is moving (in mickeys per second) and when it exceeds the acceleration threshold, the mouse driver moves the mouse at twice the normal rate. This creates a better mouse feel.

THE BUILT-IN MOUSE FUNCTIONS YOU CANNOT LIVE WITHOUT!

The following section details the functions provided by the mouse driver. These functions are called from a program by loading register AX with the function number and invoking INT 33h.

Function 00h
Reset Mouse

Input: AX = 0000h

Output: If driver is present:
                    AX = FFFFh
                    BX = number of buttons supported
                else:
                    AX = 0000h

Description: This function resets the mouse driver. It is also used to determine if the mouse driver has been loaded. If the mouse driver is present, the AX register returns with FFFFh and BX contains the number of buttons the driver supports (note that this is not necessarily the number of buttons physically on the mouse). After invoking this function, the mouse cursor is positioned at the center of the screen and is hidden. The text cursor is set to an inverse block and the graphics cursor is set to an arrow. The event handler is cleared and all movement limits and protection areas are reset to allow the mouse access to the whole screen.

Function 01h
Show Mouse Cursor

Input: AX = 0001h

Output: None

Description: This function increments the cursor visibility counter. If the counter is 0, the cursor is displayed on the screen. This function also resets the screen protection defined with function 10h, Set Mouse Protected Area (discussed shortly), as a side effect.

Function 02h
Hide Mouse Cursor

Input: AX = 0002h

Output: None

Description: This function decrements the cursor visibility counter. If the counter was originally 0, the cursor is removed from the screen. A corresponding number of calls to function 01h must be used to redisplay the cursor.

Function 03h
Poll Mouse Status

Input: AX = 0003h

Output: BX: Bit 2 reflects center button state
                          Bit 1 reflects right button state
                          Bit 0 reflects left button state
                    CX = current X coordinate
                    DX = current Y coordinate

Description: This function returns the current state of the mouse buttons and the cursor position. The cursor position is given in mouse coordinates, not screen coordinates.

Function 04h
Set Mouse Cursor Position

Input: AX − 0004h
                    CX = X coordinate
                    DX = Y coordinate

Output: None

Description: This function sets the current cursor position to the coordinate specified in CX and DX. The state of the cursor visibility counter determines whether the cursor is displayed after the movement takes place. If the new location is in a protected area (see function 10h, Set Mouse Protected Area), the cursor will not be displayed.

Function 05h
Get Mouse Button Press Info

Input: AX = 0005h
                    BX = Button of interest

Output: AX: Bit 2 reflects center button state
                         Bit 1 reflects right button state
                         Bit 0 reflects left button state
                    BX = Button press count
                    CX = X coordinate of last button press
                    DX = Y coordinate of last button press

Description: This function returns the number of times the specified button has been pressed
                    since this function was last called (from 0 to 32,767). Additionally, the location
                    of the last button press and the current state of each button is also returned.
                    Calling this function resets the count of button presses for the specified button.

Function 06h
Get Mouse Button Release Info

Input: AX = 0006h
                    BX = Button of interest

Output: AX: Bit 2 reflects center button state
                         Bit 1 reflects right button state
                         Bit 0 reflects left button state
                    BX = Button release count
                    CX = X coordinate of last button release
                    DX = Y coordinate of last button release

Description: This function returns the number of times the specified button has been
                    released since this function was last called (from 0 to 32,767). Addition-
                    ally, the location of the last button release and the current state of each
                    button is also returned. Calling this function resets the count of button
                    releases for the specified button.

Function 07h
Set Mouse X Limit

Input: AX = 0007h
                    CX = Minimum X coordinate
                    DX = Maximum X coordinate

Output: None

Description: This function sets limits to restrict the mouse movement in the X direction.
                    CX and DX specify the minimum and maximum coordinates the mouse will
                    be allowed to take.

Function 08h
Set Mouse Y Limit

Input: AX = 0008h
                    CX = Minimum Y coordinate
                    DX = Maximum Y coordinate

Output: None

Description: This function sets limits to restrict the mouse movement in the Y direction. CX and DX specify the minimum and maximum coordinates the mouse will be allowed to take.

Function 09h
Set Mouse Graphics Mode Cursor

Input: AX = 0009h
                    BX = Hot-spot X coordinate relative to upper-left corner
                    CX = Hot-spot Y coordinate relative to upper-left corner
                    ES:DX = Long pointer to cursor image bitmaps

Output: None

Description: This function sets the cursor bitmap in graphics modes. ES:DX point to a buffer containing the bitmap image. The buffer should contain a 32-byte bit mask followed by a 32-byte bit image. To draw the cursor, the mask is ANDed with the screen pixels and then the image is XORed with the result. The cursor hot-spot is specified by the BX and CX registers. The hot-spot position is specified relative to the upper-left corner of the image bitmap. BX and CX have legal values in the range -16..16. The graphics cursor defaults to an arrow.

Function 0Ah
Set Mouse Text Mode Cursor

Input: AX = 000Ah
                    BX: 0 = Software cursor
                          1 = Hardware cursor
                    CX: if BX = 0: AND mask
                          if BX = 1: cursor start line
                    DX: if BX = 0: XOR mask
                          if BX = 1: cursor end line

Output: None

Description: This function sets the cursor in text modes. The cursor can be either hardware or software derived (typically software is used since the hardware cursor is used to show where text entry will occur). When a software cursor is used, the screen character is ANDed with the value specified in CX and then XORed with the value specified in DX. Note that CX and DX are

16-bit values that can be used to alter color, intensity, and other attributes of the screen character. For instance, the default inverse block cursor is created when CX = 77FFh and DX = 7700h.

Function 0Ch
Set Mouse Event Handler

Input: AX = 000Ch

CX = Event mask
    Bit 6: Center button released
    Bit 5: Center button pressed
    Bit 4: Right button released
    Bit 3: Right button pressed
    Bit 2: Left button released
    Bit 1: Left button pressed
    Bit 0: Mouse motion

ES:DX = Event handler address

Output: None

Description: This function is used for event-driven mouse programming. An event mask and event handler address are supplied as parameters. A program should set the corresponding bits in the event mask for every type of event the program wants to be notified about. When one or more events of the types specified occur, the event handler is called. On entry to the handler, the CPU registers have the following values:

    AX = Mouse event flags
    BX = Button status
    CX = X coordinate
    DX = Y coordinate
    SI = Y raw mickeys
    DI = X raw mickeys
    DS = Mouse driver's data segment

Note that more than one event may be signaled by the driver at one time. The driver calls the handler with a CALL FAR instruction. The handler must return with a RET FAR instruction. The handler is called from the ISR of the mouse driver. Because of this, the handler must observe the same rules as a typical ISR. *The handler must preserve the contents of all registers and not call BIOS or DOS functions.* On entry to the handler, the DS register still points to the data segment of the mouse driver. Make sure that you set DS to your own program's data segment before manipulating your program's variables. If you do not, you will corrupt memory within the mouse driver's data segment. Before your program terminates, call this function with an event mask of

0000h (no events). Failure to do so will cause the mouse driver to call your event handler after your program has exited, crashing or hanging your machine. Ensure that you do this even with fatal error induced exits.

Function 0Fh
Set Mouse Sensitivity

Input:	AX = 000Fh
	CX = Number of mickeys per eight pixels in X direction
	DX = Number of mickeys per eight pixels in Y direction
Output:	None
Description:	Sets the sensitivity factor of the mouse. The sensitivity is specified as the number of mickeys needed to move the cursor eight coordinates in either the X or Y direction. With most drivers, these values default to eight mickeys in the X direction and 16 mickeys in the Y direction.

Function 10h
Set Mouse Protected Area

Input:	AX = 0010h
	CX = Left edge X coordinate
	DX = Top edge Y coordinate
	SI = Right edge X coordinate
	DI = Bottom edge Y coordinate
Output:	None
Description:	This function protects a portion of the screen from the mouse. The input parameters define a rectangular area. When the mouse moves into the protected rectangle, it becomes hidden until it is moved outside the rectangle or function 01h (Show Mouse Cursor) is used to reset the protected area.

Function 13h
Set Mouse Acceleration Threshold

Input:	AX = 0013h
	DX = Acceleration threshold in mickeys/second
Output:	None
Description:	This function sets the mouse acceleration (or double-speed) threshold. When the mouse speed exceeds the value specified in DX, the driver will double the cursor's movement distance. There is no way to disable acceleration, but programs can set the value of DX so high as to become unattainable, which creates the desired effect.

Function 24h
Get Mouse Info

Input:	AX = 0024h
Output:	BX = Version number (BH = major, BL = minor)
	CH = Type of mouse
	1 = bus mouse
	2 = serial mouse
	3 = InPort mouse
	4 = PS/2 mouse
	5 = HP mouse
	CL = Mouse IRQ (0 for PS/2 mouse)
Description:	This function is used to return information about the mouse and mouse driver. Some drivers do not support this function. To determine whether the driver supports this function, load BX with FFFFh and call the function. If the driver does not support the function, BX will still equal FFFFh upon return. A program should determine whether a mouse driver is installed before determining whether the driver supports this function.

CREATING A MOUSE INTERFACE MODULE

Now that we've looked at the major mouse functions, let's create a set of C functions so that we can easily support the mouse in our game programs. We'll actually need to create two files, MOUSE.H and MOUSE.C.

The Mouse Interface Header File

The MOUSE.H header file, shown in Listing 3.1, includes the prototypes for the key mouse functions we just explored as well as some useful constants for generating event masks and specifying buttons.

Listing 3.1   MOUSE.H

```
/* File: MOUSE.H
** Description:
**    Function declarations and miscellaneous definitions for module
**    MOUSE.C.
** Copyright:
**    Copyright 1994, David G. Roberts
*/

#ifndef _MOUSE_H
#include "gamedefs.h"
```

```
/* constants */

/* mouse events */
#define ME_CENTER_RELEASED   (0x40)
#define ME_CENTER_PRESSED    (0x20)
#define ME_RIGHT_RELEASED    (0x10)
#define ME_RIGHT_PRESSED     (0x08)
#define ME_LEFT_RELEASED     (0x04)
#define ME_LEFT_PRESSED      (0x02)
#define ME_MOVEMENT          (0x01)


/* button state masks */
#define CENTER_BUTTON_MASK   (0x04)
#define RIGHT_BUTTON_MASK    (0x02)
#define LEFT_BUTTON_MASK     (0x01)


/* prototypes for MOUSE.C */
int ResetMouse(void);
void ShowMouseCursor(void);
void HideMouseCursor(void);
UINT16 PollMouseStatus(UINT16 * x, UINT16 * y);
void SetMouseCursorPosition(UINT16 x, UINT16 y);
UINT16 GetMouseButtonPressInfo
    (
    UINT16   Button,
    UINT16 * Counter,
    UINT16 * x,
    UINT16 * y
    );
UINT16 GetMouseButtonReleaseInfo
    (
    UINT16 Button,
    UINT16 * Counter,
    UINT16 * x,
    UINT16 * y
    );
void SetMouseXLimit(UINT16 MinimumX, UINT16 MaximumX);
void SetMouseYLimit(UINT16 MinimumY, UINT16 MaximumY);
void SetMouseGraphicsCursor
    (
    int HotSpotX,
    int HotSpotY,
    void far * BitmapPtr
    );
void SetMouseTextCursor(UINT16 ANDmask, UINT16 XORmask);
void SetMouseEventHandler(UINT16 EventMask, void far * Handler);
void SetMouseSensitivity
    (
    UINT16 MickeysPer8X,
    UINT16 MickeysPer8Y
    );
void SetMouseProtectedArea
    (
```

```
        UINT16 Left,
        UINT16 Top,
        UINT16 Right,
        UINT16 Bottom
        );
void SetMouseAccelerationThreshold(UINT16 MickeysPerSecond);
UINT16 GetMouseInfo(UINT16 * Type, UINT16 * Irq);

#define _MOUSE_H

#endif
```

The Mouse Interface Main Module

The MOUSE.C module, shown in Listing 3.2, is a set of C routines to interface to a mouse driver. The C routines encapsulate the register level details of the various mouse driver function calls.

Listing 3.2   MOUSE.C

```
/* File: MOUSE.C
** Description:
**    Routines for interfacing with a standard DOS mouse driver via
**    INT 33h.
** Copyright:
**    Copyright 1994, David G. Roberts
*/

/* includes */
#include <assert.h>
#include <dos.h>
#include <stdio.h>
#include "gamedefs.h"
#include "mouse.h"

/* constants */
#define MOUSE_INT (0x33)

/* mouse driver function codes */
#define FC_RESET_MOUSE              (0x0000)
#define FC_SHOW_CURSOR              (0x0001)
#define FC_HIDE_CURSOR              (0x0002)
#define FC_POLL_STATUS              (0x0003)
#define FC_SET_CURSOR_POSITION      (0x0004)
#define FC_GET_BUTTON_PRESS_INFO    (0x0005)
#define FC_GET_BUTTON_RELEASE_INFO  (0x0006)
#define FC_SET_X_LIMIT              (0x0007)
#define FC_SET_Y_LIMIT              (0x0008)
#define FC_SET_GRAPHICS_CURSOR      (0x0009)
#define FC_SET_TEXT_CURSOR          (0x000A)
#define FC_SET_EVENT_HANDLER        (0x0C0C)
#define FC_SET_SENSITIVITY          (0x000F)
```

```
#define FC_SET_PROTECTED_AREA        (0x0010)
#define FC_SET_ACCEL_THRESHOLD       (0x0013)
#define FC_GET_INFO                  (0x0024)

/*
    Function: ResetMouse
    Description:
        Resets the mouse driver and returns the number of buttons the mouse
        driver supports (note: not necessarily the number of buttons on the
        mouse hardware itself!) or 0 if the driver is not loaded.
*/
int ResetMouse(void)
{
    union REGS regs;

    regs.x.ax = FC_RESET_MOUSE;

    int86(MOUSE_INT, &regs, &regs);

    /* if driver is present, return number of buttons from BX, else 0 */
    if (regs.x.ax == 0xFFFF) {
        return regs.x.bx;
    }
    else {
        return 0;
    }
}


/*
    Function: ShowMouseCursor
    Description:
        Increments the mouse cursor visibility variable.  If the variable
        equals 0, the driver will display the cursor on screen.
*/
void ShowMouseCursor(void)
{
    union REGS regs;

    regs.x.ax = FC_SHOW_CURSOR;

    int86(MOUSE_INT, &regs, &regs);
}

/*
    Function: HideMouseCursor
    Description:
        Decrements the mouse visibility counter.  If the counter is less than
        0, the driver will hide the mouse cursor.
*/
void HideMouseCursor(void)
{
    union REGS regs;

    regs.x.ax = FC_HIDE_CURSOR;
```

```
    int86(MOUSE_INT, &regs, &regs);
}

/*
    Function: PollMouseStatus
    Description:
        Polls the current status of the mouse.  The current X and Y locations
        of the mouse are returned in the variables pointed to by the x and y
        arguments.  The status of the buttons is given by the function
        return value.  The status of the buttons may be tested by ANDing
        the return value with the CENTER_BUTTON_MASK,
        RIGHT_BUTTON_MASK, and LEFT_BUTTON_MASK constants.
*/
UINT16 PollMouseStatus(UINT16 * x, UINT16 * y)
{
    union REGS regs;

    regs.x.ax = FC_POLL_STATUS;

    int86(MOUSE_INT, &regs, &regs);

    if (x != NULL) {
        *x = regs.x.cx;
    }
    if (y != NULL) {
        *y = regs.x.dx;
    }
    return regs.x.bx;
}

/*
    Function: SetMouseCursorPosition
    Description:
        Sets the current mouse cursor position to (x,y).
*/
void SetMouseCursorPosition(UINT16 x, UINT16 y)
{
    union REGS regs;

    regs.x.ax = FC_SET_CURSOR_POSITION;
    regs.x.cx = x;
    regs.x.dx = y;

    int86(MOUSE_INT, &regs, &regs);
}

/*
    Function: GetMouseButtonPressInfo
    Description:
        Returns information about the last press of the specified button,
        including how many times the button has been pressed since this
        function was last called, the X and Y location of the button
        when it was last pressed, and the current status of all the buttons.
        The button to test can be specified with the constants
```

```
            CENTER_BUTTON_MASK, RIGHT_BUTTON_MASK, and LEFT BUTTON_MASK.
            The current button states are returned directly by the function.
*/
UINT16 GetMouseButtonPressInfo
    (
    UINT16   Button,
    UINT16 * Counter,
    UINT16 * x,
    UINT16 * y
    )
{
    union REGS regs;

    regs.x.ax = FC_GET_BUTTON_PRESS_INFO;
    regs.x.bx = Button;

    int86(MOUSE_INT, &regs, &regs);

    if (Counter != NULL) {
        *Counter = regs.x.bx;
    }
    if (x != NULL) {
        *x = regs.x.cx;
    }
    if (y != NULL) {
        *y = regs.x.dx;
    }
    return regs.x.ax;
}


/*
    Function: GetMouseButtonReleaseInfo
    Description:
        Same as previous except for mouse button release instead of press.
*/
UINT16 GetMouseButtonReleaseInfo
    (
    UINT16 Button,
    UINT16 * Counter,
    UINT16 * x,
    UINT16 * y
    )
{
    union REGS regs;

    regs.x.ax = FC_GET_BUTTON_RELEASE_INFO;
    regs.x.bx = Button;

    int86(MOUSE_INT, &regs, &regs);

    if (Counter != NULL) {
        *Counter = regs.x.bx;
    }
    if (x != NULL) {
```

```
        *x = regs.x.cx;
    }
    if (y != NULL) {
        *y = regs.x.dx;
    }
    return regs.x.ax;
}


/*
    Function:   SetMouseXLimit
    Description:
        Restricts mouse movement between the minimum and maximum in the
        X direction.
*/
void SetMouseXLimit(UINT16 MinimumX, UINT16 MaximumX)
{
    union REGS regs;

    regs.x.ax = FC_SET_X_LIMIT;
    regs.x.cx = MinimumX;
    regs.x.dx = MaximumX;

    int86(MOUSE_INT, &regs, &regs);
}


/*
    Function:   SetMouseYLimit
    Description:
        Same as above, but in Y direction.
*/
void SetMouseYLimit(UINT16 MinimumY, UINT16 MaximumY)
{
    union REGS regs;

    regs.x.ax = FC_SET_Y_LIMIT;
    regs.x.cx = MinimumY;
    regs.x.dx = MaximumY;

    int86(MOUSE_INT, &regs, &regs);
}


/*
    Function: SetMouseGraphicsCursor
    Description:
        Sets the graphics mode cursor to the image pointed to by the
        BitmapPtr argument.
*/
void SetMouseGraphicsCursor
    (
    int HotSpotX,
    int HotSpotY,
    void far * BitmapPtr
    )
{
```

```
    union REGS regs;
    struct SREGS sregs;

    assert((-16 <= HotSpotX) && (HotSpotX <= 16));
    assert(-16 <= HotSpotY && HotSpotY <= 16);

    regs.x.ax = FC_SET_GRAPHICS_CURSOR;
    regs.x.bx = HotSpotX;
    regs.x.cx = HotSpotY;
    regs.x.dx = FP_OFF(BitmapPtr);
    sregs.es = FP_SEG(BitmapPtr);

    int86x(MOUSE_INT, &regs, &regs, &sregs);
}


/*
    Function: SetMouseTextCursor
    Description:
        Sets the mouse text cursor.  Note that this function will only set
        a software cursor, not a hardware cursor (i.e., BX always equals 0
        when this function invokes INT 033h).
*/
void SetMouseTextCursor(UINT16 ANDmask, UINT16 XORmask)
{
    union REGS regs;

    regs.x.ax = FC_SET_TEXT_CURSOR;
    regs.x.bx = 0;  /* always software cursor */
    regs.x.cx = ANDmask;
    regs.x.dx = XORmask;

    int86(MOUSE_INT, &regs, &regs);
}


/*
    Function: SetMouseEventHandler
    Description:
        Sets up a mouse event handler to respond to the events allowed by the
        event mask.
*/
void SetMouseEventHandler(UINT16 EventMask, void far * Handler)
{
    union REGS regs;
    struct SREGS sregs;

    regs.x.ax = FC_SET_EVENT_HANDLER;
    regs.x.cx = EventMask;
    regs.x.dx = FP_OFF(Handler);
    sregs.es = FP_SEG(Handler);

    int86x(MOUSE_INT, &regs, &regs, &sregs);
}
```

```
/*
    Function: SetMouseSensitivity
    Description:
        Sets the mouse sensitivity factors.  Sensitivity in each direction is
        given as the number of mickeys necessary to move the cursor eight
        mouse coordinates in either the X or Y direction.
*/
void SetMouseSensitivity
    (
    UINT16 MickeysPer8X,
    UINT16 MickeysPer8Y
    )
{
    union REGS regs;

    regs.x.ax = FC_SET_SENSITIVITY;
    regs.x.cx = MickeysPer8X;
    regs.x.dx = MickeysPer8Y;

    int86(MOUSE_INT, &regs, &regs);
}


/*
    Function: SetMouseProtectedArea
    Description:
        Sets a rectangular area protected from the mouse.
*/
void SetMouseProtectedArea
    (
    UINT16 Left,
    UINT16 Top,
    UINT16 Right,
    UINT16 Bottom
    )
{
    union REGS regs;

    regs.x.ax = FC_SET_PROTECTED_AREA;
    regs.x.cx = Left;
    regs.x.dx = Top;
    regs.x.si = Right;
    regs.x.di = Bottom;

    int86(MOUSE_INT, &regs, &regs);
}


/*
    Function: SetMouseAccelerationThreshold
    Description:
        Sets the mouse acceleration threshold to be MickeysPerSecond.
*/
void SetMouseAccelerationThreshold(UINT16 MickeysPerSecond)
{
    union REGS regs;
```

```
    regs.x.ax = FC_SET_ACCEL_THRESHOLD;
    regs.x.dx = MickeysPerSecond;

    int86(MOUSE_INT, &regs, &regs);
}

/*
    Function: GetMouseInfo
    Description:
        Returns info about the mouse driver.  Directly returns the version
        number of the mouse driver.  Returns the mouse type and IRQ via
        the pointers passed as arguments.
*/
UINT16 GetMouseInfo(UINT16 * Type, UINT16 * Irq)
{
    union REGS regs;

    regs.x.ax = FC_GET_INFO;

    int86(MOUSE_INT, &regs, &regs);

    if (Type != NULL) {
        *Type = regs.h.ch;
    }
    if (Irq != NULL) {
        *Irq = regs.h.cl;
    }

    return regs.x.bx;
}
```

WIRING THE MOUSE INTO YOUR PROGRAMS

There are two basic ways for a program to interact with a mouse. The first is to poll and the second is to install an event handler and act on mouse events.

Polling is very simple. Any time that the game program needs to know the state of the mouse, it simply calls the **PollMouseStatus** function. This function returns the current X and Y coordinates of the mouse (in mouse coordinates) and the states of the mouse buttons.

A game program can call the **PollMouseStatus** function in the main game loop, for instance. Each time through the loop, the game gets the new mouse status and can react on it during that frame.

There are problems with polling, however. The most obvious is the fact that unless the program calls the **PollMouseStatus** function during the time a button is being pressed, it is possible for a user to press a button and release it without the program ever knowing it. This could happen, for instance, if your game loop slows down because there are many objects being drawn on the screen.

Event-Driven Mouse Programming

With event-driven mouse programming, the program does not constantly poll the mouse driver for the state of the mouse. When the mouse state changes (a button is pressed, for example), the program is notified and can then take action. Those of you familiar with Microsoft Windows programming will find this model very similar since Windows also uses an event-driven interface.

Because the program receives a notification each time the mouse changes state, event-driven programming doesn't suffer from the missing button presses problem. When the program is notified that a button has been pressed, it can save that fact and act on it later if it is currently busy. As usual, the price for this is an increase in complexity. Fortunately, routines can be written to help manage the complexity, as we'll see next.

To notify the program of the change of state of the mouse, the mouse driver calls a handler function (or "callback") specified by the program. To specify the handler function, the program uses the mouse driver function 0Ch, Set Mouse Event Handler. This function takes as input a far pointer to the handler routine and an event mask. The event mask is used to specify which mouse events are interesting to the user program and which are not. The mouse driver calls the handler function for every "interesting" event specified in the event mask and simply discards those events that are not interesting. Figure 3.1 shows the layout of the mouse event mask passed to Set Mouse Event Handler and the event flags returned to the handler.

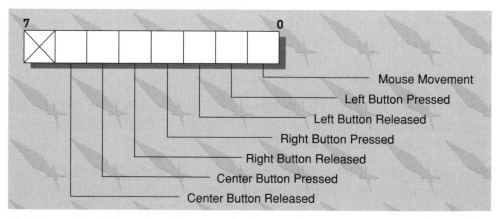

Figure 3.1   *The mouse event mask and event flags.*

The handler function is called from the mouse driver interrupt service routine, and thus must abide by the rules of an ISR. The handler function cannot call DOS or BIOS routines and should perform its work as quickly as possible. Typically, a user program just installs a handler that puts the generated mouse events into a queue.

Event-Driven Mouse Programming

The following module implements a set of routines for dealing with event-driven mouse programming. Functions are included for installing and removing an event handler that inserts mouse events into a queue. Additional functions are included for retrieving mouse events from the queue.

Creating MOUSEEVT.H

The following MOUSEEVT.H header file, shown in Listing 3.3, defines the **MOUSE_EVENT** structure used to store mouse events and declares prototypes for all the MOUSEEVT.C functions.

Listing 3.3 MOUSEEVT.H

```
/* File: MOUSEEVT.H
** Description:
**    Header file for MOUSEEVT.C.
** Copyright:
**    Copyright 1994, David G. Roberts
*/

#ifndef _MOUSEEVT_H

#include "gamedefs.h"

typedef struct {
    UINT16 InUse;
    UINT16 Event;
    UINT16 ButtonState;
    UINT16 X;
    UINT16 Y;
    UINT16 XMickeys;
    UINT16 YMickeys;
} MOUSE_EVENT;

int InstallMouseEventQueue(UINT16 Length, UINT16 EventMask);
void RemoveMouseEventQueue(void);
int QueryMouseEventWaiting(void);
int PeekMouseEvent(MOUSE_EVENT * MouseEvent);
int GetMouseEvent(MOUSE_EVENT * MouseEvent);

#define _MOUSEEVT_H

#endif
```

Creating MOUSEEVT.C

Listing 3.4 provides the complete source file for the event-driven mouse routines.

Listing 3.4   MOUSEEVT.C

```
/* File: MOUSEEVT.C
** Description:
**    Module for dealing with the mouse using event-driven programming.
** Copyright:
**    Copyright 1994, David G. Roberts
*/

#include <alloc.h>
#include <assert.h>
#include <dos.h>
#include <stdio.h>
#include "gamedefs.h"
#include "mouse.h"
#include "mouseevt.h"

/* constants */
#define ALL_EVENTS (0x7F)

/* types */
typedef struct {
    UINT16 Length;
    UINT16 Read;
    UINT16 Write;
    MOUSE_EVENT far * Queue;
} MOUSE_QUEUE;

/* module variables */
static MOUSE_QUEUE MouseQueue;
static BOOL HandlerInstalled = FALSE;

/*
    Function: MouseEventQueueHandler
    Description:
        This is the mouse event handler that is installed when
        InstallMouseEventQueue() is called.  The handler
        take the generated mouse event and adds it to the
        mouse queue specified by the MouseQueue variable.
        Note that this routine must be defined as
        "far _loadds _saveregs" to ensure that it returns
        with a RETF, that DS is loaded with the program's
        data segment (rather than leaving DS set to the
        mouse driver's data segment), and that no
        registers are modified.
*/
static void far _loadds _saveregs MouseEventQueueHandler(void)
```

```
{
    UINT16 Event;
    UINT16 ButtonState;
    UINT16 X,
    UINT16 Y;
    UINT16 XMickeys;
    UINT16 YMickeys;
    MOUSE_EVENT far * EventQueueEntry;
    UINT16 EventBit;

    /* save registers into variables */
    /* DO THIS IMMEDIATELY TO PREVENT OVERWRITING ANYTHING! */
    Event       = _AX;
    ButtonState = _BX;
    X           = _CX;
    Y           = _DX;
    XMickeys    = _SI;
    YMickeys    = _DI;


    EventBit = 1;

    /* separate all signalled events into individual queue entries */
    while (EventBit & ALL_EVENTS) {
        if (Event & EventBit) {
            EventQueueEntry = &(MouseQueue.Queue[MouseQueue.Write]);

            /* if the current write position in the queue is full, */
            /* discard all following events */
            if (EventQueueEntry->InUse == TRUE) {
                return;
            }

            /* copy info to event queue entry */
            EventQueueEntry->Event      = Event & EventBit;
            EventQueueEntry->ButtonState= ButtonState;
            EventQueueEntry->X          = X;
            EventQueueEntry->Y          = Y;
            EventQueueEntry->XMickeys    = XMickeys;
            EventQueueEntry->YMickeys    = YMickeys;

            /* mark entry as now being in use */
            EventQueueEntry->InUse = TRUE;

            /* increment write index and handle wrap-around */
            MouseQueue.Write++;
            if (MouseQueue.Write >= MouseQueue.Length) {
                MouseQueue.Write = 0;
            }
        }
        EventBit <<= 1;
    }
}
```

```
/*
    Function: InstallMouseEventQueue
    Description:
        This function takes an event mask and a queue size as
        parameters.  The function creates an event queue with
        the specified number of entries and initializes it.
        The function installs the handler using the
        SetMouseEventHandler function defined in MOUSE.C.
        The event mask parameter is passed to
        SetMouseEventHandler.  The handler is defined above,
        MouseEventQueueHandler.  The function returns TRUE if
        all went well, FALSE if memory for the queue could not
        be allocated.
*/
int InstallMouseEventQueue
    (
    UINT16 Length,
    UINT16 EventMask
    )
{
    UINT16 i;

    assert(HandlerInstalled == FALSE);
    assert(Length != 0);

    /* create queue and return error if space couldn't be allocated */
    MouseQueue.Queue = farmalloc(Length * sizeof(MOUSE_EVENT));
    if (MouseQueue.Queue == NULL) {
        return FALSE;
    }

    /* initialize queue pointers */
    MouseQueue.Length   = Length;
    MouseQueue.Write    = 0;
    MouseQueue.Read     = 0;

    /* initialize the InUse flags of each entry to not in use */
    for (i = 0; i < Length; i++) {
        MouseQueue.Queue[i].InUse = FALSE;
    }

    /* set up the handler and event mask */
    SetMouseEventHandler(EventMask, MouseEventQueueHandler);

    HandlerInstalled = TRUE;

    return TRUE;
}

/*
    Function: RemoveMouseEventQueue
    Description:
        Sets the handler function in the mouse driver to null and
```

```
        deallocates the mouse event queue memory.
*/
void RemoveMouseEventQueue(void)
{
    assert(HandlerInstalled == TRUE);

    /* Remove handler (specify all events masked, no handler address). */
    /* Note that we must do this before freeing the memory. */
    /* If we do after, we could get a mouse event after */
    /* freeing the memory. */
    SetMouseEventHandler(0, NULL);

    /* Now that there are no mouse events to be generated, */
    /* free the memory. */
    farfree(MouseQueue.Queue);

    HandlerInstalled = FALSE;
}


/*
    Function: QueryMouseEventWaiting
    Description:
        Returns TRUE if there is a mouse event in the queue,
        FALSE if not.
*/
int QueryMouseEventWaiting(void)
{
    assert(HandlerInstalled == TRUE);

    if (MouseQueue.Queue[MouseQueue.Read].InUse == TRUE) {
        return TRUE;
    }
    else {
        return FALSE;
    }
}


/*
    Function: PeekMouseEvent
    Description:
        Returns the mouse event at the head of the queue.  If
        a mouse event is present, the function returns TRUE and
        sets the InUse flag of the supplied MOUSE_EVENT structure
        to TRUE.  If no event is present, these two indicators
        are false.
*/
int PeekMouseEvent
    (
    MOUSE_EVENT * MouseEvent
    )
{
    MOUSE_EVENT far * CurrentEvent;
```

```
    assert(MouseEvent != NULL);
    assert(HandlerInstalled == TRUE);

    CurrentEvent = &(MouseQueue.Queue[MouseQueue.Read]);

    /* unconditionally copy what's sitting in the read spot */
    MouseEvent->InUse       = CurrentEvent->InUse;
    MouseEvent->Event       = CurrentEvent->Event;
    MouseEvent->ButtonState = CurrentEvent->ButtonState;
    MouseEvent->X           = CurrentEvent->X;
    MouseEvent->Y           = CurrentEvent->Y;
    MouseEvent->XMickeys    = CurrentEvent->XMickeys;
    MouseEvent->YMickeys    = CurrentEvent->YMickeys;

    /* indicate whether there was really anything there */
    return CurrentEvent->InUse;
}


/*

    Function: GetMouseEvent
    Description:
        Copies the mouse event at the head of the event queue to
        the MOUSE_EVENT structure supplied as a parameter and
        removes the event from the queue.  It returns TRUE if all
        goes well, FALSE if there is no event on the queue.
        The InUse flag of the MOUSE_EVENT structure will also
        indicate whether an event was waiting.  If InUse is
        TRUE, and event was pending, the other info in
        the MOUSE_EVENT structure is valid.
*/
int GetMouseEvent
    (
    MOUSE_EVENT * MouseEvent
    )
{
    assert(MouseEvent != NULL);
    assert(HandlerInstalled == TRUE);

    /* copy the mouse event using PeekMouseEvent */
    PeekMouseEvent(MouseEvent);

    /* if an event was present, free the queue position and */
    /* bump the read pointer (account for wrap) */
    if (MouseEvent->InUse == TRUE) {
        MouseQueue.Queue[MouseQueue.Read].InUse = FALSE;
        MouseQueue.Read++;
        if (MouseQueue.Read >= MouseQueue.Length) {
            MouseQueue.Read = 0;
        }
    }

    return MouseEvent->InUse;
}
```

Note that a program should never leave a mouse-event handler installed after it has terminated, even if the termination was caused by a fatal error or user intervention (pressing Ctrl+C, for instance). The mouse driver will not know that the program has terminated and will continue to call the handler when mouse events occur. Since the program memory has been deallocated and may be overwritten, this could cause the computer to crash. The function **RemoveMouseEventQueue** takes care of removing the event handler and should be called before a program terminates.

A Demonstration Mouse Program

The MOUSEDMO program, shown in Listing 3.5, demonstrates how to use the mouse very simply. The program simply initializes the mouse and polls for the cursor position and state of the buttons. These are then printed to the screen in text mode. Striking any key ends the program immediately. Event-driven programming is not demonstrated in MOUSEDMO but a later example, VGADEMO will use event-driven mouse programming.

Compiling and Linking:

You can compile the MOUSEDEMO program using the Borland C++ 3.1 IDE by typing "bc mousedemo.prj" and then selecting Compile I Make from the menus. If you would rather use the command line compiler, convert the MOUSEDEMO.PRJ file to a makefile using the PRJ2MAK program supplied with Borland C++ 3.1. Type "prj2mak mousedemo.prj" to create the MOUSEDEMO.MAK and MOUSEDEMO.CFG files.

If you are using Borland C++ 4.0, choose Project I Open Project from the IDE menus. Open the MOUSEDEMO.PRJ file. Borland C++ will convert the version 3.1 .PRJ file to a version 4.0 .IDE file. Compile and link the program by choosing Project I Make All from the IDE menus.

Listing 3.5 MOUSEDEMO.C

```
/* File: MOUSEDMO.C
** Description:
**    Demonstrates polled mouse programming.
** Copyright:
**    Copyright 1994, David G. Roberts
*/

#include <assert.h>
#include <conio.h>
```

```c
#include <dos.h>
#include <stdio.h>
#include "gamedefs.h"
#include "mouse.h"

int main(void)
{
    UINT16 Buttons;
    UINT16 x;
    UINT16 y;

    /* check for mouse driver and initialize it if present */
    if (ResetMouse() == 0) {
        printf("You must have a mouse to run this program.\n");
        return 1;
    }

    /* display the cursor */
    ShowMouseCursor();

    /* do this until the user hits a key */
    while (!kbhit()) {
        Buttons = PollMouseStatus(&x, &y);
        /* hide cursor while we print so we don't draw over it or scroll */
        HideMouseCursor();
        printf("X:%4d  Y:%4d  LB:%d  CB:%d  RB:%d\n", x, y,
            (Buttons & LEFT_BUTTON_MASK) != 0,
            (Buttons & CENTER_BUTTON_MASK) != 0,
            (Buttons & RIGHT_BUTTON_MASK) != 0);
        ShowMouseCursor();
        /* wait 100 ms or so */
        delay(100);
    }

    /* eat the character */
    if (getch() == 0) {
        getch();
    }

    /* hide it when we exit so it's not seen */
    HideMouseCursor();

    return 0;
}
```

JOYSTICK MAGIC

Find out how to incorporate joysticks into your programs and you'll be on the road to writing fast-action games.

The joystick is a very common input device for fast-action games, especially jet-fighter flight simulators. Although many PCs support only keyboards and mice, the joystick is standard issue for any serious game player and should be supported whenever possible. Although at first glance the joystick looks like a complicated piece of hardware, it is not. From a software view, it is simpler than the keyboard or the mouse.

The basic technology used by the IBM PC joystick is very simple. Rather than using a driver to interact with the hardware, like the mouse, the joystick is programmed through a single I/O port, which the game program itself manipulates. In fact, the IBM PC game port allows two joysticks to be plugged into the same computer, and both are controlled through the same I/O port.

A "standard" joystick has two axes of motion, X and Y, and two buttons. When two separate joysticks are plugged into the same computer using a "Y adapter," four axes of motion and four buttons are then available. The two joysticks are commonly named A and B. Some high-end joysticks actually feature more than two axes of motion or two buttons on the same joystick. To do this, they use the axes and buttons of the second logical joystick and just put the hardware into one physical unit. For instance, my joystick controls three axes and two buttons. Like a standard joystick, the axes and buttons of joystick A are provided. Further, axis Y of joystick B is controlled by a wheel on the joystick base. Some flight simulator games use axis Y of joystick B to control the throttle of the simulated plane.

eXPLORER OVERVIEW In this chapter we'll create the modules JSTICK.H and JSTICK.C to help you use the joystick in your game programs. Then, keep your eyes out for the fun projects CALJOY.C and INPUTDEV.C which will show you how to use the joystick modules.

JOYSTICK ELECTRICAL STUFF

Unlike a mouse or keyboard, which have encoded their information in digital form by the time a program has to process it, the joystick axes use a very simple resistor-capacitor electrical circuit (shown in Figure 4.1 for you electrical engineering types). Each axis of the joystick is connected to an identical circuit.

When a write is performed to the joystick I/O port address, the switch closes momentarily, shorting the capacitor (C) for each axis to ground. The capacitor discharges, causing the voltage across it to be zero. The zero voltage causes the output of the inverter to go to a logic 1. When the write strobe is removed—when the write cycle completes on the bus—the switch returns to its normal position and the capacitor begins to recharge. The mechanical part of the joystick controls the setting of the variable resistor (RV). Depending on the joystick position, the capacitor charges at a faster or slower rate. Eventually, the capacitor charges enough to reach a logic 1 state, which causes the inverter to output a logic 0.

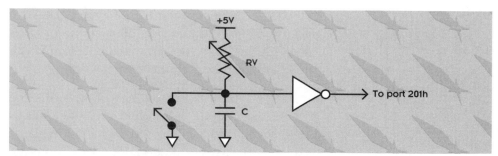

Figure 4.1 *The joystick axis circuit.*

READING A JOYSTICK

What all this means to you as a game programmer is that a program can detect the relative position of the joystick by timing how long it takes the output of the inverter to switch to a 0 after first writing to the joystick I/O port. You use a simple software timing loop to detect this switch. The logic states of the four inverters from each of the axes' circuits are mapped to the lower-order four bits of the joystick I/O port.

Reading the buttons is a simple matter of testing bits in the joystick I/O port location. A set button bit indicates that the button is *not* pressed (note the inversion). A clear button bit indicates that the button *is* pressed. The states of the four buttons are mapped to the high-order four bits of the joystick I/O port.

Figure 4.2 shows the layout of the button and axis bits in the joystick I/O port. The port is located at I/O location 201h. Writing any data (the value is ignored) to location 201h discharges the capacitors. A read of location 201h returns the present state of the capacitors and the buttons.

eXPLORER PROJECT

Reading and Checking Joysticks

Now that we know how the joystick operates, let's create a few routines to read the current state of a joystick and check to see if a joystick is attached to a game port. These functions, **SenseJoysticks** and **ReadJoysticks**, can be called from any C/C++ program. The two files we'll create are JSTICK.H and JSTICK.C, shown in Listings 4.1 and 4.2.

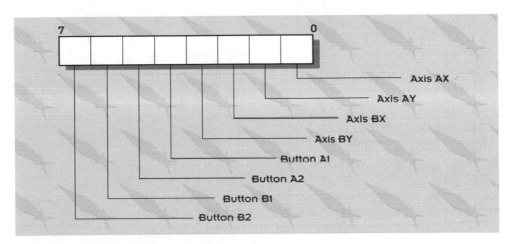

Figure 4.2   *The joystick I/O port bit locations.*

The following file contains the function and global variable prototypes necessary for other modules to call the joystick routines.

Listing 4.1   JSTICK.H

```
/* File: JSTICK.H
** Description:
**    Header file for JSTICK.C.  Defines global variables which
**    are updated with the current values of the joystick positions
**    and button states.
*/

#ifndef _JSTICK_H

#include "gamedefs.h"

typedef struct {
    UINT8 JsMask;
    UINT8 JsButtonA1;
    UINT8 JsButtonA2;
    UINT8 JsButtonB1;
    UINT8 JsButtonB2;
    UINT16 JsAxisAX;
    UINT16 JsAxisAY;
    UINT16 JsAxisBX;
    UINT16 JsAxisBY;
} JOYSTICK_STATE;

void SenseJoysticks(JOYSTICK_STATE * JsState);
void ReadJoysticks(JOYSTICK_STATE * JsState);

#define _JSTICK_H

#endif
```

Each of the joystick routines manipulates a **JOYSTICK_STATE** structure passed to it via a pointer. The **JOYSTICK_STATE** structure contains members that indicate the current state of the joystick buttons and the current axes' values. An additional member, **JsMask**, is used to indicate which joysticks are present in the system.

Listing 4.2   JSTICK.C

```
/* File: JSTICK.C
** Description:
**    Defines routines for reading the state of the joystick and
**    sensing if a joystick is attached to the game port.
*/
```

```
#include <stdio.h>
#include <dos.h>
#include "gamedefs.h"
#include "jstick.h"

/* constants */
#define JOYSTICK_PORT (0x201)

/*
    Function: SenseJoysticks
    Description:
        Tries to determine which joystick axes are available to
        be read.  The routine works by repeatedly reading the
        joystick port location for a very long time.  Those
        axes that time out before we are done reading are assumed
        to be present.  Axes that don't time out by the time that
        we're done are assumed to not be present.  Note that on
        a very fast machine, this routine could be fooled.
*/

void SenseJoysticks(JOYSTICK_STATE * JsState)
{
    register UINT8 portval;
    UINT16 limit;

    /* initialize counters */
    JsState->JsAxisAX = JsState->JsAxisAY = 0;
    JsState->JsAxisBX = JsState->JsAxisBY = 0;
    limit = 0xFFFF;

    /* don't let interrupts happen while we're reading */
    asm cli;

    /* start the timers — data value of write is unimportant */
    outportb(JOYSTICK_PORT, 0x00);

    /* do until interesting bits all drop to zero */
    while (limit) {
        portval = inportb(JOYSTICK_PORT);
        JsState->JsAxisAX += portval & 1;
        portval >>= 1;
        JsState->JsAxisAY += portval & 1;
        portval >>= 1;
        JsState->JsAxisBX += portval & 1;
        portval >>= 1;
        JsState->JsAxisBY += portval & 1;
        limit--;
    }

    /* enable interrupts */
    asm sti;
```

```
        JsState->JsMask = 0;
    if ((JsState->JsAxisAX != 0xFFFF) && (JsState->JsAxisAX != 0))
        JsState->JsMask |= 0x1;
    if ((JsState->JsAxisAY != 0xFFFF) && (JsState->JsAxisAY != 0))
        JsState->JsMask |= 0x2;
    if ((JsState->JsAxisBX != 0xFFFF) && (JsState->JsAxisBX != 0))
        JsState->JsMask |= 0x4;
    if ((JsState->JsAxisBY != 0xFFFF) && (JsState->JsAxisBY != 0))
        JsState->JsMask |= 0x8;

}


/*

    Function: ReadJoysticks
    Description:
        Reads the current values of the joystick positions and
        button states.  Axis values are returned in the JS structure
        variables JsAxisAX/AY/BX/BY and button states in
        the structure variables JsButtonA1/A2/B1/B2.  Note that
        the structure variable JsMask controls which axes of
        which joysticks (either A or B) should be waited for.
        If the B joystick, for instance, is not present, and
        JsMask indicates that JsAxisBY should be waited
        for, the routine will wait an excessively long time.
        The routine SenseJoysticks, above, can be used to try to
        automatically determine which axes of which joysticks
        are present.  Note that for joystick axes not present,
        JsAxisAX/AY/BX/BY are set to garbage values.
*/
void ReadJoysticks(JOYSTICK_STATE * JsState)
{
    register UINT8 portval;
    UINT16 limit;

    /* initialize counters */
    JsState->JsAxisAX = JsState->JsAxisAY = 0;
    JsState->JsAxisBX = JsState->JsAxisBY = 0;
    limit = 0xFFFF;

    /* don't let interrupts happen while we're reading */
    asm cli;

    /* start the timers — data value of write is unimportant */
    outportb(JOYSTICK_PORT, 0x00);

    /* do until interesting bits all drop to zero */
    while ((((portval = inportb(JOYSTICK_PORT)) & JsState->JsMask) && limit) {
        JsState->JsAxisAX += portval & 1;
        portval >>= 1;
        JsState->JsAxisAY += portval & 1;
        portval >>= 1;
        JsState->JsAxisBX += portval & 1;
        portval >>= 1;
```

```
        JsState->JsAxisBY += portval & 1;
        limit--;
    }

    /* recognize interrupts again */
    asm sti;

    /* update button variables - note these are inverted from the port */
    (portval & 0x10) ? (JsState->JsButtonA1 = 0) : (JsState->JsButtonA1 = 1);
    (portval & 0x20) ? (JsState->JsButtonA2 = 0) : (JsState->JsButtonA2 = 1);
    (portval & 0x40) ? (JsState->JsButtonB1 = 0) : (JsState->JsButtonB1 = 1);
    (portval & 0x80) ? (JsState->JsButtonB2 = 0) : (JsState->JsButtonB2 = 1);

}
```

The joystick module includes a routine to sense which joystick axes are available for use in the current system. If a joystick axis is missing, the variable resistor in the above circuit is not present and when the capacitor is discharged, it will never recharge. The detection code makes use of this fact to determine which joystick axes are present on the joystick plugged into the PC's game port. The routine discharges each of the capacitors and then waits the maximum amount of time, corresponding to a count of 0FFFFh. At the end of this long wait, the joystick counters are checked. If a joystick axis is installed, the axis circuit will have recharged at some point, and the counter corresponding to it will be much less than 0FFFFh. If a joystick axis is not installed, the capacitor will never have charged and the joystick's counter will equal 0FFFFh.

The detection routine sets **JsMask** to indicate which joysticks are present and which are not. **JsMask** is later used to ensure that the reading routine only waits for joysticks that are present. A program should either call **SenseJoysticks** or set **JsMask** before calling **ReadJoysticks**.

Some PC joystick ports don't implement the hardware for joystick B. This condition can often be detected because the hardware frequently pulls the input to the inverters for the B axes high. This causes the bits for joystick B's axes to always appear as zero when read from the joystick port. This condition is tested for in the sensing routine listed previously. This test could incorrectly report the absense of joystick B if the sensing routine was run on a *very* slow machine with joystick B pushed all the way to the upper-left corner when the sensing was taking place. In this case, the joystick might time out before the sensing routine had a chance to read the joystick port a single time. This is very unlikely, however. First, not many machines slow machines remain in the world and the joystick would have to be in the correct position for the routine to detect its presence.

Now let's take a look at the joystick routine, **ReadJoysticks**. This routine first clears the axes counter variables and sets the overflow limit (I'll explain the overflow limit in a second).

Next, the routine turns off processor interrupts. This routine converts the recharge time of the joystick circuit (shown in Figure 4.1) into a number using a software loop. If an interrupt were to occur as the loop was running, the loop would be suspended for a period of time, which would lead to an inconsistent count value—lower than would normally be reported. By shutting off interrupts temporarily, we can ensure that the CPU won't take any unexpected detours and the count value will be accurate.

After shutting off interrupts, the routine next writes to the joystick port location (0201h). The data value associated with the write is unimportant. The act of writing to the port discharges each of the joystick axis capacitors and starts the timing cycle.

The most important part of the routine comes next. The **while** loop repeatedly reads the value of the joystick port. The value returned by the port is logically ANDed with the **JsMask** variable that was set in the **SenseJoysticks** routine (described shortly). **JsMask** contains a set bit for each joystick that is installed in the machine and is of interest. When each bit in the joystick port corresponding to a set bit in **JsMask** falls to zero, indicating that the joystick axis circuit has recharged, the loop terminates. Remember that if a joystick axis is not present, its circuit will never recharge. By ANDing the port value with **JsMask**, the routine only waits for joystick axes that it knows are present, eliminating needless delay. The loop also terminates when the limit counter has expired.

It's important to note that an axis value returned by the joystick reading routine is not an absolute number. Because it was determined with the timing of a software loop, the value returned will vary depending on the speed of the computer the code is run on. Faster computers will return larger numbers, while slower computers will return smaller numbers. In fact, a fast computer may never return zero. If the computer is very fast, it executes the loop one or more times even if the joystick is set such that the capacitor charges very quickly. A very fast computer might even be able to overflow the 16-bit counter values that are used in the routine. If this happens, the values returned from the routine are useless. There are two ways to fix this problem. The first is to increase the size of the counters used in the routine to 32-bits. The second is to force users to buy good-quality "speed compensating" joystick cards. These cards use smaller adjustable resistance values in the joystick circuit to allow the capacitor to charge at a faster rate than normal joystick cards do, which brings the counter value into an acceptable range that does not overflow the 16-bit counters.

Using the **limit** counter is a non-ideal way to try to detect this problem. If the **limit** counter times out, it means that the machine is very fast (or that **JsMask** is set to wait for a non-existent axis). In this case, the values of the axes counters that have not timed out are simply clipped to the maximum value possible (0FFFFh).

In the body of the loop, a series of shifts and adds are used to increment the axes counters. This behavior takes advantage of the fact that the bit corresponding to an axis is set to 1 in the joystick port while the axis circuit is recharging. Thus, the counters for those axes that have not timed-out are incremented, while those that have timed-out simply have 0 added to them and remain unchanged. Note that using this trick keeps the length of the code in the body of the loop constant, even when some axes have timed-out. The alternative to this approach is to use multiple **if** statements to check each bit corresponding to each axis and increment the counters of those axes that are still recharging. The problem with this approach, however, is that as more counters time-out, less code is executed, the loop runs faster, and later counts can be influenced.

As soon as the loop has terminated, the routine re-enables interrupts and updates the global button variables to reflect the button states.

Joystick Calibration

Because a program can't know beforehand the minimum and maximum values that the joystick routine can return, many commercial game programs have a small joystick calibration routine that must be run before play begins. During the calibration routine, the player is asked to move the joystick to the upper-left and lower-right corners. As the player does this, the joystick routine is used to read the joystick. The minimum and maximum values returned by the routine during this procedure are stored in variables for later use.

Note that some programs avoid the calibration routine by assuming that the joystick is self-centering. When the program starts, it reads the state of the joystick and records the values. The program assumes that the joystick was centered when these values were read. It uses zero as the minimum value of each axis and twice the centered value as the maximum. Note that the various assumptions may or may not be valid. For instance, the user might be fiddling with the joystick when the program starts and the program might read an incorrect value. The program might be run on a very fast machine where zero can never be returned from the joystick routine. Finally, rarely is it the case that the maximum value is exactly twice the midpoint value on any axis.

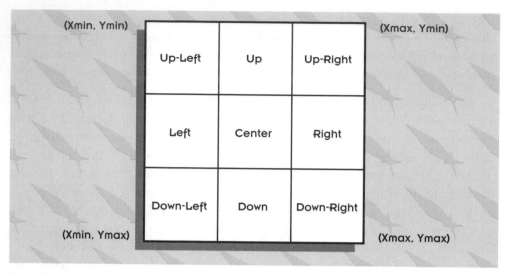

Figure 4.3 *Joystick mapping areas.*

In many instances, the assumptions made by an automatic calibration routine are fine, however. Frequently, only rough values are needed to implement a game. For instance, the values returned from the joystick routine might be mapped to nine different actions, as shown in Figure 4.3. Nine areas, each corresponding to a particular action, can be formed by dividing both the X and Y ranges of the joystick into thirds.

If the joystick is roughly in the upper-left corner of its range, it would cause the player to move up and to the left. Having nine distinct areas is far more important than knowing exactly where the cutoff between each area occurs.

Calibrating the Joystick

The CALJOY.C program, shown in Lising 4.3, demonstrates how a joystick can be calibrated using both the midpoint method and the corners method.

Compiling and Linking:

You can compile the CALJOY program using the Borland C++ 3.1 IDE by typing "bc caljoy.prj" and then selecting Compile | Make from the menus. If you would rather use the command line compiler, convert the CALJOY.PRJ file to a makefile using the PRJ2MAK program supplied with Borland C++ 3.1. Type "prj2mak caljoy.prj" to create the CALJOY.MAK and CALJOY.CFG files.

If you are using Borland C++ 4.0, choose Project | Open Project from the IDE menus. Open the CALJOY.PRJ file. Borland C++ will convert the version 3.1 .PRJ file to a version 4.0 .IDE file. Compile and link the program by choosing Project | Make All from the IDE menus.

Listing 4.3   CALJOY.C

```c
/* File: CALJOY.C
** Description:
**    Demonstrates two methods for calibrating a joystick.
**    The first method simply assumes that the user is holding
**    the joystick in the center.  The second method asks the
**    user to move the joystick to the upper-left and lower-right
**    corners and hit a button.
** Copyright:
**    Copyright 1994, David G. Roberts
*/

#include <assert.h>
#include <dos.h>
#include <stdio.h>
#include <stdlib.h>
#include "gamedefs.h"
#include "jstick.h"

/*
    Function: WaitJoystickButton
    Description:
        Waits for a joystick button to be pressed and then
        returns the current X and Y position of the joystick.
        Assumes that a joystick is installed and joystick A
        is to be read.
*/
void WaitJoystickButton
    (
    JOYSTICK_STATE * JsState,
    UINT16 * x,
    UINT16 * y
    )
{

    assert(JsState != NULL);
    assert(x != NULL);
    assert(y != NULL);

    /* wait until both buttons aren't pressed */
    /* which prevents us from detecting another button */
    /* press when the user is just holding a button down */
    /* from the last time */
    do {
        ReadJoysticks(JsState);
    } while (JsState->JsButtonA1 || JsState->JsButtonA2);
```

```
    /* read joystick until button is pressed */
    do {
        ReadJoysticks(JsState);
    } while (! (JsState->JsButtonA1 || JsState->JsButtonA2));

    /* return x and y values when button was pressed */
    *x = JsState->JsAxisAX;
    *y = JsState->JsAxisAY;

    printf("%d, %d\n", JsState->JsAxisAX, JsState->JsAxisAY);
}


/*
    Function: GetJsCorners
    Description:
        Asks the user to move the joystick to the upper-left and
        lower-right corners of its range and press a button.
        The function returns the minimum and maximum numbers
        received.
*/
void GetJsCorners
    (
    JOYSTICK_STATE * JsState,
    UINT16 * Xmin,
    UINT16 * Ymin,
    UINT16 * Xmax,
    UINT16 * Ymax
    )
{
    UINT16 XminTemp;     /* Temp variables are used to store the */
    UINT16 YminTemp;     /* results until error checking can be  */
    UINT16 XmaxTemp;     /* done on the values. */
    UINT16 YmaxTemp;
    BOOL Miscalibration;

    assert(JsState != NULL);
    assert(Xmin != NULL);
    assert(Ymin != NULL);
    assert(Xmax != NULL);
    assert(Ymax != NULL);

    Miscalibration = FALSE;

    do {
        if (Miscalibration) {
            printf("MISCALIBRATION!! Try again.\n");
        }
        printf("Move joystick to upper left and hit a button.\n");
        WaitJoystickButton(JsState, &XminTemp, &YminTemp);

        printf("Move joystick to lower right and hit a button.\n");
        WaitJoystickButton(JsState, &XmaxTemp, &YmaxTemp);
```

```
        /* if the values don't make sense, indicate miscalibration */
        Miscalibration = FALSE;
        if (XminTemp > XmaxTemp) {
            Miscalibration = TRUE;
        }
        if (YminTemp > YmaxTemp) {
            Miscalibration = TRUE;
        }
    } while (Miscalibration);

    /* return values to caller */
    *Xmin = XminTemp;
    *Ymin = YminTemp;
    *Xmax = XmaxTemp;
    *Ymax = YmaxTemp;
}


/*
    Function: CalibrateJsCorners
    Description:
        Gets the value of the joystick at the upper-left and
        lower-right corners and computes a midpoint point.
        Returns minimum, midpoint, and maximum value for
        the joystick.
*/
void CalibrateJsCorners
    (
    JOYSTICK_STATE * JsState,
    UINT16 * Xmin,
    UINT16 * Ymin,
    UINT16 * Xmid,
    UINT16 * Ymid,
    UINT16 * Xmax,
    UINT16 * Ymax
    )
{
    assert(JsState != NULL);
    assert(Xmin != NULL);
    assert(Ymin != NULL);
    assert(Xmid != NULL);
    assert(Ymid != NULL);
    assert(Xmax != NULL);
    assert(Ymax != NULL);

    /* get the corner points.  Note that we pass the pointers */
    /* straight through.  Don't pass addresses by mistake */
    /* (e.g., &Xmin). */
    GetJsCorners(JsState, Xmin, Ymin, Xmax, Ymax);

    /* calculate midpoint as average of min and max points */
    *Xmid = (*Xmin + *Xmax) / 2;
    *Ymid = (*Ymin + *Ymax) / 2;
}
```

```
/*
    Function: CalibrateJsMidpoint
    Description:
        Calibrates a joystick's range using the midpoint method.
        Reads the value of the joystick at the time it is
        called and computes a min and max range from this.
        Note that this assumes that the joystick is centered
        when the routine is called.
*/
void CalibrateJsMidpoint
    (
    JOYSTICK_STATE * JsState,
    UINT16 * Xmin,
    UINT16 * Ymin,
    UINT16 * Xmid,
    UINT16 * Ymid,
    UINT16 * Xmax,
    UINT16 * Ymax
    )
{
    assert(JsState != NULL);
    assert(Xmin != NULL);
    assert(Ymin != NULL);
    assert(Xmid != NULL);
    assert(Ymid != NULL);
    assert(Xmax != NULL);
    assert(Ymax != NULL);

    /* read midpoint value */
    ReadJoysticks(JsState);
    *Xmid = JsState->JsAxisAX;
    *Ymid = JsState->JsAxisAY;

    /* assume min coordinate is (0,0) and max is twice midpoint */
    *Xmin = *Ymin = 0;

    *Xmax = 2 * *Xmid;
    *Ymax = 2 * *Ymid;
}

int main(void)
{
    UINT16 Xmin;
    UINT16 Ymin;
    UINT16 Xmax;
    UINT16 Ymax;
    UINT16 Xmid;
    UINT16 Ymid;
    JOYSTICK_STATE JsState;

    /* must call this before reading joysticks! */
    SenseJoysticks(&JsState);

    printf("\n\n*** Joystick calibration ***\n\n");
```

```
if ((JsState.JsMask & 0x3) == 0) {
    printf("Joystick A not installed.  Exiting...\n");
    exit(1);
}

/* do it by assuming joystick at midpoint and performing */
/* a sample read */
printf("Midpoint method:\n");
CalibrateJsMidpoint(&JsState, &Xmin, &Ymin, &Xmid, &Ymid, &Xmax, &Ymax);
printf("Upper left: (%d, %d)  Lower right: (%d, %d)  "
    "Midpoint: (%d, %d)\n",
    Xmin, Ymin, Xmax, Ymax, Xmid, Ymid);

/* do it by corners method */
printf("Corners method:\n");
CalibrateJsCorners(&JsState, &Xmin, &Ymin, &Xmid, &Ymid, &Xmax, &Ymax);
printf("Upper left: (%d, %d)  Lower right: (%d, %d)  "
    "Midpoint: (%d, %d)\n",
    Xmin, Ymin, Xmax, Ymax, Xmid, Ymid);

return 0;
}
```

MULTIPLE INPUT DEVICE EXAMPLE

Listing 4.4 is a simple demonstration program that shows how input can be retrieved from all three input devices. In a real program, the **do-while** loop would be the equivalent to the main program loop. Before each new frame of animation is drawn, new input would be retrieved from each of the possible input devices and used to update player direction, speed, and so on.

Multiple Input Devices

The INPUTDEV program simply uses **printf** function calls to print the state of the Space and Enter keys, the joystick axes position and button state, and the mouse position and state of the right mouse button. Note that the Space and Enter keys can be held down at the same time and that the mouse and joystick can be moved simultaneously. Mouse input is retrieved via polling rather than events.

Compiling and Linking:

You can compile the INPUTDEV program using the Borland C++ 3.1 IDE by typing "bc inputdev.prj" and then selecting Compile | Make from the menus. If you would rather use the command line compiler, convert the INPUTDEV.PRJ file to a makefile using the PRJ2MAK program supplied with Borland C++ 3.1. Type "prj2mak inputdev.prj" to create the INPUTDEV.MAK and INPUTDEV.CFG files.

If you are using Borland C++ 4.0, choose Project | Open Project from the IDE menus. Open the INPUTDEV.PRJ file. Borland C++ will convert the version 3.1 .PRJ file to a version 4.0 .IDE file. Compile and link the program by choosing Project | Make All from the IDE menus.

Listing 4.4   INPUTDEV.C

```c
/* File: INPUTDEV.C
** Description:
**    Example of how to use keyboard, mouse, and joystick function
**    libraries.
** Author:
**    Dave Roberts
**    Copyright 1994, David G. Roberts
*/

#include <dos.h>
#include <stdio.h>
#include "gamedefs.h"
#include "keyboard.h"
#include "jstick.h"
#include "mouse.h"


int main(void)
{
    int KeyState;
    JOYSTICK_STATE JsState;
    int MousePresent;
    UINT16 MouseX;
    UINT16 MouseY;
    UINT16 MouseButtonStatus;
    int MouseLeftButtonState;

    /* figure out if there are any joysticks present, and if so, */
    /* which axes are present. */
    SenseJoysticks(&JsState);

    /* figure out if a mouse is present, and if so, reset it */
    MousePresent = (ResetMouse() > 0);
    ShowMouseCursor();

    SetButtonKeysMode();

    do {

        /* delay a bit so things don't scroll too fast */
        delay(75);

        /* hide the mouse cursor so that we don't print over it */
        /* or scroll the screen when it's visible */
        HideMouseCursor();
```

```c
        /* check the state of the Space and Enter keys */
        KeyState = GetKeyState(KEY_SPACE);
        if (KeyState) {
            printf("SPACE D  |  ");
        }
        else {
            printf("SPACE U  |  ");
        }

        KeyState = GetKeyState(KEY_ENTER);
        if (KeyState) {
            printf("ENTER D  |  ");
        }
        else {
            printf("ENTER U  |  ");
        }

        /* if a joystick is present (assume joystick A), */
        /* read its state */
        if ((JsState.JsMask & 0x3) != 0) {
            ReadJoysticks(&JsState);
            printf("AX:%4x AY:%4x BA1:%d BA2:%d  |  ",
                JsState.JsAxisAX,
                JsState.JsAxisAY,
                JsState.JsButtonA1,
                JsState.JsButtonA2);
        }

        /* if a mouse is present, read its state */
        if (MousePresent) {
            MouseButtonStatus = PollMouseStatus(&MouseX, &MouseY);
            MouseLeftButtonState =
                (MouseButtonStatus & LEFT_BUTTON_MASK) != 0;
            printf("MX:%4x MY:%4x MLB:%d",
                MouseX,
                MouseY,
                MouseLeftButtonState);
        }

        printf("\n");
        ShowMouseCursor();

        /* check if Esc is pressed—if so, exit loop */
        KeyState = GetKeyState(KEY_ESC);
    } while (!KeyState);

    /* clean up */
    SetNormalKeysMode();
    HideMouseCursor();

    return 0;
}
```

PART 2

THE GRAPHICS ADVENTURE

VGA BASICS

The VGA provides many display modes. Take a look at this chapter to see which one is right for each gaming task.

At this point you should have a good idea of how player input is read by a game program. That is, you now have the necessary knowledge to tell when a player wants to fire a missile, jump, or move left. But how do you go about drawing a missile or the game's main character on the screen? What must be done to draw the monsters and objects present in your game landscape?

This chapter explores the PC's primary graphics output device, the Video Graphics Adapter (VGA). After mastering the VGA, at the end of Part 2, you'll be able to draw missiles, aliens, explosions, frogs, dogs, logs, and just about any other object you think your game might require.

This chapter describes the various graphics modes the VGA supports, explains which features are the most useful for game programming, and presents a very useful undocumented VGA graphics mode—Mode X. We'll learn about the organization of video memory in the standard VGA graphics modes as well as Mode X and some of the more important VGA registers.

This chapter is not a reference work on the VGA. It simply introduces the game-specific knowledge about the VGA that is necessary to understand later chapters. You can find an in-depth description of the VGA in several of the reference books.

eXPLORER OVERVIEW This chapter develops a couple of re-usable modules that assist in entering the various graphics modes, setting VGA registers to specific values, and plotting points on the screen. Along the way, we'll build two simple graphics sketch programs that use our routines. The sketch programs also use the mouse modules from Chapter 3 and demonstrate event-driven mouse programming.

GETTING ORGANIZED

All bitmapped video adapters use computer memory to store an encoded version of the screen image for display on the video monitor. The display hardware uses the stored information to update the display during each video refresh cycle.

The key to understanding how to manipulate the VGA is to understand how the VGA organizes its display memory. The term "organization" refers to how the memory and pixel color values logically relate to each other. By thoroughly understanding the organization of the display memory, you can ensure that a program is manipulating pixels in the most efficient manner.

VGA display adapters support two primary memory organizations: linear and planar. Each video mode supported by the VGA uses one of these organizations. At the end of this chapter, we'll also look at Mode X, a video mode that combines both of the these organizations and creates some very useful side effects in the process.

Linear Organization

The VGA linear memory organization is very easy to understand and use. Each byte of display memory is used to store one pixel. Each byte is mapped to a single memory address in the microprocessor's memory address space. The first row of pixels is stored sequentially, in ascending order, followed by the second and all subsequent rows. The value stored in each video memory byte is used to control the color of the corresponding pixel on the screen. Essentially, the screen is a two-dimensional array of bytes, as shown in Figure 5.1.

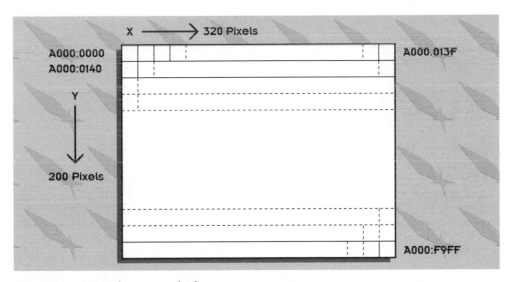

Figure 5.1   *Linear, byte-per-pixel video memory organization.*

In Mode 13h, the only mode where the linear organization is used, the screen resolution is 320x200 pixels. The Mode 13h screen starts at segment 0A000h and is 64,000 bytes long (320 times 200).

Because each pixel is represented by a whole byte, a pixel can take on 256 different color values. We'll explain more about how to control the various colors in Chapter 8.

The following function demonstrates how to plot a pixel in Mode 13h.

```
#include <assert.h>
#include <dos.h>
#include "gamedefs.h"

#define LINEAR_SEGMENT (0xA000)
#define MODE_13H_HORIZ (320)
#define MODE_13H_VERT (200)

/*
    Function: PlotMode13h
    Description:
        Plots a pixel in mode 13h (assumes that the VGA has already
        been set to that mode).
*/
void PlotMode13h
    (
    uint16 X,
    uint16 Y,
```

```
    uint16 Color
    )
{
    uint16 Offset;
    uint8 far * GraphicsBase;

    /* make sure parameters are in range */
    assert(X <= (MODE_13H_HORIZ - 1));
    assert(Y <= (MODE_13H_VERT - 1));

    /* create a far pointer to the base of Mode 13h memory */
    GraphicsBase = (uint8 far *) MK_FP(LINEAR_SEGMENT,0);

    /* compute offset from X,Y coordinates */
    Offset = Y * MODE_13H_HORIZ + X;

    /* set pixel to color */
    *(GraphicsBase + Offset) = Color;
}
```

Simple! The function creates a far pointer to the base of the video memory area and computes an offset using the X and Y coordinates of the point. The far pointer and offset are then used to set a byte of video memory to a particular color value.

Planar Organization

The planar video modes of the VGA are mostly artifacts of the VGA's evolution from the older Enhanced Graphics Adapter (EGA) standard. As we'll see in the discussion of Mode X, however, the planar organization still has very useful properties that can be exploited for game programming.

In explaining the planar memory organization, it's useful to first examine a hypothetical organization that resembles the linear organization described previously. Imagine a memory organization that is linear in nature, but represents a pixel's color by a single bit. Eight of these bits can fit into a single byte, and thus eight pixels can be accessed at one time. Obviously, since a pixel can only have two states, the organization represents a monochrome organization; that is, there are only two colors—black and white. Figure 5.2 shows what this organization would look like for a 640x480 pixel screen, mapped into segment 0A000h.

Now, this organization is very useful. With it, up to eight individual pixels can be manipulated with a single byte-sized write. Unfortunately, because this organization has only two colors, it is very dull. Since computer games aren't supposed to be dull, it just won't do, as is.

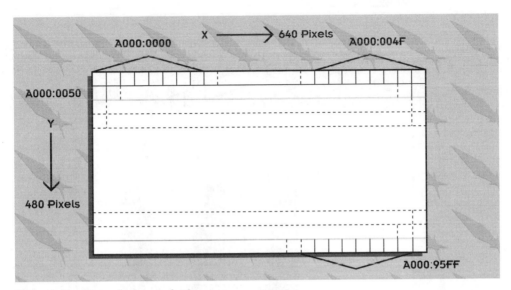

Figure 5.2 *Linear, bit-per-pixel video memory organization.*

To correct the color deficiency, imagine multiple two-dimensional arrays stacked on top of one another. Each pixel is represented by one bit in each of the arrays. Color is represented in the third, depth dimension. In this configuration, the arrays are commonly called *color planes*.

For example, when four planes are stacked atop one another, as shown in Figure 5.3, each pixel can have one of 16 possible color values. If the value 0100b represents the color red, a 0 would be stored in the pixel bit of plane 3, a 1 in plane 2, another 0 in plane 1, and a final 0 in plane 0.

The organization that we've just arrived at corresponds to VGA mode 12h. This is a 640x480 pixel mode that supports 16 possible colors, using four color planes and starting at segment 0A000h. In fact, the use of four planes is hardwired into the VGA hardware and most VGA planar modes allow a maximum of 16 colors. VGA modes allowing greater than 16 colors use the byte-per-pixel organization described earlier.

The next question is, how are the planes mapped into host memory? Are they mapped in one after another? Are the bytes from each plane interleaved with one another?

The answer is that they are mapped *on top of one another*. Each plane occupies the same set of addresses in host memory as each of the other planes. An access from the host CPU to the video memory can manipulate data in one or more planes at a given memory location simultaneously.

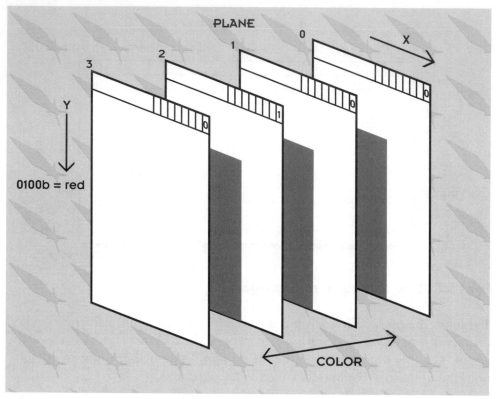

Figure 5.3 *Planar memory organization.*

UNDERSTANDING MULTIPLE DISPLAY PAGES

As we'll see later, the planar structure of the VGA can be very handy for animation techniques. In particular, because the multiple color planes are mapped on top of another, a screen's worth of display memory doesn't take up as much address space in the host address map as it would if it were mapped linearly. For instance, in the linear Mode 13h, each byte of video memory occupies one byte of address space in the host address map. In the planar video modes, four bytes of video memory are all mapped to the same byte of host memory. This attribute allows multiple screen-sized pages of video memory to be accessed from the host.

For example, Figure 5.4 shows the memory map of Mode 0Eh versus the memory map of Mode 13h. Mode 0Eh is a 640x200 pixel, 16-color planar mode. In each case, the video memory on the VGA adapter is mapped into

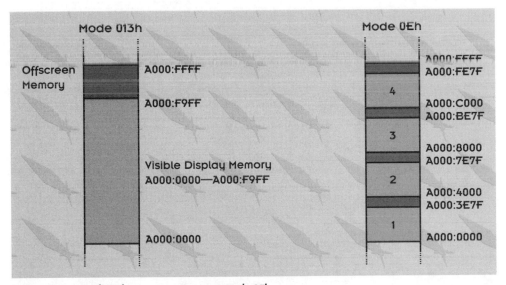

Figure 5.4 *Mode 13h memory map versus Mode 0Eh memory map.*

the 0A000h segment, but in Mode 0Eh, a single screen of memory only occupies 3E80h bytes of host memory address space ((640 * 200) / 8) = 16000 = 3E80h). Typically, this 3E80h bytes worth of memory is rounded upward to 4000h bytes, which is used for the display page size. Four display pages of 4000h bytes can fit in the 64K display memory segment.

We'll see why having multiple display pages is important in a later chapter when we discuss animation techniques that employ "page flipping" to reduce flicker.

A LOOK AT THE VGA DATA PATH

The VGA data path is used to control the manipulation of memory corresponding to pixels in each of the four color planes. The basic VGA data path is shown in Figure 5.5. Because of space limitations, only the logic connected to a single memory plane (in this case, plane 3) is shown. The logic connected to the other three memory planes is identical in function to the logic shown here and operates in parallel.

In truth, the VGA has much more logic than is shown in Figure 5.5, but the block diagram details the components most useful for game programming. You can find a more detailed block diagram of VGA hardware in one of the reference texts.

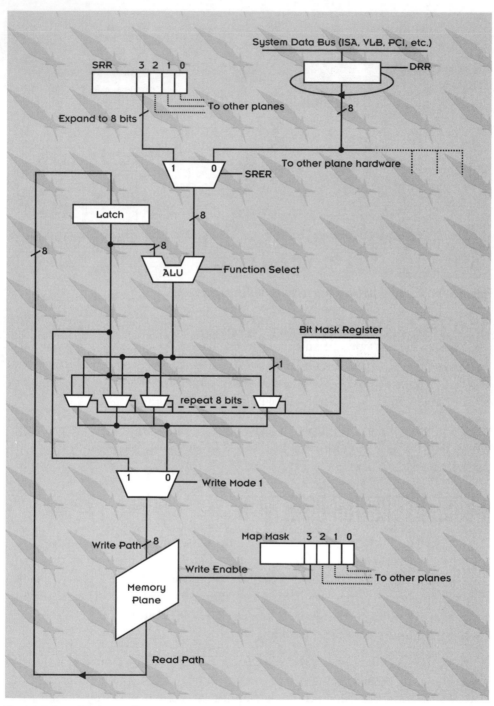

Figure 5.5   *VGA data path.*

Basic Dataflow

Let's take a look at the basic dataflow through the VGA block diagram. Note that the operation of the logic surrounding each memory plane is the same and they all operate in parallel.

Ignoring the SRR, SRER, and Write Mode 1 functions on the block diagram, the data flow is very simple. The key to the VGA block diagram are the plane latches. Whenever the VGA memory is read, each latch is loaded from its corresponding memory plane. The data returned to the host comes from one of the memory planes (explained shortly). Whenever VGA memory is written to, the data in the latches is logically combined with the host provided data and the result written back into the memory planes.

As the block diagram shows, the data is combined in an ALU, controlled by a function select code. The function select code is programmed into a VGA I/O register before the write takes place.

Next, a final data value is created on a bit-by-bit basis by optionally selecting the result of the ALU operation or the original data stored in the latch. Control for the selection is performed by the Bit Mask Register (BMR). A set bit in the BMR indicates that the bit should come from the ALU. A clear bit indicates that the original data bit, stored in the latch, should be rewritten back into memory. Note that the BMR controls the hardware for each memory plane simultaneously. Since each memory byte contains eight pixels, the BMR can be used to only manipulate some of the pixels in the byte, while leaving the others untouched.

Finally, the result of the bit masking operation is optionally written to the corresponding memory plane, subject to the Map Mask Register (MMR). The lower-order four bits of the MMR each control the write enable signal of a memory plane. If the MMR bit corresponding to a plane is set, the plane will be updated with the result of the BMR operation. If the MMR bit is clear, nothing will be written into the memory plane.

Whew! Got all that? If not, here's the summary.

To set a given pixel (or set of pixels in the same byte) to a color, follow these steps:

1. Read the VGA memory corresponding to the pixel location. This will load the VGA latches for each plane with the data from VGA memory. The result of the read returned to the CPU is ignored.
2. Select the pixels to be modified using the BMR.

3. Set the MMR to ensure that all color planes are enabled to be modified.

4. Write 0 to the VGA memory location corresponding to the pixel location. This sets each bit corresponding to the enabled pixels in each color plane to 0.

5. Set the MMR equal to the color to which you want to set the pixels. Note that this enables each color plane with a set bit in the color value and disables each plane with a clear bit in the color value.

6. Write an 0FFh to the VGA memory location corresponding to the pixel location. This sets each color plane bit for the pixel to 1. Note that this only occurs where there is a corresponding 1 in the color value, which is programmed into the MMR.

Set/Reset Register

Notice that the procedure for setting a pixel to a given color using the BMR and MMR requires one read of video memory and two writes. The Set/Reset Register (SRR) and Set/Reset Enable Register (SRER) are used to make setting a pixel (or set of pixels) to a single color very easy.

As indicated in Figure 5.5, when bits in the SRER are set, a multiplexer selects an 8-bit expanded version of the corresponding bit from the SRR to enter the ALU, rather than the data written by the CPU. The SRR represents a color value. By setting the SRER and BMR to the correct values, the color contained in the SRR can be written into selected pixels.

The procedure goes likes this:

1. Read the VGA memory corresponding to the pixel location to load the plane latches.

2. Set the BMR to select the desired pixel or pixels.

3. Set the SRR to the desired color.

4. Set the SRER to 0Fh to enable each bit of the SRR to pass through each plane ALU.

5. Write something (anything, since the CPU data is ignored for each plane where SRER contains a set bit) to the VGA memory location corresponding to the pixel location.

That's it.

When you examine the number of steps of the Set/Reset procedure versus the BMR/MMR procedure, it doesn't seem like we've saved a lot. There are still five steps in the Set/Reset procedure compared to the six steps from the BMR/MMR procedure. That's true when a single pixel is set to a given color.

The Set/Reset procedure really shines, however, when multiple pixels in multiple bytes need to be set to the same color. In this case, you can set up the SRR and SRER once and leave them alone until you finish drawing a particular color. Only the BMR needs to be manipulated to correspond to the interesting pixels in the next byte.

Here's the procedure for drawing multiple pixels:

1. Set the SRR to the desired color.
2. Set the SRER to 0Fh.
3. Read from VGA memory.
4. Set the BMR to select desired pixels.
5. Write to VGA memory.
6. Repeat steps 3 through 5 as many times as needed.

Rotation and ALU Functions

The Data Rotate Register (DRR), shown in Figure 5.6, controls a barrel rotator at the input to the data path logic. The rotator is common to each of the display plane data paths. The rotator is used to shift incoming CPU data before it passes through the ALU. Because multiple pixels are stored per byte of display memory, the data that the CPU wants to write may be misaligned. The rotator can help eliminate some extra processing by the CPU in certain cases.

The Rotate Count field of the DRR is used to select the amount of rotation that is performed. The rotation is a right rotation. Bits rotated out of the least significant bit are put back into the most signficant bit.

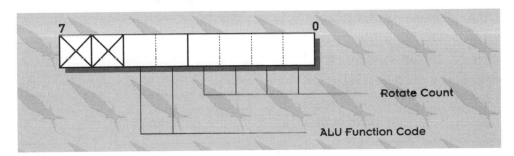

Figure 5.6 *Data rotate register layout.*

Table 5.1   *ALU Operations*

Function Code	Description
0	Pass host data unchanged
1	Host data AND latch data
2	Host data OR latch data
3	Host data XOR latch data

The ALU can perform four operations on the latch and processor supplied data, as shown in Table 5.1.

Typically, the ALU is set to simply pass through the host data, unchanged.

Default Register Values and Cleaning Up

We left out one last step in the previous procedures—resetting all the registers to their default values. Imagine the consequences of leaving the SRER set to 0Fh and then executing some code that tried to write CPU data into the display planes. Obviously, with the SRER set to 0Fh, the CPU supplied data is ignored and the SRR value is written to the planes. In order to prevent situations like this, it's customary for routines to be good citizens and reset all the registers used in the routine back to their default states.

The default state for each of the registers is shown in Table 5.2.

Read Map Select Register

One final register that is not shown in the VGA data path block diagram is the Read Map Select Register (RMSR). Remember that each byte of host address space in the video memory range corresponds to four bytes of display memory, one in each plane. What happens when the CPU reads video memory when the VGA is in a planar video mode?

Table 5.2   *Default Register Values*

Register	Default Value
BMR	0FFh — all pixels selected
MMR	0Fh — all planes selected
SRER	00h — Set/Reset operation disabled
SRR	Don't care, since SRER = 00h
DRR	0h — no rotate, no ALU function

The RMSR is used to specify which color plane data value is returned to the CPU as the result of a read. To retrieve all four bytes of display memory, the RMSR must be programmed and the video memory read once for each plane.

It turns out, however, that this capability is not used very often. Most reads of the VGA are just for the purpose of loading the plane latches rather than actually retrieving any useful information, so we won't use this register in our code.

Write Mode 1 and Fast Copies

The VGA has four different write modes defined, each with slightly different characteristics. So far, we've detailed the operation of Write Mode 0.

Write Mode 1 is used to quickly copy bytes from one region of VGA memory to another. As we'll see when we discuss video memory bitmaps, this mode is very useful. As the VGA data path block diagram shows, when Write Mode 1 is selected the Set/Reset function, the ALU, and the BMR are all bypassed. The data to be written into video memory comes directly from the plane latches. Only the MMR is honored when Write Mode 1 is selected.

Copying from one region to another is simple.

1. Set Write Mode 1.
2. Make sure the MMR is 0Fh (all planes selected).
3. Read from video memory at the source location to load the plane latches.
4. Write to video memory at the destination location to write the data contained in the latches to video memory. Since all the data comes from the latches, the data value written by the CPU is unimportant.

Because each of the plane latches is read and written with a single instruction, 32 bits of data are moved at once. This vastly speeds up data movement from one region of video memory to another.

The Write Mode 1 is set by accessing the Mode Register. The Mode Register has the layout shown in Figure 5.7. Note that there are other bits in the register that should not be modified when changing the Write Mode 1. To modify the Write Mode 1, a program should first read the Mode Register, modify just the Write Mode field, and then write it back to the Mode Register.

As we delve into offscreen bitmaps in a later chapter, we'll become much more familiar with Write Mode 1. The other two write modes, 2 and 3, are less useful for game programming than these first two. You can find out more about these modes by reading one of the reference texts.

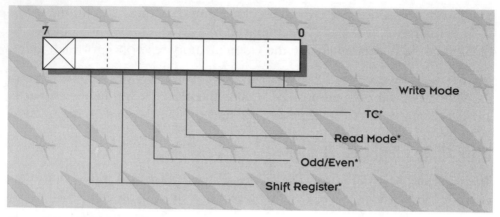

Figure 5.7 *Mode Register layout.*

THE VGA REGISTER MAP

Now that you understand some of the various VGA registers, let's find out how to access them.

The VGA has six major groups of registers: General, Sequencer, CRT Controller, Graphics Controller, Attribute Controller, and Color.

In the first group of registers, the General Registers, each individual register has a corresponding address in the host's I/O address space. The next five groups all use an indexed addressing scheme. This scheme uses two I/O ports. The first port is the index port and the second is the data port. Each VGA register in the five groups that use this scheme is given an index value. The registers are accessed by first writing the appropriate index to the index port and then reading or writing the data port. Each register of a group shares the same index and data ports. Different groups use different index and data ports.

Table 5.3 lists the I/O port addresses corresponding to the General Registers.

Table 5.3 *The General Registers I/O Port Addresses*

General Registers	Read Port	Write Port
Miscellaneous Output Register	3CCh	3C2h
Feature Control Register	3CAh	3DAh
Input Status #0 Register	3C2h	—
Input Status #1 Register	3DAh	—

Table 5.4 *The Sequencer Registers*

Group	Register	Index Port	Data Port	Index Value
Sequencer		3C4h	3C5h	
	Reset			00h
	Clocking Mode			01h
	Map Mask (MMR)			02h
	Character Map Select			03h
	Memory Mode			04h

Tables 5.4, 5.5, 5.6, and 5.7 detail the Index Port and Data Port for the Sequencer, CRT Controller, Graphics Controller, and Attribute Controller registers, and the Index Values for each of the specific registers of those groups. The Color Register group, shown in Table 5.8, is covered more extensively in Chapter 8.

The Attribute Controller group differs from the other register groups. The Index Port and Data Port of this group are mapped to the same host location. An internal flip-flop on the VGA card controls whether writes to the combined port actually go to the Index or Data port. To write to a register, the flip-flop is first cleared by reading the Input Status #1 Register (in the General Register group) and then the index value is written to the combined port. When the index value is written, the internal flip-flop changes state and indicates that the next value written to the combined port will go to the actual register whose index was just written. When the data value is written, the flip-flop again changes state and indicates that the next value will be an index value.

Note that not all of the registers listed in this table are described fully in this text. Some registers are described in a later chapters. If you are interested, consult one of the reference texts for detailed information about all the VGA registers.

The header file VGA.H, shown in Listing 5.1, contains constant definitions for the VGA register and index values detailed in Tables 5.4 through 5.8. It also includes some macros for setting some of the common VGA registers (BMR, SRR, SRER, and MMR).

Creating VGA Support Modules

Before we get deeper into the VGA, let's create a few support files, VGA.H and VGA.C, that implement some useful functions for accessing registers.

Table 5.5 *The CRT Controller Registers*

Group	Register	Index Port	Data Port	Index Value
CRT Controller		3D4h	3D5h	
	Horizontal Total			00h
	Horizontal Display End			01h
	Start Horizontal Blanking			02h
	End Horizontal Blanking			03h
	Start Horizontal Retrace			04h
	End Horizontal Retrace			05h
	Vertical Total			06h
	Overflow			07h
	Preset Row Scan			08h
	Maximum Scan Line			09h
	Cursor Start			0Ah
	Cursor End			0Bh
	Start Address High			0Ch
	Start Address Low			0Dh
	Cursor Location High			0Eh
	Cursor Location Low			0Fh
	Vertical Retrace Start			10h
	Vertical Retrace End			11h
	Vertical Display End			12h
	Offset			13h
	Underline Location			14h
	Start Vertical Blank			15h
	End Vertical Blank			16h
	Mode Control			17h
	Line Compare			18h

Table 5.6   *The Graphics Controller Registers*

Group	Register	Index Port	Data Port	Index Value
Graphics Controller		3CEh	3CFh	
	Set/Reset (SRR)			00h
	Set/Reset Enable (SRER)			01h
	Color Compare			02h
	Data Rotate (DRR)			03h
	Read Map Select (RMSR)			04h
	Mode			05h
	Miscellaneous			06h
	Color (Don't Care)			07h
	Bit Mask (BMR)			08h

Table 5.7   *The Attribute Controller Registers*

Group	Register	Index Port	Data Port	Index Value
Attribute Controller		3C0h	3C0h	
	Palette			00h - 0Fh
	Mode Control			10h
	Overscan Color			11h
	Color Plane Enable			12h
	Horizontal Pixel Panning			13h
	Color Select			14h

Table 5.8   *The Color Registers*

Group	Register	Port
Color	Color Address Write Register	3C8h
	Color Address Read Register	3C7h
	Color Data Register	3C9h

Listing 5.1   VGA.H

```
/* File: VGA.H
** Description:
**    Register definitions and constants for the VGA.
** Copyright:
**    Copyright 1994, David G. Roberts
*/

#ifndef _VGA_H

#include <dos.h>
#include "gamedefs.h"

/* constants */
#define VGA_BIOS_INT      (0x10)  /* VGA BIOS interrupt */

#define VIDEO_MEM_SEGMENT   (0xA000) /* Segment for video memory */

#define MODE13H_WIDTH   (320)    /* width of mode 013h */
#define MODE13H_HEIGHT  (200)    /* height of mode 013h */

#define MODEX_WIDTH     (320)    /* width of mode X */
#define MODEX_HEIGHT    (240)    /* height of mode X */

#define MODEY_WIDTH     (320)    /* width of mode Y */
#define MODEY_HEIGHT    (200)    /* height of mode Y */

#define MODE_X          (0xFF)   /* mode numbers for Modes X & Y */
#define MODE_Y          (0xFE)

/* General Registers */
#define MISC_OUTPUT_REG (0x3C2) /* Write port for Misc. Output Register */
#define MISC_OUTPUT_REG_READ (0x3CC) /* Read port for Misc. Output Reg. */

#define FEATURE_CNTRL_REG (0x3DA) /* Write port for Feature Control Reg. */
#define FEATURE_CNTRL_REG_READ (0x3CA) /* Read port for FC Reg. */

#define INPUT_STAT_0_REG (0x3C2) /* Input Status Reg. #0 */
#define INPUT_STAT_1_REG (0x3DA) /* Input Status Reg. #1 */

/* Sequencer Registers */
#define SEQ_INDEX_REG   (0x3C4) /* Sequencer Index Register */
#define SEQ_DATA_REG    (0x3C5) /* Sequencer Data Register */

#define RESET_INDEX                 (0)
#define CLOCKING_MODE_INDEX         (1)
#define MAP_MASK_INDEX              (2)
#define CHARACTER_MAP_SELECT_INDEX  (3)
#define MEMORY_MODE_INDEX           (4)

/* CRTC Registers */
#define CRTC_INDEX_REG  (0x3D4) /* CRTC Index Register */
#define CRTC_DATA_REG   (0x3D5) /* CRTC Data Register */
```

```
#define HORIZ_TOTAL_INDEX              (0x00)
#define HORIZ_DISPLAY_END_INDEX        (0x01)
#define START_HORIZ_BLANK_INDEX        (0x02)
#define END_HORIZ_BLANK_INDEX          (0x03)
#define START_HORIZ_RETRACE_INDEX      (0x04)
#define END_HORIZ_RETRACE_INDEX        (0x05)
#define VERT_TOTAL_INDEX               (0x06)
#define OVERFLOW_INDEX                 (0x07)
#define PRESET_ROW_SCAN_INDEX          (0x08)
#define MAX_SCAN_LINE_INDEX            (0x09)
#define CURSOR_START_INDEX             (0x0A)
#define CURSOR_END_INDEX               (0x0B)
#define START_ADDRESS_HIGH_INDEX       (0x0C)
#define START_ADDRESS_LOW_INDEX        (0x0D)
#define CURSOR_LOCATION_HIGH_INDEX     (0x0E)
#define CURSOR_LOCATION_LOW_INDEX      (0x0F)
#define VERT_RETRACE_START_INDEX       (0x10)
#define VERT_RETRACE_END_INDEX         (0x11)
#define VERT_DISPLAY_END_INDEX         (0x12)
#define OFFSET_INDEX                   (0x13)
#define UNDERLINE_LOCATION_INDEX       (0x14)
#define START_VERT_BLANK_INDEX         (0x15)
#define END_VERT_BLANK_INDEX           (0x16)
#define MODE_CONTROL_INDEX             (0x17)
#define LINE_COMPARE_INDEX             (0x18)


/* Graphics Control Registers */
#define GC_INDEX_REG    (0x3CE) /* Graphics Control Index Register */
#define GC_DATA_REG     (0x3CF) /* Graphics Control Data Register */

#define SET_RESET_INDEX               (0)
#define SET_RESET_ENABLE_INDEX        (1)
#define COLOR_COMPARE_INDEX           (2)
#define DATA_ROTATE_INDEX             (3)
#define READ_MAP_SELECT_INDEX         (4)
#define MODE_INDEX                    (5)
#define MISC_INDEX                    (6)
#define COLOR_DONT_CARE_INDEX         (7)
#define BIT_MASK_INDEX                (8)

/* Color Registers */
#define COLOR_ADDRESS_WRITE (0x3C8)
#define COLOR_ADDRESS_READ  (0x3C7)
#define COLOR_DATA          (0x3C9)

/* Macros for setting frequently used VGA registers directly */
#define SetBMR(val) outport(GC_INDEX_REG, BIT_MASK_INDEX | (val << 8))
#define SetSRR(val) outport(GC_INDEX_REG, SET_RESET_INDEX | (val << 8))
#define SetSRER(val) outport(GC_INDEX_REG,\
                    SET_RESET_ENABLE_INDEX | (val <<8))
#define SetMMR(val) outport(SEQ_INDEX_REG, MAP_MASK_INDEX | (val << 8))
```

```
/* Function prototypes */
void SetVGAReg(UINT16 IndexReg, UINT8 Index, UINT16 DataReg, UINT8 Data);
void SetVGAMode(UINT16 Mode);
void SetMode13h(void);
BOOL DetectVGA(void);

/* exported global variables */
extern UINT16    GScreenWidth;
extern UINT16    GScreenHeight;
extern UINT16    GScreenVirtualWidth;
extern UINT16    GScreenVirtualHeight;
extern UINT8     GVGAMode;

#define _VGA_H

#endif
```

The file VGA.C, shown in Listing 5.2, contains a set of short routines for
setting VGA registers, setting VGA modes, and detecting the VGA. The file
also defines four global variables, **GScreenWidth**, **GScreenHeight**,
GScreenVirtualWidth, and **GVGAMode**, which are used in a later chapter
by some animation functions. These variables are set by some of the functions
the put the VGA into a video mode, such as **SetMode13h**.

Listing 5.2   VGA.C

```
/* File: VGA.C
** Description:
**    Miscellaneous VGA functions.
** Copyright:
**    Copyright 1994, David G. Roberts
*/

#include <dos.h>
#include "gamedefs.h"
#include "vga.h"

/* global variables describing screen parameters */
UINT16  GScreenWidth;
UINT16  GScreenHeight;
UINT16  GScreenVirtualWidth;
UINT8   GVGAMode;


/*
    Function: SetVGAReg
    Description:
        Sets a VGA register, identified by the IndexReg, DataReg, and
        Index parameters to the value specified by the Data parameter.
*/
```

```
void SetVGAReg(UINT16 IndexReg, UINT8 Index, UINT16 DataReg, UINT8 Data)
{
    outportb(IndexReg, Index);
    outportb(DataReg, Data);
}

/*
    Function: SetVGAMode
    Description:
        Uses the video BIOS to set the VGA video mode.
*/
void SetVGAMode(UINT16 Mode)
{
    union REGS regs;

    regs.x.ax = Mode;

    int86(VGA_BIOS_INT, &regs, &regs);
}

/*
    Function: SetMode13h
    Description:
        Puts the VGA into Mode 13h and sets the global variables
        describing the screen state appropriately.
*/
void SetMode13h(void)
{
    SetVGAMode(0x13);

    GScreenWidth        = MODE13H_WIDTH;
    GScreenHeight       = MODE13H_HEIGHT;
    GScreenVirtualWidth = MODE13H_WIDTH;
    GVGAMode            = 0x13;
}

/*
    Function: DetectVGA
    Description:
        Returns TRUE if a VGA is detected, FALSE otherwise.
*/
BOOL DetectVGA(void)
{
    union REGS regs;

    /* try a BIOS call only the VGA understands */
    regs.x.bx = 0xFFFF;
    regs.x.ax = 0x101A;

    int86(VGA_BIOS_INT, &regs, &regs);

    /* if the card didn't understand, it's not a VGA */
    if (regs.x.bx == 0xFFFF) {
```

```
        return FALSE;
    }
    else {
        return TRUE;
    }
}
```

The **DetectVGA** function deserves a little explanation. The VGA BIOS supports many BIOS functions that previous graphics adapters like the EGA did not. The **DetectVGA** function calls one of these functions and checks to see whether the graphics card BIOS handled the call or simply returned. In particular, **DetectVGA** calls the Read Current Color Page Number BIOS function. If the BIOS handles the call, it will overwrite the FFFFh value which BX is initialized to previously. If not, the card is not a VGA. The Read Current Color Page Number function is not special. Any one of a number of VGA BIOS functions would serve equally well. The Read Current Color Page Number function just happens to work and be very easy to test.

THE STANDARD VGA MODES

There are several different standard video modes that the VGA supports. Each of these modes has a different resolution, numbers of colors, and style of memory organization. Table 5.9 lists a few of the various modes (not all; just the ones most likely to be used for game programming) and some relevant information about each.

A program configures the VGA into one of the modes in Table 5.9 by setting register AX to the correct mode number and calling INT 10h.

To return back to text mode (typically just before a program exits back to DOS), call INT 10h with AX equal to 0x03. Note that if you do not return to text mode before the program exits, the screen will become garbled and users will be upset.

Table 5.9 *Standard VGA Modes*

Mode Number	Resolution	Pixels per Byte	Bytes per Row	Number of Colors
0Dh	320x200	8	40	16
0Eh	640x200	8	80	16
10h	640x350	8	80	16
12h	640x480	8	80	16
13h	320x200	1	320	256

Note that in each of these modes, video memory is mapped into the 0A000 host address segment.

The **SetVGAMode** and **SetMode13h** functions from VGA.C can be used to easily set a particular mode.

A Standard VGA Mode Example

The program VGADEMO.C, shown in Listing 5.3, demonstrates how to manipulate the hardware of the standard VGA modes. The program takes the mode number specified on the command line, and enters that VGA mode. The program then allows the user to draw on the graphics screen using the mouse. The left mouse button is used to draw pixels and the right mouse button is used to change the drawing color.

The mode number supplied on the command line must be specified in the format "0xM", where M is the mode number in hex digits. Hitting any key will end the program and return to DOS.

VGA Sketch

Our first project in this chapter is a simple VGA sketch program. The user can draw pixels on the VGA screen using the mouse. The program supports several standard VGA modes, including linear Mode 13h and a few planar modes.

Compiling and Linking:

You can compile the VGADEMO program using the Borland C++ 3.1 IDE by typing "bc vgademo.prj" and then selecting Compile | Make from the menus. If you would rather use the command line compiler, convert the VGADEMO.PRJ file to a makefile using the PRJ2MAK program supplied with Borland C++ 3.1. Type "prj2mak vgademo.prj" to create the VGADEMO.MAK and VGADEMO.CFG files.

If you are using Borland C++ 4.0, choose Project | Open Project from the IDE menus. Open the VGADEMO.PRJ file. Borland C++ will convert the version 3.1 .PRJ file to a version 4.0 .IDE file. Compile and link the program by choosing Project | Make All from the IDE menus.

Listing 5.3   VGADEMO.C

```c
/* File: VGADEMO.C
** Description:
**      VGA sketch demo program.
** Copyright:
**      Copyright 1994, David G. Roberts
*/

#include <assert.h>
#include <conio.h>
#include <dos.h>
#include <stdio.h>
#include <stdlib.h>
#include "gamedefs.h"
#include "mouse.h"
#include "mouseevt.h"
#include "vga.h"

/* constants */
#define TEXT_MODE_NUMBER           (0x03)
#define MOUSE_EVENT_QUEUE_LENGTH    (100)
#define MODE_13H_HORIZ             (320)
#define MODE_13H_VERT              (200)
#define VIDEO_MEM_SEGMENT        (0xA000)

/* types */
typedef struct {
    int Mode;
    int XDim;
    int YDim;
    int BytesPerLine;
    int PixelsPerByte;
    int MaxColors;
    int MouseXDivisor;
    int MouseYDivisor;
} MODE_INFO;

/* module variables */
UINT8 PenColor;
int PenDown;
UINT16 ModeNumber;
MODE_INFO CurrentModeInfo;
static MODE_INFO ModeInfoTable[] = {
    {0xD, 320, 200, 40, 8, 16, 4, 1},
    {0xE, 640, 200, 80, 8, 16, 1, 1},
    {0x10, 640, 350, 80, 8, 16, 1, 1},
    {0x12, 640, 480, 80, 8, 16, 1, 1},
    {0x13, 320, 200, 320, 1, 256, 2, 1}
};

/*
    Function: GetModeInfo
```

```
Description:
    When supplied with a valid mode, the function returns
    information about it.  The info is returned in the
    MODE_INFO structure pointed to by ModeInfoReturn.
    If the supplied mode number is invalid, the function
    returns FALSE, otherwise it returns TRUE.
*/
int GetModeInfo(UINT16 Mode, MODE_INFO * ModeInfoReturn)
{
    int i;

    for (i = 0; i <= DIM(ModeInfoTable); i++) {
        if (Mode == ModeInfoTable[i].Mode) {
            *ModeInfoReturn = ModeInfoTable[1];
            return TRUE;
        }
    }
    return FALSE;
}


/*
    Function: PlotMode13h
    Description:
        Plots a pixel in mode 013h (assumes that the VGA has already
        been set to that mode).
*/
void PlotMode13h(UINT16 X, UINT16 Y, UINT16 Color)
{
    UINT16 Offset;
    UINT8 far * GraphicsBase;

    /* make sure parameters are in range */
    assert(X <= (MODE_13H_HORIZ - 1));
    assert(Y <= (MODE_13H_VERT - 1));

    /* create a far pointer to the base of Mode 13h memory */
    GraphicsBase = (UINT8 far *) MK_FP(VIDEO_MEM_SEGMENT,0);

    /* compute offset from X,Y coordinates */
    Offset = Y * MODE_13H_HORIZ + X;

    /* set pixel to color */
    *(GraphicsBase + Offset) = Color;
}


/*
    Function: PlotPlanarMode
    Description:
        Plots a point in a planar mode.
*/
void PlotPlanarMode(MODE_INFO * ModeInfo, UINT16 X, UINT16 Y, UINT16 Color)
{
    UINT16 Offset;
```

```
    UINT8 far * GraphicsBase;
    UINT8 PixelNumber;
    UINT8 PixelMask;
    UINT8 Dummy;

    assert(X <= (ModeInfo->XDim - 1));
    assert(Y <= (ModeInfo->YDim - 1));

    /* compute VGA memory location */
    GraphicsBase = (UINT8 far *) MK_FP(VIDEO_MEM_SEGMENT, 0);
    Offset = (Y * ModeInfo->BytesPerLine) + (X / ModeInfo->PixelsPerByte);
    PixelNumber = X % ModeInfo->PixelsPerByte;

    /* read VGA (load latches) */
    Dummy = GraphicsBase[Offset];

    /* set BMR to enable correct pixel location */
    PixelMask = 0x80 >> PixelNumber;
    SetBMR(PixelMask);

    /* set SRR to color */
    SetSRR((UINT8) Color);

    /* set SRER to enable SR function on all planes */
    SetSRER(0xF);

    /* write anything to VGA memory location */
    GraphicsBase[Offset] = Dummy;

    /* clean up */
    SetBMR(0xFF);   /* all pixels */
    SetSRER(0x00);  /* SR function disabled */
}

/*
    Function: VGAPlotPoint
    Description:
        Plots a point on the screen.
*/
void VGAPlotPoint(MODE_INFO * ModeInfo, UINT16 X, UINT16 Y, UINT16 Color)
{
    if (ModeInfo->Mode == 0x13) {
        PlotMode13h(X, Y, Color);
    }
    else {
        PlotPlanarMode(ModeInfo, X, Y, Color);
    }
}

/*
    Function: GetCommandLineMode
    Description:
        Examines the first parameter supplied on the command line
```

```
                    and converts it from a string to an integer.  The integer
                    is then returned to the caller.  If an error occurs, 0
                    is returned instead.
*/
UINT16 GetCommandLineMode(char *argv[])
{
    UINT16 Mode;
    int ScanStatus;

    /* convert argv[1] from ASCII to an integer */
    ScanStatus = sscanf(argv[1], "0x%x", &Mode);

    if (ScanStatus == 1) {
        return Mode;
    }
    else {
        return 0;
    }
}


/*
    Function: IncrementPenColor
    Description:
        Increments the current color of the pen and handles
        wrap-around when the pen has reached the maximum
        number of colors supported by the current mode.
*/
void IncrementPenColor(void)
{
    PenColor++;
    if (PenColor >= CurrentModeInfo.MaxColors) {
        PenColor = 0;
    }
}


/*
    Function: PlotPointAtCursor
    Description:
        Takes care of plotting a point at the cursor location
        given the MouseEvent parameter.
*/
void PlotPointAtCursor(MOUSE_EVENT * MouseEvent)
{
    int Xlocation;
    int Ylocation;

    assert(CurrentModeInfo.MouseXDivisor != 0);
    assert(CurrentModeInfo.MouseYDivisor != 0);

    /* convert mouse coordinates from event to screen coordinates */
    Xlocation = MouseEvent->X / CurrentModeInfo.MouseXDivisor;
    Ylocation = MouseEvent->Y / CurrentModeInfo.MouseYDivisor;
```

```
    /* plot the point, hiding the mouse cursor temporarily while */
    /* we do the screen update */
    HideMouseCursor();
    VGAPlotPoint(&CurrentModeInfo, Xlocation, Ylocation, PenColor);
    ShowMouseCursor();
}


/*
    Function: DispatchMouseEvent
    Description:
        Respond to a mouse event by calling the appropriate
        handling function.
*/
void DispatchMouseEvent(MOUSE_EVENT * MouseEvent)
{
    switch (MouseEvent->Event) {
        case ME_RIGHT_RELEASED:
            IncrementPenColor();
            break;
        case ME_LEFT_PRESSED:
            PenDown = TRUE;
            PlotPointAtCursor(MouseEvent);
            break;
        case ME_LEFT_RELEASED:
            PenDown = FALSE;
            break;
        case ME_MOVEMENT:
            if (PenDown == TRUE) {
                PlotPointAtCursor(MouseEvent);
            }
            break;
        default:
            break;
    }
}

int main(int argc, char *argv[])
{
    int ModeSupported;
    int MouseDriverPresent;
    int DummyKey;
    MOUSE_EVENT MouseEvent;

    /* detect VGA */
    if (!DetectVGA()) {
        printf("You must have a VGA to run this program.\n");
        return 1;
    }

    /* See if we have a command line parameter.  If not, exit. */
    if (argc < 2) {
        printf("You must supply a graphics mode on the command line.\n");
        return 1;
    }
```

```
/* get vga mode from command line */
ModeNumber = GetCommandLineMode(argv);

/* make sure people know what format to use */
if (ModeNumber == 0) {
    printf("Enter mode number as \"0xM\"\n");
    return 1;
}

/* if mode is one we support, initialize mode */
/* else print error and exit */
ModeSupported = GetModeInfo(ModeNumber, &CurrentModeInfo);
if (ModeSupported == FALSE) {
    printf("Mode 0x%x is not supported.\n", ModeNumber);
    return 1;
}
SetVGAMode(CurrentModeInfo.Mode);

/* initialize mouse */
MouseDriverPresent = ResetMouse();
if (MouseDriverPresent == 0) {
    SetVGAMode(TEXT_MODE_NUMBER);
    printf("Mouse needed for this program.\n");
    return 1;
}

/* Install a handler.  Note that we don't respond to */
/* right button press events (only right release). */
InstallMouseEventQueue(MOUSE_EVENT_QUEUE_LENGTH,
    ME_RIGHT_RELEASED | ME_LEFT_PRESSED | ME_LEFT_RELEASED |
    ME_MOVEMENT);

/* initialize pen */
PenDown = FALSE;
PenColor = 1;   /* note 0 = black */

ShowMouseCursor();

/* Do polling loop. When key is hit, exit. */
while (!kbhit()) {
    if (QueryMouseEventWaiting()) {
        GetMouseEvent(&MouseEvent);
        DispatchMouseEvent(&MouseEvent);
    }
}

/* read this so it isn't left hanging around for DOS to find */
DummyKey = getch();

/* clean up mouse */
HideMouseCursor();
RemoveMouseEventQueue();
```

```
    /* enter text mode again */
    SetVGAMode(TEXT_MODE_NUMBER);

    /* terminate program */
    return 0;
}
```

The program reads the VGA mode number from the command line, puts the VGA into that mode, initializes the mouse, and then waits for mouse events. To handle mouse events, the program uses the MOUSEEVT.C module described in Chapter 4. As mouse events occur, they are dispatched and the appropriate action is taken. If the left mouse button is pressed, the program puts the pen down and draws pixels wherever the mouse is moved. If the right mouse button is pressed, the pen color is incremented. The program exits the mouse event loop when a key is pressed. As the program exits, the mouse handler is removed, the mouse cursor is hidden, and the VGA is returned to text mode.

The **ModeInfoTable** holds information about the various modes supported by the program. The **GetModeInfo** function finds an entry in the **ModeInfoTable** based on the supplied mode number and returns it. The data in the **MODE_INFO** structure returned is used in the main module to convert from mouse coordinates to screen coordinates and by the drawing routines to handle the various resolutions.

The actual work of putting a pixel on the screen is performed by the **PlotMode13h** and **PlotPlanarMode** functions. The **PlotMode13h** function, presented earlier in the chapter, simply identifies the byte corresponding to the (x,y) location supplied to the function and changes it to the appropriate color. **PlotPlanarMode** is generalized to deal with any of the 16-color planar modes that the VGA supports. **PlotPlanarMode** uses the Set/Reset technique described earlier to change the specified pixel's color. Note that the function is limited to plotting on the first display page of the mode. If you want to plot to another display page, you can add another parameter to the function to specify the display page. The function can then use this parameter to add an offset of the display page to the **Offset** variable.

INTRODUCING MODE X

At this point, you should have a pretty good idea of the difference between the linear Mode 13h and the planar VGA modes. With respect to game programming, Mode 13h is, generally speaking, better than the other planar modes. Mode 13h has the following advantages.

- It has a medium resolution. Having too low or too high a resolution is a disadvantage: If the resolution is too low, graphic images look "blocky" and unrealistic. An artist won't be able to include detail in the image to enhance its look. High resolution, on the other hand, implies that a large number of pixels might have to be drawn during each animation frame. More pixels implies more time to draw them, which in turn implies less frames of animation per second. As we'll see in the next chapter, having an acceptable number of animation frames per second is important to making the animation smooth. Increasing the resolution above a given amount does nothing more than make animation less smooth—it doesn't contribute to the enjoyment of the game.

- Mode 13h has a large number of colors. Although the 256 colors that this mode supports may not seem like a lot, a 256-color palette is much more desirable than the 16-color palette the other VGA modes support. In fact, a clever artist can use the increased number of colors to include detailed shading into images that can actually help make Mode 13h's resolution seem higher than it is.

- Mode 13h is a much easier mode to work with. It does not need to deal with Map Mode Registers, Bit Mask Registers, or any other kind of register. Plotting a pixel is as simple as writing a single byte, corresponding to the pixel color, to memory. Easy!

There are two things that Mode 13h can't provide, however: multiple display pages and fast copies between video RAM using the display latches.

Remember that each byte of display memory corresponding to a screen pixel is individually addressable in Mode 13h's linear organization. At Mode 13h's 320x200 resolution, this corresponds to 64,000 bytes of memory. Only one display page can fit into the 64K video memory segment at address A000:0000. Remember that Mode 0Eh (Figure 5.4) can support four display pages. As we'll see in the next chapter, having multiple display pages helps make animation smooth.

Additionally, the general VGA data path is turned off when Mode 13h operates. In particular, the latches can't be used for fast video-memory to video-memory copies. As the next chapter will show, this can be an effective way to draw graphic images very quickly.

So a logical question is, can we get all the advantages of both Mode 13h and the planar modes in a single mode?

The answer is no, we can't. But we can get most of the advantages of both Mode 13h and the planar modes using an undocumented VGA mode called Mode X. Although Mode X was not documented as a standard VGA mode, it will function on all VGA cards. Strictly speaking, Mode X is one of a family of similar modes, all sharing the same video memory organization but differing with respect to screen resolution.

In particular, Mode X has the following properties:

- 256 colors
- 320x240 pixel resolution with square pixels
- Multiple display pages (between 3 and 4 pages)
- Allows using the VGA latches for fast copies

Mode X's resolution is about the same as Mode 13h, but uses 240 pixels in the vertical direction rather than Mode 13h's 200. This addition makes the pixels square; the pixels in Mode 13h are slightly taller than they are wide. This can create a problem when you want to move a graphic object across the screen at the same speed both vertically and horizontally. With non-square pixels you'd have to correct for the distortion and move slower in the vertical direction than in the horizontal. With Mode X, you just move the object the same number of pixels in both the X and Y directions. Additionally, when you draw a square in Mode 13h using the same number of pixels in both the X and Y directions, you will end up with a rectangle. In Mode X, you get a square. The use of 240 pixels in the vertical direction may not seem like a big feature at first glance, but it eliminates many minor annoyances.

Mode X supports a little less than four display pages. The number of pages is not strictly four because we used some additional display memory to make the resolution 320x240. A sibling mode to Mode X, named Mode Y, uses the same 320x200 resolution as Mode 13h, and has four display pages. Typically, only two display pages are necessary to create high-quality animation. Having three pages rather than four does not create a problem.

So, the next question is, how much did we have to give up to get Mode X? Well, we had to give up the simple linear memory organization of Mode 13h and trade it for a planar memory organization *similar* to that of the standard planar modes. Note that I said similar to that of the other planar modes, not exactly the same. What are the differences? Read on.

Mode X Memory Organization—A Hybrid

The memory organization of Mode X is a sort of hybrid combination of the byte-per-pixel Mode 13h and the other planar modes. In Mode X, each pixel occupies a byte of display memory, but instead of the bytes being mapped into consecutive host memory locations, they are mapped into four display planes with a byte from each display plane all occupying the same host address location.

Figure 5.8 diagrams how this mapping occurs. Pixel (0,0) is located in the first byte of display plane 0. Pixel (1,0) is located in the first byte of display plane 1, and so on. Pixel (4,0) is located at the second byte of plane 0. From the host's point of view, pixels (0,0) through (3,0) are all located at the same host address. Unlike the typical VGA planar modes where depth represents color, Mode X uses depth to hold pixels with increasing X coordinate values. Increasing X coordinates sequence through the four display planes and then move to the next host memory location.

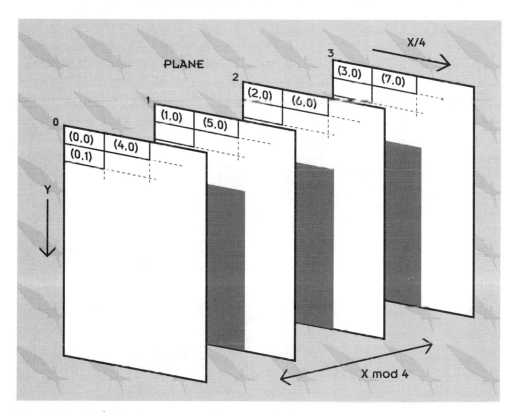

Figure 5.8 *Mode X memory organization.*

Mode X uses the MMR, described earlier, to enable the host to write a color value for a pixel into the correct display plane. Because each pixel occupies a whole byte of a display plane, the BMR and SRR are not used in Mode X operation.

From the host's point of view, the multiple display pages of Mode X look like that shown in Figure 5.9.

As you can see, each display page is 4B00h bytes in length ((320 * 240) / 4 = 19200 = 4B00h). At the end of display memory there are 7936 (1F00h) bytes of of extra memory. As we'll see later, this memory is useful for storing graphic images to be drawn quickly using the VGA display latches.

Entering and Exiting Mode X

Okay, now that we understand how video memory is organized in Mode X, just how do we go about getting the VGA into Mode X? If this mode is undocumented, we can't just call an INT 10h video BIOS function, can we? Well, yes and no.

Putting the VGA into a given video mode by hand is one of the most difficult things to do with the VGA. Over 60 registers have to be programmed with exactly the right values; otherwise, the adapter will not generate the correct video signals to the monitor. It's for this reason that we always let the VGA BIOS handle the task of putting the VGA into a given mode, as we did in the VGA example program. Typically, this operation is only done a couple of times during the run of a program (usually at the beginning to get into a

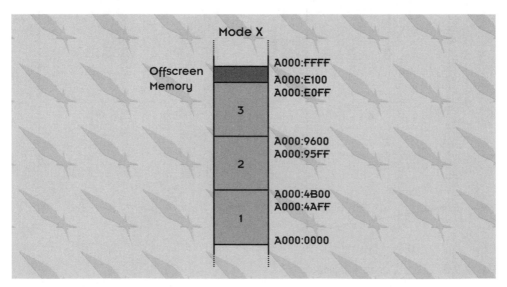

Figure 5.9   *Mode X display pages.*

graphics mode and at the end to return to text mode). Since speed is not an issue, using the BIOS ensures that the operation is done correctly.

eXplorer PROJECT

Gettin Into Mode X

It turns out that Mode X is a fairly simple modification to Mode 13h. To put the VGA into Mode X, we'll call the VGA BIOS to enter Mode 13h, as usual, and then modify a few registers. The code in Listings 5.4 and 5.5 show how this is done.

Listing 5.4   SETMODEX.H

```
/* File: SETMODEX.H
** Description:
**    Header file for module SETMODEX.C.  Routines for entering
**    undocumented modes, X and Y in particular.
** Copyright:
**    Copyright 1994, David G. Roberts
*/

#ifndef _SETMODEX_H

#include "gamedefs.h"

void SetUndocMode(int NumParams, UINT8 ModeParams[], UINT8 DotClock);
void SetModeX(void);
void SetModeY(void);

#define _SETMODEX_H

#endif
```

Listing 5.4   SETMODEX.C

```
/* File: SETMODEX.C
** Description:
**    Routines for putting the VGA into Mode X (and Y).
** Copyright:
**    Copyright 1994, David G. Roberts
** Acknowledgements:
**    Table driven method inspired by source from Themie Gouthas.
*/

#include <assert.h>
#include <dos.h>
#include <stdio.h>
#include "gamedefs.h"
#include "setmodex.h"
#include "vga.h"

/* constants */
```

```c
static UINT8 ModeXParams[] = {
    VERT_TOTAL_INDEX,            0x0D,
    OVERFLOW_INDEX,              0x3E,
    MAX_SCAN_LINE_INDEX,         0x41,
    VERT_RETRACE_START_INDEX,    0xEA,
    VERT_RETRACE_END_INDEX,      0xAC,
    VERT_DISPLAY_END_INDEX,      0xDF,
    UNDERLINE_LOCATION_INDEX,    0x00,
    START_VERT_BLANK_INDEX,      0xE7,
    END_VERT_BLANK_INDEX,        0x06,
    MODE_CONTROL_INDEX,          0xE3
};

static UINT8 ModeYParams[] = {
    UNDERLINE_LOCATION_INDEX,    0x00,
    MODE_CONTROL_INDEX,          0xE3
};

/*
    Function: SetUndocMode
    Description:
        Put the VGA into an undocumented mode.
*/
void SetUndocMode(int NumParams, UINT8 ModeParams[], UINT8 DotClock)
{
    union REGS regs;
    UINT8 VertRetraceEnd;
    unsigned i;
    UINT8 Index;
    UINT8 Data;
    UINT8 far * GraphicsBase;

    assert(ModeParams != NULL);

    /* set Mode 13h using VGA BIOS */
    regs.x.ax = 0x13;
    int86(VGA_BIOS_INT, &regs, &regs);

    /* disable Chain 4 */
    outportb(SEQ_INDEX_REG, MEMORY_MODE_INDEX);
    outportb(SEQ_DATA_REG, 0x06);

    /* enable synchronous reset */
    /* note: this avoids problems while twiddling MISC_OUTPUT_REG */
    outportb(SEQ_INDEX_REG, RESET_INDEX);
    outportb(SEQ_DATA_REG, 0x01);

    /* select 25 MHz dot clock and 60 Hz scan rate */
    if (DotClock != 0) {outportb(MISC_OUTPUT_REG, DotClock);
    }

    /* undo reset */
    outportb(SEQ_INDEX_REG, RESET_INDEX);
    outportb(SEQ_DATA_REG, 0x03);
```

```
    /* remove write protect on CRTC registers */
    outportb(CRTC_INDEX_REG, VERT_RETRACE_END_INDEX);
    VertRetraceEnd = inportb(CRTC_DATA_REG);
    VertRetraceEnd &= 0x7F; /* clear high bit */
    outportb(CRTC_DATA_REG, VertRetraceEnd);


    /* alter CRTC registers */
    for (i = 0; i < NumParams; i++) {
        Index = ModeParams[2 * i];
        Data = ModeParams[(2 * i) + 1];
        outportb(CRTC_INDEX_REG, Index);
        outportb(CRTC_DATA_REG, Data);
    }

    /* clear display memory to zero */
    outportb(SEQ_INDEX_REG, MAP_MASK_INDEX);
    outportb(SEQ_DATA_REG, 0xF);     /* enable all planes */
    GraphicsBase = (UINT8 far *) MK_FP(VIDEO_MEM_SEGMENT, 0);
    for (i = 0; i != 0xFFFF; i++) { /* note i must be unsigned */
        GraphicsBase[i] = 0;
    }
    GraphicsBase[0xFFFF] = 0;
}


/*
    Function: SetModeX
    Description:
        Puts the VGA into Mode X.
*/
void SetModeX(void)
{
    SetUndocMode(DIM(ModeXParams) / 2, ModeXParams, 0xE3);
    GScreenWidth = MODEX_WIDTH;
    GScreenHeight = MODEX_HEIGHT;
    GScreenVirtualWidth = MODEX_WIDTH;
    GVGAMode = MODE_X;
}

/*
    Function: SetModeY
    Description:
        Puts the VGA into Mode Y.
*/
void SetModeY(void)
{
    SetUndocMode(DIM(ModeYParams) / 2, ModeYParams, 0);
    GScreenWidth = MODEY_WIDTH;
    GScreenHeight = MODEY_HEIGHT;
    GScreenVirtualWidth = MODEY_WIDTH;
    GVGAMode = MODE_Y;
}
```

The module's main routine is **SetUndocMode**. **SetUndocMode** accepts an array of parameters that controls exactly which undocumented mode is to be set, either Mode X or Mode Y. The functions **SetModeX** and **SetModeY** are entry points that pass the correct list of parameters to **SetUndocMode**.

SetUndocMode starts by putting the VGA into Mode 13h using the VGA BIOS. **SetUndocMode** then disables the "Chain 4" bit of the Memory Mode Register.

The Chain 4 bit is used by the VGA to indicate whether the MMR is to be used to control access to the display planes. The VGA has four distinct display planes. When the VGA is put into the linear Mode 13h, however, the display planes are "chained" together to appear as linear memory.

When the Chain 4 bit is set, the lower two bits of the address on the host bus are used to select which plane the data will be written into. This allows a program using Mode 13h to simply read and write video memory in a linear fashion. When Chain 4 is reset, the MMR is used to control the host accesses to video memory instead. Resetting the Chain 4 bit is what gives Mode X its strange memory-mapping quality.

Note that in both cases, Mode 13h and Mode X, the pixels are stored in the exact same bytes of video memory; it's just the interface to them from the host's perspective that has changed.

After resetting Chain 4, **SetUndocMode** sets the VGA dot clock appropriately. Setting the dot clock to 25 MHz ensures that Mode X will work with some fixed-frequency monitors that would otherwise have problems. Prior to setting the dot clock, **SetUndocMode** puts the VGA into a reset state so that no problems occur while the dot clock is manipulated. The reset state is exited after the dot clock has been set.

Next, **SetUndocMode** removes the write protect condition on the first eight CRT Controller (CRTC) registers. When the VGA was created, a bit was added to the Vertical Retrace End Register, which controls whether writes are allowed to the first eight CRTC registers. This bit prevents older programs that expect an EGA card from modifying these registers with values inappropriate for VGA operation. In order to ensure that **SetUndocMode** can manipuate the first seven CRTC registers, the routine clears the high bit of the register, removing the write protect condition.

Next, the routine writes the values from the parameter array passed to it into the CRTC registers. Without going into a lot of detail, the parameters set the

VGA to accommodate the new 240 line screen size. This entails telling the VGA how many scan lines there will be on the screen and adjusting the timing periods for such things as vertical retrace.

Finally, **SetUndocMode** clears video memory to ensure that garbage isn't left on the display.

Note that exiting Mode X or Mode Y is as simple as calling the VGA BIOS to set a new display mode, usually text Mode 03h when a program terminates.

A Mode X Example

The MODEXDMO.C program, shown in Listing 5.5, demonstrates the usage of Mode X and Y. The program enters either Mode X or Y, as specified by the command-line parameter, and then draws random colored dots at random positions on the screen. The program terminates when any key is pressed.

Drawing in Mode X or Mode Y

Our second project in this chapter is a simple program that draws random dots on either a Mode X or Mode Y screen.

Compiling and Linking:

You can compile the MODEXDMO program using the Borland C++ 3.1 IDE by typing "bc modexdmo.prj" and then selecting Compile | Make from the menus. If you would rather use the command line compiler, convert the MODEXDMO.PRJ file to a makefile using the PRJ2MAK program supplied with Borland C++ 3.1. Type "prj2mak modexdmo.prj" to create the MODEXDMO.MAK and MODEXDMO.CFG files.

If you are using Borland C++ 4.0, choose Project | Open Project from the IDE menus. Open the MODEXDMO.PRJ file. Borland C++ will convert the version 3.1 .PRJ file to a version 4.0 .IDE file. Compile and link the program by choosing Project | Make All from the IDE menus.

Listing 5.5   MODEXDMO.C

```
/* File: MODEXDMO.C
** Description:
**      Demo program using Mode X or Mode Y.
** Copyright:
**      Copyright 1994, David G. Roberts
*/
```

```c
#include <assert.h>
#include <conio.h>
#include <ctype.h>
#include <dos.h>
#include <stdio.h>
#include <stdlib.h>
#include <time.h>
#include "gamedefs.h"
#include "setmodex.h"
#include "vga.h"


/* constants */
#define TEXT_MODE_NUMBER    (0x03)
#define MODE_XY_HORIZ       (320)
#define MODE_X_VERT         (240)
#define MODE_Y_VERT         (200)
#define PIXELS_PER_BYTE     (4)
#define BYTES_PER_LINE      (320 / PIXELS_PER_BYTE)
#define VIDEO_MEM_SEGMENT   (0xA000)

/*
    Function: PlotUndocMode
    Description:
        Plots a point in an undoc mode (either X or Y).
*/
void PlotUndocMode(UINT16 X, UINT16 Y, UINT16 Color)
{
    UINT16 Offset;
    UINT8 far * GraphicsBase;
    int PixelNumber;
    UINT8 PixelMask;

    assert(X < MODE_XY_HORIZ);
    assert(Y < MODE_X_VERT); /* still probs if mode Y and >= MODE_Y_VERT */
    /* compute VGA memory location */
    GraphicsBase = (UINT8 far *) MK_FP(VIDEO_MEM_SEGMENT, 0);
    Offset = Y * BYTES_PER_LINE + (X / PIXELS_PER_BYTE);
    PixelNumber = X % PIXELS_PER_BYTE;
    /* set MMR to enable correct pixel location */
    PixelMask = 1 << PixelNumber;
    SetMMR(PixelMask);

    /* write color to VGA memory location */
    GraphicsBase[Offset] = Color;
    /* clean up */
    SetMMR(0x0F);    /* all pixels */
}

int main(int argc, char *argv[])
{
    int X;
    int Y;
    UINT8 Color;
```

```c
    char PlotMode;
    int DummyKey;

    /* check for VGA */
    if (!DetectVGA()) {
        printf("You must have a VGA to run this program.\n");
        return 1;
    }

    /* See if we have a command line parameter.  If not, exit. */
    if (argc < 2) {
        printf("You must supply a graphics mode on the command line.\n");
        return 1;
    }
    /* get mode from command line */
    PlotMode = tolower(argv[1][0]);
    printf("**%s**\n", argv[1]);

    /* make sure people know what format to use */
    if (PlotMode != 'x' && PlotMode != 'y') {
        printf("Mode must equal 'x' or 'y'.");
        return 1;
    }
    /* initialize mode */
    if (PlotMode == 'x') {
        SetModeX();
    }
    else {
        SetModeY();
    }

    /* seed random number generator */
    randomize();
    /* Do polling loop. When key is hit, exit. */
    while (!kbhit()) {
        X = random(MODE_XY_HORIZ);
        if (PlotMode == 'x') {
            Y = random(MODE_X_VERT);
        }
        else {
            Y = random(MODE_Y_VERT);
        }
        Color = random(256);

        PlotUndocMode(X, Y, Color);
    }
    /* read this so it isn't left hanging around for DOS to find */
    DummyKey = getch();

    /* enter text mode again */
    SetVGAMode(TEXT_MODE_NUMBER);
    /* terminate program */
    return 0;
}
```

The **PlotUndocMode** function performs most of the work in this program. This routine plots a pixel in either Mode X or Mode Y. **PlotUndocMode** first calculates the offset into the graphics memory segment of the addressed pixel. In particular, it takes into account that four adjacent pixels are mapped to the same host memory location. The routine then calculates the memory plane the pixel is stored in. To plot the pixel, the MMR is first set, with the help of the **SetMMR** function, to specify the memory plane of the desired pixel and no others. Finally, the color value is written to video memory at the correct host address. In spite of the change to a Mode X/Y hybrid planar memory structure, the function is still fairly simple.

The main routine simply checks to see which mode has been selected and initializes it. It then sits in a loop, repeatedly drawing random colored pixels at random screen locations until a key has been hit. Once it detects a keypress, the routine reads the key so that it won't be left for DOS to find after the program exits, and resets the VGA mode to the standard 80 by 24 text mode. Finally, the program quits.

SOME GUIDANCE

At this point, your head is probably swimming with all the various modes that the VGA supports. A logical question is this: "Which one should I use for my programs, and why?" Well, the answer to this is that Mode 13h and the un-documented modes (either X or Y) are probably your best bet.

While the VGA provides other modes with higher resolution, they are limited to 16 colors, and higher resolution can often just mean more pixels to move around. As we'll see as we examine animation in Chapter 7, more pixels means more time drawing, which can lead to poor-quality animation. Modes 13h, X, and Y offer the best balance between color availability and resolution. This tradeoff is validated by the tremendous number of commercial games that use one of these modes in deference to the higher-resolution modes.

The next question you may ask is this: "Okay, which one of modes 13h, X, and Y should I use?" The answer is that it depends on what you're trying to do. As we'll see in later chapters, Mode 13h has some advantages that the undocumented modes don't, and vice versa. After you understand the strong points of each mode, you'll be able to make the correct choice when you're writing your own games.

So, now that we have the various VGA modes and plotting all figured out, let's take a look at bitmaps and bitblts.

BITMAPS AND BITBLTS

The secret weapon for fast game graphics is bitblts. Learn how to master the art of displaying fast bitmaps and you'll be on your way to writing fast action games.

You should now have a pretty good idea of how the VGA works. We've learned how to plot points in Mode 13h, the standard planar VGA modes, and two undocumented modes, X and Y. Theoretically, we have all the information we need to draw anything on the screen. We can draw things by calling an appropriate pixel plotting routine a number of times with the correct coordinates and color values. If you've got enough time on your hands to code up an example that uses this method, you'll find that the drawing speed will be slower than molasses. You may not notice it when drawing just a single image, but the slow speed will show itself when you have many images on the screen at once. We'll need a better technique to keep up with the future animation and speed demands of our game.

This chapter introduces the concept of *bitmaps* and shows you how to rapidly draw bitmap images, *bitblts*, in both Mode 13h and Modes X/Y. Bitmaps and bitblts will allow us to draw many images to the screen, keeping our game from moving too slowly.

As you read on, have fun experimenting with the example programs. It's easy to change the bitmaps to different images. Here's your chance to explore your artistic ability and see what you can come up with.

eXPLORER OVERVIEW In this chapter we'll develop a bitblt module, conveniently named BITBLT.C and BITBLT.H, to draw bitmaps rapidly onto the screen. In addition to routines for bitblts in both Mode 13h and Modes X/Y, BITBLT.C contains routines to use offscreen bitmaps and to convert between bitmap formats. This module will become a key component of our *Alien Alley* game as we continue.

BITMAP BASICS

If you look at any video game, you'll see many images representing the characters and objects portrayed in the game. These objects can be people, snakes, alien spaceships, or missiles. The data structure that stores the image of these objects is called a *bitmap*. In this section, we'll first focus on bitmaps that are optimized for Mode 13h. Later, we'll examine how Mode X and Y differ.

Bitmaps provide compact storage for screen images. A bitmap is simply an array of bytes that hold the color values of the screen pixels. Figure 6.1 shows a sample bitmap. The left side of the figure shows how the bitmap will look when it is drawn on the screen (a missile in this case). The right side of the figure shows the set of pixel color values that represent the bitmap. In this example, the white pixels are stored as color 0x00 and the black pixels as color 0x04.

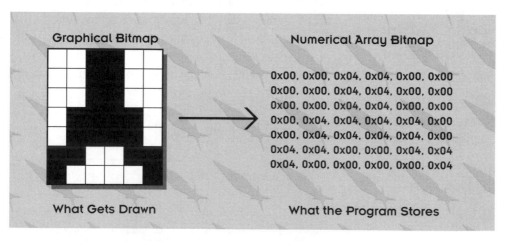

Figure 6.1 *The numerical data and graphical display of a bitmap.*

Within the array, the pixels are stored starting with the upper-left pixel, across each line, and down the rows. In other words, exactly the way English is written—left to right, top to bottom. This storage order matches the order of the pixels in video memory and makes it very easy to draw the bitmap with a minimum of complications.

Our program will use a **LINEAR_BITMAP** structure to store a bitmap. The **LINEAR_BITMAP** structure is defined in BITBLT.H, and shown next. This structure has two members, **Width** and **Height**, that represent the width and height of the bitmap. These two members are used by the bitmap drawing routines to determine the number of rows and columns in the bitmap image. The third and fourth members, **OriginX** and **OriginY**, give the origin of the local bitmap coordinate system relative to the upper-left corner of the bitmap. These two members allow calls to the drawing routine to specify the position of the bitmap on the screen relative to any pixel in the bitmap rather than simply a corner. The final member of the structure is used to mark the position of the first byte of the actual bitmap data. Since the actual number of bytes that are used to store the bitmap image is dependent on the size of the image, only a single byte is defined for the **Data** member in the structure:

```
typedef struct {
    UINT16 Width;
    UINT16 Height;
    int OriginX;
    int OriginY;
    UINT8 Data;
} LINEAR_BITMAP;
```

We'll always access the bitmap through a pointer. This technique will allow us to overlay the **LINEAR_BITMAP** structure onto the beginning of the memory space that stores the bitmap image. Figure 6.2 shows how this works, using the example bitmap image from Figure 6.1.

As shown in the figure, the **LINEAR_BITMAP** structure is accessed through a pointer, named **LinearBM** in the figure. A second pointer can be used to manipulate the bitmap data in the following way:

```
UINT8 Bitmap[] = {0x06, 0x00, 0x07, 0x00, 0x00, 0x00, 0x04, 0x04, 0x00,...};
LINEAR_BITMAP * LinearBM;
UINT8 * DataPtr;

LinearBM = (LINEAR_BITMAP *) Bitmap;
DataPtr = (UINT8 *) &(LinearBM->Data);
```

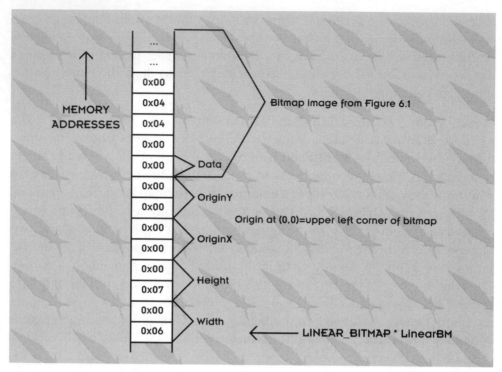

Figure 6.2 *Overlaying the LINEAR_BITMAP structure on the data.*

Now **LinearBM** can be used to access the **Width**, **Height**, **OriginX**, and **OriginY** members, and **DataPtr** + 0 is the first byte of the bitmap data, **DataPtr** + 1 is the second, and so on.

We'll use this technique of overlaying structures onto a data block many times in our code, so make sure that you understand how this works. The code will be confusing to read, otherwise.

DRAWING BITMAPS: THE BITBLT

Now that we understand how bitmaps are stored and how to access the various members of the **LINEAR_BITMAP** structure, how can we draw a bitmap onto the screen? The process is fairly easy and simply amounts to copying the pixel color values into video memory. The process is known as a bit block transfer, or *bitblt* for short.

The **BltLinear** function, shown in Listing 6.1, performs this process for VGA Mode 13h and the linear bitmap structure we defined a moment ago. The first parameter to the function, **LinearBM**, is a pointer to a linear bitmap structure. We're using a far pointer here because, as we'll soon see, it won't be possible to store all our data in a single 64K segment. We'll have to employ the far heap as well. The **x** and **y** parameters to the function indicate the position of the bitmap on the Mode 13h screen. The **ScreenBase** parameter specifies the base of the Mode 13h screen to draw into. We'll more fully explain **ScreenBase** in Chapter 7 when we discuss animation.

Listing 6.1 The BltLinear Function

```
/*
    Function: BltLinear
    Description:
        Draws a linear bitmap to the screen.
        The base of the screen is specified by the ScreenBase
        parameter and the position on that screen specified by the
        x and y parameters.
*/
void BltLinear
    (
    LINEAR_BITMAP far * LinearBM,
    int x,
    int y,
    UINT8 far * ScreenBase
    )
{
    int Top;    /* coordinate values of bitmap top-left corner */
    int Left;
    int BltWidth;   /* width of bitmap so we don't dereference pointers */
    int BltHeight;  /* height of bitmap so we don't dereference pointers */
    UINT16 TempOffset;  /* temp variable to calc far pointer offsets */
    UINT8 far * Screen; /* pointer to current screen position */
    UINT8 far * Bitmap; /* pointer to current bitmap position */
    unsigned WidthCounter;
    unsigned HeightCounter;
    unsigned ScreenIncrement;

    assert(LinearBM != NULL);
    assert(ScreenBase != NULL);

    /* calculate top-left corner position */
    Left = x - LinearBM->OriginX;
    Top  = y - LinearBM->OriginY;

    /* calculate screen pointer starting position */
    TempOffset = Top * GScreenVirtualWidth + Left;
    Screen = ScreenBase + TempOffset;

    /* calculate bitmap pointer starting position */
    Bitmap = &(LinearBM->Data);
```

```
/* blt to screen */
BltWidth = LinearBM->Width;
BltHeight = LinearBM->Height;
ScreenIncrement = GScreenVirtualWidth - BltWidth;

for (HeightCounter = 0; HeightCounter < BltHeight; HeightCounter++) {
    for (WidthCounter = 0; WidthCounter < BltWidth; WidthCounter++) {
        if (*Bitmap != 0) {
            *Screen = *Bitmap;
        }
        Screen++;
        Bitmap++;
    }
    Screen += ScreenIncrement;
}
}
```

The function first computes where the upper-left corner of the bitmap will be located. The **OriginX** and **OriginY** parameters are used to offset the upper-left corner from the **x** and **y** parameters given as arguments to the function.

Using the **Top** and **Left** variables, the routine calculates the exact offset to the first pixel location within video memory. This offset is added to the **ScreenBase** parameter to derive a final far pointer value.

The **BltWidth** and **BltHeight** variables are used to determine when to stop copying. The **BltWidth** variable is used to control the horizontal direction and the **BltHeight** variable is used to control the vertical direction. These variables are simply copies of the **Width** and **Height** members of the **LINEAR_BITMAP** structure. Separate variables are used to help optimize the C code to eliminate pointer dereferencing and structure member position calculations.

The real work happens at the end of the function, with the two nested **for** loops. Inside these loops is where the copying of pixels takes place. After each row is copied, the pointer to video memory is updated to point to the beginning of the next line.

Understanding Transparent Pixels

If you examine the inner loops of the **BltLinear** function, you'll notice that the actual statement that does the copying of the pixels from the source bitmap to the screen is contained in an **if** statement. The purpose of that **if** statement is to make zero-valued pixels in the source bitmap transparent when the copying takes place.

Transparent pixels are needed because although bitmaps are rectangular, the images that they contain rarely are. Take the missile bitmap from Figure 6.1, for instance. It is contained in a 6x7 bitmap, but there are many pixels that are part of the bitmap that are not part of the missile image itself.

Figure 6.3 shows what would happen if the missile bitmap were copied to a screen where the non-missile pixels of the bitmap were a different color than the screen background. As you can see, the missile ends up being "framed" by a set of pixels that differ from the background color of the screen. It is very easy to see the rectangle of the missile bitmap. Clearly, this is not the best result.

Figure 6.4 shows the result of copying the bitmap to the screen while taking into account the pixels of the source bitmap that should be transparent. As you can see, the image blends nicely with the screen background. The only pixels that are modified on the screen are those that actually correspond to image pixels in the source bitmap. No frame is visible around for a clearly superior image.

As the **if** statement in the inner loops of the **BltLinear** function shows, the value 0 is used to represent transparent pixels in the source bitmap. The value 0 is chosen because it is very easy to test for. In the standard VGA palette, 0 is

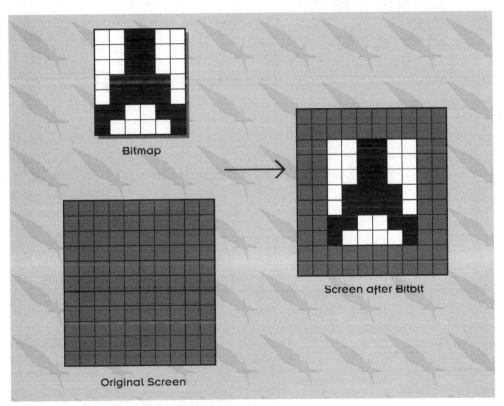

Bitmap

Screen after Bitblt

Original Screen

Figure 6.3 *Drawing an image with non-transparent pixels.*

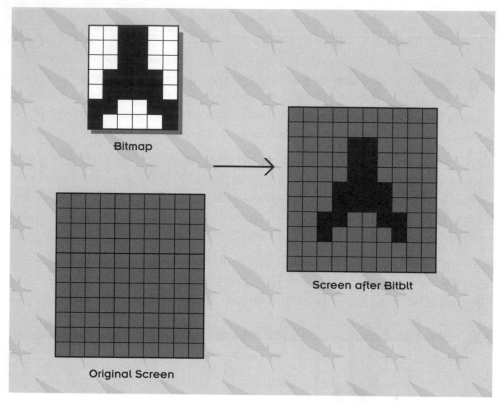

Figure 6.4 *Drawing an image with transparent pixels.*

used to represent black pixels. When transparency is needed, another pixel color value will have to be mapped to the color black. We'll learn how to do this when we discuss the VGA's color palette in a later chapter. The concept that you should take away from this section is that the color value 0 does not necessarily equal black. When transparent pixels are needed, it equals "clear."

There is a speed penalty when using transparent pixels. As each pixel is copied, its value must be tested with 0 to see whether it should be copied or not. This adds instructions to the inner loop and slows down the copying. The speed penalty can be eliminated if the original screen pixels are the same color as the pixels that would be transparent in the source bitmap. In this case, you could change the function to eliminate the **if** statement. Copying the now non-transparent pixels does not change the color values of the original screen pixels because they are the same color values.

Of course, this may force you to store your bitmaps with background colors other than zero and requires you to ensure that your bitmaps are always drawn over the same color background. Figure 6.5 shows how this is done.

Often, however, the screen background is a complex image itself, and the location of a bitmap image cannot be predicted very well. When this is the case, the only way to deal with the problem is to absorb the speed decrease and use transparent pixels.

BITBLT.C contains a routine named **BltLinearNoTransparent** that can be used to draw linear bitmaps while ignoring transparent pixels. See BITBLT.C in Listing 6.10 for more information.

Mode 13h Bitblt Example

The BLTDMO13 program, shown in Listing 6.2, demonstrates the **BltLinear** function and shows the effect of transparent pixels. The program draws a bitmap of a green ball several times. Some of the images are drawn over a red background and some over a black background. This demonstrates the transparent pixels in the bitmap.

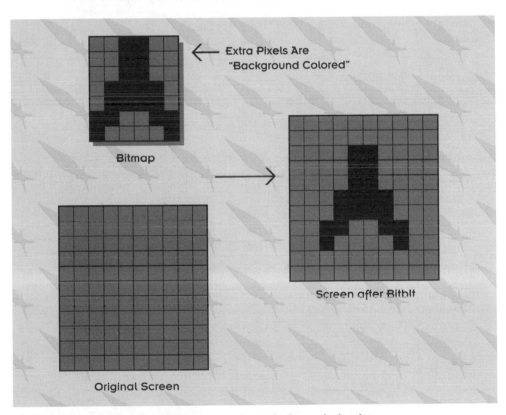

Figure 6.5 *Drawing an image when extra pixels are "background colored."*

Compiling and Linking:

You can compile the BLTDMO13 program using the Borland C++ 3.1 IDE by typing "bc bltdmo13.prj" and then selecting Compile | Make from the menus. If you would rather use the command line compiler, convert the BLTDMO13.PRJ file to a makefile using the PRJ2MAK program supplied with Borland C++ 3.1. Type "prj2mak bltdmo13.prj" to create the BLTDMO13.MAK and BLTDMO13.CFG files.

If you are using Borland C++ 4.0, choose Project | Open Project from the IDE menus. Open the BLTDMO13.PRJ file. Borland C++ will convert the version 3.1 .PRJ file to a version 4.0 .IDE file. Compile and link the program by choosing Project | Make All from the IDE menus.

Listing 6.2   BLTDMO13.C

```
/* File: BLTDMO13.C
** Description:
**    Demonstrates Mode 13h linear bitmaps.  Fills half the screen
**    with red pixels and draws a ball bitmap several times to show
**    the effect of transparent pixels and clipping.
** Copyright:
**    Copyright 1994, David G. Roberts
*/

#include <assert.h>
#include <conio.h>
#include <dos.h>
#include <stdio.h>
#include "gamedefs.h"
#include "vga.h"
#include "bitblt.h"

UINT8 BallBitmap[] = {
    10, 0,          /* Width (little endian) */
    10, 0,          /* Height (little endian) */
    0, 0,           /* X & Y origin at top left corner */
    0, 0,
    0, 0, 0, 2, 2, 2, 2, 0, 0, 0, /* color 2 = green w/ default palette */
    0, 2, 2, 2, 2, 2, 2, 2, 2, 0,
    0, 2, 2, 0, 0, 2, 2, 2, 2, 0,
    2, 2, 0, 0, 2, 2, 2, 2, 2, 2,
    2, 2, 0, 2, 2, 2, 2, 2, 2, 2,
    2, 2, 2, 2, 2, 2, 2, 2, 2, 2,
    2, 2, 2, 2, 2, 2, 2, 2, 2, 2,
    0, 2, 2, 2, 2, 2, 2, 2, 2, 0,
    0, 2, 2, 2, 2, 2, 2, 2, 2, 0,
    0, 0, 0, 2, 2, 2, 2, 0, 0, 0
};
```

```
void FillPartialScreen(UINT8 Color)
{
    UINT8 far * Screen;
    int i;

    Screen = MK_FP(VIDEO_MEM_SEGMENT, 0);

    for (i = 0; i < (MODE13H_WIDTH * (MODE13H_HEIGHT / 2)); i++) {
        *Screen++ = Color;
    }
}

int main()
{
    /* detect VGA */
    if (!DetectVGA()) {
        printf("You must have a VGA to run this program.\n");
        return 1;
    }

    SetMode13h();

    FillPartialScreen(0x04); /* 4 = red in default palette */

    BltLinear((LINEAR_BITMAP far *) &BallBitmap, 10, 10,
        (UINT8 far *) MK_FP(VIDEO_MEM_SEGMENT,0));
    BltLinear((LINEAR_BITMAP far *) &BallBitmap, 95, 95,
        (UINT8 far *) MK_FP(VIDEO_MEM_SEGMENT,0));
    BltLinear((LINEAR_BITMAP far *) &BallBitmap, 120, 120,
        (UINT8 far *) MK_FP(VIDEO_MEM_SEGMENT,0));

    getch();

    SetVGAMode(0x3);     /* return to text mode */

    return 0;
}
```

Figure 6.6 shows the graphical representation of the ball bitmap used in the demonstration program. The **BallBitmap** array reflects the bitmap in binary form. Each of the colored pixels is represented by a value of 2, which corresponds to green in the default color palette. The transparent pixels, both around the edges of the ball and also where the highlight occurs, have been represented by 0.

The **BallBitmap** array corresponds to a **LINEAR_BITMAP** structure, and thus the first four bytes of the array are the width and height values of the bitmap, 10 pixels for each in this case. The width and height values must be given in "little-endian" order (the standard convention for x86 processors) when they

Figure 6.6 *Ball bitmap.*

are included in the array of bytes (in contrast to Motorola 68000 family processors, which use big-endian format). In the little-endian format, the low-order byte of a multibyte quantity is stored in the first byte position. This is then followed by the higher-order bytes, in order. In our case, we are storing two-byte quantities and the high-order bytes are 0 because the values are less than 256 (both width and height are 10 in our case).

The **OriginX** and **OriginY** parameters are given as (0,0), which means the origin of the bitmap is the pixel in the upper-left corner of the bitmap. Calls to **BltLinear** will specify the position of this pixel on the screen.

The **main** function first checks for a VGA adapter and sets Mode 13h. It then fills the top half of the screen with the color red. The bottom of the screen remains black, following the setting of Mode 13h.

Next, **main** calls **BltLinear** three times to draw the ball images. In each case, a pointer to the **BallBitmap** array is passed to **BltLinear** after first converting its type to a **LINEAR_BITMAP far *** with a cast. **BltLinear** will use the structure overlay technique discussed earlier to access the **BallBitmap** array as a **LINEAR_BITMAP**. In all cases, a far pointer to video memory is passed as the final parameter.

The first bitmap is drawn at coordinates (10,10), which is within the top, red portion of the screen. You can see how the bitmap's transparent pixels allow the background to show through. The second call to **BltLinear** positions the bitmap straddling the red and black backgrounds, and the final call places the bitmap entirely on the black background.

Finally, the program simply waits for the user to press a key after viewing the bitmaps, resets the VGA to text mode, and exits.

Recompile the program in Listing 6.2 after changing the **BallBitmap** to your own image. Use a piece of graph paper to sketch out your new bitmap and convert it to binary form. Type the color value for each pixel into the array. Be sure to make the transparent pixels' color values equal to 0. After you've typed your own image, update the width and height fields of the array appropriately. Remember to store the width and height in little-endian format. Although all the visible pixels of the ball bitmap in the example program are green, you can make your own bitmap include many different colors. Experiment!

DEALING WITH MODE X AND Y

Great! We now understand linear bitmaps and bitblts. We can draw images onto a Mode 13h screen with ease. Unfortunately, our bitblt routine won't work in Mode X or Y and our linear bitmap structure is not well suited to the planar nature of those modes. In the next few sections we'll examine what changes must be made to accommodate Modes X and Y. In particular, we'll examine a new bitmap format, the *planar bitmap*, which is more suited to the planar nature of Modes X and Y.

Using Linear Bitmaps in Mode X and Y

The first question we have to ask ourselves is why can't we just extend our **BltLinear** function to make it work in Mode X and Y? Let's examine the problem to see what's involved.

First, remember how the video memory of Mode X and Y is structured. Four screen pixels all occupy the same host memory location. The host can select the pixel it is writing to by setting the Map Mask Register (MMR) to the appropriate value. Figure 6.7 shows how the memory is organized.

The effect of this memory organization with the organization of a linear bitmap is that we would have to set the MMR to the correct value before each pixel was copied. The loops of the bitblt routine would end up looking as like this.

```
/* blt to screen */
  for (HeightCounter = 0; HeightCounter < BltHeight; HeightCounter++) {
      XCoordinate = Left;
      for (WidthCounter = 0; WidthCounter < BltWidth; WidthCounter++) {
          if (*Bitmap != 0) {
              SetMMR(1 << (XCoordinate % 4));
              screen=XCoordinate/4 + ScreenLine;
              *Screen = *Bitmap;
          }
```

```
        Screen++;
          Bitmap++;
        XCoordinate++;
    }
    ScreenLine += MODEX_WIDTH/4;
}
```

We've added a couple new variables, **XCoordinate**, to keep track of the current x coordinate position and **ScreenLine** to keep track of the beginning address of a given screen line. Whenever a pixel needs to be copied, the MMR is set to the appropriate value. This method will work, but it will be very slow. If you were to run some tests on the relative speed of various operations on the VGA, you'd find that writing to registers is one of the slowest operations. Writing to a register once for each pixel to be copied is tremendously slow. With a little thought up front, we can structure our bitmap such that we only need to set the MMR four times, once for each plane. We'll call our new bitmap structure a *planar bitmap*.

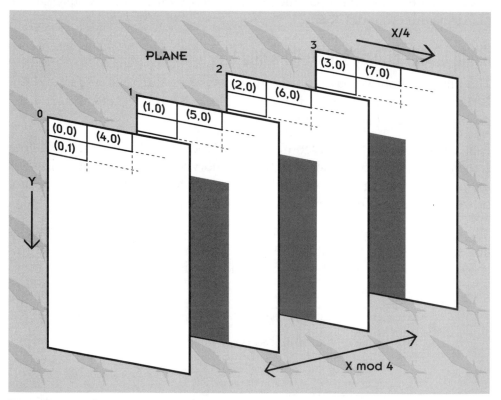

Figure 6.7 *Mode X memory organization.*

PLANAR BITMAPS

A planar bitmap is not complicated or exotic. It builds on the same concepts we saw with linear bitmaps. A planar bitmap simply rearranges the order of the pixels in the bitmap structure to more closely match the memory organization of Modes X and Y. Doing this makes it easy to quickly copy the pixels to the screen.

A planar bitmap stores all the pixels that correspond to a single memory plane in consecutive memory locations. The pixels from the first plane are stored first, followed by those from the second plane, and so on. Within the data for each plane, the pixels are stored just as they are for a linear bitmap, in ascending order, left to right, top to bottom. Figure 6.8 shows the relative ordering of pixels in our missile bitmap when it is stored in a planar bitmap structure versus the linear bitmap structure.

Notice that in the planar bitmap, two more columns of pixels have been added to the bitmap even though they were not needed to make the image fit. These extra columns were added to make the number of pixels per line in the bitmap come out to an even multiple of four. This ensures that the same number of pixels are stored for each plane. As we'll see later, this makes it easier to copy the image to video memory. The extra columns are simply assigned the color value of 0, making them invisible pixels. Since there were six original columns in the linear bitmap, two more were added, bringing the total to eight.

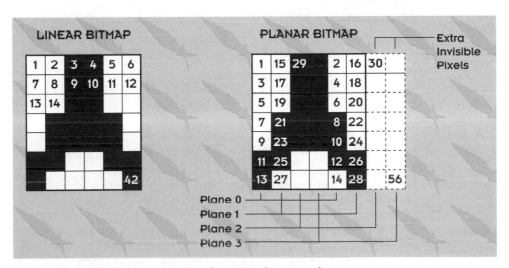

Figure 6.8   *Linear bitmap versus planar bitmap pixel storage order.*

The planar bitmap structure looks very similar to the linear bitmap structure we saw before. In fact, the header information is essentially the same.

```
typedef struct {
    UINT16 Width;               /* Bitmap width = actual width divided by 4 */
    UINT16 Height;
    int OriginX;
    int OriginY;
    UINT8 Data;
} PLANAR_BITMAP;
```

The primary difference is the **Width** member, which stores the width of the bitmap divided by four. If you're following closely, you'll notice that this equals the number of pixels per row per plane. The planar bitmap in Figure 6.8, for example, would have a **Width** of 2 (8 / 4 = 2). Once again, the **Data** member is just defined as a single byte in the structure definition but will be used to overlay the actual bitmap data in memory.

Figure 6.9 shows how the planar bitmap will be stored in memory.

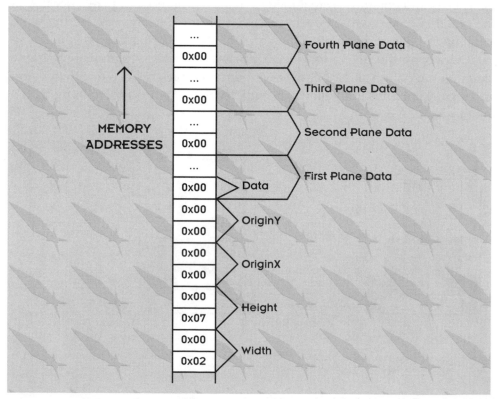

Figure 6.9   Planar bitmap memory layout.

Converting from Linear to Planar

Often, it's easier to store bitmaps in a linear format. Linear bitmaps are typically smaller because planar bitmaps have added columns of pixels if the linear width isn't a multiple of four. Most drawing packages that you'll use to create bitmaps (we'll talk more about these in a later chapter) will also store the image in a format closer to linear format than planar format.

For these reasons, it will be convenient to create and store all our bitmaps in linear format and then convert them to planar format at runtime. To create a planar bitmap, we'll use a conversion routine named **LineartoPlanar**, which is shown in Listing 6.3.

Listing 6.3   The LinearToPlanar Function

```
/*
    Function: LinearToPlanar
    Description:
        Converts a bitmap from linear format to planar format.
        The function returns a new block of memory allocated with
        farmalloc which should be farfreed when the program is finished
        with it.  Returns NULL if memory could not be allocated.  If
        the source bitmap width is not evenly divisible by four,
        the function rounds the planar bitmap width up to an even
        multiple of four and fills the new bitmap columns with 0 pixels.
*/
PLANAR_BITMAP far * LinearToPlanar(LINEAR_BITMAP far * LinearBM)
{
    unsigned PlanarWidth;
    UINT16 PlanarBMSize;
    PLANAR_BITMAP far * PlanarBM;
    unsigned PlaneCounter;
    unsigned WidthCounter;
    unsigned HeightCounter;
    UINT8 far * LinearData;
    UINT8 far * PlanarData;

    assert(LinearBM != NULL);

    /* make PlanarWidth even multiple of 4, rounding up */
    if ((LinearBM->Width % 4) != 0) {
        PlanarWidth = LinearBM->Width + (4 - (LinearBM->Width % 4));
    }
    else {
        PlanarWidth = LinearBM->Width;
    }

    /* calculate needed memory and allocate */
    /* sizeof(UINT8) correct for the dummy Data field of the */
    /* PLANAR_BITMAP structure which is already included in the */
```

```
    /* width*height term */
    PlanarBMSize = PlanarWidth * LinearBM->Height +
        sizeof(PLANAR_BITMAP) - sizeof(UINT8);
    PlanarBM = (PLANAR_BITMAP far *) farmalloc(PlanarBMSize);
    if (PlanarBM == NULL) { /* error! */
        return NULL;
    }

    /* fill in width and height info */
    PlanarBM->Width = PlanarWidth / 4;
    PlanarBM->Height = LinearBM->Height;
    PlanarBM->OriginX = LinearBM->OriginX;
    PlanarBM->OriginY = LinearBM->OriginY;

    /* store data for each plane consecutively */
    PlanarData = &(PlanarBM->Data);
    for (PlaneCounter = 0; PlaneCounter < 4; PlaneCounter++) {

        for (HeightCounter = 0; HeightCounter < PlanarBM->Height;
            HeightCounter++) {

            /* reset LinearData pointer to start of next row */
            LinearData = &(LinearBM->Data) +
                HeightCounter * LinearBM->Width + PlaneCounter;

            /* iterate over row, stepping by four */
            for (WidthCounter = PlaneCounter; WidthCounter < PlanarWidth;
                WidthCounter += 4) {

                if (WidthCounter < LinearBM->Width) {
                    *PlanarData = *LinearData;
                    LinearData += 4;
                }
                else {
                    /* fill 0's to create new rows */
                    *PlanarData = 0;
                }
                PlanarData++;
            }
        }
    }

    return PlanarBM;
}
```

LinearToPlanar takes as input a pointer to a **LINEAR_BITMAP** structure and returns a pointer to a newly allocated (with **farmalloc**) block of memory holding the equivalent **PLANAR_BITMAP** structure. Remember to free the block when you are done using it with **farfree**.

LinearToPlanar first calculates the width of the planar bitmap by rounding the linear bitmap width up to the nearest multiple of four. Memory is then allocated for the planar bitmap, and the width, height, and origin information is stored in the structure members. The actual width that is stored is the true pixel width of the planar bitmap structure divided by four.

Next, the function copies the pixels for each plane into consecutive memory locations. For each plane, the pixels are processed left to right, top to bottom.

Finally, a pointer to the **PLANAR_BITMAP** structure is returned to the calling routine.

MODE X BITBLT

The bitblt routine for planar bitmaps and Mode X, **BltPlanar**, is fairly similar in structure to the linear bitmap routine we looked at previously. The principle difference is in iterating over the bitmap for each plane that needs to be drawn.

Listing 6.4   The BitPlanar Function

```
/*
    Function: BltPlanar
    Description:
        Draws a planar bitmap to a mode X/Y screen.  The bitmap
        is positioned at (x,y) and is drawn on the mode X page
        starting at the address specified by the PageOffset parameter.
*/
void BltPlanar
    (
    PLANAR_BITMAP far * PlanarBM,
    int x,
    int y,
    UINT16 PageOffset
    )
{
    int Top;    /* coordinate values of bitmap top-left corner */
    int Left;
    unsigned BltWidth;  /* width of clipped bitmap */
    unsigned BltHeight; /* height of clipped bitmap */
    UINT16 TempOffset;  /* temp variable to calc far pointer offsets */
    /* UINT8 far * Screen; ptr to screen position - used in C version */
    UINT8 far * ScreenInit; /* used to reload screen ptr between planes */
    UINT8 far * Bitmap; /* pointer to current bitmap position */
    unsigned WidthCounter;
    unsigned HeightCounter;
    unsigned PlaneCounter;
    unsigned ScreenIncrement;
    UINT8 MMRValue;
```

```
assert(PlanarBM != NULL);

/* calculate top-left corner position */
Left = x - PlanarBM->OriginX;
Top  = y - PlanarBM->OriginY;

/* setup */
BltWidth = PlanarBM->Width;
BltHeight = PlanarBM->Height;
ScreenIncrement = GScreenVirtualWidth / 4 - BltWidth;
Bitmap = &(PlanarBM->Data);
if (Left >= 0) {
    MMRValue = 1 << (Left % 4);
}
else {
    /* correct for when bitmap moves offscreen to left */
    MMRValue = 1 << ((4 - (-Left % 4)) % 4);
}
TempOffset = (Top * (GScreenVirtualWidth / 4)) + PageOffset;
if (Left >= 0) {
    TempOffset += (Left / 4);
}
else {
    /* correct for when bitmap moves offscreen to left */
    TempOffset -= ((-Left - 1) / 4) + 1;
}
ScreenInit = MK_FP(VIDEO_MEM_SEGMENT, TempOffset);

for (PlaneCounter = 0; PlaneCounter < 4; PlaneCounter++) {
    SetMMR(MMRValue);
    Screen = ScreenInit;

    for (HeightCounter = 0; HeightCounter < BltHeight;
        HeightCounter++) {
        for (WidthCounter = 0; WidthCounter < BltWidth;
            WidthCounter++) {
            if (*Bitmap != 0) {
                *Screen = *Bitmap;
            }
            Screen++;
            Bitmap++;
        }
        Screen += ScreenIncrement;
    }

    MMRValue <<= 1;
    if (!(MMRValue & 0x0F)) {
        MMRValue = 1;
        ScreenInit++;
    }
}
}
```

This code is very similar to the bitblt code in **BltLinear** except that it is repeated for each plane and the blt width is equal to the width of each plane. The two nested loops that copy the actual plane data are virtually identical to those in **BltLinear**. On each interation through the plane loop, the MMR is set to enable the current plane and disable all others. For any sprite, we'll only end up setting the MMR four times rather than once for each pixel. Overall, the amount of time spent in the routine is greatly decreased.

The **PageOffset** parameter is added into the far pointer created to point to the screen location of the bitblt. The **PageOffset** parameter allows us to specify where in video memory we would like to blt the bitmap; it will be used when we look at the page flipping animation technique in the next chapter. You may notice that the **ScreenBase** parameter in the **BltLinear** function was a complete far pointer while **PageOffset,** in **BltPlanar** is simply an unsigned 16-bit integer. With the **ScreenBase** parameter, **BltLinear** can draw anywhere in memory while with **PageOffset**, **BltPlanar** can only draw to a different part of video memory. You'll see why the difference exists when we look at some various animation techniques in the next chapter.

BITBLT.C also contains **BltPlanarNoTransparent**, which can be used to draw planar bitmaps while ignoring transparent pixels. **BltPlanarNoTransparent** can draw an image faster than BltPlanar in those cases where transparent pixels aren't needed.

Mode X Bitblt Example

The BLTDMOX program, shown in Listing 6.5, demonstrates how to use the **LinearToPlanar** and **BltLinear** functions. The program is virtually identical in functionality to the BLTDMO13.C program presented earlier.

Compiling and Linking:

You can compile the BLTDMOX program using the Borland C++ 3.1 IDE by typing "bc bltdmox.prj" and then selecting Compile | Make from the menus. If you would rather use the command line compiler, convert the BLTDMOX.PRJ file to a makefile using the PRJ2MAK program supplied with Borland C++ 3.1. Type "prj2mak bltdmox.prj" to create the BLTDMOX.MAK and BLTDMOX.CFG files.

If you are using Borland C++ 4.0, choose Project | Open Project from the IDE menus. Open the BLTDMOX.PRJ file. Borland C++ will convert the version 3.1 .PRJ file to a version 4.0 .IDE file. Compile and link the program by choosing Project | Make All from the IDE menus.

Listing 6.5   BLTDMOX.C

```c
/* File: BLTDMOX.C
** Description:
**    Demonstration of the planar bitblt routines in Mode X.
** Author:
**    David G. Roberts
** Date:
** Copyright:
**    Copyright 1994, David G. Roberts
*/

#include <alloc.h>
#include <assert.h>
#include <conio.h>
#include <dos.h>
#include <stdio.h>
#include "gamedefs.h"
#include "bitblt.h"
#include "vga.h"
#include "setmodex.h"

UINT8 BallBitmap[] = {
    10, 0,          /* Width (little endian) */
    10, 0,          /* Height (little endian) */
    0, 0,           /* X & Y origin at top left corner */
    0, 0,
    0, 0, 0, 2, 2, 2, 2, 0, 0, 0, /* color 2 = green w/ default palette */
    0, 2, 2, 2, 2, 2, 2, 2, 2, 0,
    0, 2, 2, 0, 0, 2, 2, 2, 2, 0,
    2, 2, 0, 0, 2, 2, 2, 2, 2, 2,
    2, 2, 0, 2, 2, 2, 2, 2, 2, 2,
    2, 2, 2, 2, 2, 2, 2, 2, 2, 2,
    2, 2, 2, 2, 2, 2, 2, 2, 2, 2,
    0, 2, 2, 2, 2, 2, 2, 2, 2, 0,
    0, 2, 2, 2, 2, 2, 2, 2, 2, 0,
    0, 0, 0, 2, 2, 2, 2, 0, 0, 0
};

/*
    Function: FillPartialScreen
    Description:
        Fills the first half of the Mode X screen with the color
        specified as a parameter.  The function takes advantage of
        Mode X's ability to write to four pixels at one time by
        enabling all the display planes at once.  This allows
        fast color fills to be done in 1/4 the time normally taken.
*/
void FillPartialScreen(UINT8 Color)
{
    UINT8 far * Screen;
    int i;
```

```
        Screen = MK_FP(VIDEO_MEM_SEGMENT, 0);

        SetMMR(0xF);    /* enable all planes */
        for (i = 0; i < ((MODEX_WIDTH / 4) * (MODEX_HEIGHT / 2)); i++) {
            *Screen++ = Color;
        }
    }

    int main()
    {
        PLANAR_BITMAP far * PlanarBall;

        /* detect VGA */
        if (!DetectVGA()) {
            printf("You must have a VGA to run this program.\n");
            return 1;
        }

        SetModeX();

        FillPartialScreen(0x1); /* fill with blue */

        PlanarBall = LinearToPlanar((LINEAR_BITMAP far *) BallBitmap);

        BltPlanar(PlanarBall, 10, 10, 0);
        BltPlanar(PlanarBall, 115, 115, 0);
        BltPlanar(PlanarBall, 200, 200, 0);

        getch();

        farfree(PlanarBall);

        SetVGAMode(0x3);    /* return to text mode */

        return 0;
    }
```

The program first checks for the existence of a VGA, puts itself into Mode X and, as in BLTDMO13.C, fills the first half of the screen with a complementary color (blue this time, rather than red).

The fill routine takes advantage of one of Mode X's great strengths, the ability to do very fast color fills. Although we only enable one plane at a time when copying a bitmap to the screen, Mode X allows for all four planes, or any combination of the four, to be enabled at once. Whatever color is written to display memory gets written to all the display planes that are enabled at the time. Obviously, this is not appropriate for bitmaps because the color values can vary wildly within a bitmap and it will often be the case that four consecutive pixels won't have the same color value. When copying bitmaps, we only enable one plane at a time. When you're filling a region of the screen with a solid color, however, this technique can cause a great speedup because a routine only needs to do 25% as many writes as there are pixels to be filled.

The **FillPartialScreen** routine in BLTDMOX.C enables all four planes and then fills the first half of the screen in one-fourth the time it would have taken before.

Next, the main routine converts our ball bitmap from the linear form in which it is stored to planar format using **LinearToPlanar**. The ball is then drawn repeatedly, sometimes on the blue background and sometimes on the black. This shows the ability of **BltPlanar** to handle transparent pixels.

Notice that the balls look like circles in Mode X rather than the ellipses they were in the BLTDMO13 using Mode 13h. This is because Mode X has square pixels while Mode 13h does not.

Finally, the main routine waits for a key to be pressed, frees the planar bitmap image, sets the VGA back to text mode, and exits.

EXTRA STORAGE: VIDEO MEMORY BITMAPS

Although it may not seem like it in the simple examples from this chapter, bitmaps take a lot of memory to store. The examples we've done so far have only used a single, small bitmap. As we'll see in later chapters, a real game can have tens or even hundreds of bitmap images, each a thousand bytes or more in length. These storage requirements add up quickly, and if we aren't careful, we could develop a memory shortage.

One way to relieve the memory pressure is to use some of the RAM on the VGA card itself to hold bitmap images. Remember that a standard VGA card has 256K of memory installed. Only a portion of this memory is actually visible on the screen. The remaining offscreen memory can be used to store bitmap image data. Drawing the bitmap is as simple as copying the pixels from the offscreen video memory into onscreen memory.

Although a VGA card has 256K of memory, in Mode 13h only 64K of memory is actually mapped into the host memory space. The other 192K is inaccessible. Of the 65,536 bytes (65,536 = 64K) that are accessible, 64,000 are visible onscreen (320 * 200 = 64,000). This means that only 1,536 bytes are accessible and offscreen. The 1,536 bytes is enough to store a few bitmaps, but Mode 13h is not the best for trying to utilize video memory bitmaps.

Modes X and Y, on the other hand, allow the full 256 KB of video memory to be accessed. Remember that although the host memory window into video memory is still 64 KB in length, each host address location maps to four video memory locations with the MMR being used to specify which of the four locations should be modified. With a single screen of data in Mode X taking 76,800 bytes (320 * 240 = 76,800), there are still 185,344 bytes left over for storage of bitmaps. This is 181 KB worth of additional memory!

Because the X and Y modes have so much more space available for storing video memory bitmaps, the following sections will focus on these modes rather than Mode 13h.

Video Memory Bitmap Structure

Let's take a look at the structure used to store information about a video memory bitmap.

```
typedef struct {
    UINT16 Width;              /* Width = true width / 4 */
    UINT16 Height;
    int OriginX;
    int OriginY;
    UINT16 VideoDataOffset; /* offset to image data in video memory */
    UINTO MapMaskData,
} VIDEO_MEM_BITMAP;
```

As in the other bitmap formats, the first four members of the structure hold the width, height, and origin of the bitmap. The **Width** member actually contains the true pixel width of the bitmap divided by four. The bitblt routine for the video memory bitmap format will employ VGA Write Mode 1 to perform fast copies within video memory. Write Mode 1 uses the display latches to copy four pixels at one time. Thus, the **Width** field stores the number of four-pixel copies to be done per row. The **Height** member simply contains the pixel height of the bitmap.

Unlike the other bitmap formats, the actual pixel data is not stored in the bitmap structure itself. Of course, this makes sense. The bitmap structure is stored in main system memory while the pixel data is stored in video memory. An offset to the pixel data in video memory is stored in the bitmap structure, named **VideoDataOffset**. The **VideoDataOffset** value is used to locate the position of the pixel data in video memory.

An additional member, **MapMaskData**, that was not present in the other bitmap formats is also contained in the **VIDEO_MEM_BITMAP** structure. This field operates similarly to the **Data** member of the previous bitmap formats. It simply stores the first byte of an array of data that is accessed through the structure overlay technique described earlier.

The **MapMaskData** member is used to implement transparent pixels with video memory bitmaps. The linear and planar bitmap formats implemented transparent pixels by simply testing for a pixel value of 0 when copying the bitmap to the screen. As we'll see when we examine the bitblt routine for video memory bitmaps, the MMR will be used to specify which pixels within a four-pixel copy actually get written. The pixels that don't get written are transparent. **MapMaskData** is used to program the MMR on each four-pixel copy.

CREATING VIDEO MEMORY BITMAPS

There is no way to actually store a video memory bitmap in a file. By definition, the pixel data for a video memory bitmap is stored in video memory. Thus, we'll have to create a video memory bitmap at runtime, similar to the way we created a planar bitmap previously. As before, we'll take a linear bitmap as input. The **LinearToVideoMemory** function, shown in Listing 6.6, performs the conversion. It returns a far pointer to a **VIDEO_MEM_BITMAP** structure that has been allocated on the far heap. The main program must free the bitmap structure with a call to **farfree** when it is done with the bitmap.

Listing 6.6 The LinearToVideoMemory Function

```
/*
    Function: LinearToVideoMemory
    Description:
        Converts a linear bitmap into a video memory bitmap.  The first
        parameter points to the original linear bitmap structure while
        the second points to the address in video memory that should be
        used to hold the video bitmap.  The function returns NULL if
        no video bitmap data structure could be allocated and a
        far pointer to the structure otherwise.
*/
VIDEO_MEM_BITMAP far * LinearToVideoMemory
    (
    LINEAR_BITMAP far * LinearBM,
    UINT16 Storage,
    UINT16 * Length
    )
{
    unsigned VideoWidth;    /* width of video memory bitmap */
```

```
unsigned VideoBMSize;    /* size of video BM structure + map mask data */
VIDEO_MEM_BITMAP far * VideoBM;
unsigned WidthCounter;   /* width counter for video memory */
unsigned LinearWidthCounter; /* width counter for linear bitmap */
unsigned HeightCounter;
unsigned PlaneCounter;
UINT8 far * LinearData;
UINT8 far * VideoData;
UINT8 far * MapMaskData;
UINT8 Pixel;


assert(LinearBM != NULL);
assert(Storage != NULL);

/* make PlanarWidth even multiple of 4, rounding up */
if ((LinearBM->Width % 4) != 0) {
    VideoWidth = LinearBM->Width + (4 - (LinearBM->Width % 4));
}
else {
    VideoWidth = LinearBM->Width;
}

/* calculate length of video memory bitmap data structure */
VideoBMSize = (VideoWidth / 4) * LinearBM->Height +
    sizeof(VIDEO_MEM_BITMAP) - 1;

/* allocate video memory bitmap data structure */
VideoBM = (VIDEO_MEM_BITMAP far *) farmalloc(VideoBMSize);
if (VideoBM == NULL) { /* error! */
    return NULL;
}

/* fill in fields */
VideoBM->Width = VideoWidth / 4;
VideoBM->Height = LinearBM->Height;
VideoBM->OriginX = LinearBM->OriginX;
VideoBM->OriginY = LinearBM->OriginY;
VideoBM->VideoDataOffset = Storage;

/* copy linear data to video memory */
LinearData = &(LinearBM->Data);
VideoData = MK_FP(VIDEO_MEM_SEGMENT, Storage);
MapMaskData = &(VideoBM->MapMaskData);
for (HeightCounter = 0; HeightCounter < LinearBM->Height;
    HeightCounter++) {
    LinearWidthCounter = 0;
    for (WidthCounter = 0; WidthCounter < (VideoWidth / 4);
        WidthCounter++) {
        *MapMaskData = 0;
        for (PlaneCounter = 0; PlaneCounter < 4; PlaneCounter++) {
            if (LinearWidthCounter < LinearBM->Width) {
                Pixel = *LinearData;
                LinearData++;
```

```
            }
            else {
                Pixel = 0;  /* transparent pixel */
            }
            SetMMR(1 << PlaneCounter);
            *VideoData = Pixel;
            if (Pixel != 0) {
                *MapMaskData |= 1 << PlaneCounter;
            }
            LinearWidthCounter++;
        }
        MapMaskData++;
        VideoData++;
    }
}

if (Length != NULL) {
    *Length = VideoBM->Width * VideoBM->Height;
}

return VideoBM;
}
```

LinearToVideoMemory first ensures that the new bitmap will be a multiple of four pixels wide. This is necessary because we'll use fast video RAM to video RAM copies to actually draw the bitmap and each individual data copy will move four pixels at a time. The pixels that have to be added to bitmaps that are not multiples of four in width will be marked as transparent.

Next, the routine allocates memory for the bitmap data structure itself. The primary concern here is calculating how much memory will be needed by the **MapMaskData** array.

The standard memory allocators don't manage video memory so we can't allocate video memory for the pixel data itself. Instead, as we use the function to create more video memory bitmaps, we'll just have to keep track of the open video memory ourselves. The final routine parameter, **Length**, is used to help us. A pointer to a 16-bit unsigned integer is passed as the parameter. If the pointer is non-NULL, the integer is filled with the length of the bitmap just created. Assuming that we start with a pointer, **Storage** to empty video memory, as we create multiple video memory bitmaps we simply add the length returned after each call to **LinearToVideoMemory** to the pointer and use the resulting address in the next call.

The heart of the routine is three nested loops. The inner loop takes care of copying four pixels from the linear bitmap to video memory, one per plane, and storing the appropriate value in the **MapMaskData** array. This operation is done repeatedly until all the pixels are copied. The inner loop takes care of adding transparent pixels to the right side of the bitmap if the original bitmap width wasn't a multiple of four. The actual pixel data is stored linearly in video memory at the offset specified by **Storage**. Remember, this video memory is offscreen, so the pixel data doesn't have to account for the screen width and such.

LinearToVideoMemory is not optimized for speed. For instance, we make no attempt to cut down on the number of **SetMMR** calls as we did when bitblting a planar bitmap. We set the MMR each time a pixel is drawn. The routine will only be used during the initialization phase of a game, however, so it doesn't need to be performance conscious.

Video Memory Bitblt

The **BltVideoMem** function, shown in Listing 6.7, is used to bitblt a video memory bitmap to the screen. The routine uses VGA Write Mode 1 to copy the bitmap from offscreen video memory to onscreen video memory.

Listing 6.7   The BltVideoMem Function

```
/*
    Function: BltVideoMem
    Description:
        Performs a bitblt of a video memory bitmap to the screen.
        This routine does NOT perform clipping.  The X coordinate
        given to the routine should be a multiple of four.  If it
        is not, the routine rounds it down to the nearest multiple
        of four.
*/
void BltVideoMem
    (
    VIDEO_MEM_BITMAP far * VideoBM,
    int x,
    int y,
    UINT16 PageOffset
    )
{
    int Top;    /* coordinate values of bitmap top-left corner */
    int Left;
    UINT8 MMRCache;
    UINT8 far * MapMaskData;
    UINT8 far * Source;
    UINT8 far * Dest;
    unsigned DestOffset;
    unsigned WidthCounter;
    unsigned HeightCounter;
    unsigned BltWidth;
    unsigned BltHeight;
```

```c
   UINT8 ModeRegTemp;
   UINT8 Dummy;
   unsigned DestIncrement;

   assert(VideoBM != NULL);

   Left = x - VideoBM->OriginX;
   Top  = y - VideoBM->OriginY;

   /* initialize the various pointers */
   Source = MK_FP(VIDEO_MEM_SEGMENT, VideoBM->VideoDataOffset);
   DestOffset = (Top * (GScreenVirtualWidth / 4)) +
       (Left / 4) + PageOffset;
   Dest = MK_FP(VIDEO_MEM_SEGMENT, DestOffset);
   MapMaskData = &(VideoBM->MapMaskData);

   /* initialize MMRCache with a value that cannot occur normally */
   /* (normal values are 0x00-0x0F) which will force a reload */
   MMRCache = 0xFF;

   /* set write mode 1 for fast copying using the display latches */
   outportb(GC_INDEX_REG, MODE_INDEX);
   ModeRegTemp = inportb(GC_DATA_REG);
   ModeRegTemp = (ModeRegTemp & 0xFC) | 0x01;
   outportb(GC_DATA_REG, ModeRegTemp);

   /* setup */
   DestIncrement = (GScreenVirtualWidth / 4) - VideoBM->Width;
   BltWidth = VideoBM->Width;
   BltHeight = VideoBM->Height;

   for (HeightCounter = 0; HeightCounter < BltHeight;
       HeightCounter++) {
       for (WidthCounter = 0; WidthCounter < BltWidth;
           WidthCounter++) {
           // if current MMR value == last MMR value, don't do this
           if (MMRCache != *MapMaskData) {
               MMRCache = *MapMaskData;
               SetMMR(MMRCache);
           }
           Dummy = *Source;      // since we're using write mode 1
           *Dest = Dummy;        //    the Dummy value is ignored
           Source++;
           Dest++;
           MapMaskData++;
       }
       Dest += DestIncrement;
   }

   /* reset write mode back to write mode 0 */
   ModeRegTemp &= 0xFC;
   outportb(GC_INDEX_REG, MODE_INDEX);
   outportb(GC_DATA_REG, ModeRegTemp);
}
```

The routine starts by initializing a number of pointers that will be used in the actual drawing loops. In particular, you should notice the lines that are used to initialize the pointer to the **Dest** pointer, which keeps track of the destination location of the current pixel copy.

```
DestOffset = (Top * (GScreenVirtualWidth / 4)) +
    (Left / 4) + PageOffset;
Dest = MK_FP(VIDEO_MEM_SEGMENT, DestOffset);
```

As you can see, the **Dest** pointer is set with an offset that includes the term **Left** / 4. This has the effect of forcing the bitblt to align itself to a four-pixel boundary. As we'll see in the demonstration program in the next section, **BltVideoMem** simply rounds an x coordinate down to the nearest multiple of four. This is an artifact of using four-pixel video copies in video memory. With four pixels being moved at once, there is no way to provide arbitrary x coordinate positioning without adding some complexity.

The only way to achive arbitrary x coordinate positioning is to generate four versions of the bitmap in the **LinearToVideoMemory** routine. Each of the four video memory bitmaps would contain the linear bitmap shifted over from zero to three pixels to the right, with any additional pixels added to either side being filled with transparent pixels. Now, when the bitmap must be drawn to the screen, choose one of the four video memory bitmaps based on the x coordinate passed to the drawing routine.

As you can see, when you create the video memory bitmap in order to handle arbitrary x cooridinate positioning, you really end up creating four bitmaps and consequently taking four times the amount of video memory. Additionally, you have to select which bitmap you want to draw based on the x coordinate of the image. I chose not to add the complexity here.

Next, **BltVideoMem** initializes a variable named **MMRCache** to 0xFF. The **MMRCache** variable is used to store the last value programmed in the Map Mask Register. The **MMRCache** variable will be used to try to reduce the number of writes to the MMR that must be performed, thus improving performance. The 0xFF value is used to initialize the variable because this value cannot occur normally, and this will force the first four-pixel copy to set the MMR to the correct value.

Next, the VGA is put into Write Mode 1. In Write Mode 1, the data written to the card by the host is ignored. Instead, all data written to video memory comes from the display latches. To set Write Mode 1, we fiddle with the Write Mode field of the Graphics Control Mode Register.

Here's where the fun starts. The loops simply copy the data from the source portion of video memory into the destination, going a line at a time. Before a group of four pixels is copied, the MMR value is set to the correct value for the pixel group. The new MMR value is compared with the **MMRCache** value, and only if they are different is the value actually written to the MMR. Each read from video memory loads the four latches, which are then written to the destination video memory. The display planes that are enabled with the MMR actually have data written to them. The data that is read from the video memory and written back is garbage, since we've enabled Write Mode 1.

Finally, the routine completes by returning the VGA back to the default Write Mode 0.

BltVideoMem Optimization

Very often, video memory bitmaps are used to store rectangular bitmap tiles used to create large backgrounds. These tiles are laid out in a pattern to produce a larger image. Since the tiles are rectangular and are used for background rather than foreground images, they often don't include transparent pixels. As you can see from the **BltVideoMem** source code, the managing of the MMR puts a conditional statement into the innermost loop of the function. Even when we don't set the MMR to a new value, the conditional statement ends up slowing down the loop.

We can optimize **BltVideoMem** to draw background tiles by eliminating the support for transparent pixels. The **BltVideoMemNoTransparent** routine does just that. The **BltVideoMemNoTransparent** routine simply ignores the **MapMaskData** field of the **VIDEO_MEM_BITMAP** structure when drawing the bitmap. All pixels of color value 0 are copied to memory as color value 0. With the standard palette, color value 0 represents black.

Full source for **BltVideoMemNoTransparent** can be found in BITMAP.C.

A Video Memory Example

The BLTDMOVB program, shown in Listing 6.8, demonstrates video memory bitmaps. Like all the other examples in this chapter, BLTDMOVB will be fairly familiar. As usual, we'll use our old friend, the ball bitmap, but this time we'll convert it to a video memory bitmap.

Compiling and Linking:

You can compile the BLTDMOVB program using the Borland C++ 3. I IDE by typing "bc bltdmovb.prj" and then selecting Compile I Make from the menus. If you would rather use the command line compiler, convert the BLTDMOVB.PRJ file to a makefile using the PRJ2MAK program supplied with Borland C++ 3.1. Type "prj2mak bltdmovb.prj" to create the BLTDMOVB.MAK and BLTDMOVB.CFG files.

If you are using Borland C++ 4.0, choose Project I Open Project from the IDE menus. Open the BLTDMOVB.PRJ file. Borland C++ will convert the version 3.1 .PRJ file to a version 4.0 .IDE file. Compile and link the program by choosing Project I Make All from the IDE menus.

Listing 6.8   BLTDMOVB.C

```
/* File: BLTDMOVB.C
** Description:
**    Demonstration of video bitmap routines in Mode X.
** Copyright:
**    Copyright 1994, David G. Roberts
*/

#include <alloc.h>
#include <assert.h>
#include <conio.h>
#include <dos.h>
#include <stdio.h>
#include "gamedefs.h"
#include "bitblt.h"
#include "vga.h"
#include "setmodex.h"

UINT8 BallBitmap[] = {
    10, 0,          /* Width (little endian) */
    10, 0,          /* Height (little endian) */
    0, 0,           /* X & Y origin at top left corner */
    0, 0,
    0, 0, 0, 2, 2, 2, 2, 0, 0, 0, /* color 2 = green w/ default palette */
    0, 2, 2, 2, 2, 2, 2, 2, 2, 0,
    0, 2, 2, 0, 0, 2, 2, 2, 2, 0,
    2, 2, 0, 0, 2, 2, 2, 2, 2, 2,
    2, 2, 0, 2, 2, 2, 2, 2, 2, 2,
    2, 2, 2, 2, 2, 2, 2, 2, 2, 2,
    2, 2, 2, 2, 2, 2, 2, 2, 2, 2,
    0, 2, 2, 2, 2, 2, 2, 2, 2, 0,
    0, 2, 2, 2, 2, 2, 2, 2, 2, 0,
    0, 0, 0, 2, 2, 2, 2, 0, 0, 0
};

/*
```

```
        Function: FillPartialScreen
        Description:
            Fills the first half of the Mode X screen with the color
            specified as a parameter.  The function takes advantage of
            Mode X's ability to write to four pixels at one time by
            enabling all the display planes at once.  This allows
            fast color fills to be done in 1/4 the time normally taken.
*/
void FillPartialScreen(UINT8 Color)
{
    UINT8 far * Screen;
    int i;

    Screen = MK_FP(VIDEO_MEM_SEGMENT, 0);

    SetMMR(0xF);    /* enable all planes */
    for (i = 0; i < ((MODEX_WIDTH / 4) * (MODEX_HEIGHT / 2)); i++) {
        *Screen++ = Color;
    }
}

int main()
{
    VIDEO_MEM_BITMAP far * VideoBall;

    /* detect VGA */
    if (!DetectVGA()) {
        printf("You must have a VGA to run this program.\n");
        return 1;
    }

    SetModeX();

    FillPartialScreen(0x7); /* fill with white */

    VideoBall = LinearToVideoMemory((LINEAR_BITMAP far *) BallBitmap,
        0xC000, NULL);

    BltVideoMemNoTransparent((VIDEO_MEM_BITMAP far *) VideoBall, 10, 10, 0);
    BltVideoMem((VIDEO_MEM_BITMAP far *) VideoBall, 100,100, 0);
    BltVideoMem((VIDEO_MEM_BITMAP far *) VideoBall, 102, 115, 0);
    BltVideoMem((VIDEO_MEM_BITMAP far *) VideoBall, 103, 130, 0);

    getch();

    farfree(VideoBall);

    SetVGAMode(0x3);    /* return to text mode */

    return 0;
}
```

As you can see, this example program differs very little from the others we examined in the past. We first enter Mode X and then fill half of the screen with white, again using the Mode X fast-fill technique as we did in the planar bitmap example program.

Next, we convert the linear bitmap of the ball into a video memory bitmap. We'll store the video memory bitmap image data at offset C000h. The C000h offset indicates that the bitmap should be stored in the last quarter of video memory on the VGA card. Since there are a little less than four pages (three and change) in Mode X, the bitmap will be well off-screen.

After converting the bitmap, we draw the video memory bitmap four times. The first ball is drawn over the white background with the **BltVideoMemNoTransparent** function. This shows the full outline of the ball bitmap in video memory format. Notice that extra transparent pixels have been added to make the image width a multiple of four.

The second through fourth balls are drawn in a vertical line with slightly different x coordinates: 100, 102, and 103. Onscreen, however, these bitmaps line up vertically. You can't tell they were drawn with different x coordinates. This shows how the **BltVideoMem** function rounds all x coordinates down to a multiple of four. All three of the balls get drawn with a screen x coordinate of 100. These last images are drawn with the **BltVideoMem** function and the 0-valued pixels are treated as transparent.

Finally, the routine dutifully waits for a keypress, frees up the video memory bitmap structure, then flips the VGA back into text mode and exits.

CLIPPING

All the functions presented in this chapter so far have assumed that the whole bitmap will be located onscreen. The routines do not clip a bitmap image that may be too close to a screen edge. There are two clipping routines provided in BITBLT.C, **BltLinearClipRect** and **BltPlanarClipRect**, that will clip a sprite image to a specified rectangle. They are much slower than their non-clipping cousins and should be avoided if possible. We'll see when we build our game *Alien Alley* that they aren't needed, but if you should have a project that requires this functionality, you'll have the routines.

OPTIMIZATIONS

As we examine animation in the next chapter, we'll find that the performance of the bitblt routines we've seen here will be very important to the performance of our final animation. C code was used to describe the routines in this chapter. The actual code on disk, however, uses inline assembly language within the C routines to optimize the inner drawing loops. The gain in performance is very dramatic between the C versions and the C with assembly language versions. Some routines are about two or three times as fast in assembly language, even compared to compiling the C code with the compiler optimizations turned on.

This isn't to say that we can't do more to optimize the routines further. Like any optimization, there is always more that can be done if you've got the time and the desire. If you find that these routines aren't fast enough for your purposes, pull out your copy of *Zen Of Code Optimization* by Michael Abrash and go for it!

THE COMPLETE BITBLT.H AND BITBLT.C LISTINGS

The full source code for BITBLT.H and BITBLT.C are shown in Listings 6.9 and 6.10, respectively. These listings include the non-transparent and clipping versions of the bitblt routines as well as the assembly-language optimizations.

Listing 6.9   BITBLT.H

```
/* File: BITBLT.H
** Description:
**    Header file for BITBLT.C.  Module for bitblt'ing bitmaps to
**    the screen.
** Copyright:
**    Copyright 1994, David G. Roberts
*/

#ifndef _BITBLT_H

#include "gamedefs.h"

typedef struct {
    UINT16 Width;
    UINT16 Height;
    int OriginX;
    int OriginY;
    UINT8 Data;
} LINEAR_BITMAP;
```

```
typedef struct {
    UINT16 Width;              /* Bitmap width = actual width divided by 4 */
    UINT16 Height;
    int OriginX;
    int OriginY;
    UINT8 Data;
} PLANAR_BITMAP;

typedef struct {
    UINT16 Width;              /* Width = true width / 4 */
    UINT16 Height;
    int OriginX;
    int OriginY;
    UINT16 VideoDataOffset; /* offset to image data in video memory */
    UINT8 MapMaskData;
} VIDEO_MEM_BITMAP;

/* exported functions and variables */
void BltLinear(LINEAR_BITMAP far * LinearBM, int x, int y,
    UINT8 far * ScreenBase);
void BltLinearNoTransparent(LINEAR_BITMAP far * LinearBM, int x, int y,
    UINT8 far * ScreenBase);
PLANAR_BITMAP far * LinearToPlanar(LINEAR_BITMAP far * LinearBM);
void BltPlanar(PLANAR_BITMAP far * PlanarBM, int x, int y,
    UINT16 PageOffset);
void BltPlanarNoTransparent(PLANAR_BITMAP far * PlanarBM, int x, int y,
    UINT16 PageOffset);
VIDEO_MEM_BITMAP far * LinearToVideoMemory(LINEAR_BITMAP far * LinearBM,
    UINT16 Storage, UINT16 * Length);
void BltVideoMem(VIDEO_MEM_BITMAP far * VideoBM, int x, int y,
    UINT16 PageOffset);
void BltVideoMemNoTransparent(VIDEO_MEM_BITMAP far * VideoBM, int x, int y,
    UINT16 PageOffset);
void BltLinearClipRect(LINEAR_BITMAP far * LinearBM, int x, int y,
    UINT8 far * ScreenBase, RECT * ClipRect);
void BltPlanarClipRect(PLANAR_BITMAP far * PlanarBM, int x, int y,
    UINT16 PageOffset, RECT * ClipRect);

#define _BITBLT_H

#endif
```

Listing 6.10   BITBLT.C

```
/* File: BITBLT.C
** Description:
**     Module for bitblt'ing bitmaps to the screen.
** Copyright:
**     Copyright 1994, David G. Roberts
*/

#include <alloc.h>
#include <assert.h>
```

```c
#include <dos.h>
#include <mem.h>
#include <stdio.h>
#include "gamedefs.h"
#include "vga.h"
#include "bitblt.h"

/*
    Function: BltLinear
    Description:
        Draws a linear bitmap to the screen.
        The base of the screen is specified by the ScreenBase
        parameter and the position on that screen specified by the
        x and y parameters.
*/
void BltLinear
    (
    LINEAR_BITMAP far * LinearBM,
    int x,
    int y,
    UINT8 far * ScreenBase
    )
{
    int Top;      /* coordinate values of bitmap top-left corner */
    int Left;
    int BltWidth;    /* width of bitmap so we don't dereference pointers */
    int BltHeight;   /* height of bitmap so we don't dereference pointers */
    UINT16 TempOffset;  /* temp variable to calc far pointer offsets */
    UINT8 far * Screen; /* pointer to current screen position */
    UINT8 far * Bitmap; /* pointer to current bitmap position */
    /* unsigned WidthCounter; used for C version */
    /* unsigned HeightCounter; used for C version */
    unsigned ScreenIncrement;

    assert(LinearBM != NULL);
    assert(ScreenBase != NULL);

    /* calculate top-left corner position */
    Left = x - LinearBM->OriginX;
    Top  = y - LinearBM->OriginY;

    /* calculate screen pointer starting position */
    TempOffset = Top * GScreenVirtualWidth + Left;
    Screen = ScreenBase + TempOffset;

    /* calculate bitmap pointer starting position */
    Bitmap = &(LinearBM->Data);

    /* blt to screen */
    BltWidth = LinearBM->Width;
    BltHeight = LinearBM->Height;
    ScreenIncrement = GScreenVirtualWidth - BltWidth;
```

```
/*
This bit of C code is equivalent to the inline assembly
language, below, and is shown here for reference.

for (HeightCounter = 0; HeightCounter < BltHeight; HeightCounter++) {
    for (WidthCounter = 0; WidthCounter < BltWidth; WidthCounter++) {
        if (*Bitmap != 0) {
            *Screen = *Bitmap;
        }
        Screen++;
        Bitmap++;
    }
    Screen += ScreenIncrement;
}
*/
asm {
    push ds
    mov dx,BltWidth
    mov bx,BltHeight
    lds si,Bitmap
    les di,Screen
}
rowloop:
asm {
    mov cx,dx
}
columnloop:
asm {
    mov al,[si]
    inc si
    or al,al
    jz transparent
    mov es:[di],al
    inc di
    dec cx
    jnz columnloop
    add di,ScreenIncrement
    dec bx
    jnz rowloop
    jmp cleanup
}
transparent:
asm {
    inc di
    dec cx
    jnz columnloop
    add di,ScreenIncrement
    dec bx
    jnz rowloop
}
cleanup:
asm {
```

```
        pop ds
    }
}

/*
    Function: BltLinearNoTransparent
    Description:
        Draws a linear bitmap to the screen. Ignores transparent
        pixels.
*/
void BltLinearNoTransparent
    (
    LINEAR_BITMAP far * LinearBM,
    int x,
    int y,
    UINT8 far * ScreenBase
    )
{
    int Top;     /* coordinate values of bitmap top-left corner */
    int Left;
    int BltWidth;   /* width of bitmap so we don't dereference pointers */
    int BltHeight;  /* height of bitmap so we don't dereference pointers */
    UINT16 TempOffset;  /* temp variable to calc far pointer offsets */
    UINT8 far * Screen; /* pointer to current screen position */
    UINT8 far * Bitmap; /* pointer to current bitmap position */
    /* unsigned WidthCounter; used for C version */
    /* unsigned HeightCounter; used for C version */
    unsigned ScreenIncrement;

    assert(LinearBM != NULL);
    assert(ScreenBase != NULL);

    /* calculate top-left corner position */
    Left = x - LinearBM->OriginX;
    Top  = y - LinearBM->OriginY;

    /* calculate screen pointer starting position */
    TempOffset = Top * GScreenVirtualWidth + Left;
    Screen = ScreenBase + TempOffset;

    /* calculate bitmap pointer starting position */
    Bitmap = &(LinearBM->Data);

    /* blt to screen */
    BltWidth = LinearBM->Width;
    BltHeight = LinearBM->Height;
    ScreenIncrement = GScreenVirtualWidth - BltWidth;

    /*
    This bit of C code is equivalent to the inline assembly
    language, below, and is shown here for reference.

    for (HeightCounter = 0; HeightCounter < BltHeight; HeightCounter++) {
        for (WidthCounter = 0; WidthCounter < BltWidth; WidthCounter++) {
```

```
                *Screen++ = *Bitmap++;
            }
        Screen += ScreenIncrement;
    }
*/
asm {
    push ds
    mov dx,BltWidth
    mov bx,BltHeight
    lds si,Bitmap
    les di,Screen
}
rowloop:
asm {
    mov cx,dx

    shr cx,1
    rep movsw
    adc cx,cx
    rep movsb

    add di,ScreenIncrement
    dec bx
    jnz rowloop
    pop ds
    }
}


/*
    Function: LinearToPlanar
    Description:
        Converts a bitmap from linear format to planar format.
        The function returns a new block of memory allocated with
        farmalloc which should be farfreed when the program is finished
        with it.  Returns NULL if memory could not be allocated.  If
        the source bitmap width is not evenly divisible by four,
        the function rounds the planar bitmap width up to an even
        multiple of four and fills the new bitmap columns with 0 pixels.
*/
PLANAR_BITMAP far * LinearToPlanar(LINEAR_BITMAP far * LinearBM)
{
    unsigned PlanarWidth;
    UINT16 PlanarBMSize;
    PLANAR_BITMAP far * PlanarBM;
    unsigned PlaneCounter;
    unsigned WidthCounter;
    unsigned HeightCounter;
    UINT8 far * LinearData;
    UINT8 far * PlanarData;

    assert(LinearBM != NULL);

    /* make PlanarWidth even multiple of 4, rounding up */
    if ((LinearBM->Width % 4) != 0) {
```

```
        PlanarWidth = LinearBM->Width + (4 - (LinearBM->Width % 4));
    }
    else {
        PlanarWidth = LinearBM->Width;
    }


    /* calculate needed memory and allocate */
    /* sizeof(UINT8) correct for the dummy Data field of the */
    /* PLANAR_BITMAP structure which is already included in the */
    /* width*height term */
    PlanarBMSize = PlanarWidth * LinearBM->Height +
        sizeof(PLANAR_BITMAP) - sizeof(UINT8);
    PlanarBM = (PLANAR_BITMAP far *) farmalloc(PlanarBMSize);
    if (PlanarBM == NULL) { /* error! */
        return NULL;
    }


    /* fill in width and height info */
    PlanarBM->Width = PlanarWidth / 4;
    PlanarBM->Height = LinearBM->Height;
    PlanarBM->OriginX = LinearBM->OriginX;
    PlanarBM->OriginY = LinearBM->OriginY;

    /* store data for each plane consecutively */
    PlanarData = &(PlanarBM->Data);
    for (PlaneCounter = 0; PlaneCounter < 4; PlaneCounter++) {

        for (HeightCounter = 0; HeightCounter < PlanarBM->Height;
            HeightCounter++) {

            /* reset LinearData pointer to start of next row */
            LinearData = &(LinearBM->Data) +
                HeightCounter * LinearBM->Width + PlaneCounter;

            /* iterate over row, stepping by four */
            for (WidthCounter = PlaneCounter; WidthCounter < PlanarWidth;
                WidthCounter += 4) {

                if (WidthCounter < LinearBM->Width) {
                    *PlanarData = *LinearData;
                    LinearData += 4;
                }
                else {
                    /* fill 0's to create new rows */
                    *PlanarData = 0;
                }
                PlanarData++;
            }
        }
    }

    return PlanarBM;
}
```

```
/*
    Function: BltPlanar
    Description:
        Draws a planar bitmap to a mode X/Y screen.  The bitmap
        is positioned at (x,y) and is drawn on the mode X page
        starting at the address specified by the PageOffset parameter.
*/
void BltPlanar
    (
    PLANAR_BITMAP far * PlanarBM,
    int x,
    int y,
    UINT16 PageOffset
    )
{
    int Top;     /* coordinate values of bitmap top-left corner */
    int Left;
    unsigned BltWidth;   /* width of clipped bitmap */
    unsigned BltHeight;  /* height of clipped bitmap */
    UINT16 TempOffset;   /* temp variable to calc far pointer offsets */
    /* UINT8 far * Screen; ptr to screen position - used in C version */
    UINT8 far * ScreenInit;  /* used to reload screen ptr between planes */
    UINT8 far * Bitmap;  /* pointer to current bitmap position */
    /* unsigned WidthCounter; used for C version */
    /* unsigned HeightCounter; used for C version */
    unsigned PlaneCounter;
    unsigned ScreenIncrement;
    UINT8 MMRValue;

    assert(PlanarBM != NULL);

    /* calculate top-left corner position */
    Left = x - PlanarBM->OriginX;
    Top  = y - PlanarBM->OriginY;

    /* setup */
    BltWidth = PlanarBM->Width;
    BltHeight = PlanarBM->Height;
    ScreenIncrement = GScreenVirtualWidth / 4 - BltWidth;
    Bitmap = &(PlanarBM->Data);
    if (Left >= 0) {
        MMRValue = 1 << (Left % 4);
    }
    else {
        /* correct for when bitmap moves offscreen to left */
        MMRValue = 1 << ((4 - (-Left % 4)) % 4);
    }
    TempOffset = (Top * (GScreenVirtualWidth / 4)) + PageOffset;
    if (Left >= 0) {
        TempOffset += (Left / 4);
    }
    else {
        /* correct for when bitmap moves offscreen to left */
```

```
    TempOffset -= ((-Left - 1) / 4) + 1;
}
ScreenInit = MK_FP(VIDEO_MEM_SEGMENT, TempOffset);

/*
This bit of C code is equivalent to the inline assembly
language, below, and is shown here for reference.

for (PlaneCounter = 0; PlaneCounter < 4; PlaneCounter++) {
    SetMMR(MMRValue);
    Screen = ScreenInit;

    for (HeightCounter = 0; HeightCounter < BltHeight;
        HeightCounter++) {
        for (WidthCounter = 0; WidthCounter < BltWidth;
            WidthCounter++) {
            if (*Bitmap != 0) {
                *Screen = *Bitmap;
            }
            Screen++;
            Bitmap++;
        }
        Screen += ScreenIncrement;
    }

    MMRValue <<= 1;
    if (!(MMRValue & 0x0F)) {
        MMRValue = 1;
        ScreenInit++;
    }
}
*/

/* bitblt */
asm {
    push ds
    mov PlaneCounter,4
    lds si,Bitmap
}
planeloop:
asm {
    mov ah,MMRValue
    mov al,MAP_MASK_INDEX
    mov dx,SEQ_INDEX_REG
    out dx,ax
    mov dx,BltWidth
    mov bx,BltHeight
    les di,ScreenInit
}
rowloop:
asm {
    mov cx,dx
}
columnloop:
```

```
        asm {
            mov al,[si]
            inc si
            or al,al
            jz transparent
        }
nontransparent:
        asm {
            mov es:[di],al
            inc di
            dec cx
            jnz columnloop
        }
lineend:
        asm {
            add di,ScreenIncrement
            dec bx
            jnz rowloop
            jmp cleanup
        }
transparent:
        asm {
            inc di
            dec cx
            jz lineend
            mov al,[si]
            inc si
            or al,al
            jnz nontransparent
            jmp transparent
        }
cleanup:
        asm {
            dec PlaneCounter
            jz exit
            mov al,MMRValue
            shl al,1
            and al,0xF
            jnz noreinit
            mov al,1
            inc word ptr ScreenInit
        }
noreinit:
        asm {
            mov MMRValue,al
            jmp planeloop
        }
exit:
        asm {
            pop ds
        }

}
```

```c
/*
    Function: BltPlanarNoTransparent
    Description:
        Draws a planar bitmap to a mode X/Y screen.  The routine
        ignores transparent pixels.
*/
void BltPlanarNoTransparent
    (
    PLANAR_BITMAP far * PlanarBM,
    int x,
    int y,
    UINT16 PageOffset
    )
{
    int Top;      /* coordinate values of bitmap top-left corner */
    int Left;
    unsigned BltWidth;   /* width of clipped bitmap */
    unsigned BltHeight;  /* height of clipped bitmap */
    UINT16 TempOffset;   /* temp variable to calc far pointer offsets */
    /* UINT8 far * Screen; ptr to screen position - used in C version */
    UINT8 far * ScreenInit; /* used to reload screen ptr between planes */
    UINT8 far * Bitmap;  /* pointer to current bitmap position */
    /* unsigned WidthCounter; used for C version */
    /* unsigned HeightCounter; used for C version */
    unsigned PlaneCounter;
    unsigned ScreenIncrement;
    UINT8 MMRValue;

    assert(PlanarBM != NULL);

    /* calculate top-left corner position */
    Left = x - PlanarBM->OriginX;
    Top  = y - PlanarBM->OriginY;

    /* setup */
    BltWidth = PlanarBM->Width;
    BltHeight = PlanarBM->Height;
    ScreenIncrement = GScreenVirtualWidth / 4 - BltWidth;
    Bitmap = &(PlanarBM->Data);
    if (Left >= 0) {
        MMRValue = 1 << (Left % 4);
    }
    else {
        /* correct for when bitmap moves offscreen to left */
        MMRValue = 1 << ((4 - (-Left % 4)) % 4);
    }
    TempOffset = (Top * (GScreenVirtualWidth / 4)) + PageOffset;
    if (Left >= 0) {
        TempOffset += (Left / 4);
    }
    else {
        /* correct for when bitmap moves offscreen to left */
        TempOffset -= ((-Left - 1) / 4) + 1;
```

```
}
ScreenInit = MK_FP(VIDEO_MEM_SEGMENT, TempOffset);

/*
This bit of C code is equivalent to the inline assembly
language, below, and is shown here for reference.

for (PlaneCounter = 0; PlaneCounter < 4; PlaneCounter++) {
    SetMMR(MMRValue);
    Screen = ScreenInit;

    for (HeightCounter = 0; HeightCounter < BltHeight;
        HeightCounter++) {
        for (WidthCounter = 0; WidthCounter < BltWidth;
            WidthCounter++) {
            *Screen = *Bitmap;
            Screen++;
            Bitmap++;
        }
        Screen += ScreenIncrement;
    }

    MMRValue <<= 1;
    if (!(MMRValue & 0x0F)) {
        MMRValue = 1;
        ScreenInit++;
    }
}
*/

/* bitblt */
asm {
    push ds
    mov PlaneCounter,4
    lds si,Bitmap
}
planeloop:
asm {
    mov ah,MMRValue
    mov al,MAP_MASK_INDEX
    mov dx,SEQ_INDEX_REG
    out dx,ax
    mov dx,BltWidth
    mov bx,BltHeight
    les di,ScreenInit
}
rowloop:
asm {
    mov cx,dx
    rep movsb
    add di,ScreenIncrement
    dec bx
    jnz rowloop
```

```
        dec PlaneCounter
        jz exit
        mov al,MMRValue
        shl al,1
        and al,0xF
        jnz noreinit
        mov al,1
        inc word ptr ScreenInit
    }
    noreinit:
    asm {
        mov MMRValue,al
        jmp planeloop
    }
    exit:
    asm {
        pop ds
    }
}


/*
    Function: LinearToVideoMemory
    Description:
        Converts a linear bitmap into a video memory bitmap.  The first
        parameter points to the original linear bitmap structure while
        the second points to the address in video memory that should be
        used to hold the video bitmap.  The function returns NULL if
        no video bitmap data structure could be allocated and a
        far pointer to the structure otherwise.
*/
VIDEO_MEM_BITMAP far * LinearToVideoMemory
    (
    LINEAR_BITMAP far * LinearBM,
    UINT16 Storage,
    UINT16 * Length
    )
{
    unsigned VideoWidth;    /* width of video memory bitmap */
    unsigned VideoBMSize;    /* size of video BM structure + map mask data */
    VIDEO_MEM_BITMAP far * VideoBM;
    unsigned WidthCounter;  /* width counter for video memory */
    unsigned LinearWidthCounter; /* width counter for linear bitmap */
    unsigned HeightCounter;
    unsigned PlaneCounter;
    UINT8 far * LinearData;
    UINT8 far * VideoData;
    UINT8 far * MapMaskData;
    UINT8 Pixel;


    assert(LinearBM != NULL);
    assert(Storage != NULL);
```

```
/* make PlanarWidth even multiple of 4, rounding up */
if ((LinearBM->Width % 4) != 0) {
    VideoWidth = LinearBM->Width + (4 - (LinearBM->Width % 4));
}
else {
    VideoWidth = LinearBM->Width;
}

/* calculate length of video memory bitmap data structure */
VideoBMSize = (VideoWidth / 4) * LinearBM->Height +
    sizeof(VIDEO_MEM_BITMAP) - 1;

/* allocate video memory bitmap data structure */
VideoBM = (VIDEO_MEM_BITMAP far *) farmalloc(VideoBMSize);
if (VideoBM == NULL) { /* error! */
    return NULL;
}

/* fill in fields */
VideoBM->Width = VideoWidth / 4;
VideoBM->Height = LinearBM->Height;
VideoBM->OriginX = LinearBM->OriginX;
VideoBM->OriginY = LinearBM->OriginY;
VideoBM->VideoDataOffset = Storage;

/* copy linear data to video memory */
LinearData = &(LinearBM->Data);
VideoData = MK_FP(VIDEO_MEM_SEGMENT, Storage);
MapMaskData = &(VideoBM->MapMaskData);
for (HeightCounter = 0; HeightCounter < LinearBM->Height;
    HeightCounter++) {
    LinearWidthCounter = 0;
    for (WidthCounter = 0; WidthCounter < (VideoWidth / 4);
        WidthCounter++) {
        *MapMaskData = 0;
        for (PlaneCounter = 0; PlaneCounter < 4; PlaneCounter++) {
            if (LinearWidthCounter < LinearBM->Width) {
                Pixel = *LinearData;
                LinearData++;
            }
            else {
                Pixel = 0;  /* transparent pixel */
            }
            SetMMR(1 << PlaneCounter);
            *VideoData = Pixel;
            if (Pixel != 0) {
                *MapMaskData |= 1 << PlaneCounter;
            }
            LinearWidthCounter++;
        }
        MapMaskData++;
        VideoData++;
    }
}
```

```
    if (Length != NULL) {
        *Length = VideoBM->Width * VideoBM->Height;
    }

    return VideoBM;
}


/*

    Function: BltVideoMem
    Description:
        Performs a bitblt of a video memory bitmap to the screen.
        This routine does NOT perform clipping.  The X coordinate
        given to the routine should be a multiple of four.  If it
        is not, the routine rounds it down to the nearest multiple
        of four.
*/
void BltVideoMem
    (
    VIDEO_MEM_BITMAP far * VideoBM,
    int x,
    int y,
    UINT16 PageOffset
    )
{
    int Top;     /* coordinate values of bitmap top-left corner */
    int Left;
    UINT8 MMRCache;
    UINT8 far * MapMaskData;
    UINT8 far * Source;
    /* UINT8 far * Dest; needed in C version */
    unsigned DestOffset;
    /* unsigned WidthCounter; needed in C version */
    unsigned HeightCounter;
    unsigned BltWidth;
    unsigned BltHeight;
    UINT8 ModeRegTemp;
    /* UINT8 Dummy; used in version */
    unsigned DestIncrement;

    assert(VideoBM != NULL);

    Left = x - VideoBM->OriginX;
    Top  = y - VideoBM->OriginY;

    /* initialize the various pointers */
    Source = MK_FP(VIDEO_MEM_SEGMENT, VideoBM->VideoDataOffset);
    DestOffset = (Top * (GScreenVirtualWidth / 4)) +
        (Left / 4) + PageOffset;
    /* Dest = MK_FP(VIDEO_MEM_SEGMENT, DestOffset); needed in C version */
    MapMaskData = &(VideoBM->MapMaskData);

    /* initialize MMRCache with a value that cannot occur normally */
    /* (normal values are 0x00-0x0F) which will force a reload */
    MMRCache = 0xFF;
```

```c
/* set write mode 1 for fast copying using the display latches */
outportb(GC_INDEX_REG, MODE_INDEX);
ModeRegTemp = inportb(GC_DATA_REG);
ModeRegTemp = (ModeRegTemp & 0xFC) | 0x01;
outportb(GC_DATA_REG, ModeRegTemp);

/* setup */
DestIncrement = (GScreenVirtualWidth / 4) - VideoBM->Width;
BltWidth = VideoBM->Width;
BltHeight = VideoBM->Height;

/*
This bit of C code is equivalent to the inline assembly
language, below, and is shown here for reference.

for (HeightCounter = 0; HeightCounter < BltHeight;
    HeightCounter++) {
    for (WidthCounter = 0; WidthCounter < BltWidth;
        WidthCounter++) {
        // if current MMR value == last MMR value, don't do this
        if (MMRCache != *MapMaskData) {
            MMRCache = *MapMaskData;
            SetMMR(MMRCache);
        }
        Dummy = *Source;      // since we're using write mode 1
        *Dest = Dummy;        //   the Dummy value is ignored
        Source++;
        Dest++;
        MapMaskData++;
    }
    Dest += DestIncrement;
}
*/

/* copy data */
asm {
    push ds
    lds si,Source        /* ds:si = source */
    mov di,DestOffset    /* ds:di = dest */
    les bx,MapMaskData   /* es:bx = map mask data */
    mov dx,BltWidth
    mov ax,BltHeight
    mov HeightCounter,ax
}
rowloop:
asm {
    mov cx,dx
}
lineloop:
asm {
    mov ah,es:[bx]       /* get map mask data */
    inc bx
    cmp ah,MMRCache
    je mmrok
```

```
        mov MMRCache,ah      /* if its not the same as last time */
        push dx              /* set it and update cache */
        mov dx,SEQ_INDEX_REG
        mov al,MAP_MASK_INDEX
        out dx,ax
        pop dx
    }
    mmrok:
    asm {
        mov al,[si]          /* dummy read */
        mov [di],al          /* dummy write */
        inc si
        inc di
        dec cx
        jnz lineloop
        add di,DestIncrement
        dec HeightCounter
        jnz rowloop
        pop ds
    }

    /* reset write mode back to write mode 0 */
    ModeRegTemp &= 0xFC;
    outportb(GC_INDEX_REG, MODE_INDEX);
    outportb(GC_DATA_REG, ModeRegTemp);
}


/*
    Function: BltVideoMemNoTransparent
    Description:
        Performs a bitblt of a video memory bitmap to the screen.
        This routine does NOT perform clipping.  The X coordinate
        given to the routine should be a multiple of four.  If it
        is not, the routine rounds it down to the nearest multiple
        of four.  This routine ignores the MapMaskData field of
        the video memory bitmap structure.  Transparent pixels are
        ignored and drawn normally as color 0.
*/
void BltVideoMemNoTransparent
    (
    VIDEO_MEM_BITMAP far * VideoBM,
    int x,
    int y,
    UINT16 PageOffset
    )
{
    int Top;     /* coordinate values of bitmap top-left corner */
    int Left;
    UINT8 far * Source;
    /* UINT8 far * Dest; needed in C version */
    unsigned DestOffset;
    /* unsigned WidthCounter; needed in C version */
    /* unsigned HeightCounter; needed in C version */
    unsigned BltWidth;
```

```
unsigned BltHeight;
UINT8 ModeRegTemp;
/* UINT8 Dummy; used in C version */
unsigned DestIncrement;

assert(VideoBM != NULL);

Left = x - VideoBM->OriginX;
Top  = y - VideoBM->OriginY;

/* initialize the various pointers */
Source = MK_FP(VIDEO_MEM_SEGMENT, VideoBM->VideoDataOffset);
DestOffset = (Top * (GScreenVirtualWidth / 4)) +
    (Left / 4) + PageOffset;
/* Dest = MK_FP(VIDEO_MEM_SEGMENT, DestOffset); needed in C version */

/* set write mode 1 for fast copying using the display latches */
outportb(GC_INDEX_REG, MODE_INDEX);
ModeRegTemp = inportb(GC_DATA_REG);
ModeRegTemp = (ModeRegTemp & 0xFC) | 0x01;
outportb(GC_DATA_REG, ModeRegTemp);

/* setup */
DestIncrement = (GScreenVirtualWidth / 4) - VideoBM->Width;
BltWidth = VideoBM->Width;
BltHeight = VideoBM->Height;
SetMMR(0x0F);

/*
This bit of C code is equivalent to the inline assembly
language, below, and is shown here for reference.

for (HeightCounter = 0; HeightCounter < BltHeight;
    HeightCounter++) {
    for (WidthCounter = 0; WidthCounter < BltWidth;
        WidthCounter++) {
        Dummy = *Source;     // since we're using write mode 1
        *Dest = Dummy;       //   the Dummy value is ignored
        Source++;
        Dest++;
        MapMaskData++;
    }
    Dest += DestIncrement;
}
*/

/* copy data */
asm {
    push ds
    lds si,Source        /* ds:si = source */
    mov di,DestOffset    /* ds:di = dest */
    mov bx,BltHeight
    mov dx,BltWidth
}
```

```
        rowloop:
        asm {
            mov cx,dx
        }
        lineloop:
        asm {
            mov al,[si]          /* dummy read */
            mov [di],al          /* dummy write */
            inc si
            inc di
            dec cx
            jnz lineloop
            add di,DestIncrement
            dec bx
            jnz rowloop
            pop ds
        }

        /* reset write mode back to write mode 0 */
        ModeRegTemp &= 0xFC;
        outportb(GC_INDEX_REG, MODE_INDEX);
        outportb(GC_DATA_REG, ModeRegTemp);
}


/*
    Function: BltLinearClipRect
    Description:
        Draws a linear bitmap to the screen, clipping as appropriate.
        The base of the screen is specified by the ScreenBase
        parameter and the position on that screen specified by the
        x and y parameters.
*/
void BltLinearClipRect
    (
    LINEAR_BITMAP far * LinearBM,
    int x,
    int y,
    UINT8 far * ScreenBase,
    RECT * ClipRect
    )
{
    int Top;     /* coordinate values of bitmap top-left corner */
    int Left;
    unsigned BMOffsetX; /* starting offset into clipped bitmap */
    unsigned BMOffsetY;
    unsigned ClippedLeft;/* top-left corner position of clipped bitmap */
    unsigned ClippedTop;
    int BltWidth;    /* width of clipped bitmap */
    int BltHeight; /* height of clipped bitmap */
    UINT16 TempOffset;  /* temp variable to calc far pointer offsets */
    UINT8 far * Screen; /* pointer to current screen position */
    UINT8 far * Bitmap; /* pointer to current bitmap position */
```

```
unsigned WidthCounter;
unsigned HeightCounter;
unsigned ScreenIncrement;
unsigned BitmapIncrement;

assert(LinearBM != NULL);

Left = x - LinearBM->OriginX;
Top  = y - LinearBM->OriginY;

if (Left >= (int) ClipRect->Right || Top >= (int) ClipRect->Bottom ||
    (Left + (int) LinearBM->Width) < ClipRect->Left ||
    (Top + (int)LinearBM->Height) < ClipRect->Top)
    return;

/* clip bitmap to upper left edge of rect */

/* if Left < ClipRect->Left, calculate starting x offset in bitmap */
if (Left < ClipRect->Left) {
    BMOffsetX = ClipRect->Left - Left;
    ClippedLeft = ClipRect->Left;
    BltWidth = LinearBM->Width - BMOffsetX;
}
else {
    BMOffsetX = 0;
    ClippedLeft = Left;
    BltWidth = LinearBM->Width;
}

/* if Top < ClipRect->Top, calculate starting y offset in bitmap */
if (Top < ClipRect->Top) {
    BMOffsetY = ClipRect->Top - Top;
    ClippedTop = ClipRect->Top;
    BltHeight = LinearBM->Height - BMOffsetY;
}
else {
    BMOffsetY = 0;
    ClippedTop = Top;
    BltHeight = LinearBM->Height;
}

/* clip bitmap to lower right edge of rect */

/* if Left + bitmap width > rect width, calc ending x point */
if ((ClippedLeft + BltWidth) > ClipRect->Right) {
    BltWidth -= ClippedLeft + BltWidth - ClipRect->Right;
}

/* if Top + bitmap height > rect height, calc ending y point */
if ((ClippedTop + BltHeight) > ClipRect->Bottom) {
    BltHeight -= ClippedTop + BltHeight - ClipRect->Bottom;
}
```

```
/* calculate screen pointer starting position based on */
/* clipped bitmap location */
TempOffset = ClippedTop * GScreenVirtualWidth + ClippedLeft;
Screen = ScreenBase + TempOffset;

/* calculate bitmap pointer starting position based on */
/* clipped bitmap location */
TempOffset = BMOffsetY * LinearBM->Width + BMOffsetX;
Bitmap = &(LinearBM->Data);
Bitmap += TempOffset;

/* blt to screen */
ScreenIncrement = GScreenVirtualWidth - BltWidth;
BitmapIncrement = LinearBM->Width - BltWidth;
for (HeightCounter = 0; HeightCounter < BltHeight; HeightCounter++) {
    for (WidthCounter = 0; WidthCounter < BltWidth; WidthCounter++) {
        if (*Bitmap != 0) {
            *Screen = *Bitmap;
        }
        Screen++;
        Bitmap++;
    }
    Screen += ScreenIncrement;
    Bitmap += BitmapIncrement;
}
}


/*
    Function: BltPlanarClipRect
    Description:
        Draws a planar bitmap to a mode X/Y screen.  The routine
        clips the bitmap to the screen.
*/
void BltPlanarClipRect
    (
    PLANAR_BITMAP far * PlanarBM,
    int x,
    int y,
    UINT16 PageOffset,
    RECT * ClipRect
    )
{
    int Top;     /* coordinate values of bitmap top-left corner */
    int Left;
    unsigned PixelWidth;
    unsigned BMOffsetX[4];  /* starting offset into clipped bitmap */
    unsigned BMOffsetY;
    unsigned ClippedLeft;/* upper left corner position of clipped bitmap */
    unsigned ClippedTop;
    unsigned BltWidth[4];   /* width of clipped bitmap */
    unsigned BltHeight; /* height of clipped bitmap */
    UINT16 TempOffset;  /* temp variable to calc far pointer offsets */
    UINT8 far * Screen; /* pointer to current screen position */
```

```
UINT8 far * Bitmap; /* pointer to current bitmap position */
unsigned WidthCounter;
unsigned HeightCounter;
unsigned PlaneCounter;
unsigned LeftClipWidth;
unsigned RightClipWidth;
unsigned ScreenIncrement;
unsigned BitmapIncrement;
int i;

assert(PlanarBM != NULL);

Left = x - PlanarBM->OriginX;
Top  = y - PlanarBM->OriginY;

PixelWidth = PlanarBM->Width * 4;

if (Left >= (int) ClipRect->Right || Top >= (int) ClipRect->Bottom ||
    (Left + (int) PixelWidth) < ClipRect->Left ||
    (Top + (int) PlanarBM->Height) < ClipRect->Top)
    return;

/* clip bitmap width */

LeftClipWidth = (Left < ClipRect->Left) ? (ClipRect->Left - Left) : 0;
ClippedLeft = Left + LeftClipWidth;
RightClipWidth = ((Left + PixelWidth) > ClipRect->Right) ?
    (Left + PixelWidth - ClipRect->Right) : 0;
for (i = 0; i < 4; i++) {
    BMOffsetX[i] = LeftClipWidth / 4;
    BltWidth[i] = PlanarBM->Width - BMOffsetX[i] - (RightClipWidth / 4);
    if (i < LeftClipWidth % 4) {
        BMOffsetX[i]++;
        BltWidth[i]--;
    }
    if (i >= (4 - (RightClipWidth % 4))) {
        BltWidth[i]--;
    }
}

/* clip bitmap height */
/* if Top < 0, calculate starting y offset in bitmap */
if (Top < ClipRect->Top) {
    BMOffsetY = ClipRect->Top - Top;
    ClippedTop = ClipRect->Top;
    BltHeight = PlanarBM->Height - BMOffsetY;
}
else {
    BMOffsetY = 0;
    ClippedTop = Top;
    BltHeight = PlanarBM->Height;
}
```

```
    /* if Top + bitmap height > screen height, calc ending y point */
    if ((ClippedTop + BltHeight) > ClipRect->Bottom) {
        BltHeight -= ClippedTop + BltHeight - ClipRect->Bottom;
    }

    /* bitblt data for each plane */
    ScreenIncrement = GScreenVirtualWidth / 4;
    BitmapIncrement = PlanarBM->Width;
    for (PlaneCounter = 0; PlaneCounter < 4; PlaneCounter++) {
        /* calculate screen pointer starting position based on */
        /* clipped bitmap and current plane */
        TempOffset = (ClippedTop * (GScreenVirtualWidth / 4)) +
            ((ClippedLeft + PlaneCounter - (LeftClipWidth % 4)) / 4) +
            PageOffset;
        if (PlaneCounter < (LeftClipWidth % 4)) {
            TempOffset++;
        }
        Screen = MK_FP(VIDEO_MEM_SEGMENT, TempOffset);
        SetMMR(1 << ((Left + PlaneCounter) % 4));

        /* calculate bitmap pointer starting position based on */
        /* clipped bitmap and current plane */
        TempOffset = (PlanarBM->Width * PlanarBM->Height * PlaneCounter) +
            (BMOffsetY * PlanarBM->Width) + BMOffsetX[PlaneCounter];
        Bitmap = &(PlanarBM->Data);
        Bitmap += TempOffset;

        /* blt to screen */
        for (HeightCounter = 0; HeightCounter < BltHeight;
            HeightCounter++) {
            for (WidthCounter = 0; WidthCounter < BltWidth[PlaneCounter];
                WidthCounter++) {
                if (*Bitmap != 0) {
                    *Screen = *Bitmap;
                }
                Screen++;
                Bitmap++;
            }
            Screen += ScreenIncrement - BltWidth[PlaneCounter];
            Bitmap += BitmapIncrement - BltWidth[PlaneCounter];
        }
    }
}
```

ADVENTURES IN ANIMATION

To get your games off the ground, you'll need to master the art of animation and this chapter will show you how.

Wow! We've learned a great deal about the VGA and bitmaps in the last couple of chapters. We've learned about the various graphics modes that the VGA supports and about two undocumented modes, X and Y. We've investigated three different bitmap formats, linear, planar, and video memory, and we've seen how to draw these onto the screen using bitblt functions.

Up to now, however, our example programs have been pretty boring. Although we've drawn bitmaps on the screen, we haven't made them move. What we'd really like to see is balls bouncing, missiles flying, frogs jumping, people walking, and aliens attacking. That is, *action*—because that's what arcade games are all about. Without movement of some kind, you don't have a very action-packed arcade game. Animation brings a game to life.

In this chapter, we'll learn how to add movement to the various objects in our game. We'll investigate the topic of animation and try to understand the factors that go into making good animation.

We'll see some of the problems that can crop up and how to fix them. We'll define the term sprite and investigate several different animation techniques, including page-flipping, virtual screen buffers, and dirty rectangles.

 In this chapter we'll develop two modules: ANIMATE.C and RETRACE.C. ANIMATE.C contains routines to implement various animation techniques. RETRACE.C includes routines to test for the current state of the VGA vertical retrace. RETRACE.C is used by ANIMATE.C and many of the example programs in this chapter to synchronize various program events with the vertical retrace. Both of these modules will be used in later chapters and as we develop *Alien Alley*.

To demonstrate each of the animation techniques described in this chapter, seven programs will be built using ANIMATE.C and RETRACE.C.

INTRODUCTION TO ANIMATION

Most people associate the word *animation* with cartoons, both the Saturday morning variety as well as the feature-length Disney variety. Before we learn the techniques that we're going to use to produce animation in our game, let's take a look at what animation means to gamers and how it works. In doing this, we'll gain an understanding of what makes some animations better than others.

What Is Animation?

In the 19th century, people discovered a human physical phenomenon called *persistance of vision*. Persistance of vision occurs when the human eye looks at a particular scene and the scene is then changed rapidly. It turns out that the eye and brain continue to see an image of the old scene for a split second after the scene has changed. That is, the vision persists.

Animation exploits the persistance of vision phenomenon to create a moving scene out of a series of still scenes. For instance, you can make a flip book, which is used to animate a series of still scenes, from a series of 3x5 index cards. On the end of the first card, draw an object, for example, a ball. On the next card, draw an image of the ball either moved or changed in some way. Continue on like this until you've created 30 or 40 cards. Put the cards in order in a stack and hold the end of the cards opposite the drawings. Now flip through the cards as you would a deck of playing cards, and watch the drawings as you do so. You should see the object move or change in the way that you've drawn it.

As you flip through the cards, persistance of vision is causing your eye to see the drawing on the card while ignoring what occurs when the card flips out of the way. The image persists long enough to make the series of images appear linked together. When these linked images are shown to your brain, you see motion.

Film and Television

Although the word *animation* usually describes hand-drawn animated films, if you think about it for a while, you'll see that all films, not just cartoons, use animation. With live action film, instead of a person drawing each frame, a movie camera takes a series of still photos. In both cases, the persistance of vision phenomenon is used to trick your eye and mind into seeing a moving scene created from a series of still pictures.

Television uses the same concept but changes the display from a projector and a screen to a video display tube. A video camera is analogous to a movie camera, except that the still photographs are captured electronically and stored on magnetic tape rather than using photo-sensitive film.

Over the years, certain standards have developed for both film and TV. These standards include size, aspect ratio, and playback rate of the material. We'll look closely at the playback rates of film and TV to have a benchmark to judge the animation frame rate in our game.

Film has gravitated toward a 24 frame per second (fps) playback rate. This means that 24 pictures are required for every second of motion playback. For a hand-drawn animated film, this means that 24 pictures must be drawn for every second of screen time. If you figure that a feature length animated film typically runs 80 to 90 minutes, that's about 129,000 (= 90 * 60 * 24) drawings! My hand is getting sore just thinking about it.

However, in show biz, time is money, and there is a great desire on the part of studios to save money. Not only is it time consuming to have all those animators drawing all those frames, it's also costly. With the exception of feature-length productions by Disney, most work is now done at 12 frames per second. They photograph each drawing twice to bring the frame rate back up to the normal 24 fps so it can be captured on film and replayed using standard motion picture equipment. Although the film runs at 24 fps, the actual animation rate is really 12 fps. This technique cuts the number of frames that have to be drawn by half, consequently reducing the time and cost of the production.

Most Saturday-morning cartoons use an even slower animation rate. Depending on the action on screen, an individual animation frame may be photographed between three and eight times! This keeps productivity up and costs down but also results in much poorer quality animation.

Television uses a 30 fps playback rate. This rate is derived by halving the frequency of the AC electricity available at standard wall plugs, 60 Hz in the U.S. The actual refresh rate of a TV is 60 Hz, but each refresh only updates every other scan-line on the display. For instance, the first refresh updates all the odd numbered lines on the screen, and the second refresh updates all the even numbered lines. This happens every 1/60th of a second, so the whole display gets refreshed every 1/30th of a second, giving us our 30 fps rate.

What happens when you see a movie on TV? Does the TV drop down from 30 fps to the 24 fps rate of the film? The answer is no. The TV still operates at 30 fps, but 24 film frames are mapped to 30 TV frames in a non-one-to-one fashion to sync up the rates. In effect, six TV frames are created from the original 24 film frames to compensate. Some of the TV frames are composed of multiple, overlapping film frames.

Computer Animation

Computer animation is very similar to film and TV animation in a number of ways. The computer acts as the electrical analog of a human animator. The computer draws each frame of animation and displays it. In some cases, the drawing process may take a very long time for each frame, and so each frame is stored to disk as it is generated, and the whole animation is played back later.

In the case of computer games, the rendering is fast enough to keep up with the playback rate, and each frame is displayed as it is generated. At least that's the goal. We'll find that depending on how many objects have to be drawn on the screen, this goal may be a hard one to meet.

Some of the cartridge game machines like those from Sega and Nintendo have dedicated hardware to help move an object bitmap image around the screen very rapidly. These moving bitmaps are called *sprites*. We'll create sprites in our game as well, but we won't have any special purpose hardware to help us out. We'll have to draw each object bitmap with our bitblt routines, moving the object between frames as needed.

So, let's take a look at the basic flow of an animation program.

The Basic Animation Cycle

The basic cycle of a computer animation program is fairly simple. First we determine the new position of our object; we then erase the old image at the old position, and then we draw the new image at the new position. We just keep repeating this sequence of steps over and over while our object is moving. The following pseudo-code demonstrates how the main program loop would be constructed:

```
Done = FALSE;
while (!Done) {
    calculate new object positions
    erase objects at old positions
    draw objects at new positions
}
```

Every time we go though this loop, we create another frame of animation.

This pseudo-code is strikingly similar to the game program pseudo-code we saw in Chapter 1, reprinted here for your reference. The "calculate new object positions" procedure of the animation pseudo-code corresponds with the **GetUserInput**, **MoveObjects**, and **CheckCollisions** functions in the game pseudo-code. The "erase objects at old positions" and "draw objects at new positions" corresponds to the **DrawAnimationFrame** function.

```
PlayerAlive = TRUE;
PlayerWon = FALSE;
while (PlayerAlive && !PlayerWon) {
    GetUserInput();
    MoveObjects();
    CheckCollisions();
    DrawAnimationFrame();
    SpeedCheck();
}
```

In effect, a game program is simply a program that performs computer animation and takes a little direction from the game player. Thus, the animation is interactive.

The **SpeedCheck** function in the game pseudo-code is used ensure that the animation doesn't move too fast. This function is used to set the animation frame rate. We'll find out more about controlling the game speed, and hence, animation speed, in a later chapter.

Now, let's take our animation cycle pseudo-code and expand it into a real program.

Simple Animation Example

The ANIDEMO1 program, shown in Listing 7.1, expands our animation cycle pseudo-code into a real program. The program takes our old friend the ball bitmap from the last chapter and bounces it around the screen until a key is pressed. The program uses linear bitmaps and operates in Mode 13h.

Compiling and Linking:

You can compile the ANIDEMO1 program using the Borland C++ 3.1 IDE by typing "bc anidemo1.prj" and then selecting Compile | Make from the menus. If you would rather use the command line compiler, convert the ANIDEMO1.PRJ file to a makefile using the PRJ2MAK program supplied with Borland C++ 3.1. Type "prj2mak anidemo1.prj" to create the ANIDEMO1.MAK and ANIDEMO1.CFG files.

If you are using Borland C++ 4.0, choose Project | Open Project from the IDE menus. Open the ANIDEMO1.PRJ file. Borland C++ will convert the version 3.1 .PRJ file to a version 4.0 .IDE file. Compile and link the program by choosing Project | Make All from the IDE menus.

Listing 7.1   ANIDEMO1.C

```
/* File: ANIDEMO1.C
** Description:
**    Simple animation demonstration.
** Copyright:
**    Copyright 1994, David G. Roberts
*/

#include <assert.h>
#include <conio.h>
#include <dos.h>
#include <stdio.h>
#include "gamedefs.h"
#include "vga.h"
#include "bitblt.h"

UINT8 BallBitmap[] = {
    10, 0,            /* Width (little endian) */
    10, 0,            /* Height (little endian) */
    0, 0,             /* X and Y origin */
    0, 0,
    0, 0, 0, 2, 2, 2, 2, 0, 0, 0, /* color 2 = green w/ default palette */
    0, 2, 2, 2, 2, 2, 2, 2, 2, 0,
    0, 2, 2, 0, 0, 2, 2, 2, 2, 0,
    2, 2, 0, 0, 2, 2, 2, 2, 2, 2,
    2, 2, 0, 2, 2, 2, 2, 2, 2, 2,
    2, 2, 2, 2, 2, 2, 2, 2, 2, 2,
```

```
        2, 2, 2, 2, 2, 2, 2, 2, 2, 2,
        0, 2, 2, 2, 2, 2, 2, 2, 2, 0,
        0, 2, 2, 2, 2, 2, 2, 2, 2, 0,
        0, 0, 0, 2, 2, 2, 2, 0, 0, 0
};

UINT8 BallEraseBitmap[] = {
    10, 0,          /* Width (little endian) */
    10, 0,          /* Height (little endian) */
    0, 0,           /* X and Y origin */
    0, 0,
    16, 16, 16, 16, 16, 16, 16, 16, 16, 16, /* color 16 = black */
    16, 16, 16, 16, 16, 16, 16, 16, 16, 16, /* with default palette */
    16, 16, 16, 16, 16, 16, 16, 16, 16, 16,
    16, 16, 16, 16, 16, 16, 16, 16, 16, 16,
    16, 16, 16, 16, 16, 16, 16, 16, 16, 16,
    16, 16, 16, 16, 16, 16, 16, 16, 16, 16,
    16, 16, 16, 16, 16, 16, 16, 16, 16, 16,
    16, 16, 16, 16, 16, 16, 16, 16, 16, 16,
    16, 16, 16, 16, 16, 16, 16, 16, 16, 16,
    16, 16, 16, 16, 16, 16, 16, 16, 16, 16
};

/* note: make these track width and height of bitmap, above */
#define BITMAP_HEIGHT   (10)
#define BITMAP_WIDTH    (10)

int main()
{
    int x, y;
    int OldX, OldY;
    int vx, vy;
    BOOL Erase;

    /* detect VGA */
    if (!DetectVGA()) {
        printf("You must have a VGA to run this program.\n");
        return 1;
    }

    SetMode13h();

    x = 0;
    y = 0;
    vx = 2;
    vy = 1;

    Erase = FALSE;

    while (!kbhit()) {
        if (Erase) {
            /* update new position */
            OldX = x;
```

```
            OldY = y;
            x += vx;
            y += vy;
            if ((x < 0) || ((x + BITMAP_WIDTH) >= MODE13H_WIDTH)) {
                vx = -vx;
                x += 2 * vx;
            }
            if ((y < 0) || ((y + BITMAP_HEIGHT) >= MODE13H_HEIGHT)) {
                vy = -vy;
                y += 2 * vy;
            }

            /* erase */
            BltLinear((LINEAR_BITMAP far *) BallEraseBitmap, OldX, OldY,
                MK_FP(VIDEO_MEM_SEGMENT, 0x0000));
        }

        /* draw */
        BltLinear((LINEAR_BITMAP far *) BallBitmap, x, y,
            MK_FP(VIDEO_MEM_SEGMENT, 0x0000));
        Erase = TRUE;

        /* delay a bit */
        delay(20);

    }

    getch();

    SetVGAMode(0x3);

    return 0;
}
```

The program starts by setting the VGA to Mode 13h and initializing the variables that hold the ball's current position and horizontal and vertical velocities: **x**, **y**, **vx**, and **vy**. On each frame of animation, the velocity variables will be added to the current position variables to update the position of the ball.

Next, the variable **Erase** is set to **FALSE**. Since the animation loop erases the previous image of the ball before it draws the new image at the new location, we have a slight problem when we first start to execute the loop. How can we erase something if we haven't drawn it yet? The **Erase** variable solves our problem. We encapsulate the updating and erasing code in the body of the loop in an **if** statement that checks if erasing and updating should be done. The first time through the loop, **Erase** will be **FALSE** and no erasing will be done. After drawing the image, **Erase** is set to **TRUE**, and erasing is done on the second and subsequent executions of the loop.

The loop continues executing until a keypress is detected by the **kbhit** function.

In place of the "calculate new object positions" operation in the animation pseudo code, there is now real code to calculate the position of the ball in the next frame. In each iteration of the loop, the old x and y coordinates are saved into the **OldX** and **OldY** variables. These will be used to erase the old bitmap position later. The **x** and **y** variables are then updated from the **vx** and **vy** variables. Next, the values of **x** and **y** are checked against the limits of the screen to ensure that the bitmap's new position will still be on the screen. If not, the velocity in the offending direction is negated to cause the ball to "bounce" off the screen edge, and the x or y coordinate is corrected to bring it back on screen.

When the new position has been calculated, the bitmap at the old location is erased by drawing a bitmap that is all black and the same size as the ball bitmap, at the same location of the ball bitmap. **BltLinear** is used to draw the linear bitmap on the Mode 13h screen. Color 16 in the default VGA palette corresponds to black. Don't forget that color 0, although black in the color palette, is used to represent transparent pixels. A bitmap consisting of nothing but color 0 won't erase anything!

Now, this brings up a question. Why did we use the **OldX** and **OldY** variables to store the previous frame's image location? Why not just erase the bitmap first using the **x** and **y** variable, and then update the position? Well, in an example this small, it really doesn't matter. In truth, it would have worked the other way as well. We'll see later, however, that depending on the animation method chosen, it pays to keep all the screen updating, both erasing and drawing, as close together as possible. If we had many sprites on the screen at once, it might take a while to update the positions of all of them. If this time was put between the screen updates, the animation quality could suffer. With only one sprite in this example, the time taken to update its position is negligible and wouldn't be noticed.

After the bitmap is erased at the old position, it is drawn at the new position. Again, **BltLinear** is used to draw the bitmap. After the drawing is done, **Erase** is set to **TRUE** to ensure that erasing takes place on the second and subsequent frames of the animation.

Finally, a short delay of 20 milliseconds is added using the **delay** library function. This ensures that the animation doesn't run too fast. Recompile the program with different values of delay to see what effect this has. With no delay, the animation runs at maximum speed and the ball is very, very fast!

A Problem with Flicker

When you run the ANIDEMO1 program, you'll see the green ball bounce around the screen. What you'll also notice is that the ball flickers every so often. The image isn't steady but sometimes seems to disappear for a second. It doesn't happen all the time, just every now and then. If you play around with the delay value at the end of the loop, you'll find that the ball flickers more the faster it moves. With a six or seven millisecond delay value, you can get the ball flickering pretty well. A value under five will have the ball flickering a lot but it'll move so fast that it's hard to see. With a delay value over 30 you'll see the flicker quite plainly.

What causes this flicker and what can we do about it? To understand the problem, we first have to understand how video displays work. Let's take a look.

UNDERSTANDING VIDEO DISPLAYS

A video display, also known as a video monitor or cathode ray tube, basically consists of an electron gun, some deflection plates, and a phosphor coated glass screen. Although from the outside it appears that the screen is just a glass plate, it's really the end of a pyramid-like glass tube. The phosphor coating is only on the screen end of the tube. The electron gun is located inside the tube, opposite from and pointing toward the screen. The deflection plates sit between the electron gun and the screen. Figure 7.1 shows the configuration.

The electron gun shoots a beam of electrons at the front of the tube. The beam of electrons strikes the phosphor coating the screen and causes it to

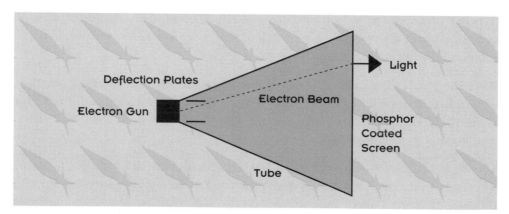

Figure 7.1 *An internal view of a video display.*

emit light, which exits through the front of the screen and is seen by the viewer. The phosphor emits light while the beam strikes it and for a fraction of a second following the removal of the beam.

The deflection plates are pieces of charged metal that serve to steer the electron beam within the tube. Using the deflection plates, it is possible to position the electron beam anywhere on the screen. By varying the intensity of the electron beam, it's possible to make the light emitted by the phosphor brighter or darker.

The previous description neglects the way in which color is created. In reality, there are three different types of phosphors coating the screen: one that emits red light, another that emits green light, and a third that emits blue light. The phosphors coat the screen in a repeating triangular pattern of dots, one for each phosphor color, as shown in Figure 7.2. Additionally, there are three electron guns. Each of the guns is used to shoot electrons at one of the phosphor dots in the triangular grouping. By varying the intensity of each of the electron beams relative to one another, different colors are created on the screen.

Now, to draw a representation of video memory onto the display, the VGA examines each pixel's color value stored in memory and sends three intensity values for the red, green, and blue components of the color to the monitor. This causes the monitor to draw the pixel on the display in the correct color. The VGA examines video memory starting at the top-left corner of the screen and moves toward the right. As it does this, the monitor causes the deflection plates to move the three electron beams to the right as well. As the beams move, the VGA card continues to output color values and a row of pixels is drawn, as shown in Figure 7.3.

Figure 7.2   *The triangle pattern of phosphor dots allows many different colors to be created on the screen.*

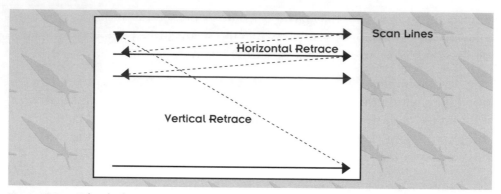

Figure 7.3 *Video display scan pattern.*

When the beam reaches the right side of the screen, it is momentarily turned off and swept back to the left side of the screen and down one row. This is called a *horizontal retrace*. The beam then traces out the next row of pixels. Turning off the beam ensures that no light is emitted while the beam sweeps back to the left side of the screen. This sequence of events, scan and horizontal retrace, occurs for each row on the screen until the last row is reached.

When the beam reaches the right side of the screen and there are no more rows of pixels to display, the monitor turns off the beam and moves it back to the top-left corner. A single video frame has been displayed or *refreshed*. The act of turning off the beam and moving it from the bottom-right corner back to the top-left corner is called a *vertical retrace*.

This process occurs 60 times per second in Mode X and 70 times per second in Mode 13h and Mode Y. Unlike TV, all the pixels are refreshed during each frame and the refresh rate is not fixed at 60 Hz.

The Cause of Flicker

The flicker we saw in the ANIDEMO1 program was caused by our updates of video memory not being synchronized with the operation of the video display. As the VGA scanned through video memory, sending color values to the display, it would sometimes catch our program in the midst of modifying video memory. For instance, perhaps the program had just finished erasing the bitmap from the previous frame but had not yet begun to draw the bitmap for the next frame when the VGA scanned through that particular region of memory. In that case, the VGA would see black pixels and would output them to the display. That display frame was effectively blank as far as our bitmap is concerned.

Sometimes the VGA will catch the program in the middle of drawing or erasing the bitmap. In either case, the VGA scans video memory and draws some pixels as being erased when they really should be drawn as containing part of our sprite bitmap. In a later frame the pixels are displayed correctly. It's this momentary display of the screen pixels in the incorrect state that causes the flicker. In effect, we are seeing not only the frames of our animation, but sometimes we also see the transitions between frames.

So, how do we eliminate the flicker?

The Key Is Vertical Retrace

Flicker occurs because the VGA finds our program in the middle of modifying video memory for the next frame. The solution to the problem is to ensure that the VGA never finds video memory in the "incorrect" state, that is, different from the way it should be at the end of drawing each of our animation frames.

Figure 7.4 shows a timeline of the sequence of events described in the previous section. In particular, notice the period labeled "vertical retrace" and remember that during both horizontal and vertical retrace periods the electron beam is off and the VGA temporarily stops scanning video memory while the beam moves back to the start of the next scanline. The period for vertical retrace is greater than the period for horizontal retrace, because the beam has to move a greater distance to get back to the top of the screen.

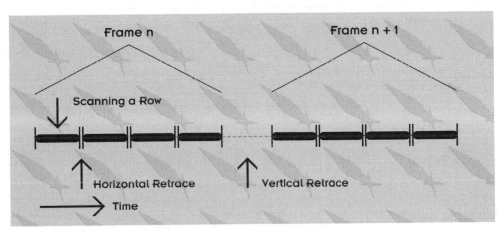

Figure 7.4 *Video display timeline.*

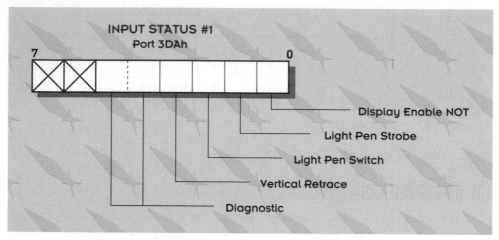

Figure 7.5 *Layout of the Input Status #1 register.*

To ensure that the VGA won't find memory in a partially modified state, we can do all our screen modifications while the display is in a retrace period. In particular, we could use *vertical* retrace since it gives us more time than horizontal retrace to make our changes. The question is, how can our program detect when vertical retrace is occurring so that we can synchronize our erasing and drawing?

Well, we can simply ask the VGA. The Input Status #1 register of the VGA, Port 3DAh, contains a bit that reflects the current state of vertical retrace. Figure 7.5 shows the bit layout of the Input Status #1 register. If the Vertical Retrace bit contains a 1, vertical retrace is occurring. If the bit contains a 0, either the VGA is scanning pixels or a horizontal retrace is occurring.

A horizontal retrace can be detected by using the Display Enable NOT bit in conjunction with the Vertical Retrace bit. The possible combinations are shown in Table 7.1.

Table 7.1 *Vertical Retrace and Display Enable NOT Bit Combinations*

Vertical Retrace	Display Enable NOT	VGA Operation
0	0	Scanning pixels
1	0	Not possible
0	1	Horizontal Retrace
1	1	Vertical Retrace

The Input Status #1 register is located at 3DAh. It is one of the few VGA registers that is *not* accessed through an index and data register pair.

A Vertical Retrace Demo

Now that we understand where our flicker is coming from, let's modify our program to do its screen modification while vertical retrace is going on. The program ANIDEMO2, shown in Listing 7.2, is a simple modification of the ANIDEMO1 program we looked at earlier.

Compiling and Linking:

You can compile the ANIDEMO2 program using the Borland C++ 3.1 IDE by typing "bc anidemo2.prj" and then selecting Compile | Make from the menus. If you would rather use the command line compiler, convert the ANIDEMO2.PRJ file to a makefile using the PRJ2MAK program supplied with Borland C++ 3.1. Type "prj2mak anidemo2.prj" to create the ANIDEMO2.MAK and ANIDEMO2.CFG files.

If you are using Borland C++ 4.0, choose Project | Open Project from the IDE menus. Open the ANIDEMO2.PRJ file. Borland C++ will convert the version 3.1 .PRJ file to a version 4.0 .IDE file. Compile and link the program by choosing Project | Make All from the IDE menus.

Listing 7.2   ANIDEMO2.C

```
/* File: ANIDEMO2.C
** Description:
**    Demonstrates animation while drawing and erasing sprites during
**    video retrace.
** Copyright:
**    Copyright 1994, David G. Roberts
*/

#include <assert.h>
#include <conio.h>
#include <dos.h>
#include <stdio.h>
#include "gamedefs.h"
#include "vga.h"
#include "bitblt.h"
#include "retrace.h"

UINT8 BallBitmap[] = {
    10, 0,          /* Width (little endian) */
```

```
    10, 0,          /* Height (little endian) */
    0, 0,           /* X and Y origin */
    0, 0,
    0, 0, 0, 2, 2, 2, 2, 0, 0, 0, /* color 2 = green w/ default palette */
    0, 2, 2, 2, 2, 2, 2, 2, 2, 0,
    0, 2, 2, 0, 0, 2, 2, 2, 2, 0,
    2, 2, 0, 0, 2, 2, 2, 2, 2, 2,
    2, 2, 0, 2, 2, 2, 2, 2, 2, 2,
    2, 2, 2, 2, 2, 2, 2, 2, 2, 2,
    2, 2, 2, 2, 2, 2, 2, 2, 2, 2,
    0, 2, 2, 2, 2, 2, 2, 2, 2, 0,
    0, 2, 2, 2, 2, 2, 2, 2, 2, 0,
    0, 0, 0, 2, 2, 2, 2, 0, 0, 0
};

UINT8 BallEraseBitmap[] = {
    10, 0,          /* Width (little endian) */
    10, 0,          /* Height (little endian) */
    0, 0,           /* X and Y origin */
    0, 0,
    16, 16, 16, 16, 16, 16, 16, 16, 16, 16, /* color 16 = black */
    16, 16, 16, 16, 16, 16, 16, 16, 16, 16, /* with default palette */
    16, 16, 16, 16, 16, 16, 16, 16, 16, 16,
    16, 16, 16, 16, 16, 16, 16, 16, 16, 16,
    16, 16, 16, 16, 16, 16, 16, 16, 16, 16,
    16, 16, 16, 16, 16, 16, 16, 16, 16, 16,
    16, 16, 16, 16, 16, 16, 16, 16, 16, 16,
    16, 16, 16, 16, 16, 16, 16, 16, 16, 16,
    16, 16, 16, 16, 16, 16, 16, 16, 16, 16,
    16, 16, 16, 16, 16, 16, 16, 16, 16, 16
};

/* note: make these track width and height of bitmap, above */
#define BITMAP_HEIGHT   (10)
#define BITMAP_WIDTH    (10)

int main()
{
    int x, y;
    int OldX, OldY;
    int vx, vy;
    BOOL Erase;

    /* detect VGA */
    if (!DetectVGA()) {
        printf("You must have a VGA to run this program.\n");
        return 1;
    }

    SetMode13h();

    x = 0;
    y = 0;
```

```
        vx = 2;
        vy = 1;

        Erase = FALSE;

        while (!kbhit()) {
            if (Erase) {
                /* update new position */
                OldX = x;
                OldY = y;
                x += vx;
                y += vy;
                if ((x < 0) || ((x + BITMAP_WIDTH) >= MODE13H_WIDTH)) {
                    vx = -vx;
                    x += 2 * vx;
                }
                if ((y < 0) || ((y + BITMAP_HEIGHT) >= MODE13H_HEIGHT)) {
                    vy = -vy;
                    y += 2 * vy;
                }

                /* wait for vertical retrace before we erase and draw */
                WaitVerticalRetraceStart();

                /* erase */
                BltLinear((LINEAR_BITMAP far *) BallEraseBitmap, OldX, OldY,
                    MK_FP(VIDEO_MEM_SEGMENT, 0x0000));
            }

            /* draw */
            BltLinear((LINEAR_BITMAP far *) BallBitmap, x, y,
                MK_FP(VIDEO_MEM_SEGMENT, 0x0000));
            Erase = TRUE;
        }

        getch();

        SetVGAMode(0x3);

        return 0;
    }
```

The only difference between ANIDEMO1 and ANIDEMO2 is that ANIDEMO2 includes a call to **WaitVerticalRetraceStart** right before the previous frame's bitmap is erased and removes the call to **delay**.

As you might guess, **WaitVerticalRetraceStart** is used to stall the program until the VGA begins a vertical retrace period. **WaitVerticalRetraceStart** is located in the RETRACE.C module, shown in Listing 7.13. RETRACE.C contains other routines related to vertical retrace that we'll use during the rest of this chapter and in following chapters.

```
#define VR_BIT  (0x08)

/*
    Function: WaitVerticalRetraceStart
    Description:
        Waits for the VGA to begin vertical retrace.  Note that if the
        VGA is already in vertical retrace, the routine will wait all
        during the next display frame until vertical retrace begins
        again.
*/
void WaitVerticalRetraceStart(void)
{
    UINT8 InputStatus1;

    /* make sure we aren't in retrace already */
    do {
        InputStatus1 = inportb(INPUT_STAT_1_REG);
    } while (InputStatus1 & VR_BIT);

    /* wait for retrace to start */
    do {
        InputStatus1 = inportb(INPUT_STAT_1_REG);
    } while (!(InputStatus1 & VR_BIT));
}
```

WaitVerticalRetraceStart begins by checking that the VGA isn't in a vertical retrace period already. If it is, the routine waits until the next vertical retrace period begins. We need this functionality because we want to ensure that our program has the maximum possible time to perform the screen manipulations. If the routine simply returned when vertical retrace was active while it was in the middle of a retrace period, the routine would return immediately. Our drawing functions would then have only a fraction of a retrace period to do their work. There is no way to determine what that fraction would be, however. We might call the routine right before the VGA started scanning the next video frame, and our drawing routines would then get caught modifying memory again.

Now, the last question is, why did ANIDEMO2 remove the call to **delay**? The answer is that synchronizing our program with the vertical retrace slows it down to an acceptable speed. With the call to **WaitVerticalRetraceStart** in there, the **while** loop in ANIDEMO2 can only execute once per video frame. With a video refresh rate of 70 Hz in Mode 13h, this provides a natural delay of 14.2 milliseconds between frames (1/70 Hz = 14.2 milliseconds). This is close enough to the 20 milliseconds we had before the ball bounces around the screen at roughly the same speed.

When you run ANIDEMO2, you'll find that the flicker that was present in ANIDEMO1 is no longer there. The ball in ANIDEMO2 is a nice steady image. The animation is smooth and really high quality. We did it! Or did we?

Although ANIDEMO2 produces high-quality animation without the flicker we had with ANIDEMO1, it's still vulnerable to a few problems. The technique we used, erasing and drawing all our sprite bitmap images during vertical retrace works well when the program can complete all its erasing and drawing during a single vertical retrace period.

With the single ball bitmap of ANIDEMO2, we have plenty of time to spare. But what happens when you have 10 or 20 sprites on the screen at once and the erasing and drawing period takes more time than vertical retrace?

PROJECT

We Still Have a Flicker Problem

Take a look at the ANIDEMO3 program, shown in Listing 7.3. This program functions exactly like ANIDEMO2 but draws 50 sprites on the screen instead of one.

Compiling and Linking:

You can compile the ANIDEMO3 program using the Borland C++ 3.1 IDE by typing "bc anidemo3.prj" and then selecting Compile | Make from the menus. If you would rather use the command line compiler, convert the ANIDEMO3.PRJ file to a makefile using the PRJ2MAK program supplied with Borland C++ 3.1. Type "prj2mak anidemo3.prj" to create the ANIDEMO3.MAK and ANIDEMO3.CFG files.

If you are using Borland C++ 4.0, choose Project | Open Project from the IDE menus. Open the ANIDEMO3.PRJ file. Borland C++ will convert the version 3.1 .PRJ file to a version 4.0 .IDE file. Compile and link the program by choosing Project | Make All from the IDE menus.

Listing 7.3   ANIDEMO3.C

```
/* File: ANIDEMO3.C
** Description:
**   Demonstrates problems when you try to draw a lot of sprites during
**   vertical retrace.
** Copyright:
**   Copyright 1994, David G. Roberts
*/
```

```
#include <assert.h>
#include <conio.h>
#include <dos.h>
#include <stdio.h>
#include <stdlib.h>
#include "gamedefs.h"
#include "vga.h"
#include "bitblt.h"
#include "retrace.h"

UINT8 BallBitmap[] = {
    10, 0,              /* Width (little endian) */
    10, 0,              /* Height (little endian) */
    0, 0,               /* X and Y origin */
    0, 0,
    0, 0, 0, 2, 2, 2, 2, 0, 0, 0, /* color 2 = green w/ default palette */
    0, 2, 2, 2, 2, 2, 2, 2, 2, 0,
    0, 2, 2, 0, 0, 2, 2, 2, 2, 0,
    2, 2, 0, 0, 2, 2, 2, 2, 2, 2,
    2, 2, 0, 2, 2, 2, 2, 2, 2, 2,
    2, 2, 2, 2, 2, 2, 2, 2, 2, 2,
    2, 2, 2, 2, 2, 2, 2, 2, 2, 2,
    0, 2, 2, 2, 2, 2, 2, 2, 2, 0,
    0, 2, 2, 2, 2, 2, 2, 2, 2, 0,
    0, 0, 0, 2, 2, 2, 2, 0, 0, 0
};

UINT8 BallEraseBitmap[] = {
    10,  0,             /* Width (little endian) */
    10,  0,             /* Height (little endian) */
    0, 0,               /* X and Y origin */
    0, 0,
    16, 16, 16, 16, 16, 16, 16, 16, 16, 16, /* color 16 = black */
    16, 16, 16, 16, 16, 16, 16, 16, 16, 16, /* with default palette */
    16, 16, 16, 16, 16, 16, 16, 16, 16, 16,
    16, 16, 16, 16, 16, 16, 16, 16, 16, 16,
    16, 16, 16, 16, 16, 16, 16, 16, 16, 16,
    16, 16, 16, 16, 16, 16, 16, 16, 16, 16,
    16, 16, 16, 16, 16, 16, 16, 16, 16, 16,
    16, 16, 16, 16, 16, 16, 16, 16, 16, 16,
    16, 16, 16, 16, 16, 16, 16, 16, 16, 16,
    16, 16, 16, 16, 16, 16, 16, 16, 16, 16
};

/* note: make these track width and height of bitmap, above */
#define BITMAP_HEIGHT   (10)
#define BITMAP_WIDTH    (10)

#define NUM_BALLS       (50)

int main()
{
    int x[NUM_BALLS], y[NUM_BALLS];
    int OldX[NUM_BALLS], OldY[NUM_BALLS];
```

```c
int vx[NUM_BALLS], vy[NUM_BALLS];
BOOL Erase[NUM_BALLS];
int i;

/* detect VGA */
if (!DetectVGA()) {
    printf("You must have a VGA to run this program.\n");
    return 1;
}

SetMode13h();

for (i = 0; i < NUM_BALLS; i++) {
    x[i] = random(MODE13H_WIDTH - BITMAP_WIDTH);
    y[i] = random(MODE13H_HEIGHT - BITMAP_HEIGHT);
    vx[i] = random(2) + 1;
    vy[i] = random(2) + 1;
    Erase[i] = FALSE;
}

while (!kbhit()) {
    for (i = 0; i < NUM_BALLS; i++) {
        if (Erase[i]) {
            /* update new position */
            OldX[i] = x[i];
            OldY[i] = y[i];
            x[i] += vx[i];
            y[i] += vy[i];
            if ((x[i] < 0) || ((x[i] + BITMAP_WIDTH) >= MODE13H_WIDTH)) {
                vx[i] = -vx[i];
                x[i] += 2 * vx[i];
            }
            if ((y[i] < 0) || ((y[i] + BITMAP_HEIGHT) >= MODE13H_HEIGHT)) {
                vy[i] = -vy[i];
                y[i] += 2 * vy[i];
            }
        }
    }

    /* wait for vertical retrace before we erase and draw */
    WaitVerticalRetraceStart();

    /* erase */
    for (i = 0; i < NUM_BALLS; i++) {
        if (Erase[i]) {
            BltLinear((LINEAR_BITMAP far *) BallEraseBitmap,
                OldX[i], OldY[i], MK_FP(VIDEO_MEM_SEGMENT, 0x0000));
        }
    }

    /* draw */
    for (i = 0; i < NUM_BALLS; i++) {
        BltLinear((LINEAR_BITMAP far *) BallBitmap, x[i], y[i],
            MK_FP(VIDEO_MEM_SEGMENT, 0x0000));
```

```
        Erase[i] = TRUE;
    }
}

getch();

SetVGAMode(0x3);

return 0;
}
```

What do we get when we run it? Flicker. The VGA is ending retrace and starting to scan pixels again when it catches some bitmaps still in the process of being erased and redrawn. Figure 7.6 shows the timeline for this case. Try changing the **NUM_BALLS** constant to see what effect it has on the flicker. At some number less than 50 the flicker should clear up. The exact number will depend on the speed of your system's CPU and VGA. With a 386DX-40 and an ISA VGA, I can only get five balls going before the flicker starts. If you're using a 486DX/2-66 system with a local bus VGA, you should do much better.

Is there a solution to this flicker problem that will handle lots of sprites? Of course.

PAGE-FLIPPING

The ANIDEMO1, ANIDEMO2, and ANIDEMO3 programs all used VGA Mode 13h. In this section, we'll learn about *page-flipping*, an animation technique using Mode X or Mode Y that cures the flicker problem when you have large numbers of sprites on the screen.

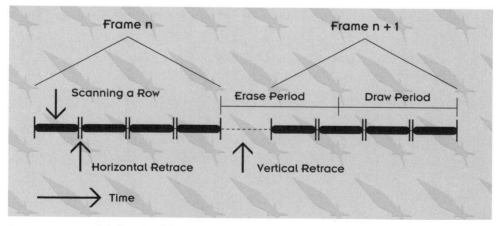

Figure 7.6 *Timeline for case of drawing 50 sprites.*

First, remember that Mode X and Mode Y have more than one display page. Mode Y supports exactly four display pages worth of memory and Mode X supports a little less than four. Of the multiple pages, one page is the *current page* and is being displayed by the VGA. The other pages are hidden offscreen. Drawing to an offscreen page has no effect on the page that is being displayed by the VGA. Because the VGA won't try to access the memory in the offscreen pages, it won't catch us if we manipulate memory in the offscreen pages.

In a nutshell, page-flipping works like this: We use two pages, named Page 0 and Page 1. Assume that Page 0 starts as the active or current page and Page 1 is the offscreen, hidden page. We compose the next frame of animation on Page 1. When we're done, we tell the VGA to make Page 1 the active page. After the next vertical retrace period, the VGA will start scanning Page 1 rather than Page 0. Page 0 will then be hidden. In essence, we're "flipping pages." We now compose the next frame of animation on Page 0, since it is offscreen. When we're done again, we tell the VGA to flip pages and make Page 0 active again. We continue this process throughout the game.

Sounds pretty easy, right? Well, most of the time it is. There is one thing to keep in mind, however. If you re-read the sequence of events carefully, you'll notice that erasing previously drawn sprites can be a problem. If we're composing our next frame on Page 1, we don't erase the sprites where they were located on the previous frame of animation. That frame of animation was drawn on Page 0. We actually have to erase the sprites from where they were located two frames previous, when we were drawing on Page 1 before. Given that you can keep all that straight in your head, and more importantly, in your programs, it's fairly straightforward.

Now that we understand the page-flipping theory, just how do we go about flipping a page? The **PageFlip** function, shown in Listing 7.4, shows how this is done.

Listing 7.4   The PageFlip Function

```
/*
    Function: PageFlip
    Description:
        Sets the VGA screen start address to the offset specified.
        The routine sets the new address while the VGA is in display
        mode and waits for retrace to become active before returning.
        This ensures that the address is set correctly (e.g., the
        VGA doesn't reload when only half of the address has been
        set) and that the old page is really invisible before we
        start manipulating things on it.
*/
```

```
void PageFlip(UINT16 Offset)
{
    WaitDisplayMode();
    SetScreenStart(Offset);
    WaitRetraceMode();
}
```

The **PageFlip** function simply makes sure that the VGA isn't in vertical retrace mode already, flips the page, and then waits for vertical retrace to start. **PageFlip** is located in the ANIMATE.C module, shown in Listing 7.11.

The **WaitDisplayMode** function returns immediately if the VGA is displaying pixels. If the VGA is in the middle of a retrace period, **WaitDisplayMode** delays returning until the VGA begins to scan pixels again. **SetScreenStart** takes the **Offset** parameter passed to **PageFlip** as its parameter. This is the actual routine that causes the VGA to flip pages. We'll see it in a moment. Before returning, the routine calls **WaitRetraceMode**, which is analogous to **WaitDisplayMode**. **WaitRetraceMode** returns if the VGA is currently vertically retracing, or it waits until retrace starts.

WaitDisplayMode and **WaitRetraceMode** are slightly different from the **WaitVerticalRetraceStart** function described earlier. **WaitVerticalRetraceStart** delays until it finds the transition from display mode to retrace mode. This means that if the VGA is currently in a vertical retrace period, **WaitVerticalRetraceStart** will delay until the start of the next retrace period. **WaitDisplayMode** and **WaitRetraceMode** return immediately if the VGA display mode they are looking for is already active. **WaitDisplayMode** and **WaitRetraceMode** are located in the RETRACE.C module, shown in Listing 7.13.

Now, why do we have to do all these waits for various VGA display modes? Why not just flip the page and be done with it?

Well, it turns out that the VGA doesn't recognize a page flip immediately. It only recognizes a page flip at the beginning or end, depending on the brand of VGA card, of the vertical retrace period. The waits are there to make sure that each page flip "takes hold," and that the VGA really displays each page we create for it. We could experience problems if we didn't wait.

For example, consider what would happen if the VGA was scanning near the top of Page 0, when we had already created our next display page on Page 1 called **PageFlip**. If **PageFlip** returned immediately, we would think that Page 1 was being displayed and that Page 0 was safe to draw on. In reality, the page flip hasn't taken hold, because the VGA hasn't done a vertical retrace yet. If we start to draw on Page 0, the VGA might catch us in the middle of our screen manipulations and display flicker. The wait calls make sure that the page flip catches.

Now, how do we actually flip pages?

The **SetScreenStart** function, shown in Listing 7.5, takes care of this.

Listing 7.5   The SetScreenStart Function

```
/*
    Function: SetScreenStart
    Description:
        Sets the VGA screen start address to the offset specified.
        This has the effect of flipping display pages or of scrolling
        the screen a few lines (a flip is really just a massive,
        page-long scroll, right?).
*/
void SetScreenStart(UINT16 Offset)
{
    UINT8 OffsetLow;
    UINT8 OffsetHigh;

    OffsetLow = LOWBYTE(Offset);
    OffsetHigh = HIGHBYTE(Offset);

    /* disable interrupts to ensure this is virtually atomic */
    asm cli;

    outportb(CRTC_INDEX_REG, START_ADDRESS_HIGH_INDEX);
    outportb(CRTC_DATA_REG, OffsetHigh);

    outportb(CRTC_INDEX_REG, START_ADDRESS_LOW_INDEX);
    outportb(CRTC_DATA_REG, OffsetLow);

    asm sti;

}
```

SetScreenStart is located in the ANIMATE.C module, along with **PageFlip**.

To actually flip pages, the **SetScreenStart** routine manipulates the Start Address High and Start Address Low registers of the VGA. These registers are located in the CRT Controller group and control what memory address the VGA starts scanning pixels from, following a vertical retrace period. The VGA has a working register that keeps track of the current scanning position. Following a retrace, this working register is reloaded from the contents of the Start Address registers. This reload is when the page flip actually "takes hold," as described previously.

There are two Start Address registers, each eight bits wide, that store the 16-bit offset value. Because of the indexing scheme used to manipulate the CRTC register bank, we must program them separately. Bad things could happen if the VGA were to start scanning after we wrote one, but not both, of these registers, however. In order to avoid taking a lengthy detour between programming the first and the second registers, interrupts are disabled while we perform the writes.

With that, we now have the knowledge and helper routines necessary to write a page-flipping demo program. Let's see what we've got.

Page-Flipping Demo

The FLIPDEMO program, shown in Listing 7.5, demonstrates how page-flipping works. The program is similar to ANIDEMO3 in that it bounces 50 balls around the screen. The difference, however, is that FLIPDEMO uses Mode X and the page-flipping technique to ensure that the balls don't flicker.

Compiling and Linking:

You can compile the FLIPDEMO program using the Borland C++ 3.1 IDE by typing "bc flipdemo.prj" and then selecting Compile | Make from the menus. If you would rather use the command line compiler, convert the FLIPDEMO.PRJ file to a makefile using the PRJ2MAK program supplied with Borland C++ 3.1. Type "prj2mak flipdemo.prj" to create the FLIPDEMO.MAK and FLIPDEMO.CFG files.

If you are using Borland C++ 4.0, choose Project | Open Project from the IDE menus. Open the FLIPDEMO.PRJ file. Borland C++ will convert the version 3.1 .PRJ file to a version 4.0 .IDE file. Compile and link the program by choosing Project | Make All from the IDE menus.

Listing 7.5   FLIPDEMO.C

```
/* File: FLIPDEMO.C
** Description:
**   Demonstrates page-flipping.
** Copyright:
**   Copyright 1994, David G. Roberts
*/

#include <alloc.h>
#include <assert.h>
#include <conio.h>
#include <stdio.h>
```

```c
#include <stdlib.h>
#include "gamedefs.h"
#include "vga.h"
#include "bitblt.h"
#include "retrace.h"
#include "setmodex.h"
#include "animate.h"

UINT8 BallBitmap[] = {
    10, 0,          /* Width (little endian) */
    10, 0,          /* Height (little endian) */
    0, 0,           /* X and Y origin */
    0, 0,
    0, 0, 0, 2, 2, 2, 2, 0, 0, 0, /* color 2 = green w/ default palette */
    0, 2, 2, 2, 2, 2, 2, 2, 2, 0,
    0, 2, 2, 0, 0, 2, 2, 2, 2, 0,
    2, 2, 0, 0, 2, 2, 2, 2, 2, 2,
    2, 2, 0, 2, 2, 2, 2, 2, 2, 2,
    2, 2, 2, 2, 2, 2, 2, 2, 2, 2,
    2, 2, 2, 2, 2, 2, 2, 2, 2, 2,
    0, 2, 2, 2, 2, 2, 2, 2, 2, 0,
    0, 2, 2, 2, 2, 2, 2, 2, 2, 0,
    0, 0, 0, 2, 2, 2, 2, 0, 0, 0
};

UINT8 BallEraseBitmap[] = {
    10, 0,          /* Width (little endian) */
    10, 0,          /* Height (little endian) */
    0, 0,           /* X and Y origin */
    0, 0,
    16, 16, 16, 16, 16, 16, 16, 16, 16, 16, /* color 16 = black */
    16, 16, 16, 16, 16, 16, 16, 16, 16, 16, /* with default palette */
    16, 16, 16, 16, 16, 16, 16, 16, 16, 16,
    16, 16, 16, 16, 16, 16, 16, 16, 16, 16,
    16, 16, 16, 16, 16, 16, 16, 16, 16, 16,
    16, 16, 16, 16, 16, 16, 16, 16, 16, 16,
    16, 16, 16, 16, 16, 16, 16, 16, 16, 16,
    16, 16, 16, 16, 16, 16, 16, 16, 16, 16,
    16, 16, 16, 16, 16, 16, 16, 16, 16, 16,
    16, 16, 16, 16, 16, 16, 16, 16, 16, 16
};

/* note: make these track width and height of bitmap, above */
#define BITMAP_HEIGHT   (10)
#define BITMAP_WIDTH    (10)

#define PAGE0_OFFSET    (0)
#define PAGE1_OFFSET    (0x4B00)

#define NUM_BALLS       (50)

int main()
{
```

```
int x[NUM_BALLS], y[NUM_BALLS];
int OldX[NUM_BALLS][2], OldY[NUM_BALLS][2];
int vx[NUM_BALLS], vy[NUM_BALLS];
int HiddenPage;
UINT16 Offset[2];
PLANAR_BITMAP far * PlanarBallBitmap;
PLANAR_BITMAP far * PlanarBallEraseBitmap;
BOOL Erase[NUM_BALLS][2];
int i;

/* detect VGA */
if (!DetectVGA()) {
    printf("You must have a VGA to run this program.\n");
    return 1;
}

Offset[0] = PAGE0_OFFSET;
Offset[1] = PAGE1_OFFSET;

PlanarBallBitmap = LinearToPlanar((LINEAR_BITMAP far *) BallBitmap);
PlanarBallEraseBitmap =
    LinearToPlanar((LINEAR_BITMAP far *) BallEraseBitmap);

/* set Mode X and display page 0 */
SetModeX();

for (i = 0; i < NUM_BALLS; i++) {
    x[i] = random(MODEX_WIDTH - BITMAP_WIDTH);
    y[i] = random(MODEX_HEIGHT - BITMAP_HEIGHT);
    vx[i] = random(2) + 1;
    vy[i] = random(2) + 1;
    Erase[i][0] = Erase[i][1] = FALSE;
}

HiddenPage = 1;

while (!kbhit()) {
    /* update new position */
    for (i = 0; i < NUM_BALLS; i++) {
        if (Erase[i][HiddenPage]) {
            x[i] += vx[i];
            y[i] += vy[i];
            if ((x[i] < 0) || ((x[i] + BITMAP_WIDTH) >= MODEX_WIDTH)) {
                vx[i] = -vx[i];
                x[i] += 2 * vx[i];
            }
            if ((y[i] < 0) || ((y[i] + BITMAP_HEIGHT) >= MODEX_HEIGHT)) {
                vy[i] = -vy[i];
                y[i] += 2 * vy[i];
            }
        }
    }
```

```
    /* erase */
    for (i = 0; i < NUM_BALLS; i++) {
        if (Erase[i][HiddenPage]) {
            BltPlanar(PlanarBallEraseBitmap,
                OldX[i][HiddenPage], OldY[i][HiddenPage],
                Offset[HiddenPage]);
        }
    }

    /* draw */
    for (i = 0; i < NUM_BALLS; i++) {
        BltPlanar(PlanarBallBitmap, x[i], y[i], Offset[HiddenPage]);
        OldX[i][HiddenPage] = x[i];
        OldY[i][HiddenPage] = y[i];
        Erase[i][HiddenPage] = TRUE;
    }

    /* flip page */
    PageFlip(Offset[HiddenPage]);
    HiddenPage ^= 1; /* flip HiddenPage to other state */
}

getch();

farfree(PlanarBallBitmap);
farfree(PlanarBallEraseBitmap);

SetVGAMode(0x3);

return 0;
}
```

The program is fairly similar to the ANIDEMO3 program. The notable changes
are the addition of two new variables: **HiddenPage** and **Offset**. Further, the
OldX, **OldY**, and **Erase** arrays are made two-dimensional, the second dimension being used to store information on a per-page basis.

HiddenPage is used to keep track of which page is currently hidden and
which is active. The **Offset** array holds the beginning offsets into the video
memory segment (A000h) of the two video pages. The member of the **Offset**
array associated with the hidden page is passed to the bitblt functions to erase
and draw the sprite and, finally, to flip the page. Now you know why **BltPlanar**
has its **PageOffset** variable—to be able to draw on the hidden page.

The **OldX** and **OldY** variables now keep track of the last position of the sprite
on both of the display pages. This keeps us from making the mistake of
erasing the sprite from the position it was at on that last frame, rather than the
last frame on the currently hidden page.

The **Erase** variable keeps track of per-page information, because the sprite doesn't need to be erased for the first two times it is drawn, once on each page.

Instead of waiting for vertical retrace to begin drawing, the main loop starts drawing immediately and then calls **PageFlip** when it is done. (**PageFlip** takes the offset of the page to make visible as its only argument.) Similar to the way the ANIDEMO2 and ANIDEMO3 programs use **WaitVerticalRetraceStart** to control the speed of their animation loops, FLIPDEMO uses **PageFlip** to control the speed of its animation loop. **PageFlip** ensures that each animation frame is displayed for at least one VGA display frame (that is, 1/60th of a second in Mode X).

As you can see when you run FLIPDEMO, the bitmaps don't flicker when they are drawn. The page-flipping is working! You may notice that the display is not as perfect as we might want it to be. It still has some problems and we'll discuss them in a later section in this chapter.

VIRTUAL SCREEN BUFFERS

Well, page-flipping is fine—if you're going to use Mode X. But what if you want to use Mode 13h instead? There are a variety of reasons to use Mode 13h rather than Mode X: speed, simplicity, and unquestionable compatibility. In short, unless you are writing a game that involves a scrolling background (as we'll learn about in a later chapter), or you need to use offscreen video memory bitmaps, or you want to do fast color fills using Mode X's four-pixel-per-write trick, Mode 13h is probably a better choice. As we've seen previously, however, it's hard to get all your erasing and drawing done during the vertical retrace period to avoid creating flicker. Can anything be done about it, or is Mode 13h destined to have flicker whenever there are a lot of sprites on screen?

Of course, the answer is yes, something can be done about the flicker of Mode 13h.

Remember that flicker was caused when the VGA caught some of the pixels that should contain our sprite in the erased state and momentarily displayed them that way. By using page-flipping, we were able to erase and draw our sprites at our leisure and then flip pages when we were ready. The secret to eliminating flicker in Mode 13h is to use a technique similar to page-flipping.

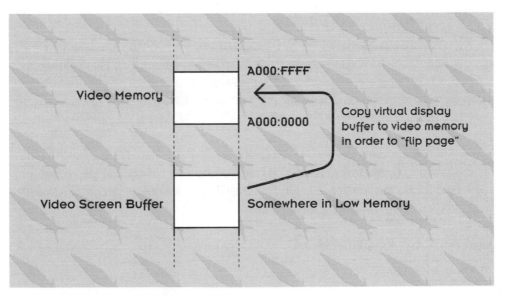

Figure 7.7 *The virtual screen animation technique.*

The Poor Man's Page Flip

To solve the flicker problem in Mode 13h, we'll actually create a "virtual screen" in system memory. This system memory display buffer will be used to create each animation frame that we wish to display. It'll be an exact replica of what the final frame will look like. All erasing and drawing will be done to the virtual screen rather than the actual screen. Once we've created each page of animation on the virtual screen, we'll simply copy it to the actual screen. Figure 7.7 shows how this is done. Because we do all of our drawing to the virtual screen, we can take as long as we want and the VGA will never find video memory in an incorrect state.

In effect, we've just created a "poor man's" page-flipping scheme. You can think of copying the virtual screen to the video memory as equivalent to flipping the page.

Let's take a look at some sample code.

A Virtual Screen Buffer Demo

The program VSCNDEMO, shown in Listing 7.6, shows the virtual screen buffer technique in action. Again, this program simply bounces 50 balls around the screen.

Compiling and Linking:

You can compile the VSCNDEMO program using the Borland C++ 3.1 IDE by typing "bc vscndemo.prj" and then selecting Compile | Make from the menus. If you would rather use the command line compiler, convert the VSCNDEMO.PRJ file to a makefile using the PRJ2MAK program supplied with Borland C++ 3.1. Type "prj2mak vscndemo.prj" to create the VSCNDEMO.MAK and VSCNDEMO.CFG files.

If you are using Borland C++ 4.0, choose Project | Open Project from the IDE menus. Open the VSCNDEMO.PRJ file. Borland C++ will convert the version 3.1 .PRJ file to a version 4.0 .IDE file. Compile and link the program by choosing Project | Make All from the IDE menus.

Listing 7.6 VSCNDEMO.C

```
/* File: VSCNDEMO.C
** Description:
**    Demonstrates the virtual screen buffer animation technique.
** Copyright:
**    Copyright 1994, David G. Roberts
*/

#include <alloc.h>
#include <assert.h>
#include <conio.h>
#include <dos.h>
#include <mem.h>
#include <stdio.h>
#include <stdlib.h>
#include "gamedefs.h"
#include "vga.h"
#include "bitblt.h"
#include "retrace.h"
#include "animate.h"

UINT8 BallBitmap[] = {
    10, 0,          /* Width (little endian) */
    10, 0,          /* Height (little endian) */
    0, 0,           /* X and Y origin */
    0, 0,
    0, 0, 0, 2, 2, 2, 2, 0, 0, 0, /* color 2 = green w/ default palette */
    0, 2, 2, 2, 2, 2, 2, 2, 2, 0,
    0, 2, 2, 0, 0, 2, 2, 2, 2, 0,
    2, 2, 0, 0, 2, 2, 2, 2, 2, 2,
    2, 2, 0, 2, 2, 2, 2, 2, 2, 2,
    2, 2, 2, 2, 2, 2, 2, 2, 2, 2,
    2, 2, 2, 2, 2, 2, 2, 2, 2, 2,
    0, 2, 2, 2, 2, 2, 2, 2, 2, 0,
    0, 2, 2, 2, 2, 2, 2, 2, 2, 0,
```

```
    0, 0, 0, 2, 2, 2, 2, 0, 0, 0
};

UINT8 BallEraseBitmap[] = {
    10,  0,           /* Width (little endian) */
    10,  0,           /* Height (little endian) */
    0, 0,             /* X and Y origin */
    0, 0,
    16, 16, 16, 16, 16, 16, 16, 16, 16, 16, /* color 16 = black */
    16, 16, 16, 16, 16, 16, 16, 16, 16, 16, /* with default palette */
    16, 16, 16, 16, 16, 16, 16, 16, 16, 16,
    16, 16, 16, 16, 16, 16, 16, 16, 16, 16,
    16, 16, 16, 16, 16, 16, 16, 16, 16, 16,
    16, 16, 16, 16, 16, 16, 16, 16, 16, 16,
    16, 16, 16, 16, 16, 16, 16, 16, 16, 16,
    16, 16, 16, 16, 16, 16, 16, 16, 16, 16,
    16, 16, 16, 16, 16, 16, 16, 16, 16, 16,
    16, 16, 16, 16, 16, 16, 16, 16, 16, 16
};

/* note: make these track width and height of bitmap, above */
#define BITMAP_HEIGHT   (10)
#define BITMAP_WIDTH    (10)

#define NUM_BALLS       (50)

#define BUFFER_SIZE     (64000)

int main()
{
    int x[NUM_BALLS], y[NUM_BALLS];
    int OldX[NUM_BALLS], OldY[NUM_BALLS];
    int vx[NUM_BALLS], vy[NUM_BALLS];
    BOOL Erase[NUM_BALLS];
    int i;
    UINT8 far * VirtualScreenBuffer;

    /* detect VGA */
    if (!DetectVGA()) {
        printf("You must have a VGA to run this program.\n");
        return 1;
    }

    for (i = 0; i < NUM_BALLS; i++) {
        x[i] = random(MODE13H_WIDTH - BITMAP_WIDTH);
        y[i] = random(MODE13H_HEIGHT - BITMAP_HEIGHT);
        vx[i] = random(2) + 1;
        vy[i] = random(2) + 1;
        Erase[i] = FALSE;
    }

    /* allocate virtual screen buffer */
    VirtualScreenBuffer = (UINT8 far *) farmalloc(BUFFER_SIZE);
```

```
    if (VirtualScreenBuffer == NULL) {
        fprintf(stderr, "Couldn't allocate memory buffer\n");
        exit(1);
    }
    /* clear buffer to 0 to match state of Mode 13h screen */
    _fmemset(VirtualScreenBuffer, 0, BUFFER_SIZE);

    SetMode13h();

    while (!kbhit()) {
        for (i = 0; i < NUM_BALLS; i++) {
            if (Erase[i]) {
                /* update new position */
                OldX[i] = x[i];
                OldY[i] = y[i];
                x[i] += vx[i];
                y[i] += vy[i];
                if ((x[i] < 0) || ((x[i] + BITMAP_WIDTH) >= MODE13H_WIDTH)) {
                    vx[i] = -vx[i];
                    x[i] += 2 * vx[i];
                }
                if ((y[i] < 0) || ((y[i] + BITMAP_HEIGHT) >= MODE13H_HEIGHT)) {
                    vy[i] = -vy[i];
                    y[i] += 2 * vy[i];
                }
            }
        }

        /* erase */
        for (i = 0; i < NUM_BALLS; i++) {
            if (Erase[i]) {
                BltLinear((LINEAR_BITMAP far *) BallEraseBitmap,
                    OldX[i], OldY[i], VirtualScreenBuffer);
            }
        }

        /* draw */
        for (i = 0; i < NUM_BALLS; i++) {
            BltLinear((LINEAR_BITMAP far *) BallBitmap, x[i], y[i],
                VirtualScreenBuffer);
            Erase[i] = TRUE;
        }

        _fmemcpy(MK_FP(VIDEO_MEM_SEGMENT,0), VirtualScreenBuffer,
            BUFFER_SIZE);
    }

    getch();

    SetVGAMode(0x3);

    return 0;
}
```

As you can see, the changes are very small. Most of the code works identically to ANIDEMO3. The only changes are that we allocate a virtual screen buffer from the far heap, we erase and draw to the virtual screen rather than the actual screen, and we copy the virtual screen to the actual screen at the end of each frame instead of waiting for vertical retrace.

When we allocate the virtual screen buffer, we call **_fmemset** to zero the virtual buffer. **_fmemset** is a library routine that sets a far memory buffer to a single value.

We erase and draw to the virtual screen by setting the last parameter in the **BltLinear** call to **VirtualScreenBuffer**. Now you know why we included **ScreenBase** as **BltLinear's** final parameter rather than simply hard-coding the routine to draw to video memory.

Finally, the routine waits for vertical retrace and copies the virtual screen buffer to VGA memory using **_fmemcpy**. In fact, we don't need to wait for vertical retrace, but it helps to slow the animation down to a reasonable speed on fast machines with fast video cards.

So, have we done it? Have we created perfect animation for Mode 13h? Well, not quite, but once again we're getting closer.

Shearing

Although it takes a steady eye to spot it, there is still a problem with our animation. If you look very carefully, every so often you'll see a slight *shear* in the middle of several of the balls on screen. The shear will appear on all the balls that intersect around a given screen line.

If you can't see shearing, it's probably because you are running with a very fast processor and a local-bus video card. If this is the case, try turning off the turbo switch on your machine and see if you can spot it. If you have a 386 machine or an ISA-bus VGA card, you should have no trouble seeing it.

The shearing, also known as *tearing*, is caused by the VGA catching up to us while we are in the middle of copying the virtual screen buffer to video memory. Remember that whenever we modify displayed video memory, we still run the risk of the VGA catching us. In this case, the effect is more subtle than the flicker we saw before. Flicker was caused by the VGA scanning some pixels in the erased state, before they were redrawn with the new sprite bitmap. We don't have flicker with the virtual screen buffer technique, because the VGA can never catch pixels in the erased state.

Shearing is caused by the VGA scanning a portion of the sprite at the new bitmap position and a portion at the old bitmap position. Figure 7.8 shows this effect.

In Figure 7.8, we're moving the ball bitmap two pixels up and two pixels to the right. As we're copying the virtual screen buffer to video memory, the VGA catches us just when we're at the square with the X in it. What actually gets displayed on the screen is a composite of the previous and current animation frames. The upper part

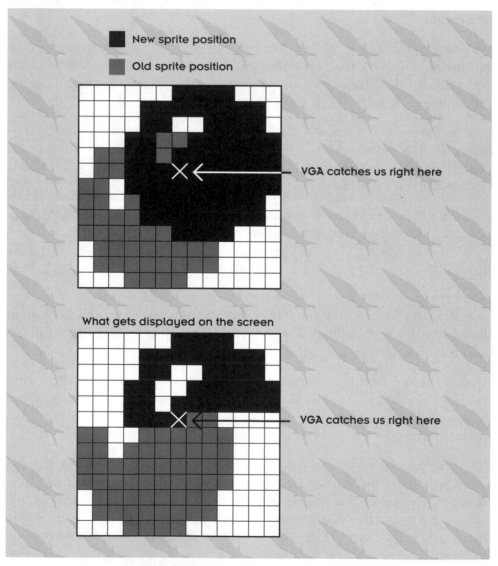

Figure 7.8 *Shearing is caused by the VGA trying to catch up during a virtual screen buffer to video memory copy.*

of the ball bitmap is from the new animation frame while the lower part is from the old. As you can see from the figure, the ball is "sheared" in half.

What if we used vertical retrace again? You'll notice that the demo program doesn't wait for vertical retrace to start before copying the virtual screen buffer to video memory. Wouldn't it eliminate the shearing if we waited until the VGA entered a vertical retrace period and then performed the copying? The answer is yes; it would help if you could copy the whole screen during the vertical retrace period. In fact, copying 64000 bytes to video memory takes longer than a normal vertical retrace period, even on fast computers with fast VGA cards. So, we'll still get shearing. The shearing can sometimes be more noticable because the copying is now synched up with the VGA display cycle and the VGA will catch the in-progess copy at virtually the same location every time. You'll find that the shearing effect doesn't move around the screen and is easier to spot.

In reality the shearing is not terrible. It's hard to spot with just a few sprites moving over a non-moving background. Although there is no general animation technique that will totally eliminate shearing for an arbitrary number of sprites, there is still one technique that we can use to reduce it if the number of sprites we have is not too large.

DIRTY RECTANGLES

The *dirty rectangle* animation technique is an optimization of the virtual screen buffer technique. In the virtual screen buffer technique, we kept a system memory block that reflected how we wanted the screen to look. We performed all of our animations into that block and then copied the system memory to video memory when we wanted to display the new frame of animation.

If you think about the situation, however, you'll quickly see that we were copying far too much memory whenever we wanted to display an animation frame. Most of the pixels on the screen remain the same from one animation frame to another. Only the pixels that make up moving objects (for example, sprites) actually change from one frame to another. So why do we copy the whole virtual screen buffer on each frame? That's a good question.

The dirty rectangle animation technique attempts to be a bit smarter about which pixels get copied to the screen. Whenever a sprite is erased or drawn, the routine computes the bounding rectangle around the area that was modified and saves it in an array. This area is "dirty," or changed, with respect to what's currently in video memory. This is where the technique gets its name.

When all the modifications have been done to the virtual screen buffer, a routine is called to copy the saved rectangles from the virtual screen to video memory. Because only the regions that have been changed are actually copied, the update takes a lot less time. As a rough calculation, consider our 50 bouncing balls example. In the virtual screen buffer technique, we'd copy the whole screen on every animation frame. That's 64,000 pixels for a 320x200 Mode 13h screen. With the dirty rectangle technique, our 50 10x10 pixel balls would only take up 10,000 pixels ([50 erase rectangles + 50 draw rectangles] * 10 pixel width * 10 pixel height). This is only about sixteen percent of the entire screen!

Note, however, that we still haven't eliminated shearing. If we simply copy while the VGA is displaying pixels, there is still the possibility that the VGA will catch us as we're updating some portion of the screen with data from a dirty rectangle. If we've reduced our copying sufficiently, however, we might be able to get all of it done while vertical retrace is going on. So, to completely eliminate shearing, we can wait until vertical retrace starts before we perform any copying of our dirty rectangles. Of course, if we have a lot of dirty rectangles, we might take longer than the vertical retrace period. As I said before, we can't eliminate the shearing in all cases, but if we don't have too many sprites moving about, we can deal with it.

So let's get to some code.

Dirty Rectangle Demo

The DIRTDEMO program, shown in Listing 7.7, demonstrates the dirty rectangle animation technique. As before, we move 50 ball sprites around the screen. If you use at least a fast 386 machine with a mediocre ISA card, you shouldn't see any shearing. If you use a 286 machine and see shearing, reduce the number of sprites until it goes away.

Compiling and Linking:

You can compile the DIRTDEMO program using the Borland C++ 3.1 IDE by typing "bc dirtdemo.prj" and then selecting Compile | Make from the menus. If you would rather use the command line compiler, convert the DIRTDEMO.PRJ file to a makefile using the PRJ2MAK program supplied with Borland C++ 3.1. Type "prj2mak dirtdemo.prj" to create the DIRTDEMO.MAK and DIRTDEMO.CFG files.

If you are using Borland C++ 4.0, choose Project | Open Project from the IDE menus. Open the DIRTDEMO.PRJ file. Borland C++ will convert the version 3.1 .PRJ file to a version 4.0 .IDE file. Compile and link the program by choosing Project | Make All from the IDE menus.

Listing 7.7   DIRTDEMO.C

```c
/* File: DIRTDEMO.C
** Description:
**    Demonstrates the dirty rectangle animation technique.
** Copyright:
**    Copyright 1994, David G. Roberts
*/

#include <alloc.h>
#include <assert.h>
#include <conio.h>
#include <dos.h>
#include <mem.h>
#include <stdio.h>
#include <stdlib.h>
#include "gamedefs.h"
#include "vga.h"
#include "bitblt.h"
#include "retrace.h"
#include "animate.h"

UINT8 BallBitmap[] = {
    10, 0,          /* Width (little endian) */
    10, 0,          /* Height (little endian) */
    0, 0,           /* X and Y origin */
    0, 0,
    0, 0, 0, 2, 2, 2, 2, 0, 0, 0, /* color 2 = green w/ default palette */
    0, 2, 2, 2, 2, 2, 2, 2, 2, 0,
    0, 2, 2, 0, 0, 2, 2, 2, 2, 0,
    2, 2, 0, 0, 2, 2, 2, 2, 2, 2,
    2, 2, 0, 2, 2, 2, 2, 2, 2, 2,
    2, 2, 2, 2, 2, 2, 2, 2, 2, 2,
    2, 2, 2, 2, 2, 2, 2, 2, 2, 2,
    0, 2, 2, 2, 2, 2, 2, 2, 2, 0,
    0, 2, 2, 2, 2, 2, 2, 2, 2, 0,
    0, 0, 0, 2, 2, 2, 2, 0, 0, 0
};

UINT8 BallEraseBitmap[] = {
    10, 0,          /* Width (little endian) */
    10, 0,          /* Height (little endian) */
    0, 0,           /* X and Y origin */
    0, 0,
    16, 16, 16, 16, 16, 16, 16, 16, 16, 16, /* color 16 = black */
    16, 16, 16, 16, 16, 16, 16, 16, 16, 16, /* with default palette */
    16, 16, 16, 16, 16, 16, 16, 16, 16, 16,
    16, 16, 16, 16, 16, 16, 16, 16, 16, 16,
    16, 16, 16, 16, 16, 16, 16, 16, 16, 16,
    16, 16, 16, 16, 16, 16, 16, 16, 16, 16,
    16, 16, 16, 16, 16, 16, 16, 16, 16, 16,
    16, 16, 16, 16, 16, 16, 16, 16, 16, 16,
    16, 16, 16, 16, 16, 16, 16, 16, 16, 16,
    16, 16, 16, 16, 16, 16, 16, 16, 16, 16
};
```

```c
/* note: make these track width and height of bitmap, above */
#define BITMAP_HEIGHT    (10)
#define BITMAP_WIDTH     (10)

#define NUM_BALLS        (30)

#define BUFFER_SIZE      (64000)

int main()
{
    int x[NUM_BALLS], y[NUM_BALLS];
    int OldX[NUM_BALLS], OldY[NUM_BALLS];
    int vx[NUM_BALLS], vy[NUM_BALLS];
    BOOL Erase[NUM_BALLS];
    int i;
    UINT8 far * VirtualScreenBuffer;
    RECT EraseRects[NUM_BALLS];
    RECT DirtyRects[NUM_BALLS];
    int Top, Left, Bottom, Right;

    /* detect VGA */
    if (!DetectVGA()) {
        printf("You must have a VGA to run this program.\n");
        return 1;
    }

    for (i = 0; i < NUM_BALLS; i++) {
        x[i] = random(MODE13H_WIDTH - BITMAP_WIDTH);
        y[i] = random(MODE13H_HEIGHT - BITMAP_HEIGHT);
        vx[i] = random(2) + 1;
        vy[i] = random(2) + 1;
        Erase[i] = FALSE;
    }

    /* allocate virtual screen buffer */
    VirtualScreenBuffer = (UINT8 far *) farmalloc(BUFFER_SIZE);
    if (VirtualScreenBuffer == NULL) {
        fprintf(stderr, "Couldn't allocate memory buffer\n");
        exit(1);
    }
    /* clear buffer to 0 to match state of Mode 13h screen */
    _fmemset(VirtualScreenBuffer, 0, BUFFER_SIZE);

    SetMode13h();

    while (!kbhit()) {

        for (i = 0; i < NUM_BALLS; i++) {
            if (Erase[i]) {
                /* update new position */
                OldX[i] = x[i];
                OldY[i] = y[i];
                x[i] += vx[i];
```

```c
            y[i] += vy[i];
            if ((x[i] < 0) || ((x[i] + BITMAP_WIDTH) >= MODE13H_WIDTH)) {
                vx[i] = -vx[i];
                x[i] += 2 * vx[i];
            }
            if ((y[i] < 0) || ((y[i] + BITMAP_HEIGHT) >= MODE13H_HEIGHT)) {
                vy[i] = -vy[i];
                y[i] += 2 * vy[i];
            }
        }
    }

    /* erase */
    for (i = 0; i < NUM_BALLS; i++) {
        if (Erase[i]) {
            BltLinear((LINEAR_BITMAP far *) BallEraseBitmap,
                OldX[i], OldY[i], VirtualScreenBuffer);

            EraseRects[i].Top = OldY[i] -
                ((LINEAR_BITMAP *) BallEraseBitmap)->OriginY;
            EraseRects[i].Left = OldX[i] -
                ((LINEAR_BITMAP *) BallEraseBitmap)->OriginX;
            EraseRects[i].Bottom = OldY[i] -
                ((LINEAR_BITMAP *) BallEraseBitmap)->OriginY +
                ((LINEAR_BITMAP *) BallEraseBitmap)->Height;
            EraseRects[i].Right = OldX[i] -
                ((LINEAR_BITMAP *) BallEraseBitmap)->OriginX +
                ((LINEAR_BITMAP *) BallEraseBitmap)->Width;
        }
    }

    /* draw */
    for (i = 0; i < NUM_BALLS; i++) {
        BltLinear((LINEAR_BITMAP far *) BallBitmap, x[i], y[i],
            VirtualScreenBuffer);

        Top = y[i] - ((LINEAR_BITMAP *) BallBitmap)->OriginY;
        Left = x[i] - ((LINEAR_BITMAP *) BallBitmap)->OriginX;
        Bottom = y[i] -
            ((LINEAR_BITMAP *) BallBitmap)->OriginY +
            ((LINEAR_BITMAP *) BallBitmap)->Height;
        Right = x[i] -
            ((LINEAR_BITMAP *) BallBitmap)->OriginX +
            ((LINEAR_BITMAP *) BallBitmap)->Width;

        if (Erase[i] == TRUE) {
            /* optimization: combine erase and draw rectangles */
            DirtyRects[i].Top = MIN(Top, EraseRects[i].Top);
            DirtyRects[i].Left = MIN(Left, EraseRects[i].Left);
            DirtyRects[i].Bottom = MAX(Bottom, EraseRects[i].Bottom);
            DirtyRects[i].Right = MAX(Right, EraseRects[i].Right);
        }
        else {
            DirtyRects[i].Top = Top;
```

```
                    DirtyRects[i].Left = Left;
                    DirtyRects[i].Bottom = Bottom;
                    DirtyRects[i].Right = Right;
                    Erase[i] = TRUE;
            }
        }

        WaitVerticalRetraceStart();
        CopyRects(DirtyRects, NUM_BALLS, VirtualScreenBuffer);
    }

    getch();

    SetVGAMode(0x3);

    return 0;
}
```

The demo program is very similar to VSCNDEMO. It creates an offscreen virtual display buffer and performs all drawing into that buffer. For each sprite, however, a draw and erase "dirty" rectangle is computed.

When the whole animation frame has been composed, the routine waits for vertical retrace to begin and then copies all the dirty rectangles to video memory using the **CopyRects** function. **CopyRects** is located in the ANIMATE.C module and is shown in Listing 7.8. **CopyRects** includes some inline assembly language optimization to ensure that the copying takes place as quickly as possible. I've placed the C source code equivalent to the assembly language in the comment inside the routine.

Listing 7.8   The CopyRects Function

```
/*
    Function: CopyRects
    Description:
        Copies an array of dirty rectangles from a virtual screen
        buffer to video memory.
*/
void CopyRects(RECT RectArray[], int NumRects, UINT8 far * VirtualBase)
{
    int RectCounter;
    /* int LineCounter; used in C version */
    /* int ColumnCounter; used in C version */
    UINT8 far * Screen;
    UINT8 far * VirtualScreen;
    UINT16 Offset;
    int LineIncrement;
    int Top, Left, Bottom, Right;
```

```
for (RectCounter = 0; RectCounter < NumRects; RectCounter++) {
    /* quickly copy these to simply the source code and */
    /* eliminate array index and structure member address */
    /* calculations */
    Top     = RectArray[RectCounter].Top;
    Left    = RectArray[RectCounter].Left;
    Bottom  = RectArray[RectCounter].Bottom;
    Right   = RectArray[RectCounter].Right;

    assert(Top <= Bottom);
    assert(Left <= Right);

    /* initialize pointers to virtual and physical screens */
    Offset = MODE13H_WIDTH * Top + Left;
    Screen = MK_FP(VIDEO_MEM_SEGMENT, Offset);
    VirtualScreen = VirtualBase + Offset;

    LineIncrement = MODE13H_WIDTH - (Right - Left);

    /*
    This bit of C code is equivalent to the inline assembly
    language, below, and is shown here for reference.

    for (LineCounter = Top; LineCounter < Bottom; LineCounter++) {
        for (ColumnCounter = Left; ColumnCounter < Right;
            ColumnCounter++) {
            *Screen++ = *VirtualScreen++;
        }
        Screen += LineIncrement;
        VirtualScreen += LineIncrement;
    }
    */

    /* do that copy in assembly because it's time critical */
    asm {
        push ds
        mov dx,Right
        sub dx,Left
        mov bx,Bottom
        sub bx,Top
        lds si,VirtualScreen
        les di,Screen
    }
    rowloop:
    asm {
        mov cx,dx
        shr cx,1
        rep movsw
        adc cx,0
        rep movsb
        add si,LineIncrement
        add di,LineIncrement
        dec bx
```

```
        jnz rowloop
        pop ds
    }
  }
}
```

A Dirty Rectangle Optimization

The demo program in Listing 7.8 does a slight optimization of the generalized dirty rectangle technique explained previously. To understand the optimization, take a look at Figure 7.9.

As Figure 7.9 shows, in most instances a sprite isn't moving too fast, and the erase rectangle and draw rectangle overlap each other. If we wanted to be naive about our copying, we'd just copy each rectangle, both erase and draw, and be done with it. This means that we'd draw each pixel in the overlap area twice, however.

The demo program takes the bounding rectangles for both erase and draw and combines them into a larger rectangle that encloses both of the update regions.

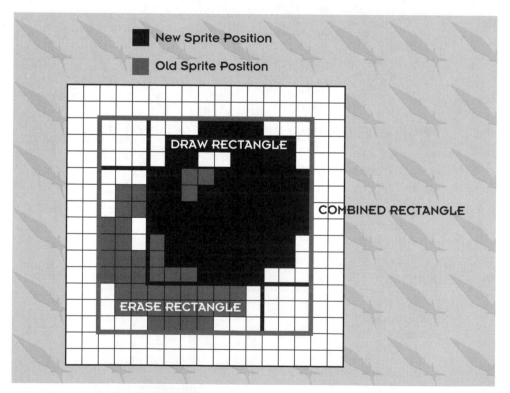

Figure 7.9 *Optimizing dirty rectangles.*

This has the effect of adding a few pixels to the combined region that were not a part of either the erase or draw rectangles. If you look at Figure 7.9, however, you'll see that the added area is actually smaller than the overlap area between the erase and draw rectangles. Overall, we've found a net savings. In fact, the savings is larger than the raw number of pixels would indicate, because by only drawing one large rectangle rather than two slightly smaller rectangles, we eliminate the overhead involved with drawing a rectangle at all.

If you really wanted to get crazy, you could try to optimize all the rectangles on the screen, such that even overlapping sprites were combined together. You could even compute the optimal set of rectangles from a set of intersecting rectangles, such that only truly dirty pixels got copied. Figure 7.10 shows how you could compute three more optimal rectangles for two overlapping sprites.

In general, added optimization is not worth very much. You'd have to test whether rectangles overlap, and the testing takes time. You'd then have to compute the optimal set of rectangles, and this takes more time. At some point it takes more time to compute the optimal set of rectangles than it does just to copy a non-optimal set.

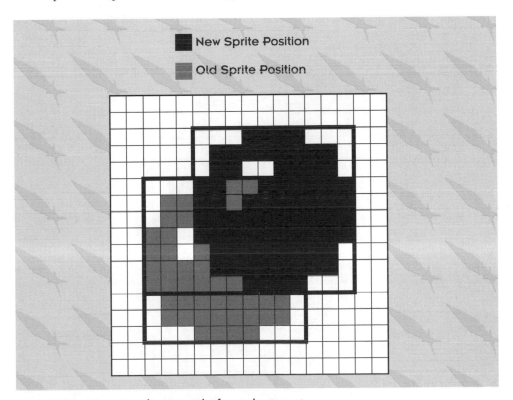

Figure 7.10 *Optimizing dirty rectangles for overlapping sprites.*

At one end of the spectrum you have full optimization and at the other you have no optimization. The technique used in the demo program falls somewhere in between. It's easy to do, because you know beforehand that the draw and erase rectangles for a single sprite will likely overlap, but it doesn't try to get too fancy.

OTHER ANIMATION PROBLEMS

Throughout this chapter, we've examined a number of animation techniques that deal with flicker and shearing. There are other animation problems that can crop up, however. In this section, we'll examine two more maladies, strobing and jerkiness, and talk about what can be done about them.

Strobing

Go back to the FLIPDEMO program and run it. If you have a faster machine, recompile the program with a larger number of balls than 50, until the speed of the balls drops from its normally zippy speed. Now, take a look at some of the faster moving balls. What do you see? If you've slowed the sprites down to a sufficient level, you should see a faint image trailing the main sprite image as it moves around the screen, as shown in Figure 7.11.

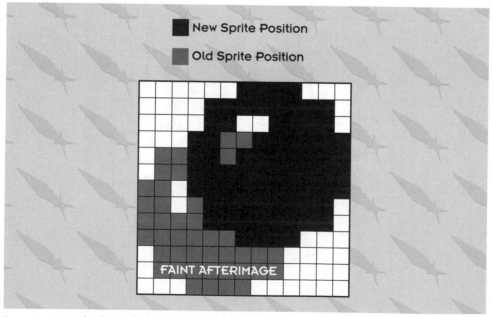

Figure 7.11   *This figure illustrates a strobing effect.*

This phenomenon, called *strobing* or *ghosting*, is not a problem with the animation or the page-flipping. Each animation frame is being displayed correctly, and the monitor is functioning just fine. The ghost image is caused by your eyes and brain, not anything involved with the animation. What you are experiencing is the point where the eye and brain are starting to break down and see through the animation illusion.

Strobing occurs when the eye begins to perceive two separate animation frames as being distinct. In addition to blending the frames and creating motion, the eye also creates a ghost image that seems to follow the sprite.

Strobing is most apparent when the sprite moves a great deal in each animation frame, when the frame rate is low, or when the sprite has a high contrast with the background.

About the only way to help eliminate strobing is to increase the frame rate of the animation by drawing fewer sprites or by optimizing the drawing routines so that they don't take as long. Increasing the frame rate helps by causing the eye to more easily blend the two images together, creating a single moving object. Additionally, if you increase the frame rate and you want your sprite to move at the same speed across the screen, you'll end up decreasing the distanced moved on each frame. A rate of 30 frames per second or higher is usually sufficient to clear up strobing effects.

Strobing does not usually occur with film or TV, because the frame rate is usually high enough (24 or 30 fps) and most film and TV video is live action rather than hand-drawn animation. In live action footage, the film or video camera tends to blur fast moving objects so that they are no longer distinct in each individual frame. This blurring helps the eye to blend frames containing the fast moving objects during film or TV playback.

If you look at fast-moving objects on Saturday-morning cartoon animation, however, you will tend to notice strobing. In this case, you are looking at hand-drawn animation frames displayed at 12 fps. The hand-drawn frames don't incorporate any blurring of fast moving objects, and the lower-quality frame rate helps bring out the effect.

Jerkiness

At some point, the frame rate of animation gets so low that the eye and brain can't effectively blend the motion at all. You won't even see the strobing effect described previously. Instead, the animation will look like a series of still frames displayed in sequence. All movement will begin to look jerky.

The only thing to do in this instance is to increase the frame rate. Typically, things start to look very poor at 15 fps or less.

If your animation is synched to the vertical retrace period because you are using the page-flipping or dirty rectangle animation techniques, for instance, you'll only be able to generate animation at certain discrete frame rates. For instance, if you're using Mode X and it takes your program less than one video frame time (1/60th of a second) to generate an animation frame, the animation frame rate will equal the VGA video frame rate of 60 fps. If your program takes more than one video frame time but less than two video frame times, your animation frame rate will be 30 fps. Table 7.2 shows other rates.

OBJECT INTERNAL ANIMATION

In the previous sections of this chapter, we've learned a great deal about several different animation techniques. We've seen how we can easily animate an object to make it move around the screen. But movement of an object isn't all there is to animation. Sometimes you may want to have movement *within* an object.

For example, what if we have a spaceship in our game? We want to move the spaceship around the screen, but at the same time, we want the spaceship to seem to rotate. What if we have a bird in our game and we want to make its wings flap as it flies? Using the techniques we've covered in previous sections, we are more than equipped to move the objects around, but what about making them seem to change shape or rotate?

Table 7.2 *Frame Drawing Time Versus Animation Frame Rate*

Time to Generate One Animation Frame	Mode X Frame Rate
< 1/60 second	60
1/60 < x < 2/60 seconds	30
2/60 < x < 3/60 seconds	20
3/60 < x < 4/60 seconds	15
4/60 < x < 5/60 seconds	12
5/60 < x < 6/60 seconds	10

Multiple Bitmap Images

Creating object internal animation is very easy. While we move the object around the screen, we simply draw different bitmaps of the object in different states to make it appear that the object is changing shape in some way. Let's take a closer look at the spaceship example.

Figures 7.12 through 7.15 show the bitmap images of our spaceship. We'll use four images of the spaceship to make it seem as if the center portion of the ship is spinning. As you can see in each bitmap image, the green window in the center section of the ship moves slightly to the right side of the ship. Additionally, notice that the red light at the bottom of the ship is darker in two of the images than in the other two. This slight color change will make the light appear to blink.

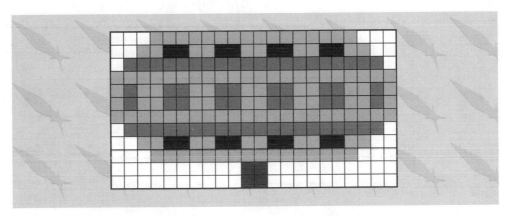

Figure 7.12　*Spaceship image #1.*

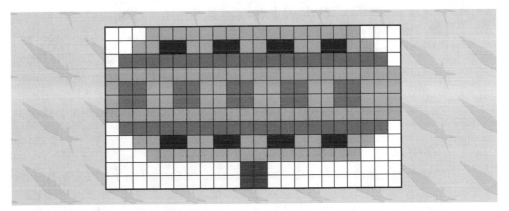

Figure 7.13　*Spaceship image #2.*

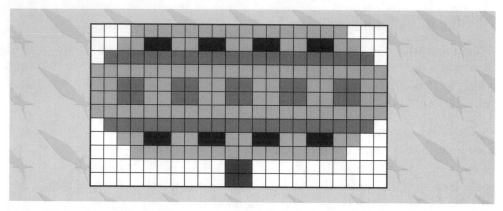

Figure 7.14 *Spaceship image #3.*

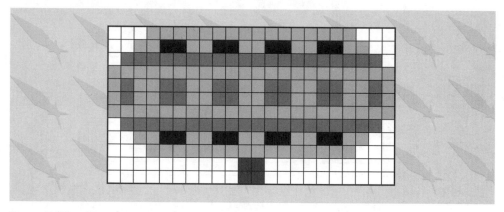

Figure 7.15 *Spaceship image #4.*

Object Internal Animation Demo

Let's take a look at a program that brings our spaceship to life. ISPANDMO.C, shown in Listing 7.9, uses the dirty rectangle animation technique to move a spaceship around the screen. At the same time, it uses the four images of the spaceship, shown in Figures 7.12 through 7.15, to make it seem as if the ship is rotating and the bottom red light is blinking.

Compiling and Linking:

You can compile the ISPANDMO program using the Borland C++ 3.1 IDE by typing "bc ispandmo.prj" and then selecting Compile | Make from the menus. If you would rather use the command line compiler, convert the ISPANDMO.PRJ file to a makefile using the PRJ2MAK program supplied with Borland C++ 3.1. Type "prj2mak ispandmo.prj" to create the ISPANDMO.MAK and ISPANDMO.CFG files.

If you are using Borland C++ 4.0, choose Project | Open Project from the IDE menus. Open the ISPANDMO.PRJ file. Borland C++ will convert the version 3.1 .PRJ file to a version 4.0 .IDE file. Compile and link the program by choosing Project | Make All from the IDE menus.

Listing 7.9   ISPANDMO.C

```c
/* File: ISPANDMO.C
** Description:
**    Demonstrates internal sprite animation.  The demo uses the
**    dirty rectangle animation method.
** Copyright:
**    Copyright 1994, David G. Roberts
*/

#include <alloc.h>
#include <assert.h>
#include <conio.h>
#include <dos.h>
#include <mem.h>
#include <stdio.h>
#include <stdlib.h>
#include "gamedefs.h"
#include "vga.h"
#include "bitblt.h"
#include "retrace.h"
#include "animate.h"
#include "pcx.h"

#define BITMAP_HEIGHT    (12)
#define BITMAP_WIDTH     (22)

#define BUFFER_SIZE      (64000)

#define NUM_IMAGES       (4)
#define FRAMES_PER_IMAGE (8)

int main()
{
    int x, y;
    int OldX, OldY;
    int vx, vy;
    BOOL Erase;
    int i;
    UINT8 far * VirtualScreenBuffer;
    RECT DirtyRects[2];
    int Top, Left, Bottom, Right;
    LINEAR_BITMAP far * ShipBitmap[4];
    LINEAR_BITMAP far * ShipEraseBitmap;
    UINT8 far * EraseBitmapData;
    unsigned SpriteImage;
    unsigned FramesCounter;
```

```
/* detect VGA */
if (!DetectVGA()) {
    printf("You must have a VGA to run this program.\n");
    return 1;
}

/* allocate virtual screen buffer */
VirtualScreenBuffer = (UINT8 far *) farmalloc(BUFFER_SIZE);
if (VirtualScreenBuffer == NULL) {
    fprintf(stderr, "Couldn't allocate memory buffer\n");
    exit(1);
}
/* clear buffer to 0 to match state of Mode 13h screen */
_fmemset(VirtualScreenBuffer, 0, BUFFER_SIZE);

ShipBitmap[0] = LoadPCX("ship1.pcx", NULL);
if (ShipBitmap[0] == NULL) {
    printf("Can't load ship bitmap.\n");
    return 1;
}

ShipBitmap[1] = LoadPCX("ship2.pcx", NULL);
if (ShipBitmap[1] == NULL) {
    printf("Can't load ship bitmap.\n");
    return 1;
}

ShipBitmap[2] = LoadPCX("ship3.pcx", NULL);
if (ShipBitmap[2] == NULL) {
    printf("Can't load ship bitmap.\n");
    return 1;
}

ShipBitmap[3] = LoadPCX("ship4.pcx", NULL);
if (ShipBitmap[3] == NULL) {
    printf("Can't load ship bitmap.\n");
    return 1;
}

/* create the erase bitmap from a real image with the bits */
/* changed to be non-transparent black (color 16 in default palette */
ShipEraseBitmap = LoadPCX("ship1.pcx", NULL);
if (ShipEraseBitmap == NULL) {
    printf("Can't load ship bitmap.\n");
    return 1;
}
EraseBitmapData = &(ShipEraseBitmap->Data);
for (i = 0; i < ShipEraseBitmap->Width * ShipEraseBitmap->Height; i++) {
    *EraseBitmapData++ = 16;
}

SetMode13h();

x = y = 0;
```

```
vx = 1;
vy = 2;

SpriteImage = 0;
FramesCounter = 0;

while (!kbhit()) {

    if (Erase) {
        /* update new position */
        OldX = x;
        OldY = y;
        x += vx;
        y += vy;
        if ((x < 0) || ((x + BITMAP_WIDTH) >= MODE13H_WIDTH)) {
            vx = -vx;
            x += 2 * vx;
        }
        if ((y < 0) || ((y + BITMAP_HEIGHT) >= MODE13H_HEIGHT)) {
            vy = -vy;
            y += 2 * vy;
        }
    }

    /* erase */
    if (Erase) {
        BltLinear(ShipEraseBitmap, OldX, OldY, VirtualScreenBuffer);

        DirtyRects[0].Top = OldY - ShipEraseBitmap->OriginY;
        DirtyRects[0].Left = OldX - ShipEraseBitmap->OriginX;
        DirtyRects[0].Bottom = OldY - ShipEraseBitmap->OriginY +
            ShipEraseBitmap->Height;
        DirtyRects[0].Right = OldX - ShipEraseBitmap->OriginX +
            ShipEraseBitmap->Width;

        /* see if it's time to go to the next sprite image */
        FramesCounter++;
        if (FramesCounter >= FRAMES_PER_IMAGE) {
            FramesCounter = 0;
            /* if so, bump image counter and handle wrap-around */
            SpriteImage++;
            if (SpriteImage >= NUM_IMAGES) {
                SpriteImage = 0;
            }
        }
    }

    /* draw */
    BltLinear(ShipBitmap[SpriteImage], x, y, VirtualScreenBuffer);

    DirtyRects[1].Top = y - ShipBitmap[SpriteImage]->OriginY;
    DirtyRects[1].Left = x - ShipBitmap[SpriteImage]->OriginX;
    DirtyRects[1].Bottom = y - ShipBitmap[SpriteImage]->OriginY +
        ShipBitmap[SpriteImage]->Height;
```

```
        DirtyRects[1].Right = x - ShipBitmap[SpriteImage]->OriginX +
            ShipBitmap[SpriteImage]->Width;

        WaitVerticalRetraceStart();
        CopyRects(DirtyRects, 2, VirtualScreenBuffer);
    }

    getch();

    SetVGAMode(0x3);

    farfree(ShipBitmap[0]);
    farfree(ShipBitmap[1]);
    farfree(ShipBitmap[2]);
    farfree(ShipBitmap[3]);
    farfree(ShipEraseBitmap);
    farfree(VirtualScreenBuffer);

    return 0;
}
```

The program begins very similarly to the DIRTDEMO program. It checks to see if a VGA is present and then allocates and clears a virtual screen buffer.

ISPANDMO then loads the four bitmap images from disk. The PCX.C module, shown in Listing 7.15, contains routines for loading and saving PCX format images (a popular bitmap file format) and creating linear bitmaps from them. The **LoadPCX** function takes a pointer to a filename and returns a far pointer to a **LINEAR_BITMAP** containing the bitmap image from the PCX file. ISPANDMO uses **LoadPCX** to get each of the spaceship images and stores the returned **LINEAR_BITMAP** pointers in the **ShipBitmap** array. An erase bitmap for the ship images, **ShipEraseBitmap**, is created by loading the first bitmap image again and setting the actual image data to color value 16 (black in the default palette). This technique is used to ensure that we get the correct width and height values from the bitmap.

The main loop of ISPANDMO is fairly similar to DIRTDEMO, except that we are only moving one object. The main difference is that after erasing the object, we change the actual bitmap image that will be drawn for it. The **SpriteImage** variable is used to hold the current index into the **ShipBitmap** array. When drawing the image, we call **BltLinear** to draw **ShipBitmap[SpriteImage]**. This causes the sprite image to change over time and makes the ship appear to rotate and the light appear to blink.

The **FramesCounter** variable and the **FRAMES_PER_IMAGE** constant are used to control how fast the ship spins and the light blinks. We don't change the **SpriteImage** variable on every animation frame. Rather, **FramesCounter** is incremented on every frame, and when it reaches **FRAMES PER IMAGE**, we increment **SpriteImage**. By altering **FRAMES_PER_IMAGE**, you can make the ship spin either faster or slower.

ANIMATE.C, RETRACE.C, AND PCX.C LISTINGS

Listing 7.10 ANIMATE.H

```
/* File: ANIMATE.H
** Description:
**    Header file for ANIMATE.C.
** Author:
**    David G. Roberts
** Copyright:
**    Copyright 1994, David G. Roberts
*/


#ifndef _ANIMATE_H

#include "gamedefs.h"

void SetScreenStart(UINT16 Offset);
void PageFlip(UINT16 Offset);
void CopyBufferToScreen(UINT8 far * Buffer, unsigned Size);
int AddRect
    (
    RECT RectArray[],
    int NumRects,
    int Top,
    int Left,
    int Bottom,
    int Right
    );
void CopyRects(RECT RectArray[], int NumRects, UINT8 far * VirtualBase);

#endif
```

Listing 7.11 ANIMATE.C

```
/* File: ANIMATE.C
** Description:
**    Routines for performing animation.  Includes routines for page
**    flipping, off-screen display buffers, and dirty rectangles.
** Author:
**    David G. Roberts
** Copyright:
**    Copyright 1994, David G. Roberts
*/
```

```
#include <assert.h>
#include <dos.h>
#include <mem.h>
#include <stdio.h>
#include "gamedefs.h"
#include "animate.h"
#include "retrace.h"
#include "vga.h"

/*
    Function: SetScreenStart
    Description:
        Sets the VGA screen start address to the offset specified.
        This has the effect of flipping display pages or of scrolling
        the screen a few lines (a flip is really just a massive,
        page-long scroll, right?).
*/
void SetScreenStart(UINT16 Offset)
{
    UINT8 OffsetLow;
    UINT8 OffsetHigh;

    OffsetLow = LOWBYTE(Offset);
    OffsetHigh = HIGHBYTE(Offset);

    /* disable interrupts to ensure this is virtually atomic */
    asm cli;

    outportb(CRTC_INDEX_REG, START_ADDRESS_HIGH_INDEX);
    outportb(CRTC_DATA_REG, OffsetHigh);

    outportb(CRTC_INDEX_REG, START_ADDRESS_LOW_INDEX);
    outportb(CRTC_DATA_REG, OffsetLow);

    asm sti;

}

/*
    Function: PageFlip
    Description:
        Sets the VGA screen start address to the offset specified.
        The routine sets the new address while the VGA is in display
        mode and waits for retrace to become active before returning.
        This ensures that the address is set correctly (e.g., the
        VGA doesn't reload when only half of the address has been
        set) and that the old page is really invisible before we
        start manipulating things on it.
*/
void PageFlip(UINT16 Offset)
{
```

```
    WaitDisplayMode();
    SetScreenStart(Offset);
    WaitRetraceMode();
}


/*
    Function: CopyRects
    Description:
        Copies an array of dirty rectangles from a virtual screen
        buffer to video memory.
*/
void CopyRects(RECT RectArray[], int NumRects, UINT8 far * VirtualBase)
{
    int RectCounter;
    /* int LineCounter; used in C version */
    /* int ColumnCounter; used in C version */
    UINT8 far * Screen;
    UINT8 far * VirtualScreen;
    UINT16 Offset;
    int LineIncrement;
    int Top, Left, Bottom, Right;

    for (RectCounter = 0; RectCounter < NumRects; RectCounter++) {
        /* quickly copy these to simplify the source code and */
        /* eliminate array index and structure member address */
        /* calculations */
        Top      = RectArray[RectCounter].Top;
        Left     = RectArray[RectCounter].Left;
        Bottom   = RectArray[RectCounter].Bottom;
        Right    = RectArray[RectCounter].Right;

        assert(Top <= Bottom);
        assert(Left <= Right);

        /* initialize pointers to virtual and physical screens */
        Offset = MODE13H_WIDTH * Top + Left;
        Screen = MK_FP(VIDEO_MEM_SEGMENT, Offset);
        VirtualScreen = VirtualBase + Offset;

        LineIncrement = MODE13H_WIDTH - (Right - Left);

        /*
        This bit of C code is equivalent to the inline assembly
        language, below, and is shown here for reference.

        for (LineCounter = Top; LineCounter < Bottom; LineCounter++) {
            for (ColumnCounter = Left; ColumnCounter < Right;
                ColumnCounter++) {
                *Screen++ = *VirtualScreen++;
            }
            Screen += LineIncrement;
            VirtualScreen += LineIncrement;
```

```
        }
    */

        /* do that copy in assembly because it's time critical */
        asm {
            push ds
            mov dx,Right
            sub dx,Left
            mov bx,Bottom
            sub bx,Top
            lds si,VirtualScreen
            les di,Screen
        }
        rowloop:
        asm {
            mov cx,dx
            shr cx,1
            rep movsw
            adc cx,0
            rep movsb
            add si,LineIncrement
            add di,LineIncrement
            dec bx
            jnz rowloop
            pop ds
        }
    }
}
```

Listing 7.12 RETRACE.H

```
/* File: RETRACE.H
** Description:
**    Header file for vertical retrace functions in RETRACE.C.
** Author:
**    David G. Roberts
** Copyright:
**    Copyright 1994, David G. Roberts
*/

#ifndef _RETRACE_H

#include "gamedefs.h"

/* exported functions and variables */
void WaitVerticalRetraceStart(void);
void WaitVerticalRetraceEnd(void);
void WaitDisplayMode(void);
void WaitRetraceMode(void);
BOOL VerticalRetraceOccuring(void);

#endif
```

Listing 7.13 RETRACE.C

```c
/* File: RETRACE.C
** Description:
**    Routines used to look for vertical retrace.
** Author:
**    David G. Roberts
** Copyright:
**    Copyright 1994, David G. Roberts
*/

#include <assert.h>
#include <dos.h>
#include <stdio.h>
#include "gamedefs.h"
#include "retrace.h"
#include "vga.h"

/* constants */
#define VR_BIT (0x08)
#define DISPLAY_ENABLE (0x01)

/*
    Function: WaitVerticalRetraceStart
    Description:
        Waits for the VGA to begin vertical retrace.  Note that if the
        VGA is already in vertical retrace, the routine will wait all
        during the next display frame until vertical retrace begins
        again.
*/
void WaitVerticalRetraceStart(void)
{
    UINT8 InputStatus1;

    /* make sure we aren't in retrace already */
    do {
        InputStatus1 = inportb(INPUT_STAT_1_REG);
    } while (InputStatus1 & VR_BIT);

    /* wait for retrace to start */
    do {
        InputStatus1 = inportb(INPUT_STAT_1_REG);
    } while (!(InputStatus1 & VR_BIT));
}

/*
    Function: WaitVerticalRetraceEnd
    Description:
        Waits for vertical retrace to complete.  If the VGA is not
        in vertical retrace, it waits until the VGA enters vertical
        retrace again and the retrace subsequently completes.
*/
```

```
void WaitVerticalRetraceEnd(void)
{
    UINT8 InputStatus1;

    /* make sure we aren't in display state (= not retrace) */
    do {
        InputStatus1 = inportb(INPUT_STAT_1_REG);
    } while (!(InputStatus1 & VR_BIT));

    /* wait for retrace to end */
    do {
        InputStatus1 = inportb(INPUT_STAT_1_REG);
    } while (InputStatus1 & VR_BIT);
}


/*
    Function: WaitDisplayMode
    Description:
        If the VGA is currently in display mode, the function returns
        immediately, else it waits until diplay mode is entered.
*/
void WaitDisplayMode(void)
{
    UINT8 InputStatus1;

    /* wait for retrace to end and display mode to start */
    do {
        InputStatus1 = inportb(INPUT_STAT_1_REG);
    } while (InputStatus1 & DISPLAY_ENABLE);
}


/*
    Function: WaitRetraceMode
    Description:
        If the VGA is currently in retrace mode, the function returns
        immediately, else it waits until retrace mode is entered.
*/
void WaitRetraceMode(void)
{
    UINT8 InputStatus1;

    /* wait for display mode to end and retrace to start */
    do {
        InputStatus1 = inportb(INPUT_STAT_1_REG);
    } while (!(InputStatus1 & VR_BIT));
}


/*
    Function: VerticalRetraceOccuring
    Description:
        Returns the current state of the VGA vertical retrace.  If
        retrace is occuring, the function returns TRUE.
*/
```

```
BOOL VerticalRetraceOccuring(void)
{
    return (inportb(INPUT_STAT_1_REG) & VR_BIT) >> 3;
}
```

Listing 7.14 PCX.H

```
/* File: PCX.H
** Description:
**    Header file for PCX.C.
** Copyright:
**    Copyright 1994, David G. Roberts
*/

#ifndef _PCX_H

#include <stdio.h>
#include "gamedefs.h"
#include "bitblt.h"

typedef struct {
    UINT8   Manufacturer;
    UINT8   Version;
    UINT8   Encoding;
    UINT8   BitsPerPixel;
    UINT16  XMin;
    UINT16  YMin;
    UINT16  XMax;
    UINT16  YMax;
    UINT16  HDpi;
    UINT16  VDpi;
    UINT8   ColorMap[16][3];
    UINT8   Reserved;
    UINT8   NPlanes;
    UINT16  BytesPerLine;
    UINT16  PaletteInfo;
    UINT16  HScreenSize;
    UINT16  VScreenSize;
    UINT8   Pad[54];
} PCX_HEADER;

LINEAR_BITMAP far * LoadPCX(char * FileName, UINT8 Palette[256][3]);
int SavePCX
    (
    char * Filename,
    LINEAR_BITMAP far * Bitmap,
    UINT8 Palette[256][3]
    );

#define _PCX_H

#endif
```

Listing 7.15   PCX.C

```c
/* File: PCX.C
** Description:
**    Routines to load, encode, and decode PCX format files.
** Copyright:
**    Copyright 1994, David G. Roberts
*/

#include <alloc.h>
#include <assert.h>
#include <dos.h>
#include <stdio.h>
#include "gamedefs.h"
#include "bitblt.h"
#include "pcx.h"

/*
    Function: DecodePCXLine
    Description:
        A module local function that decodes a lines-worth of data
        from a PCX file.
*/
static int DecodePCXLine
    (
    UINT8 far * LineBuffer,
    unsigned TotalBytes,
    FILE * File
    )
{
    unsigned Position;
    int Count;
    UINT8 Color;
    int RawData;
    int i;

    Position = 0;

    while (Position < TotalBytes) {
        RawData = fgetc(File);
        if (RawData == EOF) {
            return -1;
        }
        if ((RawData & 0xC0) == 0xC0) {
            Count = RawData & 0x3F;
            RawData = fgetc(File);
            if (RawData == EOF) {
                return -1;
            }
            Color = RawData;
        }
        else {
            Count = 1;
```

```
            Color = RawData;
        }
        for (i = 0; i < Count; i++) {
            LineBuffer[Position++] = Color;
        }
    }
}

    return 0;
}


/*
    Function: EncodeRun
    Description:
        Encodes a run length and a data value and writes them to
        a PCX file.  This routine has been adapted from the ZSoft
        PCX documentation.  The routine returns a non-zero value
        in the event of an error (typically disk full).
*/
static int EncodeRun(int Val, int RunLength, FILE * File)
{
    if (RunLength) {
        if ((RunLength == 1) && (0xC0 != (0xC0 & Val))) {
            /* run of 1 with color index < 0xC0 so no encoding */
            if (EOF == fputc(Val, File)) {
                return 1;
            }
        }
        else {
            if (EOF == fputc(0xC0 | RunLength, File)) {
                return 1;
            }
            if (EOF == fputc(Val, File)) {
                return 1;
            }
        }
    }
    return 0;
}


/*
    Function: EncodePCXLine
    Description:
        Takes a line of byte data and run-length encodes it in PCX
        format.  This routine has been adapted from the ZSoft PCX
        documentation.  The routine returns a non-zero value in
        the event of an error (typically disk full).
*/
static int EncodePCXLine
    (
    UINT8 far * LineBuffer,
    unsigned Length,
    FILE * File
    )
```

```
{
    int OldVal;
    int NewVal;
    int Count;
    unsigned LengthCounter;

    /* start us off */
    OldVal = *LineBuffer++;
    LengthCounter = 1;
    Count = 1;

    while (LengthCounter < Length) {
        NewVal = *LineBuffer++;
        if (NewVal == OldVal) {
            /* we've found a run */
            Count++;
            if (Count == 63) {
                /* this run is at least 63 long, so save off what we */
                /* have so far */
                if (EncodeRun(OldVal, Count, File)) {
                    return 1; /* error */
                }
                Count = 0;
            }
        }
        else {
            /* no run */
            if (Count) {
                /* save off the run we were working on */
                if (EncodeRun(OldVal, Count, File)) {
                    return 1;
                }
            }
            OldVal = NewVal;
            Count = 1;
        }
        LengthCounter++;
    }

    /* save off last run */
    if (Count) {
        if (EncodeRun(OldVal, Count, File)) {
            return 1;
        }
    }

    return 0;
}

/*
    Function: LoadPCX
    Description:
        Loads a PCX file into memory and converts it to LINEAR_BITMAP
```

```
            format.   The palette data for the PCX file is ignored.
*/
LINEAR_BITMAP far * LoadPCX(char * FileName, UINT8 Palette[256][3])
{
    FILE * File;
    UINT8 far * LineBuffer;
    LINEAR_BITMAP far * LinearBM;
    UINT8 far * LinearDataPointer;
    PCX_HEADER PCXHeader;
    unsigned LineCounter;
    unsigned WidthCounter;
    int Result;
    unsigned XSize;
    unsigned YSize;
    unsigned TotalBytes;
    int ColorIndex;

    assert(FileName != NULL);

    /* read in header */
    File = fopen(FileName, "rb");
    if (File == NULL) {
        return NULL;
    }
    Result = fread(&PCXHeader, 1, sizeof(PCXHeader), File);
    if (Result != sizeof(PCXHeader)) {
        fclose(File);
        return NULL;
    }

    /* compute size of image and scanline size */
    XSize = PCXHeader.XMax - PCXHeader.XMin + 1;
    YSize = PCXHeader.YMax - PCXHeader.YMin + 1;
    TotalBytes = PCXHeader.NPlanes * PCXHeader.BytesPerLine;

    /* allocate scanline buffer */
    LineBuffer = (UINT8 far *) farmalloc(TotalBytes);
    if (LineBuffer == NULL) {
        fclose(File);
        return NULL;
    }

    /* allocate and fill in LINEAR_BITMAP data structure */
    LinearBM = (LINEAR_BITMAP far *) farmalloc(sizeof(LINEAR_BITMAP) +
        XSize * YSize - 1);
    if (LinearBM == NULL) {
        fclose(File);
        farfree(LineBuffer);
        return NULL;
    }

    LinearBM->Width = XSize;
    LinearBM->Height = YSize;
```

```
LinearBM->OriginX = 0;
LinearBM->OriginY = 0;

/* decode data */
LinearDataPointer = (UINT8 far *) &(LinearBM->Data);

for (LineCounter = 0; LineCounter < YSize; LineCounter++) {
    Result = DecodePCXLine(LineBuffer, TotalBytes, File);
    if (Result != 0) {
        farfree(LineBuffer);
        farfree(LinearBM);
        return NULL;
    }
    for (WidthCounter = 0; WidthCounter < XSize; WidthCounter++) {
        *LinearDataPointer++ = LineBuffer[PCXHeader.XMin + WidthCounter];
    }
}


farfree(LineBuffer);

/* if the caller doesn't want palette information, just return */
if (Palette == NULL) {
    fclose(File);
    return LinearBM;
}

/* get the palette */
if (PCXHeader.Version != 5) {
    /* if the PCX file doesn't support the 256-color palette */
    /* use the 16-color palette instead */
    for (ColorIndex = 0; ColorIndex < 16; ColorIndex++) {
        Palette[ColorIndex][0] = PCXHeader.ColorMap[ColorIndex][0] / 4;
        Palette[ColorIndex][1] = PCXHeader.ColorMap[ColorIndex][1] / 4;
        Palette[ColorIndex][2] = PCXHeader.ColorMap[ColorIndex][2] / 4;
    }
    for (ColorIndex = 16; ColorIndex < 256; ColorIndex++) {
        Palette[ColorIndex][0] = 0;
        Palette[ColorIndex][1] = 0;
        Palette[ColorIndex][2] = 0;
    }
}
else {
    fseek(File, -((256 * 3) + 1), SEEK_END);
    Result = fgetc(File);
    if (Result != 12) {
        /* this doesn't have a 256-color palette, */
        /* so use the 16-color one */
        for (ColorIndex = 0; ColorIndex < 16; ColorIndex++) {
            /* copy entries and divide by four since PCX colors */
            /* can range from 0 to 255 and VGA colors can only */
            /* go as high as 63 */
            Palette[ColorIndex][0] =
                PCXHeader.ColorMap[ColorIndex][0] / 4;
```

```
                    Palette[ColorIndex][1] =
                        PCXHeader.ColorMap[ColorIndex][1] / 4;
                    Palette[ColorIndex][2] =
                        PCXHeader.ColorMap[ColorIndex][2] / 4;
                }
            for (ColorIndex = 16; ColorIndex < 256; ColorIndex++) {
                Palette[ColorIndex][0] = 0;
                Palette[ColorIndex][1] = 0;
                Palette[ColorIndex][2] = 0;
            }
        }
        else {
            /* read in the palette in one chunk */
            fread(Palette, sizeof(UINT8), 256 * 3, File);
            /* now divide the RGB entries down so they range */
            /* from 0 to 63 */
            for (ColorIndex = 0; ColorIndex < 256; ColorIndex++) {
                Palette[ColorIndex][0] /= 4;
                Palette[ColorIndex][1] /= 4;
                Palette[ColorIndex][2] /= 4;
            }
        }
    }

    /* clean up a bit */
    fclose(File);

    return LinearBM;
}


/*
    Function: SavePCX
    Description:
        Takes a linear bitmap and a palette as input and saves the
        linear bitmap as a PCX file with the specified name.
        The bitmap will be saved as a version 5 format PCX file with
        a palette.
*/
int SavePCX
    (
    char * Filename,
    LINEAR_BITMAP far * Bitmap,
    UINT8 Palette[256][3]
    )
{
    PCX_HEADER PCXHeader;
    FILE * File;
    int ColorIndex;
    int i;
    int Result;
    unsigned LineCounter;
    UINT8 far * Data;
    int PalData;
```

```
assert(Filename != NULL);
assert(Bitmap != NULL);
assert(Palette != NULL);

/* fill in PCX header */
PCXHeader.Manufacturer  = 10;
PCXHeader.Version       = 5;
PCXHeader.Encoding      = 1;
PCXHeader.BitsPerPixel  = 8;
PCXHeader.XMin          = 0;
PCXHeader.YMin          = 0;
PCXHeader.XMax          = Bitmap->Width - 1;
PCXHeader.YMax          = Bitmap->Height - 1;
PCXHeader.HDpi          = Bitmap->Width;
PCXHeader.VDpi          = Bitmap->Height;
PCXHeader.Reserved      = 0;
PCXHeader.NPlanes       = 1;
PCXHeader.BytesPerLine  = (Bitmap->Width + 1) & 0xFFFE; /* make even */
PCXHeader.PaletteInfo   = 1;
PCXHeader.HScreenSize   = Bitmap->Width;
PCXHeader.VScreenSize   = Bitmap->Height;
for (ColorIndex = 0; ColorIndex < 16; ColorIndex++) {
    PCXHeader.ColorMap[ColorIndex][0] = Palette[ColorIndex][0] * 4;
    PCXHeader.ColorMap[ColorIndex][1] = Palette[ColorIndex][1] * 4;
    PCXHeader.ColorMap[ColorIndex][2] = Palette[ColorIndex][2] * 4;
}
for (i = 0; i < sizeof(PCXHeader.Pad); i++) {
    PCXHeader.Pad[i] = 0;
}

/* open file */
File = fopen(Filename, "wb");
if (File == NULL) {
    return 1; /* error */
}

/* write header to file */
Result = fwrite(&PCXHeader, sizeof(PCX_HEADER), 1, File);
if (Result != 1) {
    /* write error */
    fclose(File);
    return 1;
}

/* encode data */
Data = (UINT8 far *) &(Bitmap->Data);
for (LineCounter = 0; LineCounter < Bitmap->Height; LineCounter++) {
    if (EncodePCXLine(Data, Bitmap->Width, File)) {
        fclose(File);
        return 1; /* file write error */
    }
```

```
        /* handle odd width since BytesPerLine must be even */
        if (Bitmap->Width & 1) {
            if (fputc(0, File) != 0) {
                fclose(File);
                return 1; /* file write error */
            }
        }
        Data += Bitmap->Width;
    }

    /* write palette */
    fputc(12, File);      /* palette marker */
    for (ColorIndex = 0; ColorIndex < 256; ColorIndex++) {
        PalData = Palette[ColorIndex][0] * 4;
        Result = fputc(PalData, File);
        if (Result != PalData) {
            fclose(File);
            return 1; /* write error */
        }
        PalData = Palette[ColorIndex][1] * 4;
        Result = fputc(PalData, File);
        if (Result != PalData) {
            fclose(File);
            return 1; /* write error */
        }
        PalData = Palette[ColorIndex][2] * 4;
        Result = fputc(PalData, File);
        if (Result != PalData) {
            fclose(File);
            return 1; /* write error */
        }
    }

    /* close and exit */
    fclose(File);
    return 0;
}
```

That's it for this chapter. Now that we know how to animate things, let's take a look at how we can control which colors the VGA uses to display our images and how we can create those neat fade-in and fade-out effects the professionals always use.

COLOR YOUR WORLD

Color can make or break a game. Check out this chapter to see how you can manipulate the VGA palette to produce some amazing effects.

When Picasso painted *The Old Guitarist* in blue, he did it with the color he felt best communicated his thoughts. When Michelangelo painted the Sistine Chapel, nobody told him which colors to use. In the past few chapters we've learned how to plot pixels to the VGA screen, draw bitmaps, and create smooth-running animation. In everything we've done, however, we've been limited to the default colors selected by the VGA. If Picasso or Michelangelo had to suffer such indignity, they would never have taken freelance jobs as computer game artists.

Color is a natural part of art and that applies to game art as well as any other type. Not only do game artists want to determine the shape of various objects in the game, they also want to determine their colors. The VGA's default colors place artificial limits on game artists. Further, they place artificial limits on game programmers. There are many effects that can be created simply by manipulating the various colors that the VGA can display.

In this chapter, we'll break out of the constraining mold of the VGA's default palette. We'll learn about the RGB color model and how the VGA displays different colors. We'll discover how to change the default colors of the VGA to suit our purposes and we'll investigate some of the techniques used to create fade-ins, fade-outs, and other color-based graphic effects.

eXPLORER OVERVIEW   This chapter will develop a module named PALETTE.C. This module contains routines for manipulating individual VGA palette entries as well as blocks of entries. Further, PALETTE.C includes routines to perform fades and rotations. A short program, PALDEMO, demonstrates some of the effects that can be obtained with the routines in PALETTE.C.

COMPUTERS AND COLOR

In the last chapter, we discussed how a VGA monitor creates a video image by shooting a beam of electrons at a phosphor-coated display tube. We learned that the inside of a color display tube is coated with a repeating pattern of small phosphor dots, similar to what is shown in Figure 8.1. There are three types of phosphor in the pattern, each of which emits a different color of light when it is struck with a beam of electrons generated inside the display tube. The three phosphor colors are red, green, and blue, and three electron beams are used to individually strike each of the dots in the pattern.

It's hard to believe, but the VGA makes all the rich colors you see in computer games and other programs simply by mixing together differing amounts of red, green, and blue light emitted from the phosphors. This method of creating color is called the RGB color model.

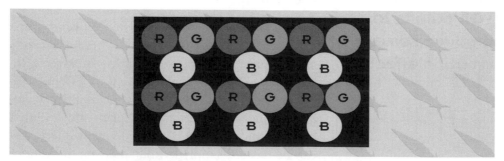

Figure 8.1   *The triangle pattern of phosphor dots.*

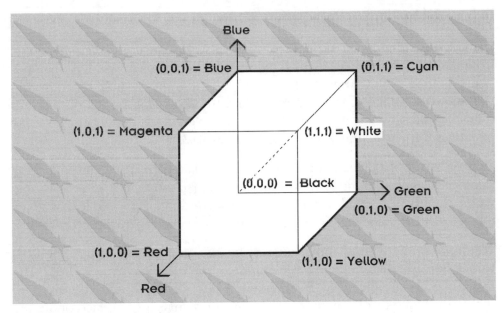

Figure 8.2 *The RGB color cube.*

The RGB color model is based on a color cube with three axes: red, green, and blue. A color may be described by its position within the cube using a standard three-valued (r, g, b) tuple, similar to (x, y, z) coordinates in three-space. Figure 8.2 shows the RGB color cube.

The cube is conceptually one unit square with each coordinate axis in RGB-space taking on a value between 0 and 1. Black is located at the origin of RGB-space, (0,0,0). White is located exactly opposite the origin at location (1,1,1). White is composed of the maximum amount of red, green, and blue light, mixed in equal proportion to each other. Black is composed of the minimum amount of light. All the grays are located along the dotted line from black to white. They occur when equal proportions of red, green, and blue light are mixed together.

When we've plotted pixels in the past few chapters, we haven't had to deal with RGB colors. Whenever we wanted to make a pixel green, we've just stored a 2 into video memory. Whenever we wanted to make the pixel red, we stored a 4 instead. As we'll see later in this chapter, we can even change the colors that these numbers represent. For instance, we'll be able to make 2 create red and 4 create green, if we like. How, do you ask, does the VGA know what color corresponds to what number? To answer the question, let's take a look at the VGA display data path.

Video RAM to Display Data Path

In the VGA, individual R, G, or B coordinates within the color cube can range from 0 to 63. White is represented by the value (63,63,63). With RGB components ranging from 0 to 63, there are 262,144 different possible colors within the VGA color cube ($64^3 = 262,144$). Since the 256 color modes of the VGA only allow us to select a subset of those possible colors, there must be some mechanism for selecting which colors are displayed.

Figure 8.3 shows a diagram of the VGA display data path. You can see that the number we stored in video RAM is actually just an index to a 256-entry table within the VGA. The table is called a *color palette* and it is this table that stores the actual RGB color that is displayed on the screen.

When presented with an input index value, the color palette dumps the RGB values stored at that index to three *digital-to-analog converters*, or DACs. The DACs convert the digital RGB components into analog signals that are then sent to the video display monitor. These analog signals are used to control the intensities of the electron beams striking the phosphor dot patterns in the display tube. A higher signal causes the electron beam to be more intense and the phosphor to emit more light.

For example, if our color value stored in video memory is 4, it will index the color palette and send the RGB value (63,0,0) to the DACs. This causes the

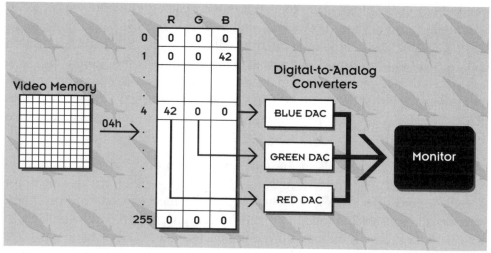

Figure 8.3　*VGA display data path.*

DACs to send a maximum signal level on the red wire leading to the monitor and minimum signal level on the green and blue wires. This in turn causes the red electron beam to be at maximum intensity and the green and blue beams to be off. The red electron beam strikes the red phosphor dot on the screen and causes it to emit red light with a high intensity. Since the green and blue electron beams are off, the green and blue phosphor dots aren't struck and don't emit any light. The result is that the user looking at the display monitor sees a red dot. This process repeats itself as the VGA scans through memory, displaying pixels.

The color palette is the key to manipulating the various colors that the VGA can display. By changing the RGB values of individual palette entries, the VGA will display a different color on the monitor when that color palette index is retrieved from video memory.

THE VGA COLOR PALETTE

In the past few chapters we've been using the default colors with our bitmaps and drawing routines. Of course we've decided that overall the colors of the default palette are nice, but limiting. In this section we'll take a look at the colors available in the default palette and the VGA registers that allow us access to the palette to change the RGB color values stored in it.

The Default Palette

Whenever the VGA is reset, a default set of RGB color entries is stored in the palette. The default colors are listed in Table 8.1.

The RGB values themselves are difficult to mentally map into colors, so Table 8.2 gives more intuitive descriptions of the first 16 colors. The first 16 default colors are identical to the 16 EGA colors and are provided for compatibility with the EGA palette. I used these colors to create the spaceship bitmap in the last chapter.

Palette Registers

The VGA has several registers that are designed to manipulate the palette RGB values. Some of the registers emulate the EGA palette registers and are provided for compatibility. These registers only allow a programmer to manipulate the first 16 color entries, since the EGA only had 16 colors. Because game programmers are interested in the 256 color modes that the VGA sup-

Table 8.1 *Default VGA Palette RGB Values*

Index	RGB	Index	RGB	Index	RGB	Index	RGB
0	(0,0,0)	64	(63,31,31)	128	(14,14,28)	192	(0,16,0)
1	(0,0,42)	65	(63,39,31)	129	(17,14,28)	193	(0,16,4)
2	(0,42,0)	66	(63,47,31)	130	(21,14,28)	194	(0,16,8)
3	(0,42,42)	67	(63,55,31)	131	(24,14,28)	195	(0,16,12)
4	(42,0,0)	68	(63,63,31)	132	(28,14,28)	196	(0,16,16)
5	(42,0,42)	69	(55,63,31)	133	(28,14,24)	197	(0,12,16)
6	(42,21,0)	70	(47,63,31)	134	(28,14,21)	198	(0,8,16)
7	(42,42,42)	71	(39,63,31)	135	(28,14,17)	199	(0,4,16)
8	(21,21,21)	72	(31,63,31)	136	(28,14,14)	200	(8,8,16)
9	(21,21,63)	73	(31,63,39)	137	(28,17,14)	201	(10,8,16)
10	(21,63,21)	74	(31,63,47)	138	(28,21,14)	202	(12,8,16)
11	(21,63,63)	75	(31,63,55)	139	(28,24,14)	203	(14,8,16)
12	(63,21,21)	76	(31,63,63)	140	(28,28,14)	204	(16,8,16)
13	(63,21,63)	77	(31,55,63)	141	(24,28,14)	205	(16,8,14)
14	(63,63,21)	78	(31,47,63)	142	(21,28,14)	206	(16,8,12)
15	(63,63,63)	79	(31,39,63)	143	(17,28,14)	207	(16,8,10)
16	(0,0,0)	80	(45,45,63)	144	(14,28,14)	208	(16,8,8)
17	(5,5,5)	81	(49,45,63)	145	(14,28,17)	209	(16,10,8)
18	(8,8,8)	82	(54,45,63)	146	(14,28,21)	210	(16,12,8)
19	(11,11,11)	83	(58,45,63)	147	(14,28,24)	211	(16,14,8)
20	(14,14,14)	84	(63,45,63)	148	(14,28,28)	212	(16,16,8)
21	(17,17,17)	85	(63,45,58)	149	(14,24,28)	213	(14,16,8)
22	(20,20,20)	86	(63,45,54)	150	(14,21,28)	214	(12,16,8)
23	(24,24,24)	87	(63,45,49)	151	(14,17,28)	215	(10,16,8)
24	(28,28,28)	88	(63,45,45)	152	(20,20,28)	216	(8,16,8)
25	(32,32,32)	89	(63,49,45)	153	(22,20,28)	217	(8,16,10)
26	(36,36,36)	90	(63,54,45)	154	(24,20,28)	218	(8,16,12)
27	(40,40,40)	91	(63,58,45)	155	(26,20,28)	219	(8,16,14)
28	(45,45,45)	92	(63,63,45)	156	(28,20,28)	220	(8,16,16)
29	(50,50,50)	93	(58,63,45)	157	(28,20,26)	221	(8,14,16)
30	(56,56,56)	94	(54,63,45)	158	(28,20,24)	222	(8,12,16)
31	(63,63,63)	95	(49,63,45)	159	(28,20,22)	223	(8,10,16)

(continued)

Table 8.1   *Default VGA Palette RGB Values (Continued)*

Index	RGB	Index	RGB	Index	RGB	Index	RGB
32	(0,0,63)	96	(45,63,45)	160	(28,20,20)	224	(11,11,16)
33	(16,0,63)	97	(45,63,49)	161	(28,22,20)	225	(12,11,16)
34	(31,0,63)	98	(45,63,54)	162	(28,24,20)	226	(13,11,16)
35	(47,0,63)	99	(45,63,58)	163	(28,26,20)	227	(15,11,16)
36	(63,0,63)	100	(45,63,63)	164	(28,28,20)	228	(16,11,16)
37	(63,0,47)	101	(45,58,63)	165	(26,28,20)	229	(16,11,15)
38	(63,0,31)	102	(45,54,63)	166	(24,28,20)	230	(16,11,13)
39	(63,0,16)	103	(45,49,63)	167	(22,28,20)	231	(16,11,12)
40	(63,0,0)	104	(0,0,28)	168	(20,28,20)	232	(16,11,11)
41	(63,16,0)	105	(7,0,28)	169	(20,28,22)	233	(16,12,11)
42	(63,31,0)	106	(14,0,28)	170	(20,28,24)	234	(16,13,11)
43	(63,47,0)	107	(21,0,28)	171	(20,28,26)	235	(16,15,11)
44	(63,63,0)	108	(28,0,28)	172	(20,28,28)	236	(16,16,11)
45	(47,63,0)	109	(28,0,21)	173	(20,26,28)	237	(15,16,11)
46	(31,63,0)	110	(28,0,14)	174	(20,24,28)	238	(13,16,11)
47	(16,63,0)	111	(28,0,7)	175	(20,22,28)	239	(12,16,11)
48	(0,63,0)	112	(28,0,0)	176	(0,0,16)	240	(11,16,11)
49	(0,63,16)	113	(28,7,0)	177	(4,0,16)	241	(11,16,12)
50	(0,63,31)	114	(28,14,0)	178	(8,0,16)	242	(11,16,13)
51	(0,63,47)	115	(28,21,0)	179	(12,0,16)	243	(11,16,15)
52	(0,63,63)	116	(28,28,0)	180	(16,0,16)	244	(11,16,16)
53	(0,47,63)	117	(21,28,0)	181	(16,0,12)	245	(11,15,16)
54	(0,31,63)	118	(14,28,0)	182	(16,0,8)	246	(11,13,16)
55	(0,16,63)	119	(7,28,0)	183	(16,0,4)	247	(11,12,16)
56	(31,31,63)	120	(0,28,0)	184	(16,0,0)	248	(0,0,0)
57	(39,31,63)	121	(0,28,7)	185	(16,4,0)	249	(0,0,0)
58	(47,31,63)	122	(0,28,14)	186	(16,8,0)	250	(0,0,0)
59	(55,31,63)	123	(0,28,21)	187	(16,12,0)	251	(0,0,0)
60	(63,31,63)	124	(0,28,28)	188	(16,16,0)	252	(0,0,0)
61	(63,31,55)	125	(0,21,28)	189	(12,16,0)	253	(0,0,0)
62	(63,31,47)	126	(0,14,28)	190	(8,16,0)	254	(0,0,0)
63	(63,31,39)	127	(0,7,28)	191	(4,16,0)	255	(0,0,0)

Table 8.2 *The First 16 Palette Entries*

Value	Description
0	Black
1	Blue
2	Green
3	Cyan
4	Red
5	Magenta
6	Brown
7	White
8	Gray
9	Light Blue
10	Light Green
11	Light Cyan
12	Light Red
13	Light Magenta
14	Yellow
15	Bright White

ports, we'll ignore the EGA compatibility registers and focus on the VGA-only registers.

The VGA supports three registers, shown in Table 8.3, for manipulating palette RGB entries: the Color Address Read register, the Color Address Write register, and the Color Data register. Each register has its own dedicated I/O port address; they do not use an indexed scheme like many of the other VGA register groups.

Table 8.3 *Color Registers*

Register	Port
Color Address Read Register	3C7h
Color Address Write Register	3C8h
Color Data Register	3C9h

The Color Address Read register and the Color Address Write register are used to select the index of the palette entry we want to read or write. All reading and writing of actual RGB color values is done through the Color Data register.

RGB values are written to the Color Data register in sequence, first red, then green, and finally blue. A counter within the VGA is used to keep track of which component of the RGB tuple is being written. This counter is reset whenever a new index value is written to the Color Address Read register or the Color Address Write register.

After a full RGB tuple has been read or written to or from the Color Data register, the current palette index value is incremented. This allows us to read or write a block of palette entries very rapidly by simply writing the first index value to one of the address registers and then manipulating the Color Data register repeatedly.

Since an internal counter is used to keep track of where we are, it's a good idea to disable interrupts around our palette setting code. This prevents some other piece of code from mistakenly manipulating the palette while we're doing the same thing.

Additionally, it's a good idea to change palette entries only while the VGA is in a retrace state. If the VGA is sending pixels to the display while a color is changed, it can cause a "snow" effect. Simply call **WaitVerticalRetraceStart** before writing to the palette. However, you can read palette entries at any time without creating snow.

SETTING YOUR OWN COLORS

Let's take a look at some routines from PALETTE.C that are used to set and get color palette entries. The functions **SetVGAPaletteEntry** and **GetVGAPaletteEntry**, shown in Listing 8.1, manipulate an individual palette entry. They both take a pointer to an **RGB_TUPLE** as input to store the RGB color components. First, the **RGB_TUPLE** is defined:

```
typedef struct {
    UINT8 r;
    UINT8 g;
    UINT8 b;
} RGB_TUPLE;
```

Listing 8.1 The SetVGAPaletteEntry and GetVGAPaletteEntry Functions

```c
/*
    Function: SetVGAPaletteEntry
    Description:
        Modifies the VGA palette entry specified by the Index
        parameter to the RGB color value specified by
        the Rgb parameter.  The individual R, G, and B values
        should be ready to be sent directly to the VGA
        (i.e., should range from 0-63).

        This function may need to be called during a vertical
        or horizontal retrace period on some VGAs to avoid
        causing snow.
*/
void SetVGAPaletteEntry(int Index, RGB_TUPLE * Rgb)
{
    assert(0 <= Index && Index <= 255);
    assert(Rgb != NULL);
    assert(Rgb->r < 64);
    assert(Rgb->g < 64);
    assert(Rgb->b < 64);

    asm cli;

    outportb(COLOR_ADDRESS_WRITE, Index);
    outportb(COLOR_DATA, Rgb->r);
    outportb(COLOR_DATA, Rgb->g);
    outportb(COLOR_DATA, Rgb->b);

    asm sti;
}

/*
    Function: GetVGAPaletteEntry
    Description:
        Gets the R, G, and B components of the color value
        currently in the VGA palette at Index.  The
        function returns the color components in the
        RGB_TUPLE pointed to by Rgb.
*/
void GetVGAPaletteEntry(int Index, RGB_TUPLE * Rgb)
{
    assert(0 <= Index && Index <= 255);
    assert(Rgb != NULL);

    asm cli;

    outportb(COLOR_ADDRESS_READ, Index);

    Rgb->r = inportb(COLOR_DATA);
```

```
    Rgb->g = inportb(COLOR_DATA);
    Rgb->b = inportb(COLOR_DATA);

    asm sti;
}
```

These functions are very simple. **SetVGAPaletteEntry** simply outputs the color index to the Color Address Write register and then outputs the R, G, and B color values to the Color Data register. **GetVGAPaletteEntry** does the reverse. It first writes the color index to the Color Address Read register and then inputs the R, G, and B color values.

Setting a block of palette entries is just about as easy as setting a single entry. The functions **SetVGAPaletteBlock** and **GetVGAPaletteBlock** are used to manipulate a block of palette entries. These functions take a pointer to a two-dimensional array and a starting index and length as parameters. The array holds RGB components for each of 256 palette entries. The starting index and length determine the block of palette entries that we're interested in.

The block functions use a bit of inline assembly language to optimize the speed of setting and getting the palette. Because these functions will be called while vertical retrace is active, they only have a limited amount of time to set a block of palette entries before the VGA begins displaying pixels again. The palette manipulations could create the "snow" effect if they are not completed before the end of the retrace period.

On ISA VGA cards, even this assembly language optimization won't be enough to allow a program to set the whole palette during a single vertical retrace period. If you find that setting a large palette block cannot fit into a single retrace period, break the block up into two or more smaller blocks and set each smaller block during multiple vertical retrace periods. **SetVGAPaletteBlock** and **GetVGAPaletteBlock** are shown in Listing 8.2.

Listing 8.2   The SetVGAPaletteBlock and GetVGAPaletteBlock Functions

```
/*
    Function: SetVGAPaletteBlock
    Description:
        Sets a subset of the VGA palette registers to new values.
        A RAM copy of the palette to load is pointed to by
        the Palette parameter.  The block of palette registers
        to transfer to the VGA is specified by the Start and
        Length parameters.  Note that Length specifies the
```

```
                number of RGB entries, not the actual length of
                the block in bytes.

                This function may need to be called during a vertical
                or horizontal retrace period on some VGAs to avoid
                causing snow.
*/
void SetVGAPaletteBlock(UINT8 Palette[256][3], int Start, int Length)
{
    UINT8 * BlockStartPtr;

    assert(Palette != NULL);
    assert(0 <= Start && Start <= 255);
    assert(Length > 0);
    assert(Start + Length <= 256);

    asm cli;

    outportb(COLOR_ADDRESS_WRITE, Start);

    BlockStartPtr = &Palette[Start][0];

#if defined(__TINY__) || defined(__SMALL__) || defined(__MEDIUM__)
    asm {
        /* near data pointers so no need to load DS with correct value */
        push ds
        mov si,BlockStartPtr
    }
#else
    asm {
        /* far data pointers, so load DS, too */
        push ds
        lds si,BlockStartPtr
    }
#endif
    asm {
        mov cx,Length
        mov dx,COLOR_DATA
    }
    Loop:
    asm {
        outsb           /* write R component */
        outsb           /* write G component */
        outsb           /* write B component */
        dec cx
        jnz Loop
        pop ds
    }

    asm sti;
}
```

```
/*
    Function: GetVGAPaletteBlock
    Description:
        Gets a subset of the VGA palette registers and stores
        them in a UINT8 array.  The subset block to retrieve
        is identified by the Start and Length parameters.
        Note that Length specifies the number of RGB entries,
        not the length of the block in bytes.
*/
void GetVGAPaletteBlock(UINT8 Palette[256][3], int Start, int Length)
{
    UINT8 * BlockStartPtr;

    assert(Palette != NULL);
    assert(0 <= Start && Start <= 255);
    assert(Length > 0);
    assert(Start + Length <= 256);

    asm cli;

    outportb(COLOR_ADDRESS_READ, Start);

    BlockStartPtr = &Palette[Start][0];

#if defined(__TINY__) || defined(__SMALL__) || defined (__MEDIUM__)
    asm {
        /* near data pointers, so move ds into es */
        mov ax,ds
        mov es,ax
        mov di,BlockStartPtr
    }
#else
    asm {
        /* far data pointers so load es,di from BlockStartPtr */
        les di,BlockStartPtr
    }
#endif
    asm {
        mov cx,Length
        mov dx,COLOR_DATA
    }
    Loop:
    asm {
        insb            /* get R component */
        insb            /* get G component */
        insb            /* get B component */
        dec cx
        jnz Loop
    }

    asm sti;
}
```

Note that **SetVGAPaletteBlock** and **GetVGAPaletteBlock** use the **insb** and **outsb** assembly language instructions. These instructions are present on 80286-based machines and above. Thus, 8088-based PC/XT machines won't be able to run these routines. A PC/AT class machine is required. If you want to make these routines work with an 8088, replace **insb** and **outsb** with **in/stos** and **lods/out** instruction pairs. If you leave them as **insb** and **outsb**, be sure to enable 80286 instruction usage in the compiler so that these routines will assemble correctly; otherwise, the compiler will report an error.

Several more routines operate on a copy of a palette residing in system memory. You'll find that an in-memory copy of the palette is useful for doing complex palette manipulations. Once you've finished with the palette copy, you can copy the affected entries back to the VGA palette using **SetVGAPaletteBlock**. Use **GetVGAPaletteBlock** to copy all the default VGA palette entries into this in-memory palette copy before the manipulations take place.

The functions shown in Listing 8.3 are analogous to those listed previously, except they just manipulate the in-memory palette copy.

Listing 8.3   The SetPaletteEntry and GetPaletteEntry Functions

```
/*
    Function: SetPaletteEntry
    Description:
        Sets the RGB components of a UINT8 entry to the values
        specified by the Rgb parameter.
*/
void SetPaletteEntry(UINT8 Palette[256][3], int Index, RGB_TUPLE * Rgb)
{
    assert(Palette != NULL);
    assert(0 <= Index && Index <= 255);
    assert(Rgb != NULL);
    assert(Rgb->r < 64);
    assert(Rgb->g < 64);
    assert(Rgb->b < 64);

    Palette[Index][0] = Rgb->r;
    Palette[Index][1] = Rgb->g;
    Palette[Index][2] = Rgb->b;
}

/*
    Function: GetPaletteEntry
    Description:
        Sets Rgb to the color components from the Palette at
```

```
        Index.
*/
void GetPaletteEntry(UINT8 Palette[256][3], int Index, RGB_TUPLE * Rgb)
{
    assert(Palette != NULL);
    assert(0 <= Index && Index <= 255);
    assert(Rgb != NULL);

    Rgb-> r = Palette[Index][0];
    Rgb-> g = Palette[Index][1];
    Rgb-> b = Palette[Index][2];
}
```

Two other functions, shown in Listing 8.4, are also useful to help manipulate in-memory palette copies: **FillPaletteBlock** and **CopyPaletteBlock**. You use **FillPaletteBlock** to set a block of palette entries to a single color, which is helpful when you want to clear a palette to all black or all white, for instance. You use **CopyPaletteBlock** to transfer palette entries between two in-memory palette copies, which is useful if you are trying to manage multiple palettes and need some entries to be identical between them.

Listing 8.4   The FillPaletteBlock and CopyPaletteBlock Functions

```
/*
    Function: FillPaletteBlock
    Description:
        Fills a block of palette entries with a single color.
        The block begins at index Start and is Length entries
        long.  The fill color is specified by Rgb.  This
        function is useful for clearing a palette to all
        black or all white to create an ending point for a
        fade.
*/
void FillPaletteBlock
    (
    UINT8 Palette[256][3],
    int Start,
    int Length,
    RGB_TUPLE * Rgb
    )
{
    int Index;

    assert(Palette != NULL);
    assert(0 <= Start && Start <= 255);
    assert(Length > 0);
    assert(Start + Length <= 256);
```

```
    assert(Rgb != NULL);
    assert(Rgb->r < 64);
    assert(Rgb->g < 64);
    assert(Rgb->b < 64);

    for (Index = Start; Index < Start + Length; Index++) {
        Palette[Index][0] = Rgb->r;
        Palette[Index][1] = Rgb->g;
        Palette[Index][2] = Rgb->b;
    }
}


/*
    Function: CopyPaletteBlock
    Description:
        Copies a block of palette entries from one palette to
        another.
*/
void CopyPaletteBlock
    (
    UINT8 DestPalette[256][3],
    UINT8 SourcePalette[256][3],
    int Start,
    int Length
    )
{
    int Index;

    assert(DestPalette != NULL);
    assert(SourcePalette != NULL);
    assert(0 <= Start && Start <= 255);
    assert(Length > 0);
    assert(Start + Length <= 256);

    for (Index = 0; Index < Start + Length; Index++) {
        DestPalette[Index][0] = SourcePalette[Index][0];
        DestPalette[Index][1] = SourcePalette[Index][1];
        DestPalette[Index][2] = SourcePalette[Index][2];
    }
}
```

FADE TO BLACK: PALETTE EFFECTS

The VGA palette doesn't have to be static. We don't have to just set up a bunch of palette entries at the beginning of our program and forget about them. Games would be most drab if this were the case. You can produce many interesting effects by manipulating the palette on a frame-by-frame basis. We'll examine three effects—fades, rotations, and palette animation—in this section.

Fades

Palette fades look similar to the fades used in movies and television. The screen typically starts out black or white and then fades in to show a scene or starts out with the scene and then slowly fades to black. This effect looks great at the beginning of a game when it's used to fade into the title screen.

A fade is easily accomplished by simply manipulating a block of palette entries so that their RGB color values move to a particular point within the color cube. For instance, if you want to fade a particular palette entry to black, simply move the RGB value of the entry along the line between the original RGB value and (0,0,0), black. Each time the VGA goes into a vertical retrace period, compute a new RGB point closer to black and set the palette entry to that RGB value. When you reach black, you're done.

If you're fading more than one palette entry, which is quite common, you simply move all the entries along the lines between their starting positions and black during each vertical retrace period. Different entries should move at different rates depending on how "close" their starting positions are to black within the color cube. In this way, each of the entries ends up being set to black at the same time and the fade looks even for all the colors in the block. Figure 8.4 shows three colors and their fade paths to black within the RGB color cube.

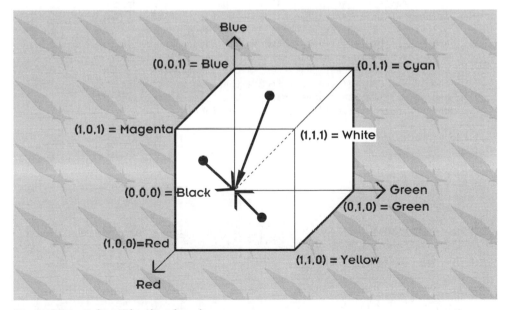

Figure 8.4   *Fading within the color cube.*

Fades to white can be accomplished the same way as fades to black except that the final RGB value should be (63,63,63) rather than (0,0,0).

Fade-ins are just fade-outs in reverse. For instance, if you start with an all-black palette and wish to fade in another palette, you just move each palette entry along the line between black and its final RGB color value within the color cube.

The code to perform a fade is very simple. First, we need a routine that will compute new RGB values for each palette entry of a block. The routine needs to be told the starting and ending RGB values for each palette entry within the block. It also needs to be told how many fade steps will be performed and for which fade step it should compute the RGB values. This technique allows the routine to calculate the new RGB values so that each entry ends up at its final RGB value at the same time. **ComputeFadeStep**, shown in Listing 8.5, performs these computations.

Listing 8.5   The ComputeFadeStep Function

```
/*
    Function: ComputeFadeStep
    Description:
        Computes a palette for a single step of a palette fade.  The
        starting palette and ending palette for the fade are given.
        The amount to fade each entry in the block is computed
        as the ratio of the current step to the number of steps
        in the fade.  Note that when step = 0, the resulting
        palette equals the starting palette and when step =
        NumSteps, the resulting palette equals the ending palette.
        Only the palette entries specified in the block will be
        altered in the FadeStepPalette.  A calling routine
        should use CopyPaletteBlock from either the starting or
        ending palettes to ensure that FadeStepPalette contains
        correct entries outside the specified block.
*/
void ComputeFadeStep
    (
    UINT8 StartPalette[256][3],
    UINT8 EndPalette[256][3],
    int Start,
    int Length,
    long NumSteps,
    long CurrentStep,
    UINT8 FadeStepPalette[256][3]
    )
{
    int Index;
    long RDelta;
    long GDelta;
    long BDelta;
```

```
assert(StartPalette != NULL);
assert(EndPalette != NULL);
assert(0 <= Start && Start <= 255);
assert(Length > 0);
assert(Start + Length <= 256);
assert(NumSteps > 0);
assert(0 <= CurrentStep && CurrentStep <= NumSteps);
assert(FadeStepPalette != NULL);

for (Index = Start; Index < Start + Length; Index++) {
    RDelta = EndPalette[Index][0] - StartPalette[Index][0];
    RDelta = (RDelta * CurrentStep) / NumSteps;

    GDelta = EndPalette[Index][1] - StartPalette[Index][1];
    GDelta = (GDelta * CurrentStep) / NumSteps;

    BDelta = EndPalette[Index][2] - StartPalette[Index][2];
    BDelta = (BDelta * CurrentStep) / NumSteps;

    FadeStepPalette[Index][0] = StartPalette[Index][0] + RDelta;
    FadeStepPalette[Index][1] = StartPalette[Index][1] + GDelta;
    FadeStepPalette[Index][2] = StartPalette[Index][2] + BDelta;
}
}
```

Actually fading the palette requires deciding how many steps will be used in the fade (using **ComputeFadeStep** to calculate the new RGB values for each step), and then setting the palette with the new RGB values with **SetVGAPaletteBlock**. The function **FadePaletteBlock**, shown in Listing 8.6, does all this.

Listing 8.6   The FadePaletteBlock Function

```
#define STEPS_PER_SECOND     (60)    /* number of fade steps per second */
                                     /*   = 1 per VGA scan frame */

/*
    Function: FadePaletteBlock
    Description:
        Fades a block of palette entries on the screen.  The starting
        and ending palettes are given as well as the block to fade
        and the length of time to fade.  The routine computes the
        number of fade steps from the length of time given.  It
        then computes each fade step and sets the block of VGA
        palette entries to the values computed for the step.
        Note that the VGA palette corresponding to the block
        specified should equal what is contained in StartPalette,
        otherwise a color jump will result when the palette is
        set on the first fade step.  The routine will leave the
        VGA palette entries corresponding to the specified block
        equal to the values in EndPalette.  If the routine is
```

```
            passed a length greater than 128, it will fade half the
            color entries on every other retrace and alternate between
            the two halves.  This avoids snow.
*/
void FadePaletteBlock
    (
    UINT8 StartPalette[256][3],
    UINT8 EndPalette[256][3],
    int Start,
    int Length,
    int Milliseconds
    )
{
    UINT8 IntermedPalette[256][3];
    long TotalSteps;
    long Step;

    assert(StartPalette != NULL);
    assert(EndPalette != NULL);
    assert(0 <= Start && Start <= 255);
    assert(Length > 0);
    assert(Start + Length <= 256);
    assert(Milliseconds > 0);

    if (Length <= 128) {
        TotalSteps = ((long) Milliseconds * STEPS_PER_SECOND) / 1000;
    }
    else {
        TotalSteps = ((long) (Milliseconds / 2) * STEPS_PER_SECOND) / 1000;
    }

    for (Step = 0; Step <= TotalSteps; Step++) {
        ComputeFadeStep(StartPalette, EndPalette, Start, Length,
            TotalSteps, Step, IntermedPalette);
        if (Length <= 128) {
            WaitVerticalRetraceStart();
            SetVGAPaletteBlock(IntermedPalette, Start, Length);
        }
        else {
            WaitVerticalRetraceStart();
            SetVGAPaletteBlock(IntermedPalette, Start, Length / 2);
            WaitVerticalRetraceStart();
            SetVGAPaletteBlock(IntermedPalette, Start + (Length / 2),
                Length - (Length / 2));
        }
    }
}
```

Rotations

Simple effects (we'll see some later) can be created by rotating palette entries.
The function **RotatePaletteBlock**, shown in Listing 8.7, will rotate a block of

palette entries. The rotation occurs only within the block itself. Positive rotation values rotate one direction and negative values rotate in the other direction.

Listing 8.7   The RotatePaletteBlock Function

```
/*
    Function: RotatePaletteBlock
    Description:
        Rotates a block of palette entries around one another.  The
        block is specified by Start and Length.  The rotation amount
        is specified by Rotation.  A positive rotation value will
        make Palette[Start] = Palette[Start + Rotation].  Rotations
        are clipped to the block specified (i.e., the rotation wraps
        around within the block).
*/
void RotatePaletteBlock
    (
    UINT8 Palette[256][3],
    int Start,
    int Length,
    int Rotation
    )
{
    UINT8 TempPalette[256][3];
    int Index;
    int SourceIndex;

    assert(Palette != NULL);
    assert(0 <= Start && Start <= 255);
    assert(Length > 0);
    assert(Start + Length <= 256);

    if (Rotation < 0) {
        Rotation = Length + Rotation;
    }

    for (Index = 0; Index < Length; Index++) {
        SourceIndex = (Index + Rotation) % Length;
        TempPalette[Start + Index][0] = Palette[Start + SourceIndex][0];
        TempPalette[Start + Index][1] = Palette[Start + SourceIndex][1];
        TempPalette[Start + Index][2] = Palette[Start + SourceIndex][2];
    }

    CopyPaletteBlock(Palette, TempPalette, Start, Length);
}
```

Palette Animation

Animation doesn't necessarily have to be done with the sprite-based techniques that we saw in the last chapter. Many striking animations can be created very simply by using palette effects instead.

For example, a blinking light on a spaceship can be created simply by using a single bitmap and changing the palette entry corresponding to the pixels making up the light. Two separate bitmaps, and all the disk and RAM storage required for them, aren't needed for such a simple effect.

We'll see an example of the blinking light animation and a "chaser light" effect in the demonstration program in Listing 8.8. The chaser light effect creates many small blocks of color that follow each other across the screen. I created both of these effects simply by manipulating the VGA palette.

Palette Demo

The PALDEMO program, shown in Listing 8.8, demonstrates many of the palette effects described previously. Let's take a look at what it does.

Compiling and Linking:

You can compile the PALDEMO program using the Borland C++ 3.1 IDE by typing "bc paldemo.prj" and then selecting Compile | Make from the menus. If you would rather use the command line compiler, convert the PALDEMO.PRJ file to a makefile using the PRJ2MAK program supplied with Borland C++ 3.1. Type "prj2mak paldemo.prj" to create the PALDEMO.MAK and PALDEMO.CFG files.

If you are using Borland C++ 4.0, choose Project | Open Project from the IDE menus. Open the PALDEMO.PRJ file. Borland C++ will convert the version 3.1 .PRJ file to a version 4.0 .IDE file. Compile and link the program by choosing Project | Make All from the IDE menus.

Listing 8.8   PALDEMO.C

```
/* File: PALDEMO.C
** Description:
**    Program to demonstrate palette manipulations including fading
**    and rotation.
** Copyright:
**    Copyright 1994, David G. Roberts
*/

#include <alloc.h>
#include <assert.h>
#include <conio.h>
#include <dos.h>
#include <stdio.h>
#include "gamedefs.h"
#include "bitblt.h"
```

```c
#include "palette.h"
#include "pcx.h"
#include "retrace.h"
#include "setmodex.h"
#include "vga.h"

#define CHASER_BLOCK_LEN    (16)
#define BLINK_RATE          (10)

/*
    Function: PlotModeX
    Description:
        Plots a pixel in Mode X.
*/
void PlotModeX
    (
    UINT16  X,
    UINT16  Y,
    UINT8   Color
    )
{
    UINT8 Plane;
    UINT8 PlaneMask;
    UINT16 Offset;
    UINT8 far * GraphicsBase;

    /* create a far pointer to the base of video memory */
    GraphicsBase = (UINT8 far *) MK_FP(VIDEO_MEM_SEGMENT,0);

    /* calculate plane and offset of pixel */
    Plane = X % 4;
    Offset = ((MODEX_WIDTH / 4) * Y) + (X / 4);

    /* plot point */
    PlaneMask = 1 << Plane;
    SetMMR(PlaneMask);
    GraphicsBase[Offset] = Color;
}

int main()
{
    LINEAR_BITMAP far * ShipLB;
    PLANAR_BITMAP far * ShipPB;
    UINT8 StandardPalette[256][3];
    UINT8 WhitePalette[256][3];
    UINT8 BlackPalette[256][3];
    RGB_TUPLE White = {63, 63, 63};
    RGB_TUPLE Black = {0, 0, 0};
    RGB_TUPLE BlinkOff = {42, 0, 0};
    RGB_TUPLE BlinkOn = {63, 21, 21};
    RGB_TUPLE Green;
    int i;
    int On;
    int BlinkCounter;
```

```
/* check for VGA */
if (!DetectVGA()) {
    printf("This program requires a VGA.\n");
    return 1;
}

/* load bitmap from PCX */
ShipLB = LoadPCX("ship1.pcx", NULL);
if (ShipLB == NULL) {
    printf("Cannot load SHIP1.PCX.\n");
    return 1;
}

/* convert bitmap to planar format */
ShipPB = LinearToPlanar(ShipLB);

/* put vga into mode X */
SetModeX();

/* draw bitmap */
BltPlanar(ShipPB, 100, 100, 0);

/* get palette from VGA */
GetVGAPaletteBlock(StandardPalette, 0, 16);

/* fade palette to white over 3 second interval */
FillPaletteBlock(WhitePalette, 0, 16, &White);
FadePaletteBlock(StandardPalette, WhitePalette, 0, 16, 3000);

/* fade palette to black */
FillPaletteBlock(BlackPalette, 0, 16, &Black);
FadePaletteBlock(WhitePalette, BlackPalette, 0, 16, 750);

/* wait a couple seconds for effect */
delay(2000);

/* fade palette back to normal in one second */
FadePaletteBlock(BlackPalette, StandardPalette, 0, 16, 1000);

/* rotate colors */
for (i = 0; i < 16; i++) {
    delay(500);
    RotatePaletteBlock(StandardPalette, 0, 16, 1);
    WaitVerticalRetraceStart();
    SetVGAPaletteBlock(StandardPalette, 0, 16);
}

/* blink light on bottom of the spaceship and create "chaser */
/* light" effect. */

/* zero out the block we'll be working on */
FillPaletteBlock(StandardPalette, 16, CHASER_BLOCK_LEN, &Black);
/* draw pixels in different colors from our block across the screen */
for (i = 0; i < MODEX_WIDTH; i++) {
```

```
            PlotModeX(i, 200, (i % CHASER_BLOCK_LEN) + 16);
            PlotModeX(i, 201, (i % CHASER_BLOCK_LEN) + 16);
            PlotModeX(i, 202, (i % CHASER_BLOCK_LEN) + 16);
    }
    /* grab a color from the VGA and stuff it into the first few */
    /* entries of our palette block */
    GetVGAPaletteEntry(2, &Green);
    FillPaletteBlock(StandardPalette, 16, 6, &Green);

    On = 0;
    BlinkCounter = 0;
    while (!kbhit()) {
        WaitVerticalRetraceStart();

        if (BlinkCounter == BLINK_RATE) {
            if (On) {
                    SetVGAPaletteEntry(4, &BlinkOn);
            }
            else {
                SetVGAPaletteEntry(4, &BlinkOff);
            }
            On = !On;
            BlinkCounter = 0;
        }
        else {
            BlinkCounter++;
        }

        /* make those "chaser lights" go! */
        SetVGAPaletteBlock(StandardPalette, 16, CHASER_BLOCK_LEN);
        RotatePaletteBlock(StandardPalette, 16, CHASER_BLOCK_LEN, -2);
    }

    /* clean up and exit */
    SetVGAMode(3);

    farfree(ShipPB);
    farfree(ShipLB);

    return 0;
}
```

The program starts by trying to detect a VGA and failing to run, with an error message, if none is found. The program then loads the spaceship bitmap from the SHIP1.PCX file, the one used in the previous chapter, and then converts it to planar bitmap format. Next, the program puts the VGA into Mode X and draws the spaceship bitmap.

After drawing the ship, the program places a copy of the default VGA palette in the **StandardPalette** array. We'll use this copy of the palette to create some of the effects.

The first effect we'll be incorporating is fading the palette to all white. The **FillPaletteBlock** function is used to fill the first 16 entries of **WhitePalette** array with the **RGB_TUPLE** corresponding to white (63, 63, 63). Next, **FadePaletteBlock** is used to fade the first 16 VGA palette entries between the standard VGA palette and the all-white palette over a three-second interval. We only have 16 entries because all the colors needed for the spaceship are contained in the first 16 entries.

The second effect we'll be adding to our program is fading the palette to all black. **FillPaletteBlock** is used to set the first 16 entries of a second palette array, **BlackPalette**, to all black. A fade is then performed between **WhitePalette** and **BlackPalette**. **WhitePalette** is used as the source since the palette is already in that state. The combination of the fade to white followed by the fade to black creates a nice effect.

After a delay of a couple seconds, the program then fades from all black back to the default VGA palette, which causes the spaceship image to fade in.

Remember that we haven't done anything with video memory all this time. Every byte in video memory has remained untouched since we drew the spaceship bitmap image.

Next, the program rotates the VGA palette. As I mentioned before, rotating the default palette produces some pretty strange results. The screen and different portions of the bitmap appear in strange, clashing colors.

Finally, the program creates a chaser light effect and blinks the light on the bottom of the spaceship bitmap. Since setting up the chaser light effect is the hardest part of the program, we'll take a closer look at this process.

The chaser lights are created by first setting a block of palette entries in the **StandardPalette** array to black. The block is **CHASER_BLOCK_LEN** in length and starts at index 16. Next, we use the **PlotModeX** function to plot a short vertical line of pixels, three pixels in height, all the way across the screen. The color index is altered to range from 16 to 16 + **CHASER_BLOCK_LEN** depending on the X coordinate.

The program then grabs an RGB tuple out of the default VGA palette. In this case, we use palette index number two, which corresponds to green in the default palette. We store this in an RGB tuple called, strangely enough, **Green**. The **Green RGB_TUPLE** is used to set six RGB values of the **StandardPalette** array to **Green**, starting at index 16.

The program then enters a loop, and on each iteration through the loop, it waits for a vertical retrace to start.

When a vertical retrace is detected, the loop continues. Every so often, palette entry number four is toggled between a light-red and a dark-red RGB tuple. The light at the bottom of the spaceship bitmap is drawn in color number four and this causes the light to appear to blink. The rate of blinking is determined by the **BLINK_RATE** constant.

Next, the block of palette entries starting at index 16 is copied from the **StandardPalette** array and these entries are rotated. The rotation causes the entries holding the **Green** color to rotate through this block of palette entries, which in turn causes different pixels on the screen to change to green or black and creates the chaser light effect. The image of motion is created, but as before, once the video memory has been set up correctly, only palette RGB values are being manipulated.

If we wanted to, we could use this chaser light effect to create the sensation of the spinning spaceship as we did in the previous chapter. The lights in the spaceship image could be drawn with different palette indexes very similar to the way we drew the vertical lines with different palette indexes for the chaser lights. Instead of the four bitmaps we used in the last chapter to create the spinning spaceship with a blinking light, we could use just one with some nifty palette effects!

The loop terminates when a keystroke is detected. The VGA is returned to text mode, the bitmap memory freed, and the program then terminates.

INTO THE ACTION

DETECTING COLLISIONS

When is a collision a collision and not just a near miss? Find out how to implement collision detection using the best, time-saving methods.

Now that we can draw objects onto the screen and move them around with the various animation techniques we have available, we'll need some way to detect whenever two or more objects collide. Collision detection is an important part of every fast-action video game, including *Alien Alley*. For instance, it's used to determine when missiles hit aliens, when the player's ship is hit by a missle and drops shield energy, or when an alien runs into the player and ends the game.

In this chapter, we'll take a look at the fundamental problem of collision detection. We need to perform collision detection for *every* frame of animation, so high performance collision detection will be important to allow us to keep up an acceptable animation frame rate. As we dive into this chapter, we'll investigate a few methods to make the collision detection in our game program run quickly. In particular, we'll investigate the use of bounding rectangles to speed up the fundamental collision detection test and various pruning techniques to reduce the number of comparisons that must be done between the objects on the screen.

 In this chapter we'll develop a module named COLLIDE.C, which contains a set of routines that help with collision detection.

I've provided a short program named COLLDEMO that demonstrates the use of the collision routines. COLLDEMO is really a very simple game, and utilizes many of the concepts we've explored in previous chapters, including animation, joystick control, and palette effects.

ANALYZING THE BASIC PROBLEM

Before we start to look at how to make collision detection run quickly, let's spend a little time examining the fundamental problem that occurs when you incorporate collision detection into a program. This way we'll be better equipped to evaluate solutions as we discuss them in later sections.

Imagine that you have a game with two objects on the screen. With only two objects on the screen, collision detection is fairly easy. Simply see if object #1 is touching object #2 or object #2 is touching object #1. (At this point, I'll leave the definition of "touching" a little vague. We'll discuss how we'll test for "touching" in later sections. Right now, the important thing to note is the number of collision checks that must be performed.) With two objects there are two checks. You'll quickly notice that we can eliminate one of the checks right off the bat; if object #1 is touching object #2, then object #2 is also touching object #1.

Imagine three objects on the screen. In this situation, three tests must be performed: #1 with #2, #1 with #3, and #2 with #3. Now imagine four objects. There are six tests: #1 with #2, #1 with #3, #1 with #4, #2 with #3, #2 with #4, and #3 with #4.

Do you notice the pattern forming here? Table 9.1 shows how many tests must be performed to check from 2 to 20 objects.

The table shows a fairly explosive growth rate. In moving from 2 objects to 20 objects, we added 189 tests that must be performed. If you study the table for a while you might be able to come up with the general formula for how many tests must be performed for each number of objects.

Table 9.1 *Objects and Collision Tests*

Number of Objects	Number of Collision Tests
2	1
3	3
4	6
5	10
6	15
7	21
8	28
9	36
10	45
15	105
20	190

But to keep you from thinking too hard, I've provided it for you here

```
(n² - n) / 2
```

where *n* is the number of objects. That is, given *n* objects, you can determine whether a given object collides with any other object by performing n^2 tests. Since we don't compare an object with itself, we eliminate *n* of the tests, giving us $n^2 - n$. Since we know that testing object #x with object #y is just the same as testing object #y with object #x, we eliminate half of the remaining tests, which gives us the final formula:

```
(n² - n) / 2
```

Computer scientists have devised a notation to easily describe the growth rates of problems like ours. The specific notation used is called "O-notation." O-notation is used to describe how a problem grows as the number of inputs or outputs, *n*, changes. In our case, *n* is the number of game objects on the screen for which we must calculate collision status. Computer scientists would say that our algorithm is $O(n^2)$, which we can read as "our algorithm is order n^2," or "our algorithm is big-oh n^2." This means that as *n* increases, the number of tests that must be performed increases roughly in the same way as n^2 and that the running time of our collision testing code will increase at roughly an n^2 rate.

Is this bad? Well, no, not strictly speaking. What it means is that having many objects on the screen at once can greatly slow our collision testing code if we aren't careful. Doubling the number of objects on the screen roughly quadruples the number of tests that we must perform. But it could be worse. Many algorithms found in computer science are $O(n^3)$ or $O(2^n)$. These algorithms increase their running time much more quickly than our collision test algorithm. Of course, it could also be better. Some algorithms are $O(n)$ or $O(1)$. An $O(n)$ algorithm increases at a constant rate depending on how many inputs are fed to it. Doubling the number of inputs doubles the running time of the algorithm. An $O(1)$ algorithm is pure joy. An $O(1)$ algorithm runs at the same rate no matter how many inputs are fed to it.

In the following sections, we'll examine ways to help us deal with the explosive growth rate that collision testing exhibits. The methods we examine won't change the fundamental nature of the algorithm, but they'll help us decrease the number of tests that we have to perform, making the process more manageable.

REDUCING TESTS WITH GAME RULES

We have already reduced a few of the tests in our collision problem. Remember that the basic collision detection algorithm has n^2 tests, but we reduced that to $(n^2 - n) / 2$ by recognizing that testing an object against itself was nonsensical and that testing object #x with object #y was the same as testing object #y with object #x.

We can further reduce the number of tests by recognizing that game rules often dictate which objects are "allowed" to collide. For instance, imagine we have a game with a spaceship flying around shooting at aliens. The game rules, as decided by the programmer, may say that aliens can't collide with each other. Further, it makes no sense to test the player's missiles with the player's spaceship, since the ship should never be able to collide with its own missiles. Likewise, alien missiles won't ever hit aliens. Player missiles won't hit other player missiles and alien missiles won't hit other alien missiles, although perhaps we should allow player missiles to hit other alien missiles.

To see how these rules can greatly reduce the amount of tests performed, let's work with some numbers. Using the previous example, let's say that we have one spaceship (the player's), five player missiles, 20 aliens, and 10 alien missiles all on the screen at once. That's 36 objects in total and would require 1296 (n^2) tests if every object had to be compared with every other object. Just using the test reduction techniques we discussed in the previous section we can reduce that to 630 tests (($n^2 - n$) / 2). But we can reduce this number even further if we take a look at the game rules.

Using the game rules, we can see that the player spaceship will have to be tested against each of the aliens and each of the alien missiles. That's 30 tests (20 aliens + 10 alien missiles). The player missiles have to be tested against the aliens and the alien missiles. Testing 5 player missiles with 20 aliens requires 100 tests. Testing 5 player missiles with the 10 alien missiles requires 50 tests. That's it. Since aliens, player missiles, and alien missiles don't collide with their same types, there is nothing more to do. The total number of tests we actually require is 180. We've managed to eliminate 450 tests, or 71%, of the 630 tests we would have had to do otherwise!

But the real advantage to this method can be seen when we decide to add just one more alien to the screen. Now we have 37 objects. Using our $(n^2 - n) / 2$ formula, this would require 666 tests, or an increase of 36 tests. Taking advantage of the game rules, we only require six additional tests (the alien with the player spaceship and with each of the five player missiles).

OTHER TEST-REDUCING TECHNIQUES

Using game rules to reduce tests is very simple and effective—when the game rules are fashioned to make it so. If the game rules require that every object be tested with every other, or nearly every other, then there are still going to be a lot of tests. The techniques described in this section can help reduce the number of tests even when the game rules don't help.

Sorting

When you have many sprites on the screen at one time, they are rarely located all at the same location. A fairly easy to way eliminate collision tests is to sort the sprites in ascending order using the X or Y axis coordinate of their left or top side as a key. To check for collisions, you simply traverse the sorted list, and for each sprite on the list, collision test it with the next few sprites following it in the list. You can stop testing a given sprite when you reach another sprite further down in the list that has a location with a key greater than the location of the first sprite plus its width or height. Boy, that's a mouthful. Let's examine this more closely.

Suppose we have five sprites, as detailed in Table 9.2. We have sorted them according to their X coordinates. When we go to test for collisions, we would start testing sprite #1 with all the other sprites in the list following it. So, we would test sprite #1 with sprite #2, then with sprite #3. When we got to sprite #4, we would stop, because sprite #4 is located at X coordinate 40, and sprite

Table 9.2 *Sprites Sorted in Ascending Order by X Coordinate*

Sprite Number	X Coordinate	Sprite Width
1	10	10
2	15	5
3	18	8
4	40	10
5	45	10

#1's right side is located at X coordinate 19 (X coordinate 10 + width of 10 - 1). Since every sprite after sprite #4 has an X coordinate greater than sprite #4, there is no need to check any further.

We would then continue with sprite #2, testing it with sprite #3, and then stopping when we reached sprite #4 because it is out of range. Sprite #3 would immediately stop when sprite #4 was reached. Sprite #4 would be tested with sprite #5 and then would stop because the end of the list was reached.

Note that the Y coordinate of each sprite is ignored for the purposes of sorting the sprites and deciding when to stop comparing sprites. The Y coordinate is used in the actual collision testing, however.

The total number of tests in this example was 4, which is less than the 10 our formula would predict. This method relies on the assumption that most of the time sprites are distributed across the screen. If the sprites are closely grouped together, however, this method will degenerate to the $(n^2 - n) / 2$ situation.

This example uses X coordinates, but you could just as easily sort the sprites by Y coordinate. Since the Y resolution of the screen is usually less, however, using the X coordinate helps to spread out the sprites—in most situations. Before using either coordinate axis for this method, you should examine your sprites and screen size to determine which axis will give you better results.

The Sector Method

The sector method is similar to the sorting method in philosophy. Like the sorting method, the sector method tries to eliminate collision tests by only testing a sprite with those other sprites that are near it and could possibly be intersecting it.

The sector method divides the screen up into a grid of "sectors." In the simplest case, the screen is divided into quadrants. For each sprite you determine which sector, or sectors, it is located in and then test it only against the other sprites in the bin.

For instance, Figure 9.1 shows six sprites located on a screen that has been divided into 16 sectors, four horizontally and four vertically. Sprites #1 and #2 are located in the same sector and would be tested against each other. Sprites #4 and #5 are also in the same sector and would be tested. Sprite #3 is all alone in its sector and so would not be tested against anything.

The primary difficulty of the sector method is in handling sprites like #6; that is sprites that fall into more than one sector. As long as your sprites are smaller than the sectors, a single sprite can only be located in one to four sectors. This allows the problem to be dealt with more easily. The locations of the corners of the sprites can be used to determine which sector the sprite is located in.

When choosing a number of sectors to use both vertically and horizontally, try to choose powers of 2 (2, 4, 8, 16, etc.). This approach makes determining which sector a sprite is located in much easier because you can simply divide its coordinate values by a power of 2. Dividing by a power of 2 is the same as left-shifting the coordinate value, so no slow division instructions or routines need to be invoked. The number of sectors in the vertical direction does not have to be the same as the number of sectors in the horizontal direction. Dividing by 16 in the horizontal direction on a 320-pixel wide screen allows sprites with a maximum width of 20 pixels. Dividing by eight in the vertical direction on a 240-pixel high screen gives a maximum sprite height of 30.

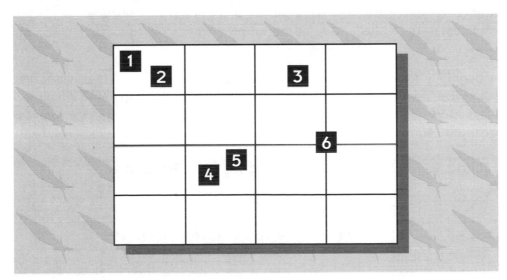

Figure 9.1   *You can use the sector method to test sprites.*

Hybrid Techniques

If you need to get really complex, consider using the sorting or sector methods described previously in conjunction with the game rule reduction technique. For instance, if you frequently end up with many sprites located in the same sector when you're using the sector technique, use game rules to reduce the number of tests among the sprites located in each bin.

> *Note:* *Don't automatically think that the hybrid technique is the best technique to use. Like any other optimization, techniques for reducing collision tests work well in some instances but not in others. If you only have a few sprites on the screen at one time, consider just testing them exhaustively or using the game rule reduction method.*

The sorting method and the sector method each have overhead in sorting the sprites or in determining in which sector a sprite is located. That overhead may not be worth it in cases where the number of tests is not that large. Even if the complex method is faster, see if your game really needs it. If your animation loop is running at full speed with a simple technique, why use a more complex one? It won't be saving you time and you'll only have to debug it.

COLLISION TESTING WITH BOUNDING RECTANGLES

Now that we've worked on reducing the numbers of sprites that have to be collision tested against one another, let's consider how we'll be doing the testing. Although we now have only a small number of tests, we still want each test to run quickly. One of the simplest ways to test for sprite collisions is to use bounding rectangles.

A bounding rectangle is the smallest rectangle that encloses all the pixels of a sprite. The bounding rectangle can be calculated from the position of the upper-left corner of the sprite and its width and height. COLLIDE.C contains the function **ComputeBoundingRect**, shown in Listing 9.1, that performs this calculation.

Listing 9.1 The ComputeBoundingRect Function

```
/*
    Function: ComputeBoundingRect
    Description:
        Calculates the bounding rectangle for a sprite given its
        position, origin offset, width, and height.
*/
void ComputeBoundingRect
```

```
    (
    int x,
    int y,
    int OriginX,
    int OriginY,
    int Width,
    int Height,
    RECT * Rect
    )
{
    int Top;
    int Left;
    int Bottom;
    int Right;

    assert(Rect != NULL);

    Top            = y - OriginY;
    Left           = x - OriginX;
    Bottom         = Top + Height - 1;
    Right          = Left + Width - 1;

    Rect->Top      = Top;
    Rect->Left     = Left;
    Rect->Bottom   = Bottom;
    Rect->Right    = Right;
}
```

Remember that the origin of the bitmap is actually specified by the X and Y coordinate values. The **OriginX** and **OriginY** parameters are used to determine the upper-left corner of the bitmap, given the X and Y coordinates. Although **OriginX** and **OriginY** have typically been zero in our past examples, *Alien Alley* will use some sprites where this is not the case.

The bounding rectangle is returned from **ComputeBoundingRect** in the rectangle structure pointed to by the **Rect** parameter.

Actually testing to see whether two bounding rectangles overlap is about as easy as computing them in the first place. The function shown in Listing 9.2, **CollisionTestRect**, also from COLLIDE.C, is used to perform the comparison.

Listing 9.2   The CollisionTestRect Function

```
/*
    Function: CollisionTestRect
    Description:
        Tests two bounding rectangles to see if they overlap.
        Returns TRUE if so, FALSE otherwise.
*/
BOOL CollisionTestRect(RECT * r1, RECT * r2)
```

```
{
    assert(r1->Left <= r1->Right);
    assert(r1->Top <= r1->Bottom);
    assert(r2->Left <= r2->Right);
    assert(r2->Top <= r2->Bottom);

    if (r1->Left > r2->Right || r2->Left > r1->Right ||
        r1->Top > r2->Bottom || r2->Top > r1->Bottom) {
        return FALSE;
    }
    else {
        return TRUE;
    }
}
```

It's important to note that bounding rectangles won't produce a perfect collision test unless the object they enclose is also rectangular. In most cases, the bounding rectangle will enclose a set of transparent pixels that fill in the "corners" of the actual object within the bounding rectangle. Technically, these pixels are not part of the object but will be considered so for the purpose of testing collisions. In some cases, a collision might be indicated between two objects when only a few of their transparent pixels have actually intersected.

In spite of this lack of precision, bounding rectangles are really quite useful for very quick collision testing. They are easy to generate for a given object, and the testing is very simple. In many cases, bounding rectangles will suffice as the sole testing method. Even if an object has a complex and non-rectangular shape, multiple rectangles more closely estimating the true outline of the object can be calculated and used for collision testing. Sometimes a better collision test is needed, however.

BITMAP TESTING

Bounding rectangles lack precision. A rectangle is a first order approximation of an object's true shape, but an especially complex shape can be difficult to deal with. If you find yourself trying to approximate an object's shape with nearly as many rectangles as there are pixels in the object, consider using bitmap testing instead. Bitmap testing is much slower than rectangle testing but provides an exact indication of when two objects have collided. Bitmap testing can be performed in many ways, but there are a couple popular methods that I'll describe here.

Bitmap testing can be performed during a bitblt. While copying pixels to video memory, the destination pixel locations are first read to determine if they contain the pixels of a previously drawn object. If so, a collision has occurred. The difficulty now is to determine which object the pixels belong to. If there are few enough objects on the screen, each object can be assigned its own block of color indexes from the color palette. By determining which color index has just collided with, a program can determine which object the collision pixel belongs to.

A second method involves storing a collision bitmap in memory for every object. A collision bitmap is a bit-per-pixel representation of the solid portions of a bitmap. That is, the solid portions of a bitmap are stored as a 1 bit, eight pixels per byte. Testing for collisions can then be performed by noting the upper-left corner of each bitmap and then shifting and ANDing bytes of the two collision bitmaps together. Whenever an AND operation produces a non-zero result, the two objects have collided.

The two functions shown in Listings 9.3 and 9.4 implement the second bitmap collision testing method. Both routines can be found in COLLIDE.C. The **COLLISION_MAP** data structure is found in COLLIDE.H and is defined here:

```
typedef struct {
    UINT16  Width;
    UINT16  Height;
    UINT8   Data;
} COLLISION_MAP;
```

CreateCollisionMap is responsible for generating the **COLLISION_MAP** from a **LINEAR_BITMAP**. The **COLLISION_MAP** contains a set bit for each pixel in the source bitmap that is not transparent. Since a **COLLISION_MAP** must represent pixels in groups of eight, the routine computes a width that is at least that of the source bitmap and then pads the extra bits with 0.

Listing 9.3   The CreateCollisionMap Function

```
/*
    Function: CreateCollisionMap
    Description:
        Given a far pointer to a LINEAR_BITMAP, the function returns
        a far pointer to a COLLISION_MAP derived from the LINEAR_BITMAP.
        All "solid" pixels from the LINEAR_BITMAP have a corresponding
        bit set to 1 in the COLLISION_MAP while "transparent" pixels
        have a corresponding bit set to 0.
*/
COLLISION_MAP far * CreateCollisionMap(LINEAR_BITMAP far * LinearBM)
{
    UINT16 CollisionMapWidth;
```

```c
    COLLISION_MAP far * CollisionMap;
    UINT8 far * CollisionMapData;
    UINT8 far * BitmapData;
    UINT16 WidthCounter;
    UINT16 HeightCounter;
    UINT8 WorkingData;
    int BitCounter;

    assert(LinearBM != NULL);
    assert(LinearBM->Width != 0);
    assert(LinearBM->Height != 0);

    /* compute size of collision map, allocate, and initialize */
    CollisionMapWidth = ((LinearBM->Width - 1) / 8) + 1;
    CollisionMap = (COLLISION_MAP far *) farmalloc(sizeof(COLLISION_MAP) +
        (CollisionMapWidth * LinearBM->Height) - 1);
    CollisionMap->Width     = CollisionMapWidth;
    CollisionMap->Height    = LinearBM->Height;

    /* initialize data pointers */
    CollisionMapData    = (UINT8 far *) &(CollisionMap->Data);
    BitmapData          = (UINT8 far *) &(LinearBM->Data);

    /* interate over all pixels in bitmap and fill in collision map */
    for (HeightCounter = 0; HeightCounter < LinearBM->Height;
        HeightCounter++) {

        WorkingData = 0;
        BitCounter = 7;
        for (WidthCounter = 0; WidthCounter < LinearBM->Width;
            WidthCounter++) {

            if (*BitmapData++ != 0) {
                WorkingData |= 1 << BitCounter;
            }
            BitCounter--;
            if (BitCounter < 0) {
                *CollisionMapData++ = WorkingData;
                WorkingData = 0;
                BitCounter = 7;
            }
        }

        /* do final save of working data at end of line unless */
        /* it's just been done */
        if (BitCounter != 7) {
            *CollisionMapData++ = WorkingData;
        }
    }

    return CollisionMap;
}
```

CollisionTestBitmap actually compares two bitmaps to each other. The relative placement of the two bitmap rectangles is computed and then individual bytes from the two **COLLISION_MAP**s are compared against one another to see if they overlap. If they do, the function returns TRUE; otherwise it returns FALSE.

Listing 9.4   The CollisionTestBitmap Function

```
/*
    Function: CollisionTestBitmap
    Description:
        Tests two objects using COLLISION_MAPs.  The upper-left corner
        of each object is specified with (x1, y1) and (x2, y2).
*/
BOOL CollisionTestBitmap
    (
    COLLISION_MAP far * Object1,
    COLLISION_MAP far * Object2,
    int x1,
    int y1,
    int x2,
    int y2
    )
{
    UINT8 far * Data1;
    UINT8 far * Data2;
    COLLISION_MAP far * SwapTemp;
    int DeltaX;
    int DeltaY;
    int Shift;
    int Skip;
    UINT16 WidthCounter1;
    UINT16 WidthCounter2;
    UINT16 HeightCounter1;
    UINT16 HeightCounter2;
    UINT8 Object1Data;
    UINT8 ShiftRegister;
    UINT8 OldObject2Data;
    UINT8 NewObject2Data;
    UINT8 FinalObject2Data;

    assert(Object1 != NULL);
    assert(Object2 != NULL);

    DeltaX = x2 - x1;
    DeltaY = y2 - y1;
    /* swap objects to make the algorithm work */
    if (DeltaX < 0) {
        SwapTemp    = Object1;
        Object1     = Object2;
        Object2     = SwapTemp;
        DeltaX      = -DeltaX;
```

```
        DeltaY        = -DeltaY;
    }

    Data1            = (UINT8 far *) &(Object1->Data);
    Data2            = (UINT8 far *) &(Object2->Data);

    HeightCounter1  = 0;
    HeightCounter2  = 0;

    /* skip rows off the object with the least Y-value */
    if (DeltaY > 0) {
        Data1 += Object1->Width * DeltaY;
        HeightCounter1 += DeltaY;
    }
    else if (DeltaY < 0) {
        Data2 += Object2->Width * -DeltaY;
        HeightCounter2 -= DeltaY;
    }

    Shift   = DeltaX % 8;   /* amount to shift object 2 data to right */
    Skip    = DeltaX / 8;   /* number of bytes to skip at beginning of */
                            /*    object 1 data line */

    while (HeightCounter1 < Object1->Height &&
        HeightCounter2 < Object2->Height) {

        /* potentially skip a few bytes 'cause obj 1 is to left of obj 2 */
        WidthCounter1   = Skip;
        Data1           += Skip;

        WidthCounter2  = 0;
        OldObject2Data  = 0;

        while (WidthCounter1 < Object1->Width &&
            WidthCounter2 < Object2->Width) {

            /* get data */
            Object1Data     = *Data1++;
            NewObject2Data  = *Data2++;
            /* shift object 2 data to correct delta X differential */
            ShiftRegister   = ((UINT16) OldObject2Data << 8) |
                (UINT16) NewObject2Data;
            ShiftRegister   >>= Shift;
            FinalObject2Data = ShiftRegister & 0xFF;

            /* return if we have a collision */
            if (Object1Data & FinalObject2Data) {
                return TRUE;
            }

            OldObject2Data = NewObject2Data;
            WidthCounter1++;
            WidthCounter2++;
        }
```

```
        /* correct pointers at end of line */
        Data1 += Object1->Width - WidthCounter1;
        Data2 += Object2->Width - WidthCounter2;

        HeightCounter1++;
        HeightCounter2++;
    }

    /* we got through all that with no collision */
    return FALSE;
}
```

The general problem with bitmap testing is that it is very slow in comparison to testing bounding rectangles. Even though **CollisionTestBitmap** is written in C and could be speeded up significantly by translating it into assembly language, it will still be slower than rectangle testing by a few orders of magnitude. Performing bitmap testing for all tests, even with the test-reducing strategies that we looked at in previous sections, can slow down an otherwise fast game. A compromise between perfect testing and speed can be reached by combining rectangle testing and bitmap testing. Recognize that in many games, things won't be colliding during most animation frames. There is no point in doing a detailed check when it probably won't indicate a collision anyway. Why not first start off with a simple rectangle test? For those in-stances when a rectangle test indicates a collision, you can then perform a more detailed bitmap test between the two objects. This approach allows most of the tests to run quickly, and only a few spend time in the more complex bitmap testing procedure.

Of the two bitmap methods we discussed earlier, the second is usually pre-ferred over the first. The first method requires the program to read video memory or an offscreen display buffer while drawing each sprite. This forces the bitblt routine to be much slower for each sprite. Additionally, because the testing code is so closely linked to the drawing code, it is hard to use bound-ing rectangles to initially test for collisions and then use bitmap testing when the rectangle test gives a positive result. The first method virtually forces you to use bitmap testing for all tests.

Collision Testing Demonstration

PROJECT The program COLLDEMO, shown in Listing 9.5, demonstrates the use of the collision routines in COLLIDE.C. The program bounces 15 magenta balls around the screen while the user moves a spaceship using the joystick. Whenever the spaceship and a ball collide, the program turns on the PC speaker for the duration of the collision.

Compiling and Linking:

You can compile the COLLDEMO program using the Borland C++ 3.1 IDE by typing "bc colldemo.prj" and then selecting Compile | Make from the menus. If you would rather use the command line compiler, convert the COLLDEMO.PRJ file to a makefile using the PRJ2MAK program supplied with Borland C++ 3.1. Type "prj2mak colldemo.prj" to create the COLLDEMO.MAK and COLLDEMO.CFG files.

If you are using Borland C++ 4.0, choose Project | Open Project from the IDE menus. Open the COLLDEMO.PRJ file. Borland C++ will convert the version 3.1 .PRJ file to a version 4.0 .IDE file. Compile and link the program by choosing Project | Make All from the IDE menus.

The demonstration uses both bounding rectangle and bitmap tests. The bitmap tests are only performed whenever the bounding rectangle test indicates that a collision might be occurring. Further, the number of tests is reduced to the minimum by not checking for collisions between the balls themselves. This means that only collisions between the spaceship and the balls are checked, giving us only one test per ball.

COLLDEMO runs in Mode X and uses the page-flipping animation technique we saw in Chapter 7. The joystick routines are from Chapter 4. Finally, in a fit of hysteria, I also made the light on the bottom of the spaceship blink using the same bit of palette animation we saw in Chapter 8. We're getting there. COLLDEMO has many of the attributes of a real game!

Listing 9.5   COLLDEMO.C

```
/* File: COLLDEMO.C
** Description:
**    Demonstration of collision routines.
** Copyright:
**    Copyright 1994, David G. Roberts
*/

#include <alloc.h>
#include <assert.h>
#include <conio.h>
#include <dos.h>
#include <stdio.h>
#include <stdlib.h>
#include "gamedefs.h"
#include "animate.h"
#include "bitblt.h"
#include "collide.h"
#include "jstick.h"
#include "palette.h"
```

```c
#include "pcx.h"
#include "retrace.h"
#include "setmodex.h"
#include "vga.h"

/* types */
struct SPRITE_tag {
    int     x;
    int     y;
    int     vx;
    int     vy;
    int     OldX[2];
    int     OldY[2];
    BOOL    Erase[2];
    BOOL    Draw;
    PLANAR_BITMAP far * Bitmap;
    PLANAR_BITMAP far * EraseBitmap;
    COLLISION_MAP far * CollisionMap;
    RECT    Bounds;
};

typedef struct SPRITE_tag SPRITE;

/* constants */
#define NUM_BALLS       15

#define PAGE0_OFFSET    0
#define PAGE1_OFFSET    0x4B00

#define SOUND_FREQUENCY 440

#define ERASE_COLOR     16

#define BLINK_RATE      15

/* globals */
SPRITE Ship;
SPRITE Ball[NUM_BALLS];
int HiddenPage;
UINT16 Offset[2];
UINT16 BallWidth;
UINT16 BallHeight;
UINT16 ShipWidth;
UINT16 ShipHeight;
UINT16 JsXmin;
UINT16 JsYmin;
UINT16 JsXmid;
UINT16 JsYmid;
UINT16 JsXmax;
UINT16 JsYmax;
JOYSTICK_STATE JsState;
UINT16 XRightThird;
UINT16 XLeftThird;
```

```
UINT16 YBottomThird;
UINT16 YTopThird;

/*
    Function: CalibrateJsMidpoint
    Description:
        Calibrates a joystick's range using the midpoint method.
        Read's the value of the joystick at the time it is
        called and computes a min and max range from this.
        Note that this assumes that the joystick is centered
        when the routine is called.
*/
void CalibrateJsMidpoint
    (
    JOYSTICK_STATE * JsState,
    UINT16 * Xmin,
    UINT16 * Ymin,
    UINT16 * Xmid,
    UINT16 * Ymid,
    UINT16 * Xmax,
    UINT16 * Ymax
    )
{
    assert(JsState != NULL);
    assert(Xmin != NULL);
    assert(Ymin != NULL);
    assert(Xmid != NULL);
    assert(Ymid != NULL);
    assert(Xmax != NULL);
    assert(Ymax != NULL);

    /* read midpoint value */
    ReadJoysticks(JsState);
    *Xmid = JsState->JsAxisAX;
    *Ymid = JsState->JsAxisAY;

    /* assume min coordinate is (0,0) and max is twice midpoint */
    *Xmin = *Ymin = 0;

    *Xmax = 2 * *Xmid;
    *Ymax = 2 * *Ymid;
}


/*
    Function: UpdateBallPositions
    Description:
        Bounces the balls around the screen.
*/
void UpdateBallPositions(void)
{
    int i;

    for (i = 0; i < NUM_BALLS; i++) {
```

```
        if (Ball[i].Erase[HiddenPage]) {
            Ball[i].x += Ball[i].vx;
            Ball[i].y += Ball[i].vy;
            if ((Ball[i].x < 0) || ((Ball[i].x + BallWidth) >=
                MODEX_WIDTH)) {
                Ball[i].vx = -Ball[i].vx;
                Ball[i].x += 2 * Ball[i].vx;
            }
            if ((Ball[i].y < 0) || ((Ball[i].y + BallHeight) >=
                MODEX_HEIGHT)) {
                Ball[i].vy = -Ball[i].vy;
                Ball[i].y += 2 * Ball[i].vy;
            }
        }
        ComputeBoundingRect(Ball[i].x, Ball[i].y, Ball[i].Bitmap->OriginX,
            Ball[i].Bitmap->OriginY, BallWidth, BallHeight,
            &(Ball[i].Bounds));
    }
}

/*
    Function: UpdateShipPosition
    Description:
        Moves the spaceship around the screen.  The velocity of
        the ship is dependent on the position of the joystick.
*/
void UpdateShipPosition(void)
{
    if (Ship.Erase[HiddenPage]) {
        ReadJoysticks(&JsState);
        if (JsState.JsAxisAX > XRightThird) {
            Ship.vx = 2;
        }
        else if (JsState.JsAxisAX > XLeftThird) {
            Ship.vx = 0;
        }
        else {
            Ship.vx = -2;
        }
        if (JsState.JsAxisAY > YBottomThird) {
            Ship.vy = 2;
        }
        else if (JsState.JsAxisAY > YTopThird) {
            Ship.vy = 0;
        }
        else {
            Ship.vy = -2;
        }
        Ship.x += Ship.vx;
        Ship.y += Ship.vy;
        if ((Ship.x < 0) || ((Ship.x + ShipWidth) >=
            MODEX_WIDTH)) {
            Ship.x -= Ship.vx;
```

```
        }
        if ((Ship.y < 0) || ((Ship.y + ShipHeight) >=
            MODEX_HEIGHT)) {
            Ship.y -= Ship.vy;
        }
    }
    ComputeBoundingRect(Ship.x, Ship.y, Ship.Bitmap->OriginX,
        Ship.Bitmap->OriginY, ShipWidth, ShipHeight,
        &(Ship.Bounds));
}

/*
    Function: CheckCollisions
    Description:
        Determine if there has been a collision between a ball and
        the ship.  If so, turn on the speaker to sound the alarm!
*/
void CheckCollisions(void)
{
    int i;

    for (i = 0; i < NUM_BALLS; i++) {
        /* the following statement uses C's short-circuit boolean */
        /* expression capability.  The CollisionTestBitmap */
        /* function call is executed if and only if the */
        /* CollisionTestRect function returns TRUE.  If */
        /* CollisionTestRect returns FALSE, the CollisionTestBitmap */
        /* call is short circuited and not executed. */
        if (CollisionTestRect(&(Ship.Bounds), &(Ball[i].Bounds)) &&
            CollisionTestBitmap(Ship.CollisionMap, Ball[i].CollisionMap,
            Ship.Bounds.Left, Ship.Bounds.Top, Ball[i].Bounds.Left,
            Ball[i].Bounds.Top)) {

            sound(SOUND_FREQUENCY);
            break; /* we know it collided, so don't check further */
        }
    }
    /* if no collisions, turn off sound */
    if (i == NUM_BALLS) {
        nosound();
    }
}

/*
    Function: Erase
    Description:
        Erase all the sprites from the screen.
*/
void Erase(void)
{
    int i;

    for (i = 0; i < NUM_BALLS; i++) {
        if (Ball[i].Erase[HiddenPage]) {
```

```
            BltPlanar(Ball[i].EraseBitmap, Ball[i].OldX[HiddenPage],
                Ball[i].OldY[HiddenPage], Offset[HiddenPage]);
        }
    }
    if (Ship.Erase[HiddenPage]) {
        BltPlanar(Ship.EraseBitmap, Ship.OldX[HiddenPage],
            Ship.OldY[HiddenPage], Offset[HiddenPage]);
    }

}

/*
    Function: Draw
    Description:
        Draw all the sprites on the screen at their new coordinates.
*/
void Draw(void)
{
    int i;

    for (i = 0; i < NUM_BALLS; i++) {
        if (Ball[i].Draw) {
            BltPlanar(Ball[i].Bitmap, Ball[i].x, Ball[i].y,
                Offset[HiddenPage]);
            Ball[i].OldX[HiddenPage]    = Ball[i].x;
            Ball[i].OldY[HiddenPage]    = Ball[i].y;
            Ball[i].Erase[HiddenPage]   = TRUE;
        }
    }
    if (Ship.Draw) {
        BltPlanar(Ship.Bitmap, Ship.x, Ship.y, Offset[HiddenPage]);
        Ship.OldX[HiddenPage]   = Ship.x;
        Ship.OldY[HiddenPage]   = Ship.y;
        Ship.Erase[HiddenPage]  = TRUE;
    }
}

/*
    Function: CreateEraseBitmap
    Description:
        Takes a bitmap as input and fills it with black.
*/
void CreateEraseBitmap(LINEAR_BITMAP far * Input)
{
    UINT8 far * Data;
    UINT16 Length;

    Length = Input->Width * Input->Height;
    Data = (UINT8 far *) &(Input->Data);

    while (Length > 0) {
        *Data++ = ERASE_COLOR;
        Length--;
```

```
    }
}

int main()
{
    LINEAR_BITMAP far * TempLinear;
    PLANAR_BITMAP far * BallBitmap;
    PLANAR_BITMAP far * BallEraseBitmap;
    COLLISION_MAP far * BallCollisionMap;
    RGB_TUPLE BlinkOff = {42, 0, 0};
    RGB_TUPLE BlinkOn = {63, 21, 21};
    int i;
    int BlinkCounter;
    BOOL On;

    /* detect VGA */
    if (!DetectVGA()) {
        printf("You must have a VGA to run this program.\n");
        return 1;
    }

    /* detect and calibrate joystick */
    SenseJoysticks(&JsState);
    JsState.JsMask &= 0x3; /* enable only A axes */
    if (JsState.JsMask == 0) {
        printf("You must have a joystick to run this program.\n");
        return 1;
    }
    CalibrateJsMidpoint(&JsState, &JsXmin, &JsYmin, &JsXmid, &JsYmid,
        &JsXmax, &JsYmax);
    XRightThird    = (2 * JsXmax) / 3;
    XLeftThird     = JsXmax / 3;
    YBottomThird   = (2 * JsYmax) / 3;
    YTopThird      = JsYmax / 3;

    /* init page offsets */
    Offset[0] = PAGE0_OFFSET;
    Offset[1] = PAGE1_OFFSET;
    HiddenPage = 1;

    /* initialize ball sprites */
    TempLinear = LoadPCX("BALL.PCX", NULL);
    if (TempLinear == NULL) {
        printf("ERROR: Can't load ball bitmap\n");
        return 1;
    }
    BallWidth   = TempLinear->Width;
    BallHeight  = TempLinear->Height;
    BallBitmap  = LinearToPlanar(TempLinear);
    if (BallBitmap == NULL) {
        printf("ERROR: Can't load ball bitmap\n");
        return 1;
    }
```

```
BallCollisionMap = CreateCollisionMap(TempLinear);
if (BallCollisionMap == NULL) {
    printf("ERROR: Can't load ball bitmap\n");
    return 1;
}
CreateEraseBitmap(TempLinear);
BallEraseBitmap = LinearToPlanar(TempLinear);
farfree(TempLinear);
if (BallEraseBitmap == NULL) {
    printf("ERROR: Can't load ball bitmap\n");
    return 1;
}
for (i = 0; i < NUM_BALLS; i++) {
    Ball[i].x          = random(MODEX_WIDTH - BallWidth);
    Ball[i].y          = random(MODEX_HEIGHT - BallHeight);
    Ball[i].vx         = random(2) + 1;
    Ball[i].vy         = random(2) + 1;
    if (random(2) == 1) {
        Ball[i].vx = - Ball[i].vx;
    }
    if (random(2) == 1) {
        Ball[i].vy = - Ball[i].vy;
    }
    Ball[i].Bitmap      = BallBitmap;
    Ball[i].EraseBitmap = BallEraseBitmap;
    Ball[i].CollisionMap= BallCollisionMap;
    Ball[i].Draw        = TRUE;
    Ball[i].Erase[0]    = FALSE;
    Ball[i].Erase[1]    = FALSE;
}

/* load ship sprite */
TempLinear  = LoadPCX("SHIP1.PCX", NULL);
if (TempLinear == NULL) {
    printf("ERROR: Can't load ship bitmap\n");
    return 1;
}
ShipWidth   = TempLinear->Width;
ShipHeight  = TempLinear->Height;
Ship.Bitmap         = LinearToPlanar(TempLinear);
if (Ship.Bitmap == NULL) {
    printf("ERROR: Can't load ship bitmap\n");
    return 1;
}
Ship.CollisionMap = CreateCollisionMap(TempLinear);
if (Ship.CollisionMap == NULL) {
    printf("ERROR: Can't load ship bitmap\n");
    return 1;
}
CreateEraseBitmap(TempLinear);
Ship.EraseBitmap    = LinearToPlanar(TempLinear);
if (Ship.EraseBitmap == NULL) {
    printf("ERROR: Can't load ship bitmap\n");
```

```
        return 1;
    }
    farfree(TempLinear);

    Ship.x        = MODE13H_WIDTH / 2;
    Ship.y        = MODE13H_HEIGHT /2;
    Ship.Draw     = TRUE;
    Ship.Erase[0] = FALSE;
    Ship.Erase[1] = FALSE;

    SetModeX();

    BlinkCounter = 0;
    On = TRUE;

    while (!kbhit()) {
        /* update positions */
        UpdateBallPositions();
        UpdateShipPosition();

        /* check collisions */
        CheckCollisions();

        /* erase old stuff */
        Erase();

        /* draw new stuff */
        Draw();

        /* flip page */
        PageFlip(Offset[HiddenPage]);
        HiddenPage ^= 1; /* flip HiddenPage to other state */

        /* blink the space ship light */
        BlinkCounter++;
        if (BlinkCounter == BLINK_RATE) {
            if (On) {
                    SetVGAPaletteEntry(4, &BlinkOn);
            }
            else {
                SetVGAPaletteEntry(4, &BlinkOff);
            }
            On = !On;
            BlinkCounter = 0;
        }
    }

    /* shut off sound just in case we were collding with a ball */
    /* when the key was hit */
    nosound();

    /* clean up keys, return to text mode, free memory, and exit */
    getch();
```

```
SetVGAMode(0x3);

farfree(Ship.Bitmap);
farfree(Ship.EraseBitmap);
farfree(Ship.CollisionMap);
farfree(BallBitmap);
farfree(BallEraseBitmap);
farfree(BallCollisionMap);

return 0;
}
```

Although COLLDEMO runs pretty fast—even with quite a few balls on a slower computer—we'll want to learn how to control the speed of a game before we dive into *Alien Alley*. In the next chapter that's just what we'll do!

CONTROLLING GAME SPEED

Now that you have your animation and game action working, it's time to learn how to control the speed of your game.

Have you ever looked down at the front of your computer case and wondered why the turbo switch is there? Why is it that every computer has this switch that everybody always leaves in the "fast" position? The switch is an example of great marketing. You see, it's really misnamed. It ought to be named the "slow" switch.

In the old days, when PCs were young, there was only one model. Programming wasn't too sophisticated then, and everybody used software timing loops in their code to slow programs down to a reasonable speed. If the game moved too quickly, for instance, well they just put:

```
for (i=0; i < 10000; i++);
```

into the code to burn a few processor cycles every so often. After developing a game, the pro grammer could alter the speed of it, and hence the difficulty, simply by changing the limit value to a counter. If the game was too easy, just speed it up. If it was too difficult, just slow it down.

When there was only one model of PC, this worked well. Everybody's computer ran at the same speed and life was good. Problems cropped up almost immediately, however, as newer PC models were brought to market, each using a more powerful microprocessor. As microprocessor clock rates climbed, the timing loops in all the software ran faster. Many game programs were unplayable on the newer machines. To help allow users to run old software that included timing loops, computer manufacturers put a switch on the front of the PC to slow the system down to near the original PC clock rate. It wasn't a perfect solution—the slow rate wasn't exactly the rate of the original PC—but it made things playable. In a stroke of marketing genius' someone decided to call it the "turbo" switch and make users think that the computer sped up, not slowed down. (Marketing people always see the glass as half-full, not half-empty.)

Since that time programmers have become a lot more sophisticated about how to control the speed of their software. In this chapter, we'll examine some of the techniques that are available to ensure that our games don't become unplayable when faster processors are developed to run them. Specifically, we'll learn about the various timing references in the PC, including the vertical retrace and the system clock timer, and how to synchronize the main animation loop of our game with one of them. We'll find out how to reprogram the system timer for different rates and how to generate an interrupt every time a vertical retrace occurs.

 This chapter will develop the TIMER.C and VRSYNC.C modules. These modules contain routines for reprogramming the PC system timer rate, intercepting the system timer interrupt, and synchronizing the system timer with the VGA's vertical retrace. Using the routines in these modules, we can limit a program's speed on all computers such that it doesn't become unplayable as more advanced PC processors are brought to market.

SYNCHRONIZING TO VERTICAL RETRACE

In Chapter 7 we learned about animation. We investigated several ways to create flicker-free animation. We learned that the general method used to eliminate flicker was to update the VGA display RAM during a vertical retrace period. A side effect of performing all our display RAM modifications during vertical retrace is that we synchronize each display frame with the vertical refresh rate of the VGA.

The VGA vertical refresh rate is a tightly controlled timing source. Vertical refresh in Mode X is standardized to occur 60 times per second, or 60 Hz. Mode 13h and Mode Y operate at 70 Hz. It may not have been obvious at the time, but when we synchronized our main animation loop with vertical retrace, we also provided ourselves with a game-speed limiting timer. Even if we run our game on a fast processor, animation frames will only be created at a rate of 60 or 70 frames per second or less. We can never exceed this rate, unless we decouple our main animation loop from the vertical retrace timing.

Of course, we can go slower than 60 fps, taking Mode X as an example. If we run our program on a slower processor, it might take more than 1/60th of a second to generate a single frame of animation. When this occurs, the program will ignore every other vertical retrace and the game will run at 30 fps.

Herein lies the problem. What if our game is synchronized to the VGA vertical retrace but is still only able to achieve 30 fps on today's fastest processor? What will occur when a faster processor is created tomorrow? Unfortunately, the game will speed up. As soon as a processor is developed that will execute our main animation loop in under 1/60th of a second, we'll generate one frame of animation per vertical retrace and our game will run at 60 fps—twice it's normal speed.

The good news is that it will never run faster than 60 fps, even if faster processors are developed. This means that if our game runs at 60 fps on today's low-end machine, we have no problem. Unfortunately, this is a rare occurrence. Since 30-fps animation is still good quality, most programmers are inclined to use extra processing power to add more features to a game and let its display rate fall to 30, or even 20, fps.

One way to correct this is to specify that the game must be run on a high-end, rather than low-end system. The "correct" speed of the game is tuned for the high-end system and when it is run on a low-end system, the gameplay seems slower. This can be an adequate solution, as today's low-end machine is tomorrow's antique, and people are likely to upgrade to faster processors over time. There is a short-term downside, however. We either force current owners of low-end systems to upgrade immediately, play on their current systems with poor performance, or forgo the enjoyment of our exciting production. In the business world this is called "limiting your market," and it is something that game companies hate to do. It is a rare game that holds a customer's attention so long that they are willing to revisit it after they have upgraded their system to a faster processor. By this time there are new games competing for the customer's attention and the sale of the older game is unlikely.

Fortunately, we can do other things to help us with our timing problem.

SYNCHRONIZING TO THE SYSTEM CLOCK

When our animation rate falls below 60 or 70 fps on today's low-end machine, we need to tune the game to run at the reduced rate and use a timing source other than the VGA vertical retrace to keep the game from speeding up when run on a faster processor. Fortunately, another timing source does exist in the PC—the system timer.

The PC/AT contains an 8254 timer chip that is used as a general system timer. The 8254 chip is a revision of the 8253 used in the original PC and XT. The 8254 includes slightly more functionality than the 8253 but is backward compatible from a software standpoint. Both the 8253 and 8254 contain three 16-bit down-counters that can be programmed with different count values. Depending on the mode specified for that particular counter, the output of the counter does different things. Figure 10.1 shows the basic schematic for this circuit in the PC. In the remainder of this chapter, I'll simply talk about the 8254, since it is included in the majority of PCs in existence (those based on the PC/AT architecture) and is a superset of the 8253.

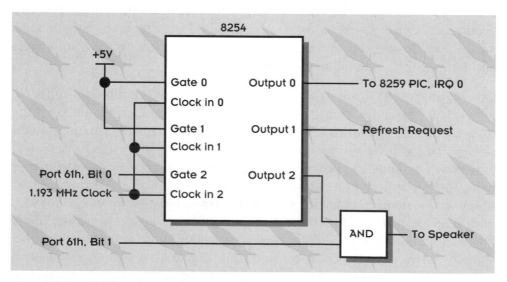

Figure 10.1 *PC/AT timer circuit schematic.*

As you can see in Figure 10.1, all the counters use the same 1.193 MHz clock source. This clock rate is the original PC/AT 4.77 MHz clock divided by four. The "Gate" input for each counter controls whether the counter is enabled and counting. You can see that counters 0 and 1 are constantly enabled, while counter 2 is enabled when bit 0 of port 61h is set. Counter 0 is used to generate a periodic interrupt, counter 1 generates DRAM refresh requests, and counter 2 generates the tone frequency that is used to drive the PC speaker.

The speaker is enabled when bits 0 and 1 of port 61h, are set. Varying the count value of counter 2 will produce different tones on the speaker.

Counter 1 controls the refresh rate of the system DRAM and should not be altered in normal operation. Changing this value can cause your computer's DRAM to be refreshed at too low of a rate, leading to random parity errors.

Counter 0 is commonly called the *system timer*. It typically is initialized with a count value of 65536, which causes it to generate a periodic interrupt on IRQ 0 at the rate of 18.2 times per second (1.193 MHz / 65,536). The periodic interrupt is commonly known as a "tick," and the 18.2 Hz rate is called the system timer *tick rate*. When the computer is turned on, the BIOS initializes a counter in low memory with the current time as read from the real-time clock (RTC) on the motherboard. The counter indicates the number of ticks that have occurred since midnight. On every tick, the BIOS increments the counter. Why does the BIOS bother keeping a separate count of timer ticks rather than reading the RTC whenever it needs to? It's really a side effect. The BIOS uses the periodic interrupt for other purposes, notably to control the floppy disk motor. The tick count is just kept because it's easy to do.

We'll use the system timer in our programs to limit the rate of our main animation loop. Unfortunately, the default rate of the system timer is only 18.2 Hz. Synchronizing directly with the system timer would leave our animation running at this same rate. In order to keep our animation flicker free, we'd like to have the VGA vertical retrace rate be an even multiple of the system timer rate. For instance, if we want our animation to run at 20 or 30 fps, we'll have to speed up the system timer to at least 20 to 30 ticks per second. Fortunately, reprogramming the system timer rate is fairly simple.

REPROGRAMMING PC TIMERS

Altering the system timer is fairly easy, as long as you know what you're doing. In this section, we'll examine the register set of the 8254, discuss the procedures necessary to redirect the system timer interrupt to your own routines, and find out what steps must be performed when exiting our program exits to set everything back to normal.

Programming 8254

The 8254 is a fairly old device and as such is very simple. It has only four 8-bit registers, as shown in Table 10.1.

The counter registers are used to read and write the current and initial counts of each counter. The Mode register is used to control the operation of the device. It determines which of several modes each counter can be in and prepare it for initialization. Programming a counter is as simple as writing to the Mode register with an encoded bit pattern and then writing the initial count values to the approriate counter register.

The encoding of the byte written to the Mode register is the important part of the programming sequence. Figure 10.2 shows the layout of the data written to the Mode register.

Table 10.2 details the encodings of the various bits in the Mode register.

Table 10.1 *8254 Registers and Port Addresses*

Register	Port Address
Counter 0	40h
Counter 1	41h
Counter 2	42h
Mode	43h

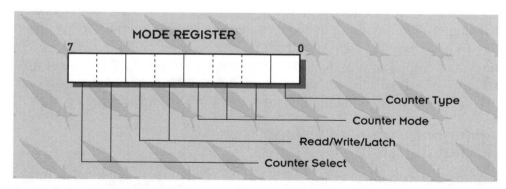

Figure 10.2 *Timer mode register layout.*

Table 10.2   *8254 Timer Mode Register Bit Encodings*

Bits	Encoding	Description
Counter Select [7,6]	00b	Select counter 0
	01b	Select counter 1
	10b	Select counter 2
	11b	Read-back command (8254)
Read/Write/Latch [5,4]	00b	Counter latch command
	01b	Read/write LSB only
	10b	Read/write MSB only
	11b	Read/write LSB and MSB
Counter Mode [3,2,1]	000b	Mode 0: Event Counter
	001b	Mode 1: Hardware-triggered One-shot
	x10b	Mode 2: Divide-by-n Counter
	x11b	Mode 3: Square-wave Generator
	100b	Mode 4: Software-triggered Strobe
	101b	Mode 5: Hardware-triggered Strobe
Counter Type [0]	0b	16-bit binary
	1b	4 decade BCD

As Table 10.2 describes, the Counter Select bits are used to determine which counter will be read or written. The read-back command is a special encoding of these bits only available on the 8254 (that is, it's unavailable for use in an original PC or PC/XT system).

The Read/Write/Latch bits determine which bytes are to be read from or written to the specific counter. It's possible to manipulate only the LSB or MSB byte of the initial count using the different commands. Except for special applications, both the MSB and the LSB are typically read and written each time. *In typical little-endian Intel fashion, the LSB is always written before the MSB.* There is no way to specify a zero count value. If 0x0000 is written as the initial count, it corresponds to a count of 0x10000, or 65,536. This maximum count value is the default value used by the system timer to produce its 18.2 Hz tick rate.

The latch command is used to store the current count of the counter for reading. If the count is not latched, then the value that will be read from the counter will be incorrect, and the read operation will interfere with the count timing. When the latch command is issued, only the Counter Select and

Read/Write/Latch bits have significance. The Counter Mode and Counter Type bits are "don't cares."

The Counter Mode bits specify a number of different modes of operation for each of the counters. The mode of a single counter is independent of the modes of the other counters. The specific operation of the counter in each of the various modes is described here:

- *Mode 0: Event Counter*—If the Gate input is 1, the counter will decrement from its initial count. The output will go to 1 when the count reaches 0. The count will remain at 0 until a new count is written.

- *Mode 1: Hardware-triggered One-shot*—Upon receiving a rising edge on the Gate input, the output will go to 0 until the count reaches 0, when the output will transition back to 1. The counter then reloads and waits for another rising edge of the Gate input.

- *Mode 2: Divide-by-n Counter*—If the Gate input is 1, the counter will count down. The output will be 1 while the counter counts down and then transition to 0 for one clock period. The initial count is then reloaded and the counter begins to count again.

- *Mode 3: Square-wave Generator*—This mode is similar to Mode 2, except that the duty cycle of the output is 50/50. That is, the output will remain at 1 for half of the countdown and go to 0 during the second half. The count is then reloaded and the counter begins to count again. If the initial count is an odd number, then the output will be 1 for one more clock cycle than it is 0.

- *Mode 4: Software-triggered Strobe*—This mode is similar to Mode 2, except that the count does not reload. If the Gate input is 1, the counter begins to count and the output is 1 until the counter counts down, when the output goes to 0 for one clock cycle. The counter then stops until it is reloaded.

- *Mode 5: Hardware-triggered Strobe*—This is similar to Mode 4, except the counter begins to count when the Gate input sees a rising edge. Like Mode 4, the output goes low for one clock period when the counter reaches terminal count. The counter then reloads and waits for another rising edge of the Gate input.

Finally, the Counter Type bit selects whether the counter should be a binary or BCD counter. Typically, all counters are programmed to be binary counters.

Programming a timer is very simple. In order to make it even more simple, there are several routines in TIMER.C to assist us. The first is **ProgramTimer**, which is shown in Listing 10.1.

Listing 10.1   The ProgramTimer Function

```c
/* MACROS */
#define GET_COUNTER(Mode)   ((Mode & SELECT_MASK) >> 6)
#define GET_RWL(Mode)   ((Mode & RWL_MASK) >> 4)

/*
    Function: ProgramTimer
    Description:
        Programs a timer with the mode and count specified.  The
        routine understands writing only the MSB or LSB and does
        the right thing.  Don't set the mode byte to latch
        counters or do the read-back command.
*/
void ProgramTimer(UINT8 Mode, UINT16 Count)
{
    int Timer;
    int Bytes;

    Timer = GET_COUNTER(Mode);
    Bytes = GET_RWL(Mode);

    assert(Timer != 0x3); /* catch read-back command */

    asm pushf;
    asm cli; /* turn off interrupts just so nobody messes with us */

    /* output mode byte */
    outportb(COUNTER_MODE, Mode);

    /* write count */
    switch (Bytes) {
        case 1: /* write MSB */
            outportb(COUNTER_0 + Timer, HIGHBYTE(Count));
            break;
        case 2: /* write LSB */
            outportb(COUNTER_0 + Timer, LOWBYTE(Count));
            break;
        case 3: /* write LSB, MSB */
            /* output in little endian order (i.e., LSB first) */
            outportb(COUNTER_0 + Timer, LOWBYTE(Count));
            outportb(COUNTER_0 + Timer, HIGHBYTE(Count));
            break;
        default:
            assert(Bytes != 0x0); /* catch latch command */
            break;
    }
```

```
    asm popf; /* interrupts back on if they were previously on */
}
```

As you can see, the **Mode** parameter passed to **ProgramTimer** must be preformatted with all the information necessary. Several symbolic constants, shown in Listing 10.2, have been defined in TIMER.H to assist us in forming a correct 8254 mode byte.

Listing 10.2 TIMER.H

```
/* File: TIMER.H
** Description:
**    Constants and declarations for use with TIMER.C.
** Copyright:
**    Copyright 1994, David G. Roberts
*/

#ifndef _TIMER_H

#include "gamedefs.h"

/* CONSTANTS */
/* counter port addresses */
#define COUNTER_0       0x40
#define COUNTER_1       0x41
#define COUNTER_2       0x42
#define COUNTER_MODE    0x43

/* mode control bit definitions */
/* select bits (bits 7 & 6) */
#define SELECT_0        0x00
#define SELECT_1        0x40
#define SELECT_2        0x80
#define READ_BACK       0xC0
#define SELECT_MASK     0xC0

/* read/write/latch bits (bits 5 & 4) */
#define LATCH_CNTR      0x00
#define RW_MSB          0x10
#define RW_LSB          0x20
#define RW_LSB_MSB      0x30
#define RWL_MASK        0x30

/* counter mode bits (bits 3, 2, & 1) */
#define MODE_EVENT          0x00
#define MODE_ONE_SHOT       0x02
#define MODE_DIV_N          0x04
#define MODE_SQUARE_WAVE    0x06
#define MODE_SW_STROBE      0x08
#define MODE_HW_STROBE      0x0A
#define MODE_MASK           0x0E
```

```
/* counter type bit (bit 0) */
#define TYPE_BINARY     0x00
#define TYPE_BCD        0x01
#define TYPE_MASK       0x01

void ProgramTimer(UINT8 Mode, UINT16 Count);
UINT16 ReadTimerCount(int Timer);
void far interrupt (*HookAndProgramSysTimer
    (
    void far interrupt (*Address)(),
    UINT8 Mode,
    UINT16 Count
    ))();
void RestoreSysTimer(void);
void UnhookAndRestoreSysTimer(void far interrupt (*Address)());
void RestoreDOSTime(void);

#define _TIMER_H

#endif
```

A mode byte can be easily formed by ORing together the correct constants. For instance, to program counter 0 with a count of 0x5577, counter type binary, using Mode 3, you would simply execute:

```
ProgramTimer(SELECT_0 | RW_LSB_MSB | MODE_DIV_N | TYPE_BINARY, 0x5577);
```

Reading a timer is even simpler than programming one. TIMER.C includes the **ReadTimerCount** function which makes this very easy. **ReadTimerCount** takes a timer number as input and, as its name suggests, returns the current count value of the timer. **ReadTimerCount**, shown in Listing 10.3, uses the counter latch command.

Listing 10.3   The ReadTimerCount Function

```
/*
    Function: ReadTimerCount.
    Description:
        Given a timer number as input, the routine returns the current
        count.
*/
UINT16 ReadTimerCount(int Timer)
{
    UINT16 Count;
    UINT8 Mode;

    Mode = (Timer << 6) | LATCH_CNTR; /* mode and type are don't cares */
```

```
    outportb(COUNTER_MODE, Mode);

    Count = inportb(COUNTER_0 + Timer); /* get LSB */
    Count |= inportb(COUNTER_0 + Timer) << 8; /* get MSB */

    return Count;
}
```

I mentioned the read-back command earlier. This command was added to the 8254 and is not present in the 8253. The read-back command allows a programmer to latch the current counts and read the current mode settings of one or more timers with a single command. When the read-back command is issued, the bits in the Mode register take on different meanings than normal. Table 10.3 shows the encodings for the various fields when the read-back command is used.

After the read-back command is issued, individual 8-bit read operations are performed to the individual counter port addresses to get the status and count values. The status byte is the first byte read, followed by the LSB of the count, followed by the MSB of the count. The status that is read as a result of the read-back command is similiar to the mode byte that was written to program the counter but with a couple of exceptions. Figure 10.3 shows the layout of the status byte.

As Figure 10.3 shows, all the fields except the Counter Select field are the same. In the status byte, we know which counter the status belongs to because we read the byte from the actual counter port rather than the Mode register port. Because of this, we don't need the Counter Select field, and the

Table 10.3 *8254 Read-Back Command Bit Encodings*

Bits	Encoding	Description
Read-Back Command [7,6]	11b	Must be 11b for read-back command
Latch [5,4]	00b	Latch count and status
	01b	Latch count
	10b	Latch status
	11b	No operation
Select Counter 2 [3]	1b	If 1, latch status and/or count of counter 2
Select Counter 1 [2]	1b	If 1, latch status and/or count of counter 1
Select Counter 0 [1]	1b	If 1, latch status and/or count of counter 0
Reserved [0]	0b	Must be 0

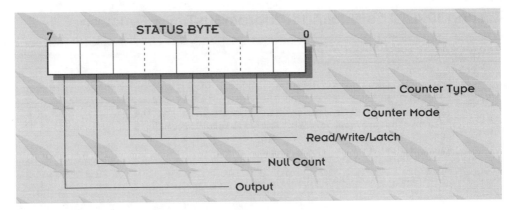

Figure 10.3   *Read-back command status byte layout.*

high two bits are used to encode the current state of the output of the counter and whether the counter is in a null state. If the Null Count bit is set, the counter has not been initialized and written to yet, and so the count value should not be read. If Null Count is clear, then the counter may be read.

There is not usually a reason to use the read-back command, so there are no C routines in TIMER.C to help us with this task.

Hooking the System Timer Interrupt

Now that we've found a way to reprogram counter 0, the system timer, what can we do with it? Right now, all we can do is speed up the system tick rate. Since counter 0 is programmed with the maximum count value of 0 (which equals 0x10000, or 65,536), we can only make it faster. Speeding up the tick rate only makes the DOS time advance at a faster rate, however. We can't do anything truly useful with the system timer unless we intercept the interrupt caused by it and direct the interrupt to one of our own routines.

Figure 10.1 shows the output of counter 0 going to the 8259 PIC, IRQ 0. This interrupt is mapped by the system to interrupt vector 8. To redirect the system timer interrupt, we need to redirect INT 8 to our own interrupt routine.

The **HookAndProgramSysTimer** function from TIMER.C, shown in Listing 10.4, will allow us to both redirect the system timer to our own routine and reprogram it to a different rate and/or operating mode using one simple call. **HookAndProgramSysTimer** returns the old INT 8 vector. This vector should be stored in our program so that we can restore it before our program quits.

Listing 10.4 The HookAndProgramSysTimer Function

```
/*
     Function: HookAndProgramSysTimer
     Description:
          Redirects the system timer and programs it with a new count.
          Note that simply redirecting the timer without reprogramming
          it can be done with the setvect command.  The routine
          returns the previous system timer vector.  BE SURE TO
          RESTORE THE TIMER INTERRUPT USING THIS VECTOR BEFORE THE
          PROGRAM EXITS!!
*/
void far interrupt (*HookAndProgramSysTimer
     (
     void far interrupt (*Address)(),
     UINT8 Mode,
     UINT16 Count
     ))()
{
     void far interrupt (*RetVal)();

     Mode &= 0x3F; /* make sure we're setting counter 0 */

     assert(GET_RWL(Mode) != 0); /* catch latch command */

     RetVal = getvect(SYS_TIMER_INT);
     ProgramTimer(Mode, Count);
     setvect(SYS_TIMER_INT, Address);

     return RetVal;
}
```

So, what sorts of things can we do in our own timer routines? Well, we'll see a more detailed example in a later section, but here are a few guidelines for writing a system timer interrupt procedure:

- Re-enable interrupts as quickly as possible once you enter the routine.

- Like any other interrupt function, avoid calling DOS functions, because the processor could have been executing a DOS function when the interrupt occured and DOS is not re-entrant.

- If you speed up the rate to a multiple of the 18.2 Hz rate, say 36.4 Hz, try to execute the original interrupt routine at the right frequency. For instance, if the rate was 36.4 Hz, call the original interrupt vector every other interrupt. This will allow other code that may have already redirected the interrupt to function. At a minimum, the normal BIOS code will function to simply update the standard tick counter. Sometimes this is very difficult, especially if the new interrupt rate is not a clean multiple of the default 18.2 Hz rate. If you don't do this, the BIOS tick count will be incorrect when your program exits. (From the BIOS point of view, time just stopped.) We'll see a way to correct for this in a moment, so attempting to execute the interrupt at the right frequency isn't strictly necessary.

- Don't put a lot of code in the interrupt function. Especially, don't put all your drawing and erasing code in the interrupt function. Try to simply increment various counters and flags and have your main animation loop check these counters and flags to figure out the time.

- Be sure to acknowledge the interrupt to the PIC. If you don't do this, you'll only get one interrupt and no others. Do this by writing 0x20 to port 0x20. (See the PIC and NONSPECIFIC_EOI constants in GAMEDEFS.H.)

Cleaning Up

You must ensure that the system timer has been reset to its normal state *before your program exits*. If you fail in this very important task, the BIOS tick counter may advance at the wrong rate. Further, the old interrupt vector pointing to a function in your now terminated program may be called, which might cause the system to crash. Restoring of the timer must be done even if your program quits because of an error or a user interrupt (Ctrl+C or Ctrl+Break, for instance).

Fortunately, TIMER.C provides several simple routines to undo whatever modifications have been done to the system timer's state. The first of these routines is **RestoreSysTimer**, shown in Listing 10.5, which simply programs counter 0 of the 8254 with the default mode and count.

Listing 10.5 The RestoreSysTimer Function

```
/*
    Function: RestoreSysTimer
    Description:
        Restores the system timer to its original settings.  Call
        this function after reprogramming the system timer but
        before quitting the application.
*/
void RestoreSysTimer(void)
{
    ProgramTimer(SELECT_0 | RW_LSB_MSB | MODE_SQUARE_WAVE | TYPE_BINARY, 0);
}
```

If your program has hooked the system timer by calling **HookAndProgram-SysTimer**, it can undo the hook by calling **UnhookAndRestoreSysTimer**, which is shown in Listing 10.6. **UnhookAndRestoreSysTimer** takes the previous INT 8 vector returned by **HookAndProgramSysTimer** as input.

Listing 10.6   The UnhookAndRestoreSysTimer Function

```
/*
    Function: UnhookAndRestoreSysTimer
    Description:
        Undoes what HookAndProgramSysTimer does.
*/
void UnhookAndRestoreSysTimer(void far interrupt (*Address)())
{
    /* NOTE: set the vector first.  If this is not done, the */
    /*   user interrupt routine could still be called between the */
    /*   timer restoration and the vector restoration.  If this */
    /*   happened, the user interrupt could reinitialize the timer */
    /*   with the user-needed mode and count, clobbering the timer. */
    setvect(SYS_TIMER_INT, Address);
    RestoreSysTimer();
}
```

Finally, we also need a way to restore the BIOS tick count and DOS date if we have not been calling the original INT 8 vector at the default 18.2 Hz rate in our own interrupt routine. **RestoreDOSTime** reads the real-time clock for the present date and time of day and reinitializes the DOS date and BIOS tick count using the values it reads. The RTC returns the date and time of day in BCD format, so **RestoreDOSTime** uses **BCD2Bin** to convert the RTC return values back to binary for use in further computations. Both **RestoreDOSTime** and **BCD2Bin** are shown in Listing 10.7.

Listing 10.7   The BCD2Bin and RestoreDOSTime Functions

```
/*
    Function: BCD2Bin
    Description:
        Module local function used in RestoreDOSTime to convert the
        BCD number format returned from the real-time clock to
        binary.  Argument is a single byte.
*/
static int BCD2Bin(UINT8 Arg)
{
    return (((Arg >> 4) & 0xF) * 10) + (Arg & 0xF);
}

/*
    Function: RestoreDOSTime
    Description:
        Restores the DOS time-of-day counter from the real-time clock.
        This alleviates the burden on the programmer to have to call
        the system timer vector (the old INT 8 vector) 18.2 times per
        second when the vector has been hooked for some reason.  This
        is particularly useful if the system timer rate has been
```

```
                reprogrammed to a non-integer multiple of the 18.2 Hz rate.
*/
void RestoreDOSTime(void)
{
    union REGS Regs;
    UINT8 Century;
    UINT8 Year;
    UINT8 Month;
    UINT8 Day;
    UINT8 Hours;
    UINT8 Mins;
    UINT8 Secs;

    /* NOTE: be sure to read both date and time from the RTC before */
    /*    setting the DOS date or time.  DOS will set the RTC date */
    /*    AND time whenever either DOS set routine is called (from */
    /*    its stored copies).  This will temporarily corrupt the RTC */
    /*    date or time (whichever is not being set) so we have to make */
    /*    a copy for ourselves first so we can set the second one */
    /*    from the correct information. */

    /* get RTC date */
    Regs.h.ah = READ_RTC_DATE;
    int86(CLOCK_INT, &Regs, &Regs);

    Century = Regs.h.ch;
    Year    = Regs.h.cl;
    Month   = Regs.h.dh;
    Day     = Regs.h.dl;

    /* get RTC time */
    Regs.h.ah = READ_RTC_TIME;
    int86(CLOCK_INT, &Regs, &Regs);

    Hours   = Regs.h.ch;
    Mins    = Regs.h.cl;
    Secs    = Regs.h.dh;

    /* set DOS date */
    Regs.x.cx = BCD2Bin(Century) * 100 + BCD2Bin(Year);
    Regs.h.dh = BCD2Bin(Month);
    Regs.h.dl = BCD2Bin(Day);
    Regs.h.ah = SET_DOS_DATE;
    int86(DOS_INT, &Regs, &Regs);

    /* set DOS time */
    Regs.h.ch = BCD2Bin(Hours);
    Regs.h.cl = BCD2Bin(Mins);
    Regs.h.dh = BCD2Bin(Secs);
    Regs.h.dl = 0; /* hunredths */
    Regs.h.ah = SET_DOS_TIME;
    int86(DOS_INT, &Regs, &Regs);
}
```

SYNCHRONIZING A TIMER TO VERTICAL RETRACE

Well, now that we know how to reprogram the system timer rate and replace its interrupt function with our own, what should we do with all this knowledge? More specifically, how can we synchronize the timer to the VGA vertical retrace period, and what specifically should our replacement timer interrupt routine do?

To keep our animation running at a slower rate than 60 or 70 fps, we need a way to be able to count how many vertical retraces have occured while we were doing the movement calculations and drawing for the current frame. For instance, if we want our animation to run at 30 fps in Mode X, even on a fast processor, we need to make sure that we only create an animation frame every other vertical retrace period. On a slow processor, this might not be a problem. If it takes us longer than 1/60th of a second to create an animation frame, we'll be doing calculations while one vertical retrace occurs, and so we can simply wait for the next one to draw our animation frame. If we move to a faster processor, however, we might be able to get our calculations done in less than 1/60th of a second. In that case, simply performing the calculations and then waiting for the next vertical retrace will have our animation running at 60 fps, rather than 30 fps.

If the VGA produced an interrupt every time it went into a vertical retrace, we could use the interrupt to increment a counter to keep track of how many vertical retraces had occured. The fast processor would then finish its calculations and wait until the counter indicated the right number of vertical retraces had been skipped before drawing the frame.

Unfortunately, the VGA has no way of generating an interrupt whenever a vertical retrace occurs. If you examine a VGA reference book, you'll find a vertical retrace interrupt mentioned, but in the real-world this is rarely implemented. In fact, even IBM's original VGA cards did not implement this feature.

Fortunately, we can use the system timer to give us almost the same result. If we set the system timer so that it times out at 1/60th of a second period and then synchronize the start of the timer countdown with a vertical retrace, a timer interrupt will occur very close to the start of the next vertical retrace.

The file VRSYNC.C, shown in Listing 10.8, can be used to help synchronize the timer to the VGA vertical retrace.

Listing 10.8 VRSYNC.C

```
/* File: VRSYNC.C
** Description:
**    Syncs the system timer to the display vertical retrace.
** Copyright:
**    Copyright 1994, David G. Roberts
** Acknowledgements:
**    The basic technique demonstrated here comes from public domain
**    code written by Petteri Kangaslampi.
*/

#include <assert.h>
#include <dos.h>
#include <stdlib.h>
#include "gamedefs.h"
#include "retrace.h"
#include "timer.h"
#include "vrsync.h"

/* constants */
#define MARGIN 500 /* 500 1.1925 MHz clocks of margin - ~420 microsec */

static BOOL    RetraceTimerInstalled = FALSE;
static UINT16  ReinitCount;
static void far interrupt (*OldSysTimerVect)();

/*
    Function: RetraceTimerInit
    Description:
        Installs a retrace interrupt procedure to be called
        whenever a retrace occurs.

        THE FUNCTION SPECIFIED BY TIMERPROC IS AN INTERRUPT
        FUNCTION.  IT SHOULD NOT CALL ANY DOS FUNCTIONS AND
        SHOULD REENABLE INTERRUPTS AS SOON AS POSSIBLE AFTER
        TAKING CONTROL OF THE SYSTEM.
*/
void RetraceTimerInit(void far interrupt (*TimerProc)())
{
    UINT16 FirstRead;
    UINT16 SecondRead;
    int Delta;

    assert(RetraceTimerInstalled == FALSE);

    /* figure out refresh rate */
    do {
        /* wait for refresh */
        WaitVerticalRetraceStart();
        /* init timer with max count */
        ProgramTimer(SELECT_0 | RW_LSB_MSB | MODE_EVENT | TYPE_BINARY, 0);
        /* wait for refresh again */
```

```
            WaitVerticalRetraceStart();
            /* check to see what the count is */
            FirstRead = ReadTimerCount(0);

            /* now do it again */
            WaitVerticalRetraceStart();
            /* init timer with max count */
            ProgramTimer(SELECT_0 | RW_LSB_MSB | MODE_EVENT | TYPE_BINARY, 0);
            /* wait for refresh again */
            WaitVerticalRetraceStart();
            /* check to see what the count is */
            SecondRead = ReadTimerCount(0);

            /* compute the delta and do this again if it's too big */
            /* if it's too big, we probably got an interrupt at some point */
            /*    that skewed our timing */
            Delta = SecondRead - FirstRead;
        } while (Delta > 2 || Delta < -2);

    /* set ReinitCount to the quickest time we got minus some margin */
    /* remember 0 = 0x10000, so 0 - FirstRead = 0x10000 - FirstRead */
    ReinitCount = MIN(0 - FirstRead, 0 - SecondRead) - MARGIN;

    /* sync timer with refresh and install user hook function */
    WaitVerticalRetraceStart();
    OldSysTimerVect = HookAndProgramSysTimer(TimerProc,
        SELECT_0 | RW_LSB_MSB | MODE_EVENT | TYPE_BINARY, ReinitCount);
    outportb(PIC, NONSPECIFIC_EOI);

    RetraceTimerInstalled = TRUE;
}


/*
    Function: RetraceTimerStop
    Description:
        Deinstalls the retrace interrupt procedure.  The original
        timer vector is put back in place and the timer is
        programmed with its default values.  Finally, the BIOS
        tick count is reinitialized from the RTC because the
        old vector was never called.
*/
void RetraceTimerStop(void)
{
    assert(RetraceTimerInstalled == TRUE);

    UnhookAndRestoreSysTimer(OldSysTimerVect);
    RestoreDOSTime();
}

/*
    Function: RetraceTimerReinit
    Description:
```

```
           This function should be called at the end of the user
           retrace timer procedure to reinitialize the timer with
           the correct count values and restart it.  Do not call
           this function before calling RetraceTimerInit to
           calculate the correct count values first.
*/
void RetraceTimerReinit(void)
{
    assert(RetraceTimerInstalled == TRUE);

    ProgramTimer(SELECT_0 | RW_LSB_MSB | MODE_EVENT | TYPE_BINARY,
        ReinitCount);
}
```

To synchronize the timer with the vertical retrace, the program must first call
RetraceTimerInit. **RetraceTimerInit** first determines the vertical retrace rate.
It's not hardcoded at 60 Hz so you can use this routine with both Mode 13h or
Mode X. It does this by starting the timer at the start of a vertical retrace and
then waiting for the next vertical retrace. When the next retrace occurs, the
routine reads the current timer count. **RetraceTimerInit** takes two samples
of the vertical retrace period to make sure the timing is correct.

The function then computes a timer count that will be used to initialize the
timer and synchronize it with the vertical retrace. The count value is made a
little smaller to ensure that the interrupt routine can take control before the next
vertical retrace occurs. This is crucial to performing tasks that must be done
before the refresh actually occurs, like flipping pages in Mode X.

When the correct count value is determined, it is saved, and **RetraceTimerInit**
waits for the next vertical retrace. When the vertical retrace occurs, the system
timer is programmed with the new count value and the user-interrupt routine
specified by the **TimerProc** parameter is installed as the system timer interrupt handler.

Notice that the system timer is programmed with the event mode rather than
its usual divide-by-n mode. This means that the counter will count down to 0,
generate an interrupt, and then not reinitialize until it is reprogrammed. We
only produce one interrupt per counter initialization.

RetraceTimerReinit is used to reinitialize the system timer after the interrupt
has occured. This function is called by the user interrupt handler after the
handler has done its work and waited for vertical retrace to occur. The timeline
for this sequence of events is shown in Figure 10.4.

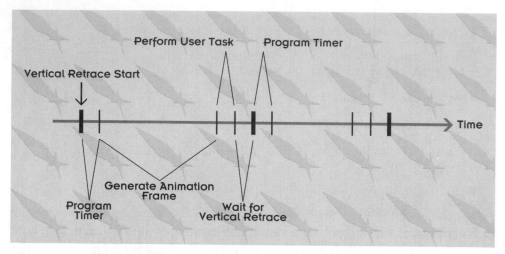

Figure 10.4 *Timeline for system timer synchronization with VGA vertical retrace.*

We'll see a more concrete example program in the next section that will demonstrate the sorts of tasks the user interrupt function should perform.

Finally, to restore the system timer and remove the user interrupt function, use **RetraceTimerStop**.

 **Timer Demonstration Program**

The program RSYNCDMO, shown in Listing 10.9, demonstrates the use of the VRSYNC.C routines and ultimately the use of the TIMER.C routines. RSYNCDMO is a modification of the FLIPDEMO program that we examined when we learned about animation techniques. RSYNCDMO bounces a number of balls around the screen in Mode X. The frame rate remains at 30 fps, even though the program only displays five balls. If you'll remember the original FLIPDEMO, most machines are able to animate many more balls than this and still run at 60 fps. Even when run on a very fast processor, RSYNCDMO won't speed up, and the animation is sychronized to the VGA vertical retrace.

Compiling and Linking:

You can compile the RSYNCDMO program using the Borland C++ 3.1 IDE by typing "bc rsyncdmo.prj" and then selecting Compile | Make from the menus. If you would rather use the command line compiler, convert the RSYNCDMO.PRJ file to a makefile using the PRJ2MAK program supplied with Borland C++ 3.1. Type "prj2mak rsyncdmo.prj" to create the RSYNCDMO.MAK and RSYNCDMO.CFG files.

If you are using Borland C++ 4.0, choose Project | Open Project from the IDE menus. Open the RSYNCDMO.PRJ file. Borland C++ will convert the version 3.1 .PRJ file to a version 4.0 .IDE file. Compile and link the program by choosing Project | Make All from the IDE menus.

Listing 10.9   RSYNCDMO.C

```
/* File: RSYNCDMO.C
** Description:
**    Demonstrates synchronization of the system timer with the VGA
**    retrace.  This is a modification of the FLIPDEMO program
**    that runs at 30 fps no matter how few balls are drawn.
** Copyright:
**    Copyright 1994, David G. Roberts
*/


#include <alloc.h>
#include <assert.h>
#include <conio.h>
#include <stdio.h>
#include <stdlib.h>
#include "gamedefs.h"
#include "animate.h"
#include "bitblt.h"
#include "retrace.h"
#include "setmodex.h"
#include "timer.h"
#include "vga.h"
#include "vrsync.h"


UINT8 BallBitmap[] = {
    10, 0,          /* Width (little endian) */
    10, 0,          /* Height (little endian) */
    0, 0,           /* X and Y origin */
    0, 0,
    0, 0, 0, 2, 2, 2, 2, 0, 0, 0, /* color 2 = green w/ default palette */
    0, 2, 2, 2, 2, 2, 2, 2, 2, 0,
    0, 2, 2, 0, 0, 2, 2, 2, 2, 0,
    2, 2, 0, 0, 2, 2, 2, 2, 2, 2,
    2, 2, 0, 2, 2, 2, 2, 2, 2, 2,
    2, 2, 2, 2, 2, 2, 2, 2, 2, 2,
    2, 2, 2, 2, 2, 2, 2, 2, 2, 2,
    0, 2, 2, 2, 2, 2, 2, 2, 2, 0,
    0, 2, 2, 2, 2, 2, 2, 2, 2, 0,
    0, 0, 0, 2, 2, 2, 2, 0, 0, 0
};

UINT8 BallEraseBitmap[] = {
    10, 0,          /* Width (little endian) */
    10, 0,          /* Height (little endian) */
    0, 0,           /* X and Y origin */
    0, 0,
```

```
        16, 16, 16, 16, 16, 16, 16, 16, 16, 16, /* color 16 = black */
        16, 16, 16, 16, 16, 16, 16, 16, 16, 16, /* with default palette */
        16, 16, 16, 16, 16, 16, 16, 16, 16, 16,
        16, 16, 16, 16, 16, 16, 16, 16, 16, 16,
        16, 16, 16, 16, 16, 16, 16, 16, 16, 16,
        16, 16, 16, 16, 16, 16, 16, 16, 16, 16,
        16, 16, 16, 16, 16, 16, 16, 16, 16, 16,
        16, 16, 16, 16, 16, 16, 16, 16, 16, 16,
        16, 16, 16, 16, 16, 16, 16, 16, 16, 16,
        16, 16, 16, 16, 16, 16, 16, 16, 16, 16
};

/* globals used in RetraceInt as well as main function */
int RetraceCount;
int HiddenPage;
UINT16 Offset[2];
BOOL FrameReady;

/* note: make these track width and height of bitmap, above */
#define BITMAP_HEIGHT    (10)
#define BITMAP_WIDTH     (10)

#define PAGE0_OFFSET     (0)
#define PAGE1_OFFSET     (0x4B00)

#define NUM_BALLS        (5)

#define FRAME_SKIP       1    /* 0 = 60 fps, 1 = 30 fps, 2 = 20 fps */

/*
    Function: RetraceProc
    Description:
        Replacement system timer interrupt called after the timer
        is sync'd with the VGA vertical retrace.
*/
void far interrupt RetraceProc(void)
{
    asm sti;    /* reenable other interrupts */

    if (RetraceCount == 0) {
        if (FrameReady) {
            /* flip page */
            PageFlip(Offset[HiddenPage]);
            RetraceTimerReinit();
            HiddenPage ^= 1; /* flip HiddenPage to other state */
            RetraceCount = FRAME_SKIP;
            FrameReady = FALSE;
        }
        else {
            /* we weren't quite ready */
            WaitVerticalRetraceStart();
            RetraceTimerReinit();
            RetraceCount = 0;
```

```
            }
        }
        else {
            /* simply do this again */
            RetraceCount--;
            WaitVerticalRetraceStart();
            RetraceTimerReinit();
        }

        /* acknowledge the int to the PIC */
        outportb(PIC, NONSPECIFIC_EOI);
}

int main()
{
    int x[NUM_BALLS], y[NUM_BALLS];
    int OldX[NUM_BALLS][2], OldY[NUM_BALLS][2];
    int vx[NUM_BALLS], vy[NUM_BALLS];
    PLANAR_BITMAP far * PlanarBallBitmap;
    PLANAR_BITMAP far * PlanarBallEraseBitmap;
    BOOL Erase[NUM_BALLS][2];
    int i;

    /* detect VGA */
    if (!DetectVGA()) {
        printf("You must have a VGA to run this program.\n");
        return 1;
    }

    Offset[0] = PAGE0_OFFSET;
    Offset[1] = PAGE1_OFFSET;
    HiddenPage = 1;

    PlanarBallBitmap = LinearToPlanar((LINEAR_BITMAP far *) BallBitmap);
    PlanarBallEraseBitmap =
        LinearToPlanar((LINEAR_BITMAP far *) BallEraseBitmap);

    /* set Mode X and display page 0 */
    SetModeX();

    for (i = 0; i < NUM_BALLS; i++) {
        x[i] = random(MODEX_WIDTH - BITMAP_WIDTH);
        y[i] = random(MODEX_HEIGHT - BITMAP_HEIGHT);
        vx[i] = random(2) + 1;
        vy[i] = random(2) + 1;
        Erase[i][0] = Erase[i][1] = FALSE;
    }

    /* start up synchronized interrupt */
    FrameReady = FALSE;
    RetraceCount = FRAME_SKIP;
    RetraceTimerInit(RetraceProc);
```

```
        while (!kbhit()) {
            /* update new position */
            for (i = 0; i < NUM_BALLS; i++) {
                if (Erase[i][HiddenPage]) {
                    x[i] += vx[i];
                    y[i] += vy[i];
                    if ((x[i] < 0) || ((x[i] + BITMAP_WIDTH) >= MODEX_WIDTH)) {
                        vx[i] = -vx[i];
                        x[i] += 2 * vx[i];
                    }
                    if ((y[i] < 0) || ((y[i] + BITMAP_HEIGHT) >= MODEX_HEIGHT)) {
                        vy[i] = -vy[i];
                        y[i] += 2 * vy[i];
                    }
                }
            }

            /* stall until retrace procedure flips page */
            while (FrameReady);

            /* erase */
            for (i = 0; i < NUM_BALLS; i++) {
                if (Erase[i][HiddenPage]) {
                    BltPlanar(PlanarBallEraseBitmap,
                        OldX[i][HiddenPage], OldY[i][HiddenPage],
                        Offset[HiddenPage]);
                }
            }

            /* draw */
            for (i = 0; i < NUM_BALLS; i++) {
                BltPlanar(PlanarBallBitmap, x[i], y[i], Offset[HiddenPage]);
                OldX[i][HiddenPage] = x[i];
                OldY[i][HiddenPage] = y[i];
                Erase[i][HiddenPage] = TRUE;
            }

            /* flip page */
            FrameReady = TRUE;
        }

        RetraceTimerStop();

        getch();

        farfree(PlanarBallBitmap);
        farfree(PlanarBallEraseBitmap);

        SetVGAMode(0x3);

        return 0;
    }
```

The routines in VRSYNC.C are used to set up a vertical retrace synchonized interrupt routine, **RetraceProc**. This routine does nothing other than decrement **RetraceCount**, reinitialize the system timer using **RetraceTimerReinit**, and acknowledge the interrupt to the PIC on every other vertical retrace. When **RetraceCount** is zero, however, **RetraceProc** flips Mode X pages if the main program has prepared an animation frame, as indicated by the state of **FrameReady**.

FrameReady is used to control the speed of the main animation loop. The main loop sets **FrameReady** after preparing an animation frame, rather than flip pages itself. When two retraces have been counted off and **FrameReady** is set, **RetraceProc** flips pages and clears **FrameReady**.

After setting **FrameReady**, the main routine continues to execute until it gets ready to draw the next frame. Before drawing, however, the main loop checks the state of **FrameReady** to see if **RetraceProc** has flipped pages yet. If not, the main loop stalls until **RetraceProc** flips pages and clears **FrameReady**. The main loop can't draw on the next hidden page until it becomes hidden! The main loop could have stalled just after setting **FrameReady**, but there is no harm in doing a little work for the next page before the pages are flipped. Overlapping the movement calculations with the wait for **FrameReady** to be reset allows us to get a head start on the next frame and make use of the time that otherwise would have been wasted delaying for the page flip.

Now you understand one of the reasons we do our movement calculations before we erase our sprites. If we erased the sprites first, we couldn't start executing the movement code while we were waiting for the page flip to occur.

As written, RSYNCDMO runs at 30 fps. You can easily make it run at 20 fps by changing the **FRAME_SKIP** contant. Changing **FRAME_SKIP** to 2 makes **RetraceProc** skip two vertical retraces between page flips, giving a frame rate of 20 fps. Of course, you can also speed the program up to 60 fps by setting **FRAME_SKIP** to 0, but then you've just added a bunch of complexity relating to the timer to get back to where FLIPDEMO was originally.

We finally have all the pieces necessary to write a game! In the next chapter, we'll get down to it.

Creating
Alien Alley

Our gaming adventure has finally arrived. In this chapter we'll create the fun game *Alien Alley*.

When I was 12 years old, I went on a ski trip to Lake Tahoe with my church youth group. Although I had been to the snow a few times before, my parents didn't ski and I had never learned before. I was extremely excited about the event and couldn't wait to get on the slopes. After driving up from near San Francisco late Friday night, the morning finally arrived and the event was at hand!

After impatiently waiting in line to rent skis, I rushed outside and put the equipment on. I had dreamed of this moment for years and now the time had come. I promptly stood up outside the ski rental hut at the resort and started sliding toward the parking lot. My hands were waving back and forth, and I had no idea what was happening or how to stop. Just before I would have careened off a 12 foot snow cliff onto the concrete parking lot below, I fell down and stopped. Clearly, there was more to this than I had thought.

I dusted myself off and turned around to find my friend's older sister laughing at me hysterically. She kept giggling as I struggled to stand up but tried to keep myself from moving further toward the parking lot. Finally, she walked over and helped me up.

"This is your first time, right? Do you need a quick lesson?" she asked.

"Ummm... yea," I replied, smiling sheepishly.

She got me standing up and showed me how to position my skis so that I wouldn't slide any further. She then had me shuffle a small way up the main slope. She showed me how to position my skis when I wanted to go straight, how to turn to the left and right, and, most importantly, how to stop. After about 10 minutes of instruction, she turned me loose and walked away saying, "Now practice."

I spent the whole day on a short beginner run at the bottom of the hill. I kept riding the lift up to the top and spending a half hour getting down the 50 yards to the bottom again. I would turn to the left and then fall. I would successfully turn to the left and then start turning to the right, end up with my skis straight down the hill, and then have to fall to stop because I couldn't get the left turn completed. Although I remembered how to perform each of the maneuvers she had shown me and could do each of them in isolation, I couldn't link them together to actually ski. At the end of the first day, I had finally gotten to the point where I could get down the whole beginner run without falling. I was cold and tired—and triumphant!

At this point in our exploration, we're at the top of the ski slope, about to take our first run. When we started, you may have been heading toward the parking lot, enthusiastic about getting started, but unsure of what to do.

In previous chapters, we've had a number of short lessons. We've learned how to interface with the three major game input devices: the keyboard, the mouse, and the joystick. We understand how the VGA operates, its various modes and memory organizations. We've examined several ways to encode bitmap images and draw them on the screen rapidly. We've looked at several different animation techniques, and we are able to manipulate the VGA palette to make the VGA display images in the colors that we define. The example programs that we've played with so far have demonstrated individual techniques, but they were the equivalent of making a single turn on the ski slope.

In this chapter, we'll combine many of these techniques to create *Alien Alley*. *Alien Alley* will be a complete game that makes use of multiple input devices, performs high speed animation, and manipulates the palette to create a number of effects. In this chapter, we'll finally link our turns together, center our weight over our skis, and get down to the bottom of the hill without falling.

eXPLORER PROJECT

Alien Alley is a type of game frequently called a "vertical shooter." It is similar to many games that have appeared in arcades and on the PC for years. The player controls a spaceship that can move around the screen, up, down, left, and right. The alien spaceships emerge from the top of the screen, moving from side to side as they approach the player spaceship. The object of the game is to destroy as many of these alien spaceships as possible before the player is destroyed.

The player's ship is equipped with plasma cannons to reduce the alien invaders to nothing but a few fast-moving elementary particles. Unfortunately, the aliens also pack firepower of their own and have no trouble using it. Both the player and the aliens fire two shots at a time.

The player's ship comes equipped with a shield generator that can dissipate the energy of five alien shots before burning out. The sixth shot destroys the ship and ends the game. Additionally, the aliens have no qualms about ramming the player's ship. Running into an alien destroys the player's ship immediately, no matter how much shield energy remains.

The player receives 10 points for each alien destroyed. There is currently only one type of alien ship. Others could be added and different point values assigned to them to make the scoring more varied.

Alien Alley keeps track of high scores. If a player's performance is sufficient to be among the top 10, a high-score entry screen is displayed that allows the player's name to be entered. The high-score file is saved to disk between sessions.

The remainder of this chapter is devoted to exploring the *Alien Alley* code itself. Because of the length of the code, the body of the chapter contains only small excerpts that deal with the concept at hand. You will find the full source code module, ALIEN1.C, at the end of the chapter.

THE MAIN GAME LOOP

The best way for us to start examining *Alien Alley*'s code is to take a look at the first function to be executed: **main**. *Alien Alley* starts by initializing some program-wide variables and then displaying the introduction credit screens.

The functions **ProgramInit** and **IntroCredits** perform these tasks. Listing 11.1 shows the **main** function:

Listing 11.1 The main Function

```
/*
    Function: main
    Description:
        Main program loop.  Init's the program, draws intro screens
        and title pages, and waits for user to hit keystroke
        to indicate what they want to do.
*/
int main()
{
    BOOL    Quit;
    BOOL    DrawTitle;
    char    Key;


    ProgramInit();

    IntroCredits();

    Quit = FALSE;
    DrawTitle = TRUE;

    while (!Quit) {
        if (DrawTitle) {
            TitlePage();
            DrawTitle = FALSE;
        }

        Key = getch();
        Key = tolower(Key);

        randomize(); /* make sure we get a different game */

        switch (Key) {
            case 0: /* extended key (F1, for instance) */
                /* burn next key input which should be */
                /* a scan code corresponding to the key */
                getch();
                break;
            case 0x1B: /* escape */
            case 'q':
                Quit = TRUE;
                break;
            case 'j':
                if (JoystickPresent) {
                    Play(Key);
                    NewHighScore(Score);
                    DrawTitle = TRUE;
```

```
            }
            break;
    case 'm':
        if (MousePresent) {
            Play(Key);
            NewHighScore(Score);
            DrawTitle = TRUE;
        }
        break;
    case ' ': /* space */
        Key = 'k';
        /* fall through */
    case 'k':
        Play(Key);
        NewHighScore(Score);
        DrawTitle = TRUE;
        break;
    case 's':
        DisplayHighScoreScreen();
        DrawTitle = TRUE;
        break;
    default:
        DrawTitle = FALSE;
        break;
    }
}

SaveHighScores();

SetVGAMode(0x3);

return 0;
}
```

After initialization and the display of the introductory credits, the program enters the main loop. The main loop displays the title screen and then waits for a keypress. When the user presses a key, one of three things can happen, depending on the key pressed: the game is started, the high-score screen is displayed, or the keypress is ignored. When the user presses the key that starts the game, the main loop first checks to see that the specified input device is present. If not, then the keypress is ignored. The mouse and joystick are initialized in **ProgramInit** and the **MousePresent** and **JoystickPresent** variables set appropriately. The keyboard is always present.

The program calls the function **Play** to get the game going. When this function returns, the **Score** variable reflects the player's score and this value is passed to the **NewHighScore** function to determine if the user has enough points to get on the high-score list. If so, **NewHighScore** allows the player's name to be entered. After the actual game play ends and the high score has been input, the title page is redrawn and the main loop waits for another keypress.

If the user presses "Q" or the Esc key, the main loop exits, the high scores are saved, the VGA is returned to text mode, and the program quits as the **main** function completes.

INTRO SCREENS AND TITLE

The introduction and title screens are a requirement for any professional-looking game, but don't worry, they are simple to create. The introduction screens are drawn using the VGA BIOS, and the title screen is a PCX file that is loaded into memory and then drawn using **BltLinear**. Before displaying any of the screens, the VGA palette is set to all black so that the image doesn't appear suddenly. The palette is then faded in slowly to create a more pleasing transition.

IntroCredits and **TitlePage** are shown in Listing 11.2. **IntroCredits** uses the **CenterString** function to draw a centered line of text on the display, using the VGA BIOS to draw the individual characters. The **CenterString** function can be found in Listing 11.11, the full ALIEN1.C listing at the end of this chapter. The title page is drawn by a separate routine so that it can be drawn by itself again at the end of the game. The introduction sequence only occurs when the game first starts.

Listing 11.2 The IntroCredits and TitlePage Functions

```
/*
    Function: IntroCredits
    Description:
        Displays the introduction credits.
*/
void IntroCredits(void)
{
    /* get into mode 13h */
    SetMode13h();

    /* load palette with VGA defaults */
    GetVGAPaletteBlock(GamePalette, 0, 256);

    /* set everything to black so we can draw without being seen */
    /* use two SetVGAPaletteBlock calls to avoid snow */
    SetVGAPaletteBlock(BlackPalette, 0, 128);
    SetVGAPaletteBlock(BlackPalette, 128, 128);
```

```
/* first page of stuff */
CenterString("Coriolis Group Books", 7, INTRO_TEXT_COLOR);
CenterString("Presents", 10, INTRO_TEXT_COLOR);
if (kbhit()) {
    getch();
    return;
}
FadeIn(1500);
if (kbhit()) {
    getch();
    return;
}
delay(1500);
if (kbhit()) {
    getch();
    return;
}
FadeOut(1500);
if (kbhit()) {
    getch();
    return;
}
delay(500);

/* second page of stuff */
ClearMode13hScreen();
CenterString("A", 7, INTRO_TEXT_COLOR);
CenterString("Dave Roberts", 10, INTRO_TEXT_COLOR);
CenterString("Production", 13, INTRO_TEXT_COLOR);
if (kbhit()) {
    getch();
    return;
}
FadeIn(1500);
if (kbhit()) {
    getch();
    return;
}
if (kbhit()) {
    getch();
    return;
}
delay(1500);
if (kbhit()) {
    getch();
    return;
}
FadeOut(1500);
if (kbhit()) {
    getch();
    return;
```

```
    }
    delay(500);
}

/*
    Function: TitlePage
    Description:
        Displays the Alien Alley title page.
*/
void TitlePage(void)
{
    LINEAR_BITMAP far * Image;

    /* clear screen */
    ClearMode13hScreen();

    /* set everything to black so we can draw without being seen */
    /* use two function calls to avoid snow */
    SetVGAPaletteBlock(BlackPalette, 0, 128);
    SetVGAPaletteBlock(BlackPalette, 128, 128);

    /* first page of stuff */
    Image = LoadPCX("title.pcx", GamePalette);
    if (Image == NULL) {
        FatalError("Can't load 'title.pcx'", "TitlePage", __LINE__);
    }
    BltLinear(Image, 0, 0, MK_FP(VIDEO_MEM_SEGMENT, 0));
    farfree(Image);
    if (kbhit()) {
        getch();
        SetVGAPaletteBlock(GamePalette, 0, 128);
        SetVGAPaletteBlock(GamePalette, 128, 128);
        return;
    }
    FadeIn(1500);
}
```

THE ANIMATION LOOP

The animation loop is contained in the **Play** function, which is shown in
Listing 11.3. This is where the actual game code is executed, after we've
displayed all the credits and title pages and the user's input control choice has
been accepted. In short, this is where the action is.

Listing 11.3   The Play Function

```
/*
    Function: Play
    Description:
        Play the game!
```

```
*/
void Play(int Control)
{
    BOOL    UserInputUp;
    BOOL    UserInputDown;
    BOOL    UserInputLeft;
    BOOL    UserInputRight;
    BOOL    UserInputFire;
    int     GunBlinkCounter;
    int     GunBlinkState;
    RGB_TUPLE Black = {0, 0, 0};
    RGB_TUPLE GunColor;
    BOOL    GameOver;
    BOOL    GameOverInput;
    BOOL    GameOverDeath;
    LINEAR_BITMAP far * Image;

    /* fade screen to remove title page */
    FadeOut(500);

    /* load sprites */
    LoadSprites();

    /* initialize all counters, etc. */
    Score = 0;
    AlienGenCounter = ALIEN_GEN_RATE_BASE;
    HeroShields = MAX_HERO_SHIELDS;

    /* set mode X */
    SetModeX();
    SetUpModeX();

    /* set up palette stuff */
    /* palette.pcx is a single pixel bitmap with the palette */
    /*    this is done because it's easy to load the palette */
    /*    using LoadPCX */
    Image = LoadPCX("palette.pcx", GamePalette);
    if (Image == NULL) {
        FatalError("Can't load 'palette.pcx'", "ProgramInit", __LINE__);
    }
    farfree(Image); /* ignore the single pixel bitmap */
    SetVGAPaletteBlock(GamePalette, 0, 128);
    SetVGAPaletteBlock(GamePalette, 128, 128);

    /* install keyboard or mouse handlers */
    /* do nothing for joystick */
    if (Control == 'm') {
    }
    else if (Control == 'k') {
        SetButtonKeysMode();
    }

    /* set up gun blink stuff */
```

```
GetPaletteEntry(GamePalette, GUN_COLOR, &GunColor);
GunBlinkCounter      = GUN_BLINK_RATE;
GunBlinkState        = 1; /* gun blink on */

/* initialize the status screen */
InitStatus();

/* enter main animation loop */
GameOver = FALSE;
while (!GameOver) {
    /* get user input */
    GameOverInput = GetInput(Control, &UserInputUp, &UserInputDown,
        &UserInputLeft, &UserInputRight, &UserInputFire);

    /* move sprites */
    MoveSprites(UserInputUp, UserInputDown, UserInputLeft,
        UserInputRight, UserInputFire);

    /* check for collisions */
    CheckCollisions();

    /* erase */
    GameOverDeath = EraseSprites();

    /* draw */
    DrawSprites();

    /* update status */
    DrawStatus();

    /* wait for page flip */
    PageFlip(PageOffset[HiddenPage]);
    HiddenPage ^= 1; /* flip HiddenPage to other state */

    /* blink the guns */
    if (GunBlinkCounter == 0) {
        if (GunBlinkState == 1) {
            SetVGAPaletteEntry(GUN_COLOR, &Black);
        }
        else {
            SetVGAPaletteEntry(GUN_COLOR, &GunColor);
        }
        GunBlinkState ^= 1; /* flip it to other state */
        GunBlinkCounter = GUN_BLINK_RATE;
    }
    else {
        GunBlinkCounter--;
    }

    /* player either aborts or dies */
    GameOver = GameOverInput || GameOverDeath;
}

/* uninstall mouse and/or keyboard handlers */
```

```
if (Control == 'm') {
}
else if (Control == 'k') {
    SetNormalKeysMode();
}

/* free all memory used to play */
FreeSprites();

/* fade to black... */
FadeOut(250);

/* return to Mode 13h, as we were */
SetMode13h();
}
```

Play first loads the sprite bitmaps necessary for the game objects, initializes a few counters and flags, sets up the VGA in Mode X, and draws the status area at the bottom of the display. *Alien Alley* uses Mode X and the page-flipping animation technique discussed in Chapter 7. If the keyboard is used, our special keyboard handler from Chapter 2 is installed to allow multiple keys to be held down at once.

The heart of **Play**, however, is the main animation loop. In sequence, the main animation loop gets the player's input, moves the various sprite objects around the screen, checks for collisions between them, erases the sprites at their old positions, and draws them at their new positions. After the sprite images have been drawn, the status area at the bottom is updated to reflect the player's current score and shield level.

Once all the screen updates have been performed, the hidden page is ready to be displayed. The actual page flip is done using **PageFlip** rather than installing a vertical retrace interrupt handler. It turns out that *Alien Alley* runs at 60 fps on my Am386DX-40 and ISA VGA card. With the rise of fast 486s and local bus video, I made the decision that I would only support a 386DX-40 or above. Because *Alien Alley* already runs at the maximum rate, there is no point in trying to limit its performance on faster systems.

Once the page flip has occurred, the VGA is in a vertical retrace state, and some palette manipulations are performed to create a blinking light effect for the ships' guns. This code is almost identical to that in PALDEMO.EXE in Chapter 8. We simply toggle a single palette entry between two RGB values representing red and black.

There are two ways to exit the animation loop: either the player's ship is destroyed or the player presses the Esc key.

When the animation loop exits, the keyboard handler is removed, the sprite memory is freed, and the screen is faded to black.

SETTING UP MODE X

Alien Alley uses Mode X for its animation. The Mode X setup in the game is, however, a bit more complicated than what has been used in previous demo programs. *Alien Alley* doesn't simply set Mode X and then initialize the **PageOffset** variables to the start of two consecutive blocks of VGA memory. The specific initialization used is shown in Listing 11.4 and described in the subsequent text:

Listing 11.4   The SetUpModeX Function

```
/* screen parameters */
#define SCREEN_WIDTH            MODEX_WIDTH
#define SCREEN_HEIGHT           MODEX_HEIGHT
#define SCREEN_WIDTH_BYTES      (SCREEN_WIDTH / 4)
#define VERTICAL_BORDER_LINES   (MAX_OBJECT_HEIGHT + MAX_MOVE_STEP)
#define VERTICAL_BORDER_BYTES   (VERTICAL_BORDER_LINES * SCREEN_WIDTH_BYTES)
#define REDUCED_SCREEN_HEIGHT   (SCREEN_HEIGHT - STATUS_HEIGHT)
#define REDUCED_SCREEN_BYTES    (REDUCED_SCREEN_HEIGHT * SCREEN_WIDTH_BYTES)
#define STATUS_BYTES            (STATUS_HEIGHT * SCREEN_WIDTH_BYTES)

/*
    Function: SetUpModeX
    Description:
        Initializes the mode X page start variables and sets up the
        status area.
*/
void SetUpModeX(void)
{
    unsigned    LineCompare;
    UINT8       VGARegTemp;

    /* calculate offsets */
    PageOffset[0] = STATUS_BYTES + VERTICAL_BORDER_BYTES;
    PageOffset[1] = PageOffset[0] + REDUCED_SCREEN_BYTES +
        VERTICAL_BORDER_BYTES;

    /* set start address to page 0 */
    PageFlip(PageOffset[0]);
    HiddenPage = 1;

    /* set line compare register */

    /* Mode X (and Mode Y and Mode 13h) are double scan modes, so */
    /*    the number of lines in terms of the VGA is actually */
    /*    double the pixel height */
    LineCompare = 2 * REDUCED_SCREEN_HEIGHT;
    WaitVerticalRetraceStart();
```

```
    asm cli;
    /* write lower eight bits of line compare */
    outportb(CRTC_INDEX_REG, LINE_COMPARE_INDEX);
    outportb(CRTC_DATA_REG, LineCompare & 0xFF);
    /* ninth bit is in bit 4 of overflow register */
    outportb(CRTC_INDEX_REG, OVERFLOW_INDEX);
    VGARegTemp = inportb(CRTC_DATA_REG);
    VGARegTemp = (VGARegTemp & 0xEF) | ((LineCompare >> 4) & 0x10);
    outportb(CRTC_DATA_REG, VGARegTemp);
    /* tenth bit is in bit 6 of max scan line register */
    outportb(CRTC_INDEX_REG, MAX_SCAN_LINE_INDEX);
    VGARegTemp = inportb(CRTC_DATA_REG);
    VGARegTemp = (VGARegTemp & 0xBF) | ((LineCompare >> 3) & 0x40);
    outportb(CRTC_DATA_REG, VGARegTemp);
    asm sti;
}
```

Eliminating the Need for Clipping

Figure 11.1 gives an overview of how *Alien Alley* organizes VGA memory in Mode X. In particular, notice that the two pages of video memory are not located at the beginning of VGA memory, nor are they located back-to-back. There is some space ahead of the first page of memory (divided into two sections), some space between the first and the second, and some space after the second. The initial memory region is used for the status area at the bottom of the screen and is discussed next. First, let's examine the areas labeled "Offscreen Border" before, between, and after the two pages.

The space before, between, and after the two pages eliminates the need for bitblt routines that clip a sprite to the edges of the screen. The extra space allows a sprite to be fully drawn but only have the correct portion of it appear on the screen. Figure 11.2 shows how this occurs.

If extra space was not placed before, between, and after pages, the sprite would need to be clipped to fit the visible screen area. Figure 11.3 shows what would happen if no space was provided and clipping was not performed. A sprite bitmap drawn on the hidden page would also have a portion drawn on the visible page in the wrong position, creating an incorrect display. Bitblt routines that perform clipping can be used to limit the drawing of the bitmap image to the correct screen area, but such routines are typically slower than their non-clipping counterparts and may reduce the animation frame rate if many objects are on screen at once.

Alien Alley defines a constant named **MAX_OBJECT_HEIGHT** that, as its name suggests, is set to the maximum height of all the objects in the game.

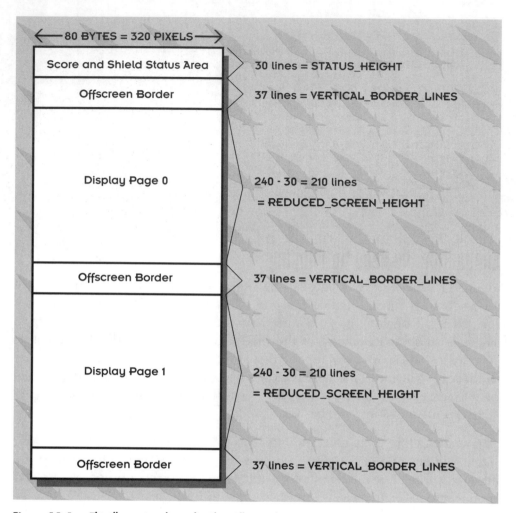

Figure 11.1 *This illustration shows the Alien Alley Mode X VGA memory organization.*

This constant, along with **MAX_MOVE_STEP**, which specifies the maximum number of pixels that any object will move in a single animation frame, is used to calculate the height of the vertical border, **VERTICAL_BORDER_LINES**. From this value, we compute the number of display memory bytes in the vertical border area, **VERTICAL_BORDER_BYTES**.

The Status Display

Before setting the **PageOffset** array with the beginning offsets of the two pages, **SetUpModeX** compensates for the amount of video memory needed by the status display at the bottom of the screen. Although it appears onscreen

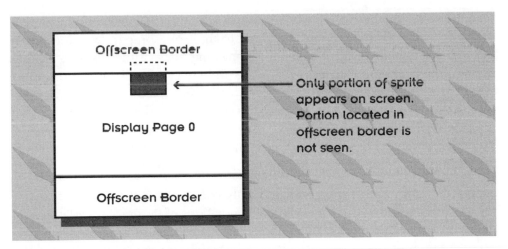

Figure 11.2 *Sprite fully drawn partially on screen.*

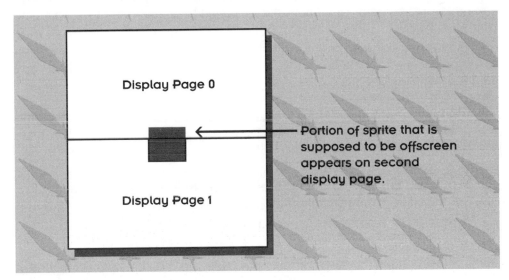

Figure 11.3 *Problems result if no extra space is provided.*

that the status display is just the lower portion of each display page, *Alien Alley* uses a feature of the VGA to make the status display area unified in video memory. The reason that we use this approach will become clear when we look at scrolling in Chapter 13.

The VGA includes a register called the Line Compare register (CRTC index 18h). This register is used to create the status display at the bottom of the screen. As the VGA scans down the screen, it keeps a count of all the lines it has scanned so far on the current video frame. After each row of pixels is scanned, the VGA compares the current line count to the Line Compare register. When the two are equal, the VGA scans the remaining lines of the display, starting from offset 0 in video memory. This has the effect of creating a portion of screen area at the bottom of the display that remains fixed in video memory at offset 0—a split screen. Page flipping has no effect on this portion of the display. Normally, the Line Compare register is initialized with a line count that is greater than that of the current display mode and thus the split-screen effect does not occur. Figure 11.4 shows how this looks on the display.

Setting the Line Compare register is slightly complicated. It turns out that this register has existed through a couple of generations of PC graphics adapters. In the EGA, the register was 9 bits wide. Of the 9 bits, 8 are located in the Line Compare register at CRTC index 18h. Bit 8 (the 9th bit) is located at bit 4 of the Overflow register (CTRC index 7). When the VGA was created, higher resolution modes were created and the register needed to be extended to 10 bits. The 10th bit is located at bit 6 of the Max Scanline register (CRTC index 9). Setting the Line Compare register requires that a program read the Overflow and Max Scanline registers, set the appropriate bits of the Line Compare register, and then write back the result without disturbing the other bits in those registers.

Note that before actually setting the Line Compare register, the routine multiplies the actual line count where the split screen will occur by 2. This is needed because Mode X (like Mode Y and Mode 13h) is a double-scanned mode. This means that as far as the VGA is concerned, Mode X is really a 320x480 mode but each row of pixels is output twice. Thus, the line counts that the VGA keeps internally are all multiplied by two, and so our program has to provide its line counts in the same manner.

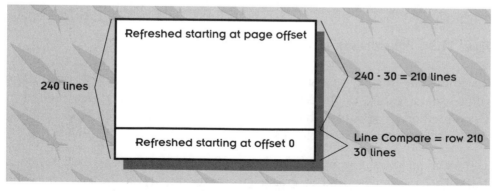

Figure 11.4 *Using the Line Compare register to create a split screen display.*

Once Mode X has been initialized, the display page starting offsets are initialized correctly, and the split-screen mode of the VGA is set up using the Line Compare register, **Play** enters the animation loop.

GETTING INPUT

The first thing to do in the animation loop is to get the user's input. The function **GetInput** takes care of getting input for a specific input device, depending on which one the user has specified. **GetInput** calls **GetJoystickInput**, **GetMouseInput**, or **GetKeyboardInput** as appropriate, as shown in Listing 11.5.

Listing 11.5   The GetJoystickInput, GetMouseInput, GetKeyboardInput, and GetInput Functions

```
/*
    Function: GetJoystickInput
    Description:
        Reads the current joystick position and button state and
        sets UserInput... accordingly.
*/
BOOL GetJoystickInput
    (
    BOOL * UserInputUp,
    BOOL * UserInputDown,
    BOOL * UserInputLeft,
    BOOL * UserInputRight,
    BOOL * UserInputFire
    )
{

    ReadJoysticks(&JsState);

    *UserInputUp    = JsState.JsAxisAY < JsThresholdUp;
    *UserInputDown  = JsState.JsAxisAY > JsThresholdDown;
    *UserInputLeft  = JsState.JsAxisAX < JsThresholdLeft;
    *UserInputRight = JsState.JsAxisAX > JsThresholdRight;
    *UserInputFire  = JsState.JsButtonA1;

    if (kbhit()) {
        if (getch() == 0) {
            getch();
        }
        return TRUE;
    }
    else {
        return FALSE;
    }
}
```

```
/*
    Function: GetMouseInput
    Description:
        Reads the position of the mouse and the current button state
        and sets UserInput... accordingly.
*/
BOOL GetMouseInput
    (
    BOOL * UserInputUp,
    BOOL * UserInputDown,
    BOOL * UserInputLeft,
    BOOL * UserInputRight,
    BOOL * UserInputFire
    )
{
    UINT16 Buttons;
    UINT16 x;
    UINT16 y;

    Buttons = PollMouseStatus(&x, &y);

    *UserInputUp    = y < MOUSE_THRESHOLD_UP;
    *UserInputDown  = y > MOUSE_THRESHOLD_DOWN;
    *UserInputLeft  = x < MOUSE_THRESHOLD_LEFT;
    *UserInputRight = x > MOUSE_THRESHOLD_RIGHT;
    *UserInputFire  = (Buttons & LEFT_BUTTON_MASK) != 0;

    if (kbhit()) {
        if (getch() == 0) {
            getch();
        }
        return TRUE;
    }
    else {
        return FALSE;
    }
}


/*
    Function: GetKeyboardInput
    Description:
        Updates the "UserInput..." variables used by the MoveSprites
        routine from the keyboard input device.
*/
BOOL GetKeyboardInput
    (
    BOOL * UserInputUp,
    BOOL * UserInputDown,
    BOOL * UserInputLeft,
    BOOL * UserInputRight,
    BOOL * UserInputFire
    )
{
    *UserInputUp    = GetKeyState(KEY_UP);
```

```
    *UserInputDown  = GetKeyState(KEY_DOWN);
    *UserInputRight = GetKeyState(KEY_RIGHT);
    *UserInputLeft  = GetKeyState(KEY_LEFT);
    *UserInputFire  = GetKeyState(KEY_SPACE) ||
        GetKeyState(KEY_CONTROL) || GetKeyState(KEY_ALT);

    return GetKeyState(KEY_ESC);
}

/*

    Function: GetInput
    Description:
        Get's player input and updates the hero's x & y variables
        as well as the variable to start a new missile firing.
        Control is a character specifying the method of input
        gathering.  Returns whether the user wants to quit the
        program or not.
*/
BOOL GetInput
    (
    int Control,
    BOOL * UserInputUp,
    BOOL * UserInputDown,
    BOOL * UserInputLeft,
    BOOL * UserInputRight,
    BOOL * UserInputFire
    )
{
    BOOL Quit;

    switch (Control) {
        case 'j':
            Quit = GetJoystickInput(UserInputUp, UserInputDown,
                UserInputLeft, UserInputRight, UserInputFire);
            break;
        case 'm':
            Quit = GetMouseInput(UserInputUp, UserInputDown,
                UserInputLeft, UserInputRight, UserInputFire);
            break;
        case 'k':
            Quit = GetKeyboardInput(UserInputUp, UserInputDown,
                UserInputLeft, UserInputRight, UserInputFire);
            break;
    }
    return Quit;
}
```

MOVING SPRITES

Once the user's input has been fetched, the animation loop moves all the
sprites currently on the screen. **MoveSprites**, shown in Listing 11.6, is called
to do the actual work.

The sprites are defined as follows:

```
typedef struct {
    BOOL    Active;
    int     x;
    int     y;
    int     vx;
    int     vy;
    int     OldX[2];
    int     OldY[2];
    BOOL    Erase[2];
    BOOL    Draw;
    unsigned ObjectSpec;        /* object specific use */
    unsigned ObjectSpec2;
    RECT    Bounds;
} SPRITE;
```

Each type of object in the game has a dedicated array of **SPRITE** structures. A single large array could have been defined to hold all the sprites, with a **Type** member used to distinguish between them. By using individual arrays, however, we are able to bound the exact number of each type of object—alien missiles, for instance—on the screen at one time. Further, collision detection is simplified by not having to search through a large list trying to determine whether two objects are allowed to collide, according to the game rules. We'll see this later when we look at collision detection.

```
SPRITE              Hero;
SPRITE              Alien[MAX_ALIENS];
SPRITE              HeroMissile[MAX_HERO_MISSILES];
SPRITE              AlienMissile[MAX_ALIEN_MISSILES];
SPRITE              Explosion[MAX_EXPLOSIONS];
```

The first thing that **MoveSprites** does is update the player position based on the input just received from **GetInput**. Next, the player's missiles are moved up the screen and the alien missiles are moved down the screen. If the player is requesting that a missile be fired, one is generated. A player missile is fired only when the routine detects that the button (either joystick, mouse, or key) has just been pressed. If the button is held down, it will not generate repeated missiles.

After the missile positions are updated, **MoveSprites** moves all the aliens currently on the screen. As each alien is handled, **MoveSprites** randomly decides whether the alien should change course or fire a missile. The exact frequency of these events is controlled by the **ALIEN_MOVE_TIME_BASE**, **ALIEN_MOVE_TIME_VAR**, **ALIEN_PROX_THRESHOLD**, **ALIEN_FIRE_PROB_HERO**, and **ALIEN_FIRE_PROB_RANDOM** constants.

Every so often, **MoveSprites** tries to create another alien. If there is a free alien sprite in the **Alien** array, then the creation succeeds. If not, then there are already the maximum number of aliens on the screen at the current instant and no new alien is created.

Finally, **MoveSprites** updates explosion animation. Although explosions don't actually move, they are animated and need to have successive frames drawn. **MoveSprites** makes sure that the explosion animation progresses and keeps track of when it's time to move to the next frame for any given explosion. The number of times that a frame of explosion animation is repeated by the main animation loop is controlled by **EXPLOSION_FRAME_REPEAT_COUNT**. Ideally, the explosion animation would be advanced every time another game animation frame was drawn, but this would force an artist to draw a large number of explosion animation frames. By repeating each frame of explosion animation more than once, the number of explosion bitmaps is reduced, along with the amount of memory needed to store them.

Listing 11.6 The MoveSprites Function

```
/*
    Function: MoveSprites
    Description:
        Takes care of moving hero ship and alien sprites, based on
        user input and their behavioral algorithms.  MoveSprites
        is also where missiles are generated and off-screen images
        are removed from play.
*/
void MoveSprites
    (
    BOOL UserInputUp,
    BOOL UserInputDown,
    BOOL UserInputLeft,
    BOOL UserInputRight,
    BOOL UserInputFire
    )
{
    int i;
    static LastFireInput;
    int AlienFireResult;
    int AlienProximity;

    /* first, take care of the hero */
    if (UserInputUp) {
        Hero.y -= HERO_Y_VELOCITY;
    }
    if (UserInputDown) {
        Hero.y += HERO_Y_VELOCITY;
    }
```

```
if (UserInputLeft) {
    Hero.x -= HERO_X_VELOCITY;
}
if (UserInputRight) {
    Hero.x += HERO_X_VELOCITY;
}
/* limit player movement */
Hero.y = MAX(HeroYMin, MIN(HeroYMax, Hero.y));
Hero.x = MAX(HeroXMin, MIN(HeroXMax, Hero.x));
/* update hero bounding rect */
ComputeBoundingRect(Hero.x, Hero.y, HeroBitmap->OriginX,
    HeroBitmap->OriginY, HeroWidth, HeroHeight,
    &(Hero.Bounds));

/* update hero missiles */
for (i = 0; i < MAX_HERO_MISSILES; i++) {
    if (HeroMissile[i].Draw) {
        /* update position */
        HeroMissile[i].y += HeroMissile[i].vy;
        /* stop drawing when it's off screen */
        if (HeroMissile[i].y < - (MAX_OBJECT_HEIGHT / 2)) {
            HeroMissile[i].Draw = FALSE;
        }
        else {
            /* if still onscreen, update bounding rect */
            ComputeBoundingRect(HeroMissile[i].x, HeroMissile[i].y,
                MissileBitmap->OriginX, MissileBitmap->OriginY,
                MissileWidth, MissileHeight, &(HeroMissile[i].Bounds)
        }
    }
}


/* generate hero missiles */
if (UserInputFire && !LastFireInput && Hero.Draw) {
    CreateHeroMissile(Hero.x - HERO_GUN_OFFSET_LEFT,
        Hero.y - HERO_GUN_OFFSET_UP);
    CreateHeroMissile(Hero.x + HERO_GUN_OFFSET_RIGHT,
        Hero.y - HERO_GUN_OFFSET_UP);
}
LastFireInput = UserInputFire;

/* update alien missiles */
for (i = 0; i < MAX_ALIEN_MISSILES; i++) {
    if (AlienMissile[i].Draw) {
        /* update position */
        AlienMissile[i].y += AlienMissile[i].vy;
        /* stop drawing when it's off screen */
        if (AlienMissile[i].y > (REDUCED_SCREEN_HEIGHT +
            (MAX_OBJECT_HEIGHT / 2))) {
            AlienMissile[i].Draw = FALSE;
        }
        else {
            /* if still onscreen, update bounding rect */
```

```
                    ComputeBoundingRect(AlienMissile[i].x, AlienMissile[i].y,
                        MissileBitmap->OriginX, MissileBitmap->OriginY,
                        MissileWidth, MissileHeight, &(AlienMissile[i].Bounds));
                }
            }
        }

        /* move aliens */
        for (i = 0; i < MAX_ALIENS; i++) {
            if (Alien[i].Draw) {
                if (Alien[i].ObjectSpec == 0) {
                    /* pick a new direction */
                    Alien[i].vx = random((2 * ALIEN_X_VELOCITY) + 1) -
                        ALIEN_X_VELOCITY;
                    Alien[i].ObjectSpec = ALIEN_MOVE_TIME_BASE +
                        random(ALIEN_MOVE_TIME_VAR);
                }
                else {
                    Alien[i].ObjectSpec--;
                }
                /* update alien position */
                Alien[i].x += Alien[i].vx;
                Alien[i].y += Alien[i].vy;

                /* clip alien movement horizontally */
                Alien[i].x = MAX(MAX_OBJECT_WIDTH / 2, MIN(Alien[i].x,
                    SCREEN_WIDTH - (MAX_OBJECT_WIDTH / 2)));

                /* move alien to top when it gets to bottom */
                if (Alien[i].y > (REDUCED_SCREEN_HEIGHT +
                    (MAX_OBJECT_HEIGHT / 2))) {
                    Alien[i].y = - (MAX_OBJECT_HEIGHT / 2);
                }

                /* update alien bounding rect */
                ComputeBoundingRect(Alien[i].x, Alien[i].y,
                    AlienBitmap->OriginX, AlienBitmap->OriginY,
                    AlienWidth, AlienHeight, &(Alien[i].Bounds));

                /* generate alien missiles */
                if (Alien[i].ObjectSpec2 == 0) {
                    AlienFireResult = random(100); /* in percent */
                    AlienProximity  = Alien[i].x - Hero.x;
                    if (AlienProximity < 0) {
                        AlienProximity = -AlienProximity;
                    }
                    if (((AlienProximity < ALIEN_PROX_THRESHOLD) &&
                        (AlienFireResult < ALIEN_FIRE_PROB_HERO)) ||
                        (AlienFireResult < ALIEN_FIRE_PROB_RANDOM)) {
                        CreateAlienMissile(Alien[i].x -
                            ALIEN_GUN_OFFSET_LEFT, Alien[i].y +
                            ALIEN_GUN_OFFSET_DOWN);
                        CreateAlienMissile(Alien[i].x +
```

```
                          ALIEN_GUN_OFFSET_RIGHT, Alien[i].y +
                          ALIEN_GUN_OFFSET_DOWN);
                      Alien[i].ObjectSpec2 = ALIEN_FIRE_LOCKOUT;
                  }
              }
              else {
                  Alien[i].ObjectSpec2-;
              }
          }
      }


      /* generate aliens */
      if (AlienGenCounter == 0) {
          /* generate an alien */
          CreateAlien();
          /* reinit generate counter */
          AlienGenCounter = ALIEN_GEN_RATE_BASE +
              random(ALIEN_GEN_RATE_VAR);
      }
      else {
          AlienGenCounter-;
      }


      /* update explosions - note, we don't really "move" them, just */
      /* make the animation go */
      for (i = 0; i < MAX_EXPLOSIONS; i++) {
          if (Explosion[i].Draw) {
              if (Explosion[i].ObjectSpec2 == 0) {
                  Explosion[i].ObjectSpec++;
                  Explosion[i].ObjectSpec2 = EXPLOSION_FRAME_REPEAT_COUNT;
                  if (Explosion[i].ObjectSpec >= MAX_EXPLOSION_BITMAPS) {
                      Explosion[i].Draw = FALSE;
                  }
              }
              else {
                  Explosion[i].ObjectSpec2-;
              }
          }
      }
}
```

COLLISION DETECTION

Once all the objects have been moved around the screen, it's time to determine what hit what. **CheckCollisions** is responsible for determining which objects have collided during this animation frame. **CheckCollisions** uses both rectangle and bitmap collision testing. Rectangles are used first as a quick test and then bitmap testing is used when the rectangle test indicates that a possible collision has occurred. Bounding rectangles are computed by the **MoveSprites** routine after each object position is updated.

CheckCollisions consists of several loops that each check a number of different types of objects against one another. The first loop checks the player's ship against alien ships, the second checks alien ships against the player's missiles, and the final loop checks the player's ship against alien missiles. Separating the different objects into different arrays allows these loops to be very simple.

Once a collision is detected, the objects that collided are removed from the game and explosions are created at the collision location.

The collision testing is very fast. Only objects that the game rules allow collisions between are checked, and the bounding rectangle test eliminates non-collisions very quickly. The slower bitmap test is only invoked when it needs to be.

The code makes good use of C's ability to do short-circuit boolean expression evaluation. If two tests are connected with a logical AND (&&), then C stops evaluating the expression the moment it finds a portion that is false. By putting the bitmap test later in the expression, it will be evaluated only if the rectangle test is found to be true. If the rectangle test is false, the remaining portions of the expression are not evaluated. The **CheckCollisions** function is shown in Listing 11.7.

Listing 11.7 The CheckCollisions Function

```
/*
    Function: CheckCollisions
    Description:
        Check for collisions between various objects and start
        explosions if they collide.  Collision detection is
        performed between:
            * aliens and hero
            * aliens and hero missiles
            * hero and alien missiles
        Note that all tests are performed between objects that are
        currently being drawn, not just active objects.
*/
void CheckCollisions(void)
{
    int i, j;

    /* check between hero and aliens */
    for (i = 0; i < MAX_ALIENS; i++) {
        /* Use C short circuit boolean evaluation in a big way. */
        /* Make sure both hero and alien are still being drawn */
        /* (they may still be active but have been removed */
        /* from the screen and are just being erased). */
        /* If they are still onscreen, then perform a rectangle test. */
        /* If the rectangle collision indicates a possible hit, then */
        /* perform a bitmap test. */
```

```
        if (Hero.Draw && Alien[i].Draw &&
            CollisionTestRect(&(Hero.Bounds), &(Alien[i].Bounds)) &&
            CollisionTestBitmap(HeroCollisionMap, AlienCollisionMap,
                Hero.Bounds.Left, Hero.Bounds.Top,
                Alien[i].Bounds.Left, Alien[i].Bounds.Top)) {

            Hero.Draw = FALSE;
            CreateExplosion(Hero.x, Hero.y);
            Alien[i].Draw = FALSE;
            CreateExplosion(Alien[i].x, Alien[i].y);
        }
    }


    /* check between aliens and hero missiles */
    for (i = 0; i < MAX_ALIENS; i++) {
        if (!Alien[i].Draw) {
            continue;
        }
        for (j = 0; j < MAX_HERO_MISSILES; j++) {
            /* do similiar short circuit, mondo huge test as above */
            if (HeroMissile[j].Draw &&
                CollisionTestRect(&(Alien[i].Bounds),
                    &(HeroMissile[j].Bounds)) &&
                CollisionTestBitmap(AlienCollisionMap,
                    MissileCollisionMap, Alien[i].Bounds.Left,
                    Alien[i].Bounds.Top, HeroMissile[j].Bounds.Left,
                    HeroMissile[j].Bounds.Top)) {

                Alien[i].Draw      = FALSE;
                HeroMissile[j].Draw = FALSE;
                CreateExplosion(Alien[i].x, Alien[i].y);
                Score += POINTS_PER_ALIEN;
                break; /* alien is destroyed */
            }
        }
    }


    /* check between hero and alien missiles */
    for (i = 0; i < MAX_ALIEN_MISSILES; i++) {
        /* again, rely on short circuiting */
        if (AlienMissile[i].Draw && Hero.Draw &&
            CollisionTestRect(&(AlienMissile[i].Bounds),
                &(Hero.Bounds)) &&
            CollisionTestBitmap(MissileCollisionMap, HeroCollisionMap,
                AlienMissile[i].Bounds.Left, AlienMissile[i].Bounds.Top,
                Hero.Bounds.Left, Hero.Bounds.Top)) {

            AlienMissile[i].Draw    = FALSE; /* destroy missile in any case */
            if (HeroShields == 0) {
                Hero.Draw           = FALSE;
                CreateExplosion(Hero.x, Hero.y);
                break; /* hero is destroyed */
```

```
        }
        else {
            /* take away a bit of shields */
            HeroShields--;
        }
    }
  }
}
```

ERASING AND DRAWING

After all the onscreen objects have been moved and have been tested for collisions, it's time to erase the sprites at their previous positions on the hidden page. **EraseSprites** is called to perform this task.

In general, **EraseSprites**, shown in Listing 11.8, is fairly simple. To erase a sprite, we simply draw its erase bitmap, an all-black bitmap the same size as the sprite, at its location on the hidden page. The **OldX** and **OldY** arrays for each sprite keep track of where a sprite has been drawn on each page. The erase bitmap is drawn with **BltPlanarNoTransparent**, since the erase bitmap doesn't need to have any transparent pixels. This makes the bitblt of the erase bitmap much faster than if we had used **BltPlanar**.

Listing 11.8   The EraseSprites Function

```
/*
    Function: EraseSprites
    Description:
        Erase all current bitmaps from the hidden screen.  If the
        erasure marks the last time that the object will be erased
        because it is no longer being drawn, deactivate the object.
*/
BOOL EraseSprites(void)
{
    int i;
    static unsigned DeathCounter;

    /* do player and possibly deactivate */
    if (Hero.Active && Hero.Erase[HiddenPage]) {
        BltPlanarNoTransparent(HeroEraseBitmap, Hero.OldX[HiddenPage],
            Hero.OldY[HiddenPage], PageOffset[HiddenPage]);
        Hero.Erase[HiddenPage] = FALSE;
        if (!(Hero.Draw || Hero.Erase[0] || Hero.Erase[1])) {
            Hero.Active = FALSE;
            DeathCounter = DEATH_DELAY;
        }
    }
```

```
        /* erase and deactivate hero missiles */
        for (i = 0; i < MAX_HERO_MISSILES; i++) {
            if (HeroMissile[i].Active && HeroMissile[i].Erase[HiddenPage]) {
                /* erase missile itself */
                BltPlanarNoTransparent(MissileEraseBitmap,
                    HeroMissile[i].OldX[HiddenPage],
                    HeroMissile[i].OldY[HiddenPage],
                    PageOffset[HiddenPage]);
                /* erase missile trail */
                BltPlanarNoTransparent(MissileTrailUpEraseBitmap,
                    HeroMissile[i].OldX[HiddenPage],
                    HeroMissile[i].OldY[HiddenPage],
                    PageOffset[HiddenPage]);
                HeroMissile[i].Erase[HiddenPage] = FALSE;
            }
            /* deactivate missile if we aren't going to draw or */
            /*    erase it anymore */
            if (!(HeroMissile[i].Draw || HeroMissile[i].Erase[0] ||
                HeroMissile[i].Erase[1])) {
                HeroMissile[i].Active = FALSE;
            }
        }

        /* erase and deactivate aliens */
        for (i = 0; i < MAX_ALIENS; i++) {
            if (Alien[i].Active && Alien[i].Erase[HiddenPage]) {
                BltPlanarNoTransparent(AlienEraseBitmap,
                    Alien[i].OldX[HiddenPage],
                    Alien[i].OldY[HiddenPage],
                    PageOffset[HiddenPage]);
                Alien[i].Erase[HiddenPage] = FALSE;
            }
            /* deactive alien if it's been destroyed */
            if (!(Alien[i].Draw || Alien[i].Erase[0] ||
                Alien[i].Erase[1])) {
                Alien[i].Active = FALSE;
            }
        }

        /* erase and deactivate alien missiles */
        for (i = 0; i < MAX_ALIEN_MISSILES; i++) {
            if (AlienMissile[i].Active && AlienMissile[i].Erase[HiddenPage]) {
                /* erase missile itself */
                BltPlanarNoTransparent(MissileEraseBitmap,
                    AlienMissile[i].OldX[HiddenPage],
                    AlienMissile[i].OldY[HiddenPage],
                    PageOffset[HiddenPage]);
                /* erase missile trail */
                BltPlanarNoTransparent(MissileTrailDnEraseBitmap,
                    AlienMissile[i].OldX[HiddenPage],
                    AlienMissile[i].OldY[HiddenPage],
                    PageOffset[HiddenPage]);
```

```
                AlienMissile[i].Erase[HiddenPage] = FALSE;
        }
        /* deactivate missile if we aren't going to draw or */
        /*   erase it anymore */
        if (!(AlienMissile[i].Draw || AlienMissile[i].Erase[0] ||
            AlienMissile[i].Erase[1])) {
            AlienMissile[i].Active = FALSE;
        }
    }

    /* erase and deactivate explosions */
    for (i = 0; i < MAX_EXPLOSIONS; i++) {
        if (Explosion[i].Active && Explosion[i].Erase[HiddenPage]) {
            BltPlanarNoTransparent(ExplosionEraseBitmap,
                Explosion[i].OldX[HiddenPage],
                Explosion[i].OldY[HiddenPage],
                PageOffset[HiddenPage]);
            Explosion[i].Erase[HiddenPage] = FALSE;
        }
        /* deactivate if explosion has run its course */
        if (!(Explosion[i].Draw || Explosion[i].Erase[0] ||
            Explosion[i].Erase[1])) {
            Explosion[i].Active = FALSE;
        }
    }

    /* hero has died - signal game over after brief delay */
    if (!Hero.Active) {
        if (DeathCounter == 0) {
            return TRUE;
        }
        else {
            DeathCounter--;
        }
    }
    return FALSE;
}
```

Drawing sprites is just as easy as erasing them. **DrawSprites**, shown in List-ing 11.9, does the work very quickly. It simply iterates through each of the object arrays, looking for objects that need to be drawn and then calling **BltPlanar** with the object's **x** and **y** coordinates and the hidden page offset as arguments.

DrawSprites handles the objects in a back-to-front order. Objects that should appear "on top" are drawn last. Because explosions are not really important to the actual game play, they are drawn first. By doing this, they don't obscure missiles or alien spaceships from the player's view. Following the explosions, first missiles, then aliens, and finally the player's ship are drawn.

Once a sprite is drawn, **DrawSprites** updates the **OldX** and **OldY** arrays with the **x** and **y** variables, so that the sprite can be erased from this display page at the appropriate time.

Listing 11.9   The DrawSprites Function

```
/*
    Function: DrawSprites
    Description:
        Draw all active objects that should be drawn on the
        screen.
*/
void DrawSprites(void)
{
    int i;

    /* do explosions */
    for (i = 0; i < MAX_EXPLOSIONS; i++) {
        if (Explosion[i].Draw) {
            /* draw explosion */
            BltPlanar(ExplosionBitmap[Explosion[i].ObjectSpec],
                Explosion[i].x, Explosion[i].y, PageOffset[HiddenPage]);
            Explosion[i].Erase[HiddenPage]  = TRUE;
            Explosion[i].OldX[HiddenPage]   = Explosion[i].x;
            Explosion[i].OldY[HiddenPage]   = Explosion[i].y;
        }
    }

    /* draw hero missiles */
    for (i = 0; i < MAX_HERO_MISSILES; i++) {
        if (HeroMissile[i].Draw) {
            /* draw missile itself */
            BltPlanar(MissileBitmap, HeroMissile[i].x, HeroMissile[i].y,
                PageOffset[HiddenPage]);
            /* draw missile trail */
            BltPlanar(MissileTrailUpBitmap, HeroMissile[i].x, HeroMissile[i].y,
                PageOffset[HiddenPage]);
            HeroMissile[i].Erase[HiddenPage]   = TRUE;
            HeroMissile[i].OldX[HiddenPage] = HeroMissile[i].x;
            HeroMissile[i].OldY[HiddenPage] = HeroMissile[i].y;
        }
    }

    /* draw alien missiles */
    for (i = 0; i < MAX_ALIEN_MISSILES; i++) {
        if (AlienMissile[i].Draw) {
            /* draw missile itself */
            BltPlanar(MissileBitmap, AlienMissile[i].x, AlienMissile[i].y,
                PageOffset[HiddenPage]);
            /* draw missile trail */
            BltPlanar(MissileTrailDnBitmap, AlienMissile[i].x,
```

```
                AlienMissile[i].y, PageOffset[HiddenPage]);
            AlienMissile[i].Erase[HiddenPage]   = TRUE;
            AlienMissile[i].OldX[HiddenPage]    = AlienMissile[i].x;
            AlienMissile[i].OldY[HiddenPage]    = AlienMissile[i].y;
        }
    }

    /* do aliens */
    for (i = 0; i < MAX_ALIENS; i++) {
        if (Alien[i].Active && Alien[i].Draw) {
            BltPlanar(AlienBitmap, Alien[i].x, Alien[i].y,
                PageOffset[HiddenPage]);
            Alien[i].Erase[HiddenPage]  = TRUE;
            Alien[i].OldX[HiddenPage]   = Alien[i].x;
            Alien[i].OldY[HiddenPage]   = Alien[i].y;
        }
    }

    /* do player */
    if (Hero.Active && Hero.Draw) {
        BltPlanar(HeroBitmap, Hero.x, Hero.y, PageOffset[HiddenPage]);
        Hero.Erase[HiddenPage]  = TRUE;
        Hero.OldX[HiddenPage]   = Hero.x;
        Hero.OldY[HiddenPage]   = Hero.y;
    }
}
```

Activation and Deactivation

In addition to simply erasing and drawing sprites, **EraseSprites** and **DrawSprites** handle the activation and deactivation of sprites. Remember, because we're using page flipping as our animation technique, we can't simply stop drawing an object once it is destroyed as the result of a collision. Let's take a look at an example.

Let's say that we've got an alien onscreen, we're displaying page 0, and page 1 is the hidden page. During **CheckCollisions**, we find that one of the player's missiles has collided with the alien and that it should now be removed from the screen. Even if we don't draw the alien to page 1 during this animation frame, we have to remember to erase it from page 0 during the next animation frame when page 0 is the hidden page. If we simply stop drawing, we'll leave an image of the alien on page 0 by mistake.

Alien Alley uses three boolean variables for each object to make sure that they are drawn, erased, and made available for re-use at the proper times. These variables are part of the **SPRITE** data structure and named **Active**, **Draw**, and **Erase**. **Erase** is a two-element array, each element corresponding to a display page.

Active is used to mark a sprite as being, well, active. That is, portions of *Alien Alley* are still manipulating it for some reason. A non-active sprite can be re-used. The **CreateExplosion**, **CreateAlien**, **CreateAlienMissile**, and **CreateHeroMissile** functions search the appropriate sprite arrays for an object that is not active.

Draw is used to indicate that the **DrawSprites** routine should draw the sprite to the screen. If this variable is **FALSE**, even if the sprite is still active, **DrawSprites** won't put it on the screen. **Draw** is set to **TRUE** when an object is created.

Finally, the **Erase** array is used to indicate that a sprite should be erased in **EraseSprites**. When **DrawSprites** draws an object, it sets the **Erase** flag corresponding to the hidden page to **TRUE**. During a subsequent animation frame, **EraseSprites** will see the flag set and know that it should erase the sprite from this display page. **EraseSprites** then sets the flag back to **FALSE**.

EraseSprites also takes care of deactivating an object once it has been removed from play. After erasing an object, **EraseSprites** checks to see if **Draw** and both **Erase** flags are all set to **FALSE**. If so, then **EraseSprites** knows that the sprite will never be drawn again and has been removed from both display pages. **EraseSprites** then sets the **Active** flag to **FALSE** to allow the **CreateXXX** routines to re-use the object.

Let's see how this works by re-examining the sequence of events that occurs when an alien is created and then destroyed.

1. The hidden page is currently page 0.
2. A call to **CreateAlien** is made. **CreateAlien** searches the **Alien SPRITE** array to find an entry that has **Active** set to **FALSE**.
3. **CreateAlien** finds an entry and sets **Active** and **Draw** to TRUE. It also sets both **Erase** flags to **FALSE**.
4. **EraseSprites** is called. The **Erase** flag for page 0 is **FALSE**, so the alien is not erased.
5. **DrawSprites** is called. The **Draw** flag for the alien is **TRUE,** so it is drawn to page 0 and the **Erase** flag for page 0 is set to **TRUE**.
6. A page flip occurs, making page 0 visible and page 1 hidden.
7. **EraseSprites** is called. The **Erase** flag for page 1 is **FALSE**, so the alien is not erased.
8. **DrawSprites** is called. The **Draw** flag for the alien is **TRUE,** so it is drawn to page 1 and the **Erase** flag for page 1 is set to **TRUE**. The sprite has now been drawn to both pages.

9. A page flip occurs, making page 1 visible and page 0 hidden.

10. **EraseSprites** is called. The **Erase** flag for page 0 is **TRUE**, so the alien is erased. The **Erase** flag for page 0 is set to **FALSE**.

11. **DrawSprites** is called. The **Draw** flag for the alien is **TRUE**, so it is drawn to page 0, and the **Erase** flag for page 0 is set to **TRUE**.

11. A page flip occurs, making page 0 visible and page 1 hidden.

13. **EraseSprites** is called. The **Erase** flag for page 1 is **TRUE**, so the alien is erased. The **Erase** flag for page 1 is set to **FALSE**.

14. **DrawSprites** is called. The **Draw** flag for the alien is **TRUE**, so it is drawn to page 1, and the **Erase** flag for page 1 is set to **TRUE**.

15. Events 9 through 14 repeat while the alien is on the screen.

Now, when a player's missile hits the alien ship, the following events happen:

1. The hidden page is page 1.

2. **CheckCollisions** sets the alien's **Draw** flag to **FALSE**.

3. **EraseSprites** is called. The **Erase** flag for page 1 is **TRUE**, so the alien is erased. The **Erase** flag for page 1 is set to **FALSE**.

4. **DrawSprites** is called. Since the **Draw** flag is **FALSE**, the alien is not drawn and the **Erase** flag for page 1 remains **FALSE**.

5. A page flip occurs, making page 1 visible and page 0 hidden.

6. **EraseSprites** is called. The **Erase** flag for page 0 is **TRUE**, so the alien is erased. The **Erase** flag for page 0 is set to **FALSE**. Now, both **Erase** flags and the **Draw** flag are **FALSE**. The alien has been erased from both display pages and no longer needs to be redrawn. **EraseSprites** detects this condition and sets the **Active** flag to **FALSE**, to indicate that this alien **SPRITE** is no longer being used.

Death

Just as when aliens are destroyed, **EraseSprites** detects that the player's ship has been removed from the game and sets its **Active** flag to **FALSE**. Instead of immediately ending the game, however, **EraseSprites** starts a short timer. This timer allows the game to progress for a few more frames after the player's death so that the explosion from the player's ship can run its course and there is not an abrupt halt of the game.

To create the delay, **EraseSprites** initializes **DeathCounter** with the number of animation frames that should be displayed before the game ends.

Every time **EraseSprites** is called after that point, **DeathCounter** is decremented once.

Finally, when **DeathCounter** reaches zero, **EraseSprites** returns **TRUE** to the animation loop in **Play**, which signals that the player has been destroyed and that the animation loop should exit.

THE HIGH-SCORE SCREEN

After **Play** returns, **main** calls **NewHighScore**, shown in Listing 11.10, to see if the player has enough points to displace one of the top 10 scores. If so, **NewHighScore** adjusts the high-score array to make room for the player's new entry and allows the player to type his name.

The display of the high-score text is done using the VGA's BIOS routines. **SetCursorPosition** and **DrawChar** are C wrappers for these BIOS routines. The BIOS routines draw text equally well in graphics mode as they do in text modes and make it very easy to get text onto the screen. Using the BIOS has some limitations: the characters cannot be drawn at arbitrary X offsets, and each character must be a solid color. In spite of these limitations, the BIOS routines are quick and easy. If you want to draw more sophisticated text, you could write custom routines that bitblt character bitmaps to the screen. In this way, each character would be a complete bitmap and could be drawn at any position and could use multiple colors at once.

Listing 11.10 The NewHighScore Function

```
/*
    Function: NewHighScore
    Description:
        Manipulates the HighScore array to make room for the
        users score and gets the new text.
*/
void NewHighScore(int NewScore)
{
    int i;
    int Row;
    int Column;
    int StrLen;
    int Key;

    /* check to see if it's really a high score */
    if (NewScore <= HighScore[9].Score) {
        return;
    }
```

```
/* move other scores down to make room */
for (i = 8; i >= 0; i-) {
    if (NewScore > HighScore[i].Score) {
        strcpy(HighScore[i + 1].Text, HighScore[i].Text);
        HighScore[i + 1].Score = HighScore[i].Score;
    }
    else {
        break;
    }
}
i++;

/* blank out text of correct slot */
HighScore[i].Text[0] = '\0';
HighScore[i].Score = NewScore;

/* display the text and fade in */
SetMode13h();
GetVGAPaletteBlock(GamePalette, 0, 256);
SetVGAPaletteBlock(BlackPalette, 0, 128);
SetVGAPaletteBlock(BlackPalette, 128, 128);
DisplayHighScores();
FadeIn(500);

/* get user text string */
Row      = HIGH_SCORE_LINE + i;
Column   = 8;
StrLen   = 0;
do {
    SetCursorPosition(Row, Column);
    DrawChar(127, 9);
    Key = getch();
    if (Key == 0) {
        getch();
    }
    if (' ' <= Key && Key <= 126 && StrLen < HIGH_SCORE_TEXT_LEN) {
        DrawChar(Key, 9);
        HighScore[i].Text[StrLen] = Key;
        StrLen++;
        HighScore[i].Text[StrLen] = '\0';
        Column++;
    }
    else if (Key == '\b' && StrLen > 0) {
        DrawChar(' ', 9);
        StrLen-;
        Column-;
        HighScore[i].Text[StrLen] = '\0';
    }
} while (Key != '\r');

/* erase cursor */
DrawChar(' ', 9);
```

```
    /* fade to black... */
    FadeOut(500);
}
```

CREATING THE GRAPHICS

All the sprite bitmaps in *Alien Alley* are stored in individual PCX files for easy loading and manipulation. The PCX format is used because it is easy to manipulate, and most drawing packages understand it. *Alien Alley* uses the **LoadPCX** function, documented in Chapter 7, to bring each bitmap into memory as a **LINEAR_BITMAP**. The sprite bitmaps were not originally created as individual PCX files, however.

Although it is convenient for game programs to manipulate sprite bitmaps as small individual bitmap files, most commercial and shareware drawing programs can't deal with bitmap images that aren't standard screen sizes, 320x200 pixels for instance. It's difficult to have these programs save a 32x32 sprite bitmap. Those programs that have been developed specifically to draw sprite images typically lack the advanced drawing tools of the more professional programs. Additionally, since all the alien, hero, missile, and explosion bitmaps must appear on the screen at the same time, they must all use the same palette or they will not look correct. Managing the individual palettes in 10 or more individual bitmap files is cumbersome at best.

There are ways around these issues, however. A common technique in the game programming world is to draw multiple sprites on a single 320x200 canvas using high quality drawing programs. The drawing programs don't have a problem, because a standard screen size is used for the image. Palette management is also simplified because there is only one palette for the entire drawing, which covers all the sprites. The question is, how do we convert our single bitmap containing all the sprite images to individual sprite bitmap files?

Typically, a small program is written to extract the individual sprites out of the larger image and save them off to their own files. I've written such a utility, named CLIPSPR, which is included on the companion disk.

CLIPSPR

CLIPSPR is a small DOS program that extracts individual sprite bitmaps from a larger PCX file and saves them in one of a few different formats. CLIPSPR searches for sprite bitmaps within the larger bitmap by looking for a rectangular box of a special color that surrounds the sprite images. For instance, the program defaults to searching for color 255. When CLIPSPR finds a rectangle of color 255 in the large bitmap image, it assumes that what is enclosed by the rectangle is a sprite bitmap and allows it to be saved to an individual file.

CLIPSPR first processes the input file by loading it and trying to identify where the sprite-bounding rectangles are located. Once CLIPSPR finds all the sprite bitmaps, it saves them to individual files using user-supplied filenames. Before CLIPSPR exits, it records the locations and output filenames of the sprite bitmaps it has found, in a file that ends with a ".CSD" ("CLIPSPR data"). If CLIPSPR is run again on the file, it will automatically identify those sprites that have been seen before and save them out using the same names. This allows small changes to be made to an individual sprite image, without having to retype the names of all the other sprites when CLIPSPR is run again.

If there is no .CSD file present, CLIPSPR will ask the user to name each sprite image. CLIPSPR will allow the user to preview the sprite image before naming, however, as the coordinate values that CLIPSPR displays are rarely helpful in identifying individual sprites from a source file that may contain 20 or more individual images. To preview a sprite, type "?" at the naming prompt. If you wish to skip the sprite that CLIPSPR has found, enter ">" at the naming prompt. When naming the sprite, type only the basename; do not include a filename extension. The filename extension will be added by CLIPSPR based on the output file format. This allows CLIPSPR to be run multiple times to create images of multiple types while using the same .CSD file.

CLIPSPR takes up to three command-line parameters. The first parameter is the source file in which all the sprite images are located. This file must be in PCX format. You need not supply the ".PCX" extension; CLIPSPR will use ".PCX" as a default if no extension is supplied. To supply a filename with no extension, use "filename." with nothing following the period.

The second parameter is the output file format and is optional. CLIPSPR defaults to saving the sprite bitmaps in PCX format. The bitmaps may also be saved in LINEAR_BITMAP or PLANAR_BITMAP format. When these formats are used, the datafile will be a strict binary dump of the memory image of these formats. Linear and planar data files use ".LIN" and ".PLN" extensions. No palette information is included in the linear and planar formats. The desired format can be specified by including "pcx," "planar," or "linear" on the command line.

The final parameter to CLIPSPR is the color index to search for. This parameter is an integer value from 0 to 255 and defaults to 255. Each sprite in the PCX source file should be completely outlined in a rectangle of this color. The outline color should not be used for any other purpose than to outline the individual sprites. If the color appears as part of a sprite image, CLIPSPR will become confused when it performs its search. Although it tries to detect errors of this sort, the overall error handling of the program is not very robust (it's a simple utility, after all), and strange things can occur.

You can create the sprites used in *Alien Alley* by running CLIPSPR, using the ALIENSPR.PCX file as input. ALIENSPR.PCX contains all the sprites used in *Alien Alley*, each outlined in a rectangle of color 255. ALIENSPR.PCX is located in the SPRITES subdirectory.

Give the command "..\clipspr alienspr" to create the individual PCX bitmap files. Since ALIENSPR.CSD is already present, CLIPSPR will extract the individual sprites based on the information contained in ALIENSPR.CSD.

If you already have a utilities directory of some sort that is on your DOS path, you might want to move CLIPSPR.EXE to that directory, so that DOS can automatically find the program when you run it.

About the Art

The art in *Alien Alley* was created by Kevin Long of AIR Design. Kevin used a combination of Autodesk Animator and Corel Draw 4 for various elements of the artwork.

Corel Draw was used to create the font and alien character for the title screen. Both images were then imported into Autodesk Animator where color was added and their edges softened.

Autodesk Animator was also used to create the sprite bitmaps and small digital font used for the high score numbers. "Autodesk Animator is a great tool to use when you want to have many images all share the same pallette," says Kevin. "It takes all the images you create and makes them share one pallette. It also gives you a great degree of control when creating custom pallettes. This was used to get the rich greens of the aliens and the red-orange-yellow transitions in the explosions."

About the Artist

Kevin Long has been an entrepeneur in the computer industry for the last 10 years. After some soul searching and a quick reevaluation of life, Kevin has returned to doing what he loved in high school: Staying up late, creating beautiful art and listening to obnoxious music.

You can contact Kevin at:
AIR Design
3354 N.E. 83rd Ave
Portland, OR 97220
VoiceMail: 800-223-3737x594
E-Mail: air@netcom.com

POSSIBLE IMPROVEMENTS

There are many possible improvements that can be made to *Alien Alley*. We'll add two of them, sound and a scrolling background, in the next couple of chapters. In addition to these two, there are several others that would make the game more interesting.

First, *Alien Alley* currently supports only one type of alien. Many different aliens could be defined and different point values assigned to them. Each alien could have different capabilities. Some could be faster or slower or shoot more or fewer missiles.

Second, many "power ups" could be added. There is currently no way for the player to recharge theshield generators. Once they are depleted, they are gone forever. You might want to add a special capsule that, when the player contacts it, fully or partially re-energizes the shields. Another type of power up might give the player more powerful weapons. For instance, when the player gets the power up, a temporary super bomb could provide a chance to destroy all the aliens on screen with one single shot—a super bomb.

There are many other enhancements that can be made to *Alien Alley*. Your imagination is the limit. Now let's get on to making some of the more obvious ones happen!

ALIEN1.C

Listing 11.11 is the full ALIEN1.C listing. All the smaller support functions that have been neglected in the previous sections can be found in this listing.

Compiling and Linking:

You can compile the ALIEN1 program using the Borland C++ 3.1 IDE by typing "bc alien1.prj" and then selecting Compile I Make from the menus. If you would rather use the command line compiler, convert the ALIEN1.PRJ file to a makefile using the PRJ2MAK program supplied with Borland C++ 3.1. Type "prj2mak alien1.prj" to create the ALIEN1.MAK and ALIEN1.CFG files.

If you are using Borland C++ 4.0, choose Project | Open Project from the IDE menus. Open the ALIEN1.PRJ file. Borland C++ will convert the version 3.1 .PRJ file to a version 4.0 .IDE file. Compile and link the program by choosing Project | Make All from the IDE menus.

Listing 11.11 ALIEN1.C

```
/* File: ALIEN1.C
** Description:
**    Alien Alley, version 1.  Demonstration game.
** Copyright:
**    Copyright 1994, David G. Roberts
*/

#include <alloc.h>
#include <assert.h>
#include <conio.h>
#include <ctype.h>
#include <dos.h>
#include <stdio.h>
#include <stdlib.h>
#include <string.h>
#include <time.h>    /* for randomize() */
#include "gamedefs.h"
#include "animate.h"
#include "bitblt.h"
#include "collide.h"
#include "digmidif.h"
#include "digplay.h"
#include "jstick.h"
#include "keyboard.h"
#include "midpak.h"
#include "mouse.h"
#include "palette.h"
#include "pcx.h"
#include "retrace.h"
#include "setmodex.h"
#include "vga.h"
#include "vrsync.h"

/* CONSTANTS */
#define MOUSE_RANGE_Y         (MODE13H_HEIGHT)
#define MOUSE_RANGE_X         (2 * MODE13H_WIDTH)
#define MOUSE_THRESHOLD_UP    (MOUSE_RANGE_Y / 3)
#define MOUSE_THRESHOLD_DOWN  (2 * (MOUSE_RANGE_Y / 3))
#define MOUSE_THRESHOLD_LEFT  (MOUSE_RANGE_X / 3)
#define MOUSE_THRESHOLD_RIGHT (2 * (MOUSE_RANGE_X / 3))
```

```
#define INTRO_TEXT_COLOR        0x4
#define MAX_ALIENS              4
#define MAX_ALIEN_MISSILES      20
#define MAX_HERO_MISSILES       10
#define MAX_EXPLOSIONS          (MAX_ALIENS + 1) /* +1 for hero */
#define MAX_EXPLOSION_BITMAPS 5
#define ERASE_COLOR             0    /* color to use to erase sprites */
#define GUN_COLOR               8
#define GUN_BLINK_RATE          10
#define MAX_OBJECT_WIDTH        32
#define MAX_OBJECT_HEIGHT       32
#define HERO_X_VELOCITY         3
#define HERO_Y_VELOCITY         3
#define ALIEN_X_VELOCITY        2
#define ALIEN_Y_VELOCITY        2
#define HERO_MISSILE_VELOCITY   5
#define ALIEN_MISSILE_VELOCITY  4
#define MAX_MOVE_STEP           5    /* max sprite movement (hero missile) */
#define ALIEN_MOVE_TIME_VAR     50
#define ALIEN_MOVE_TIME_BASE    20
#define ALIEN_GEN_RATE_BASE     40
#define ALIEN_GEN_RATE_VAR      40
#define ALIEN_FIRE_LOCKOUT      60
#define ALIEN_FIRE_PROB_HERO    20
#define ALIEN_FIRE_PROB_RANDOM  10
#define ALIEN_PROX_THRESHOLD    20
#define HERO_GUN_OFFSET_LEFT    12
#define HERO_GUN_OFFSET_RIGHT   11
#define HERO_GUN_OFFSET_UP      4
#define ALIEN_GUN_OFFSET_LEFT   11
#define ALIEN_GUN_OFFSET_RIGHT  10
#define ALIEN_GUN_OFFSET_DOWN   3
#define DEATH_DELAY             60 /* 1 sec delay after player death */
#define POINTS_PER_ALIEN        10
#define MAX_HERO_SHIELDS        5
#define STATUS_HEIGHT           30 /* height of the bottom status window */
#define SHIELD_STATUS_COLOR     47
#define SHIELD_STATUS_INVERT_COLOR 173
#define STATUS_VERT_BORDER      5
#define STATUS_HORIZ_BORDER     8
#define SHIELDS_TEXT_LEFT       (STATUS_HORIZ_BORDER + 16)
#define SHIELDS_TEXT_TOP        (STATUS_VERT_BORDER + 5)
#define SCORE_TEXT_LEFT         190
#define SCORE_TEXT_TOP          (STATUS_VERT_BORDER + 7)
#define SCORE_NUMBERS_LEFT      237
#define SCORE_NUMBERS_TOP       (STATUS_VERT_BORDER + 7)
#define SHIELD_STATUS_WIDTH_MULT 2
#define SHIELD_STATUS_HEIGHT    10
#define SHIELD_STATUS_LEFT      96
#define SHIELD_STATUS_TOP       (STATUS_VERT_BORDER + 5)
#define SHIELD_STATUS_RIGHT     (SHIELD_STATUS_LEFT + (MAX_HERO_SHIELDS * \
    4 * SHIELD_STATUS_WIDTH_MULT) - 1)
#define SHIELD_STATUS_BOTTOM    (SHIELD_STATUS_TOP + \
```

```
      SHIELD_STATUS_HEIGHT - 1)
#define SHIELD_STATUS_OUTLINE_COLOR 7
#define STATUS_BACKGROUND_COLOR 27
#define EXPLOSION_FRAME_REPEAT_COUNT 5
#define HIGH_SCORE_TEXT_LEN        20
#define HIGH_SCORE_FILENAME        "AAHSCORE.DAT"
#define HIGH_SCORE_LINE            7
#define HIGH_SCORE_COLOR           2

/* screen parameters */
#define SCREEN_WIDTH               MODEX_WIDTH
#define SCREEN_HEIGHT              MODEX_HEIGHT
#define SCREEN_WIDTH_BYTES         (SCREEN_WIDTH / 4)
#define VERTICAL_BORDER_LINES      (MAX_OBJECT_HEIGHT + MAX_MOVE_STEP)
#define VERTICAL_BORDER_BYTES      (VERTICAL_BORDER_LINES * SCREEN_WIDTH_BYTES)
#define REDUCED_SCREEN_HEIGHT      (SCREEN_HEIGHT - STATUS_HEIGHT)
#define REDUCED_SCREEN_BYTES       (REDUCED_SCREEN_HEIGHT * SCREEN_WIDTH_BYTES)
#define STATUS_BYTES               (STATUS_HEIGHT * SCREEN_WIDTH_BYTES)

/* STRUCTURES AND TYPES */
typedef struct {
    BOOL     Active;
    int      x;
    int      y;
    int      vx;
    int      vy;
    int      OldX[2];
    int      OldY[2];
    BOOL     Erase[2];
    BOOL     Draw;
    unsigned ObjectSpec;           /* object specific use */
    unsigned ObjectSpec2;
    RECT     Bounds;
} SPRITE;

typedef struct {
    char Text[HIGH_SCORE_TEXT_LEN + 1];
    int Score;
} HIGH_SCORE;

/* GLOBAL VARIABLES */
BOOL               MousePresent;
BOOL               JoystickPresent;
JOYSTICK_STATE     JsState;
UINT16             JsThresholdUp;
UINT16             JsThresholdDown;
UINT16             JsThresholdLeft;
UINT16             JsThresholdRight;
UINT8              BlackPalette[256][3];
UINT8              GamePalette[256][3];
int                Score;
SPRITE             Hero;
SPRITE             Alien[MAX_ALIENS];
```

```
SPRITE              HeroMissile[MAX_HERO_MISSILES];
SPRITE              AlienMissile[MAX_ALIEN_MISSILES];
SPRITE              Explosion[MAX_EXPLOSIONS];
PLANAR_BITMAP far * HeroBitmap;
PLANAR_BITMAP far * HeroEraseBitmap;
COLLISION_MAP far * HeroCollisionMap;
PLANAR_BITMAP far * AlienBitmap;
PLANAR_BITMAP far * AlienEraseBitmap;
COLLISION_MAP far * AlienCollisionMap;
PLANAR_BITMAP far * MissileBitmap;
PLANAR_BITMAP far * MissileEraseBitmap;
COLLISION_MAP far * MissileCollisionMap;
PLANAR_BITMAP far * MissileTrailUpBitmap;
PLANAR_BITMAP far * MissileTrailDnBitmap;
PLANAR_BITMAP far * MissileTrailUpEraseBitmap;
PLANAR_BITMAP far * MissileTrailDnEraseBitmap;
PLANAR_BITMAP far * ExplosionBitmap[MAX_EXPLOSION_BITMAPS];
PLANAR_BITMAP far * ExplosionEraseBitmap;
PLANAR_BITMAP far * Numbers[10];
unsigned            HeroWidth, HeroHeight;
unsigned            HeroXMin, HeroXMax;
unsigned            HeroYMin, HeroYMax;
unsigned            AlienWidth, AlienHeight;
unsigned            MissileWidth, MissileHeight;
unsigned            MissileTrailWidth, MissileTrailHeight;
int                 HiddenPage;
UINT16              PageOffset[2];
int                 AlienGenCounter;
int                 HeroShields;
HIGH_SCORE          HighScore[10];


/*
    Function: FatalError
    Description:
        Handle a fatal error.
*/
void FatalError(char * Error, char * Routine, int Line)
{
    SetVGAMode(0x3);
    fprintf(stderr, "ERROR: %s in %s, line %d!\n", Error, Routine, Line);
    exit(1);
}


/*
    Function: CalibrateJsMidpoint
    Description:
        Calibrates a joystick's range using the midpoint method.
        Read's the value of the joystick at the time it is
        called and computes a min and max range from this.
        Note that this assumes that the joystick is centered
        when the routine is called.
*/
void CalibrateJsMidpoint
```

```
    (
    JOYSTICK_STATE * JsState,
    UINT16 * Xmin,
    UINT16 * Ymin,
    UINT16 * Xmid,
    UINT16 * Ymid,
    UINT16 * Xmax,
    UINT16 * Ymax
    )
{
    assert(JsState != NULL);
    assert(Xmin != NULL);
    assert(Ymin != NULL);
    assert(Xmid != NULL);
    assert(Ymid != NULL);
    assert(Xmax != NULL);
    assert(Ymax != NULL);

    /* read midpoint value */
    ReadJoysticks(JsState);
    *Xmid = JsState->JsAxisAX;
    *Ymid = JsState->JsAxisAY;

    /* assume min coordinate is (0,0) and max is twice midpoint */
    *Xmin = *Ymin = 0;

    *Xmax = 2 * *Xmid;
    *Ymax = 2 * *Ymid;
}


/*
    Function: DefaultHighScores
    Description:
        Fills in the HighScore array with some defaults.
        Have fun with this.
*/
void DefaultHighScores(void)
{
    HighScore[0].Text[0] = '\0';
    strcat(HighScore[0].Text, "George Washington");
    HighScore[0].Score = 100;

    HighScore[1].Text[0] = '\0';
    strcat(HighScore[1].Text, "John Adams");
    HighScore[1].Score = 90;

    HighScore[2].Text[0] = '\0';
    strcat(HighScore[2].Text, "Thomas Jefferson");
    HighScore[2].Score = 80;

    HighScore[3].Text[0] = '\0';
    strcat(HighScore[3].Text, "James Madison");
    HighScore[3].Score = 70;
```

```
    HighScore[4].Text[0] = '\0';
    strcat(HighScore[4].Text, "James Monroe");
    HighScore[4].Score = 60;

    HighScore[5].Text[0] = '\0';
    strcat(HighScore[5].Text, "John Quincy Adams");
    HighScore[5].Score = 50;

    HighScore[6].Text[0] = '\0';
    strcat(HighScore[6].Text, "Andrew Jackson");
    HighScore[6].Score = 40;

    HighScore[7].Text[0] = '\0';
    strcat(HighScore[7].Text, "Martin Van Buren");
    HighScore[7].Score = 30;

    HighScore[8].Text[0] = '\0';
    strcat(HighScore[8].Text, "William H. Harrison");
    HighScore[8].Score = 20;

    HighScore[9].Text[0] = '\0';
    strcat(HighScore[9].Text, "John Tyler");
    HighScore[9].Score = 10;
}

/*
    Function: LoadHighScores
    Description:
        Loads the high-score file from disk.  If a high-score file
        cannot be found or cannot be read, a default list of
        high-score entries is created.
*/
void LoadHighScores(void)
{
    FILE * HighScoreFile;
    char TextLine[81]; /* make sure high score lines are <= 80 chars */
    int i;
    int Result;

    HighScoreFile = fopen(HIGH SCORE FILENAME, "rt");
    if (HighScoreFile == NULL) { /* error on open, so default */
        DefaultHighScores();
        return;
    }

    for (i = 0; i < 10; i++) {
        if (fgets(TextLine, 81, HighScoreFile) == NULL) {
            /* there aren't enough entries, fill in default */
            DefaultHighScores();
            return;
        }
        Result = sscanf(TextLine, "%20c %d", HighScore[i].Text,
            &(HighScore[i].Score));
```

```
            if (Result != 2) {
                /* corrupt file — not a string and an integer on */
                /*   the same line */
                DefaultHighScores();
                return;
            }
        }

    fclose(HighScoreFile);
}

/*
    Function: SaveHighScores
    Description:
        Writes the HighScore array out to the high-score file.
*/
void SaveHighScores(void)
{
    FILE * HighScoreFile;
    int i;

    HighScoreFile = fopen(HIGH_SCORE_FILENAME, "wt");
    if (HighScoreFile == NULL) {
        /* error writing file, just ignore it */
        return;
    }

    for (i = 0; i < 10; i++) {
        fprintf(HighScoreFile, "%-20s %d\n", HighScore[i].Text,
            HighScore[i].Score);
    }

    fclose(HighScoreFile);
}

/*
    Function: ProgramInit
    Description:
        Performs all the program-wide initialization at start-up
        time.  This includes sensing the presence of alternate input
        devices and ensuring they are calibrated.
*/
void ProgramInit(void)
{
    UINT16 Xmin, Xmid, Xmax;
    UINT16 Ymin, Ymid, Ymax;
    RGB_TUPLE Black = {0, 0, 0};

    /* get into graphics */
    SetMode13h();

    /* detect mouse presence */
    if (ResetMouse() != 0) {
```

```
            MousePresent = TRUE;
        }
        else {
            MousePresent = FALSE;
        }

        /* detect and calibrate joystick */
        SenseJoysticks(&JsState);
        JsState.JsMask &= 0x3;  /* only enable joystick A */
        if (JsState.JsMask != 0) {
            JoystickPresent = TRUE;
            CalibrateJsMidpoint(&JsState, &Xmin, &Ymin, &Xmid, &Ymid,
                &Xmax, &Ymax);
            JsThresholdUp       = Ymax / 3;
            JsThresholdDown     = (Ymax * 2) / 3;
            JsThresholdLeft     = Xmax / 3;
            JsThresholdRight    = (Xmax * 2) / 3;
        }
        else {
            JoystickPresent = FALSE;
        }

        /* initialize palette */
        FillPaletteBlock(BlackPalette, 0, 256, &Black);

        /* load high-score file */
        LoadHighScores();
}

/*
    Function: ClearMode13hScreen
    Description:
        Clears a mode 13h screen to color 0 (typically black).
*/
void ClearMode13hScreen(void)
{
    unsigned i;
    UINT8 far * Screen;

    Screen = MK_FP(VIDEO_MEM_SEGMENT, 0);

    for (i = 0; i < (320U * 200U); i++) {
        *Screen++ = 0;
    }
}

/*
    Function: FadeIn
    Description:
        Fades from black to the game palette in the
        specified amount of time.
*/
void FadeIn(int MilliSec)
```

```
{
    FadePaletteBlock(BlackPalette, GamePalette, 0, 256, MilliSec);
}

/*
    Function: FadeOut
    Description:
        Fades from the current VGA palette to black.
*/
void FadeOut(int MilliSec)
{
    FadePaletteBlock(GamePalette, BlackPalette, 0, 256, MilliSec);
}

/*
    Function: SetCursorPosition
    Description:
        Moves the cursor position to the indicated row and column
        using the VGA BIOS, function #2.  This BIOS routine
        works even in graphics mode and is used to position the
        cursor for drawing text to the screen in graphics
        modes.
*/
void SetCursorPosition(int Row, int Column)
{
    union REGS Regs;

    Regs.h.bh = 0; /* page */
    Regs.h.dh = Row; /* row */
    Regs.h.dl = Column; /* column */
    Regs.h.ah = 2; /* set cursor position */
    int86(VGA_BIOS_INT, &Regs, &Regs);
}

/*
    Function: DrawChar
    Description:
        Draws a character onto the screen using the VGA BIOS calls.
        The character is drawn in the specified color.
*/
void DrawChar(char Char, int Color)
{
    union REGS Regs;

    Regs.h.bh = 0; /* page */
    Regs.h.al = Char; /* character */
    Regs.h.bl = Color; /* attribute byte (= color) */
    Regs.x.cx = 1; /* repeat count */
    Regs.h.ah = 9; /* write character/attribute pair */
    int86(VGA_BIOS_INT, &Regs, &Regs);
}

/*
    Function: DrawString
```

```
        Description:
            Draws a string to the graphics screen using the VGA BIOS
            calls.  The string is drawn at the row and column indicated
            using the specified color.
*/
void DrawString(char *String, int Row, int Column, int Color)
{

    while (*String != '\0') {
        /* set cursor location */
        SetCursorPosition(Row, Column);
        Column++; /* advance cursor */

        /* draw the character */
        DrawChar(*String++, Color);
    }
}


/*
    Function: CenterString
    Description:
        Centers a string on the screen.  The function calculates
        the correct starting column position to center the string
        on the screen and then calls DrawString to do the actual
        drawing of the text.
*/
void CenterString(char *String, int Row, int Color)
{
    int Len;
    int Col;

    Len = strlen(String);
    Col = (40 - Len) / 2;

    DrawString(String, Row, Col, Color);
}


/*
    Function: IntroCredits
    Description:
        Displays the introduction credits.
*/
void IntroCredits(void)
{
    /* get into mode 13h */
    SetMode13h();

    /* load palette with VGA defaults */
    GetVGAPaletteBlock(GamePalette, 0, 256);

    /* set everything to black so we can draw without being seen */
    /* use two SetVGAPaletteBlock calls to avoid snow */
    SetVGAPaletteBlock(BlackPalette, 0, 128);
    SetVGAPaletteBlock(BlackPalette, 128, 128);
```

```
/* first page of stuff */
CenterString("Coriolis Group Books", 7, INTRO_TEXT_COLOR);
CenterString("Presents", 10, INTRO_TEXT_COLOR);
if (kbhit()) {
    getch();
    return;
}
FadeIn(1500);
if (kbhit()) {
    getch();
    return;
}
delay(1500);
if (kbhit()) {
    getch();
    return;
}
FadeOut(1500);
if (kbhit()) {
    getch();
    return;
}
delay(500);

/* second page of stuff */
ClearMode13hScreen();
CenterString("A", 7, INTRO_TEXT_COLOR);
CenterString("Dave Roberts", 10, INTRO_TEXT_COLOR);
CenterString("Production", 13, INTRO_TEXT_COLOR);
if (kbhit()) {
    getch();
    return;
}
FadeIn(1500);
if (kbhit()) {
    getch();
    return;
}
if (kbhit()) {
    getch();
    return;
}
delay(1500);
if (kbhit()) {
    getch();
    return;
}
FadeOut(1500);
if (kbhit()) {
    getch();
    return;
}
delay(500);
}
```

```
/*
    Function: TitlePage
    Description:
        Displays the Alien Alley title page.
*/
void TitlePage(void)
{
    LINEAR_BITMAP far * Image;

    /* clear screen */
    ClearMode13hScreen();

    /* set everything to black so we can draw without being seen */
    /* use two function calls to avoid snow */
    SetVGAPaletteBlock(BlackPalette, 0, 128);
    SetVGAPaletteBlock(BlackPalette, 128, 128);

    /* first page of stuff */
    Image = LoadPCX("title.pcx", GamePalette);
    if (Image == NULL) {
        FatalError("Can't load 'title.pcx'", "TitlePage", __LINE__);
    }
    BltLinear(Image, 0, 0, MK_FP(VIDEO_MEM_SEGMENT, 0));
    farfree(Image);
    if (kbhit()) {
        getch();
        SetVGAPaletteBlock(GamePalette, 0, 128);
        SetVGAPaletteBlock(GamePalette, 128, 128);
        return;
    }
    FadeIn(1500);
}


/*
    Function: DisplayHighScores
    Description:
        Displays the HighScore array on the screen.
*/
void DisplayHighScores(void)
{
    char DisplayLine[41]; /* max 40 characters wide + 1 for '\0' */
    int i;

    CenterString("*** High Scores ***", 2, 4);
    for (i = 0; i < 10; i++) {
        sprintf(DisplayLine, "%2d. %-20s  %5d", i + 1, HighScore[i].Text,
            HighScore[i].Score);
        CenterString(DisplayLine, HIGH_SCORE_LINE + i, HIGH_SCORE_COLOR);
    }
}

/*
    Function: DisplayHighScoreScreen
    Description:
```

```
            Displays the high score screen from the title page.
*/
void DisplayHighScoreScreen(void)
{
    SetMode13h();
    GetVGAPaletteBlock(GamePalette, 0, 256);
    SetVGAPaletteBlock(BlackPalette, 0, 128);
    SetVGAPaletteBlock(BlackPalette, 128, 128);
    DisplayHighScores();
    FadeIn(500);
    if (getch() == 0)
        getch();
    FadeOut(500);
}


/*
    Function: NewHighScore
    Description:
        Manipulates the HighScore array to make room for the
        user's score and gets the new text.
*/
void NewHighScore(int NewScore)
{
    int i;
    int Row;
    int Column;
    int StrLen;
    int Key;

    /* check to see if it's really a high score */
    if (NewScore <= HighScore[9].Score) {
        return;
    }

    /* move other scores down to make room */
    for (i = 8; i >= 0; i--) {
        if (NewScore > HighScore[i].Score) {
            strcpy(HighScore[i + 1].Text, HighScore[i].Text);
            HighScore[i + 1].Score = HighScore[i].Score;
        }
        else {
            break;
        }
    }
    i++;

    /* blank out text of correct slot */
    HighScore[i].Text[0] = '\0';
    HighScore[i].Score = NewScore;

    /* display the text and fade in */
    SetMode13h();
    GetVGAPaletteBlock(GamePalette, 0, 256);
```

```
        SetVGAPaletteBlock(BlackPalette, 0, 128);
        SetVGAPaletteBlock(BlackPalette, 128, 128);
        DisplayHighScores();
        FadeIn(500);

        /* get user text string */
        Row    = HIGH_SCORE_LINE + i;
        Column = 8;
        StrLen = 0;
        do {
            SetCursorPosition(Row, Column);
            DrawChar(127, 9);
            Key = getch();
            if (Key == 0) {
                getch();
            }
            if (' ' <= Key && Key <= 126 && StrLen < HIGH_SCORE_TEXT_LEN) {
                DrawChar(Key, 9);
                HighScore[i].Text[StrLen] = Key;
                StrLen++;
                HighScore[i].Text[StrLen] = '\0';
                Column++;
            }
            else if (Key == '\b' && StrLen > 0) {
                DrawChar(' ', 9);
                StrLen--;
                Column--;
                HighScore[i].Text[StrLen] = '\0';
            }
        } while (Key != '\r');

        /* erase cursor */
        DrawChar(' ', 9);

        /* fade to black... */
        FadeOut(500);
}


/*
    Function: SetUpModeX
    Description:
        Initializes the mode X page start variables and sets up the
        status area.
*/
void SetUpModeX(void)
{
    unsigned    LineCompare;
    UINT8       VGARegTemp;

    /* calculate offsets */
    PageOffset[0] = STATUS_BYTES + VERTICAL_BORDER_BYTES;
    PageOffset[1] = PageOffset[0] + REDUCED_SCREEN_BYTES +
        VERTICAL_BORDER_BYTES;
```

```c
        /* set start address to page 0 */
        PageFlip(PageOffset[0]);
        HiddenPage = 1;

        /* set line compare register */

        /* Mode X (and Mode Y and Mode 13h) are double scan modes, so */
        /*    the number of lines in terms of the VGA is actually */
        /*    double the pixel height */
        LineCompare = 2 * REDUCED_SCREEN_HEIGHT;
        WaitVerticalRetraceStart();
        asm cli;
        /* write lower eight bits of line compare */
        outportb(CRTC_INDEX_REG, LINE_COMPARE_INDEX);
        outportb(CRTC_DATA_REG, LineCompare & 0xFF);
        /* ninth bit is in bit 4 of overflow register */
        outportb(CRTC_INDEX_REG, OVERFLOW_INDEX);
        VGARegTemp = inportb(CRTC_DATA_REG);
        VGARegTemp = (VGARegTemp & 0xEF) | ((LineCompare >> 4) & 0x10);
        outportb(CRTC_DATA_REG, VGARegTemp);
        /* tenth bit is in bit 6 of max scan line register */
        outportb(CRTC_INDEX_REG, MAX_SCAN_LINE_INDEX);
        VGARegTemp = inportb(CRTC_DATA_REG);
        VGARegTemp = (VGARegTemp & 0xBF) | ((LineCompare >> 3) & 0x40);
        outportb(CRTC_DATA_REG, VGARegTemp);
        asm sti;
}


/*
    Function: CreateEraseBitmap
    Description:
        Takes a bitmap as input and fills it with black.
*/
void CreateEraseBitmap(LINEAR_BITMAP far * Input)
{
    UINT8 far * Data;
    UINT16 Length;

    Length = Input->Width * Input->Height;
    Data = (UINT8 far *) &(Input->Data);

    while (Length > 0) {
        *Data++ = ERASE_COLOR;
        Length--;
    }
}

/*
    Function: LoadSprites
    Description:
        Loads the hero, alien, and missile sprites and initializes the
        sprite structures.
*/
```

```
void LoadSprites(void)
{
    LINEAR_BITMAP far * LoadBitmap;
    int i;

    /* load hero spaceship */
    LoadBitmap = LoadPCX("hero.pcx", NULL);
    if (LoadBitmap == NULL) {
        FatalError("Can't load 'hero.pcx'", "LoadSprites", __LINE__);
    }
    HeroWidth           = LoadBitmap->Width;
    HeroHeight          = LoadBitmap->Height;
    HeroBitmap          = LinearToPlanar(LoadBitmap);
    HeroBitmap->OriginX = HeroWidth / 2;
    HeroBitmap->OriginY = HeroHeight / 2;
    HeroCollisionMap    = CreateCollisionMap(LoadBitmap);
    CreateEraseBitmap(LoadBitmap);
    HeroEraseBitmap     = LinearToPlanar(LoadBitmap);
    HeroEraseBitmap->OriginX = HeroWidth / 2;
    HeroEraseBitmap->OriginY = HeroHeight / 2;
    farfree(LoadBitmap);
    HeroXMin    =   0 + (HeroWidth / 2) + 1;
    HeroXMax    =   SCREEN_WIDTH - ((HeroWidth / 2) + 1);
    HeroYMin    =   0 + (HeroHeight / 2) + 1;
    HeroYMax    =   REDUCED_SCREEN_HEIGHT - ((HeroHeight / 2) + 1);

    /* load alien spaceship */
    LoadBitmap = LoadPCX("alien.pcx", NULL);
    if (LoadBitmap == NULL) {
        FatalError("Can't load 'alien.pcx'", "LoadSprites", __LINE__);
    }
    AlienWidth          = LoadBitmap->Width;
    AlienHeight         = LoadBitmap->Height;
    AlienBitmap         = LinearToPlanar(LoadBitmap);
    AlienBitmap->OriginX    = AlienWidth / 2;
    AlienBitmap->OriginY    = AlienHeight / 2;
    AlienCollisionMap   = CreateCollisionMap(LoadBitmap);
    CreateEraseBitmap(LoadBitmap);
    AlienEraseBitmap    = LinearToPlanar(LoadBitmap);
    AlienEraseBitmap->OriginX   = AlienWidth / 2;
    AlienEraseBitmap->OriginY   = AlienHeight / 2;
    farfree(LoadBitmap);

    /* load missile */
    LoadBitmap = LoadPCX("missile.pcx", NULL);
    if (LoadBitmap == NULL) {
        FatalError("Can't load 'missile.pcx'", "LoadSprites", __LINE__);
    }
    MissileWidth            = LoadBitmap->Width;
    MissileHeight       = LoadBitmap->Height;
    MissileBitmap       = LinearToPlanar(LoadBitmap);
    MissileBitmap->OriginX = MissileWidth / 2;
    MissileBitmap->OriginY = MissileHeight / 2;
```

```
MissileCollisionMap = CreateCollisionMap(LoadBitmap);
CreateEraseBitmap(LoadBitmap);
MissileEraseBitmap  = LinearToPlanar(LoadBitmap);
MissileEraseBitmap->OriginX = MissileWidth / 2;
MissileEraseBitmap->OriginY = MissileHeight / 2;
farfree(LoadBitmap);

/* load missile trails */
LoadBitmap = LoadPCX("mtrailu.pcx", NULL);
if (LoadBitmap == NULL) {
    FatalError("Can't load 'mtrailu.pcx'", "LoadSprites", __LINE__);
}
MissileTrailWidth   = LoadBitmap->Width;
MissileTrailHeight  = LoadBitmap->Height;
MissileTrailUpBitmap    = LinearToPlanar(LoadBitmap);
MissileTrailUpBitmap->OriginX = MissileTrailWidth / 2;
MissileTrailUpBitmap->OriginY = -MissileHeight + MissileBitmap->OriginY;
CreateEraseBitmap(LoadBitmap);
MissileTrailUpEraseBitmap = LinearToPlanar(LoadBitmap);
MissileTrailUpEraseBitmap->OriginX = MissileTrailWidth / 2;
MissileTrailUpEraseBitmap->OriginY = -MissileHeight +
    MissileBitmap->OriginY;
farfree(LoadBitmap);


LoadBitmap = LoadPCX("mtraild.pcx", NULL);
if (LoadBitmap == NULL) {
    FatalError("Can't load 'mtraild.pcx'", "LoadSprites", __LINE__);
}
MissileTrailDnBitmap    = LinearToPlanar(LoadBitmap);
MissileTrailDnBitmap->OriginX = MissileTrailWidth / 2;
MissileTrailDnBitmap->OriginY = MissileTrailHeight +
    MissileBitmap->OriginY;
CreateEraseBitmap(LoadBitmap);
MissileTrailDnEraseBitmap = LinearToPlanar(LoadBitmap);
MissileTrailDnEraseBitmap->OriginX = MissileTrailWidth / 2;
MissileTrailDnEraseBitmap->OriginY = MissileTrailHeight +
    MissileBitmap->OriginY;
farfree(LoadBitmap);

/* load explosion bitmaps */
LoadBitmap = LoadPCX("exp1.pcx", NULL);
if (LoadBitmap == NULL) {
    FatalError("Can't load 'exp1.pcx'", "LoadSprites", __LINE__);
}
ExplosionBitmap[0] = LinearToPlanar(LoadBitmap);
ExplosionBitmap[0]->OriginX = LoadBitmap->Width / 2;
ExplosionBitmap[0]->OriginY = LoadBitmap->Height / 2;
farfree(LoadBitmap);
LoadBitmap = LoadPCX("exp2.pcx", NULL);
if (LoadBitmap == NULL) {
    FatalError("Can't load 'exp2.pcx'", "LoadSprites", __LINE__);
}
ExplosionBitmap[1] = LinearToPlanar(LoadBitmap);
```

```
ExplosionBitmap[1]->OriginX = LoadBitmap->Width / 2;
ExplosionBitmap[1]->OriginY = LoadBitmap->Height / 2;
farfree(LoadBitmap);
LoadBitmap = LoadPCX("exp3.pcx", NULL);
if (LoadBitmap == NULL) {
    FatalError("Can't load 'exp3.pcx'", "LoadSprites", __LINE__);
}
ExplosionBitmap[2] = LinearToPlanar(LoadBitmap);
ExplosionBitmap[2]->OriginX = LoadBitmap->Width / 2;
ExplosionBitmap[2]->OriginY = LoadBitmap->Height / 2;
farfree(LoadBitmap);
LoadBitmap = LoadPCX("exp4.pcx", NULL);
if (LoadBitmap == NULL) {
    FatalError("Can't load 'exp4.pcx'", "LoadSprites", __LINE__);
}
ExplosionBitmap[3] = LinearToPlanar(LoadBitmap);
ExplosionBitmap[3]->OriginX = LoadBitmap->Width / 2;
ExplosionBitmap[3]->OriginY = LoadBitmap->Height / 2;
farfree(LoadBitmap);
LoadBitmap = LoadPCX("exp5.pcx", NULL);
if (LoadBitmap == NULL) {
    FatalError("Can't load 'exp5.pcx'", "LoadSprites", __LINE__);
}
ExplosionBitmap[4] = LinearToPlanar(LoadBitmap);
ExplosionBitmap[4]->OriginX = LoadBitmap->Width / 2;
ExplosionBitmap[4]->OriginY = LoadBitmap->Height / 2;
CreateEraseBitmap(LoadBitmap);
ExplosionEraseBitmap = LinearToPlanar(LoadBitmap);
ExplosionEraseBitmap->OriginX   = LoadBitmap->Width / 2;
ExplosionEraseBitmap->OriginY   = LoadBitmap->Height / 2;
farfree(LoadBitmap);

/* load numbers */
LoadBitmap = LoadPCX("0.pcx", NULL);
if (LoadBitmap == NULL) {
    FatalError("Can't load '0.pcx'", "LoadSprites", __LINE__);
}
Numbers[0] = LinearToPlanar(LoadBitmap);
farfree(LoadBitmap);
LoadBitmap = LoadPCX("1.pcx", NULL);
if (LoadBitmap == NULL) {
    FatalError("Can't load '1.pcx'", "LoadSprites", __LINE__);
}
Numbers[1] = LinearToPlanar(LoadBitmap);
farfree(LoadBitmap);
LoadBitmap = LoadPCX("2.pcx", NULL);
if (LoadBitmap == NULL) {
    FatalError("Can't load '2.pcx'", "LoadSprites", __LINE__);
}
Numbers[2] = LinearToPlanar(LoadBitmap);
farfree(LoadBitmap);
LoadBitmap = LoadPCX("3.pcx", NULL);
if (LoadBitmap == NULL) {
```

```
        FatalError("Can't load '3.pcx'", "LoadSprites", __LINE__);
    }
    Numbers[3] = LinearToPlanar(LoadBitmap);
    farfree(LoadBitmap);
    LoadBitmap = LoadPCX("4.pcx", NULL);
    if (LoadBitmap == NULL) {
        FatalError("Can't load '4.pcx'", "LoadSprites", __LINE__);
    }
    Numbers[4] = LinearToPlanar(LoadBitmap);
    farfree(LoadBitmap);
    LoadBitmap = LoadPCX("5.pcx", NULL);
    if (LoadBitmap == NULL) {
        FatalError("Can't load '5.pcx'", "LoadSprites", __LINE__);
    }
    Numbers[5] = LinearToPlanar(LoadBitmap);
    farfree(LoadBitmap);
    LoadBitmap = LoadPCX("6.pcx", NULL);
    if (LoadBitmap == NULL) {
        FatalError("Can't load '6.pcx'", "LoadSprites", __LINE__);
    }
    Numbers[6] = LinearToPlanar(LoadBitmap);
    farfree(LoadBitmap);
    LoadBitmap = LoadPCX("7.pcx", NULL);
    if (LoadBitmap == NULL) {
        FatalError("Can't load '7.pcx'", "LoadSprites", __LINE__);
    }
    Numbers[7] = LinearToPlanar(LoadBitmap);
    farfree(LoadBitmap);
    LoadBitmap = LoadPCX("8.pcx", NULL);
    if (LoadBitmap == NULL) {
        FatalError("Can't load '8.pcx'", "LoadSprites", __LINE__);
    }
    Numbers[8] = LinearToPlanar(LoadBitmap);
    farfree(LoadBitmap);
    LoadBitmap = LoadPCX("9.pcx", NULL);
    if (LoadBitmap == NULL) {
        FatalError("Can't load '9.pcx'", "LoadSprites", __LINE__);
    }
    Numbers[9] = LinearToPlanar(LoadBitmap);
    farfree(LoadBitmap);

    /* initialize Hero SPRITE */
    Hero.Active        = TRUE;
    Hero.x             = (HeroXMin + HeroXMax) / 2;
    Hero.y             = (HeroYMin + HeroYMax) / 2;
    Hero.Erase[0]      = FALSE;
    Hero.Erase[1]      = FALSE;
    Hero.Draw          = TRUE;

    /* initialize alien sprites */
    for (i = 0; i < MAX_ALIENS; i++) {
        Alien[i].Active = FALSE;
        Alien[i].Draw   = FALSE;
    }
```

```
    /* initialize alien missiles */
    for (i = 0; i < MAX_ALIEN_MISSILES; i++) {
        AlienMissile[i].Active  = FALSE;
        AlienMissile[i].Draw       = FALSE;
    }

    /* initialize hero missiles */
    for (i = 0; i < MAX_HERO_MISSILES; i++) {
        HeroMissile[i].Active  = FALSE;
        HeroMissile[i].Draw    = FALSE;
    }

    /* initialize explosions */
    for (i = 0; i < MAX_EXPLOSIONS; i++) {
        Explosion[i].Active = FALSE;
        Explosion[i].Draw   = FALSE;
    }
}

/*
    Function: FreeSprites
    Description:
        Frees the memory occupied by the sprites.
*/
void FreeSprites(void)
{
    int i;

    farfree(HeroBitmap);
    farfree(HeroEraseBitmap);
    farfree(HeroCollisionMap);
    farfree(AlienBitmap);
    farfree(AlienEraseBitmap);
    farfree(AlienCollisionMap);
    farfree(MissileBitmap);
    farfree(MissileEraseBitmap);
    farfree(MissileCollisionMap);
    farfree(MissileTrailUpBitmap);
    farfree(MissileTrailDnBitmap);
    farfree(MissileTrailUpEraseBitmap);
    farfree(MissileTrailDnEraseBitmap);
    for (i = 0; i < MAX_EXPLOSION_BITMAPS; i++) {
        farfree(ExplosionBitmap[i]);
    }
    farfree(ExplosionEraseBitmap);
    for (i = 0; i < 10; i++) {
        farfree(Numbers[i]);
    }
}

/*
    Function: GetJoystickInput
    Description:
        Reads the current joystick position and button state and
```

```
                    sets UserInput... accordingly.
*/
BOOL GetJoystickInput
    (
    BOOL * UserInputUp,
    BOOL * UserInputDown,
    BOOL * UserInputLeft,
    BOOL * UserInputRight,
    BOOL * UserInputFire
    )
{
    ReadJoysticks(&JsState);

    *UserInputUp    = JsState.JsAxisAY < JsThresholdUp;
    *UserInputDown  = JsState.JsAxisAY > JsThresholdDown;
    *UserInputLeft  = JsState.JsAxisAX < JsThresholdLeft;
    *UserInputRight = JsState.JsAxisAX > JsThresholdRight;
    *UserInputFire  = JsState.JsButtonA1;

    if (kbhit()) {
        if (getch() == 0) {
            getch();
        }
        return TRUE;
    }
    else {
        return FALSE;
    }
}


/*
    Function: GetMouseInput
    Description:
        Reads the position of the mouse and the current button state
        and sets UserInput... accordingly.
*/
BOOL GetMouseInput
    (
    BOOL * UserInputUp,
    BOOL * UserInputDown,
    BOOL * UserInputLeft,
    BOOL * UserInputRight,
    BOOL * UserInputFire
    )
{
    UINT16 Buttons;
    UINT16 x;
    UINT16 y;

    Buttons = PollMouseStatus(&x, &y);

    *UserInputUp    = y < MOUSE_THRESHOLD_UP;
    *UserInputDown  = y > MOUSE_THRESHOLD_DOWN;
```

```
    *UserInputLeft  = x < MOUSE_THRESHOLD_LEFT;
    *UserInputRight = x > MOUSE_THRESHOLD_RIGHT;
    *UserInputFire  = (Buttons & LEFT_BUTTON_MASK) != 0;

    if (kbhit()) {
        if (getch() == 0) {
            getch();
        }
        return TRUE;
    }
    else {
        return FALSE;
    }
}

/*
    Function: GetKeyboardInput
    Description:
        Updates the "UserInput..." variables used by the MoveSprites
        routine from the keyboard input device.
*/
BOOL GetKeyboardInput
    (
    BOOL * UserInputUp,
    BOOL * UserInputDown,
    BOOL * UserInputLeft,
    BOOL * UserInputRight,
    BOOL * UserInputFire
    )
{
    *UserInputUp    = GetKeyState(KEY_UP);
    *UserInputDown  = GetKeyState(KEY_DOWN);
    *UserInputRight = GetKeyState(KEY_RIGHT);
    *UserInputLeft  = GetKeyState(KEY_LEFT);
    *UserInputFire  = GetKeyState(KEY_SPACE) ||
        GetKeyState(KEY_CONTROL) || GetKeyState(KEY_ALT);

    return GetKeyState(KEY_ESC);
}

/*
    Function: GetInput
    Description:
        Get's player input and updates the hero's x & y variables
        as well as the variable to start a new missile firing.
        Control is a character specifying the method of input
        gathering.  Returns whether the user wants to quit the
        program or not.
*/
BOOL GetInput
    (
    int Control,
    BOOL * UserInputUp,
```

```
        BOOL * UserInputDown,
        BOOL * UserInputLeft,
        BOOL * UserInputRight,
        BOOL * UserInputFire
        )
{
    BOOL Quit;

    switch (Control) {
        case 'j':
            Quit = GetJoystickInput(UserInputUp, UserInputDown,
                UserInputLeft, UserInputRight, UserInputFire);
            break;
        case 'm':
            Quit = GetMouseInput(UserInputUp, UserInputDown,
                UserInputLeft, UserInputRight, UserInputFire);
            break;
        case 'k':
            Quit = GetKeyboardInput(UserInputUp, UserInputDown,
                UserInputLeft, UserInputRight, UserInputFire);
            break;
    }
    return Quit;
}


/*
    Function: CreateHeroMissile
    Description:
        Finds a non-active hero missile in the HeroMissile
        array and initializes it.
*/
void CreateHeroMissile(int x, int y)
{
    int i;

    for (i = 0; i < MAX_HERO_MISSILES; i++) {
        if (!HeroMissile[i].Active) {
            HeroMissile[i].Active   = TRUE;
            HeroMissile[i].x             = x;
            HeroMissile[i].y             = y;
            HeroMissile[i].vx       = 0;
            HeroMissile[i].vy         = -HERO_MISSILE_VELOCITY;
            HeroMissile[i].Erase[0] = FALSE;
            HeroMissile[i].Erase[1] = FALSE;
            HeroMissile[i].Draw     = TRUE;
            /* initialize bounding rect */
            ComputeBoundingRect(HeroMissile[i].x, HeroMissile[i].y,
            MissileBitmap->OriginX, MissileBitmap->OriginY,
                MissileWidth, MissileHeight, &(HeroMissile[i].Bounds));
            return;
        }
    }
}
```

```
/*
    Function: CreateAlien
    Description:
        Finds a free alien in the Alien array and initializes it.
*/
void CreateAlien(void)
{
    int i;

    for (i = 0; i < MAX_ALIENS; i++) {
        if (!Alien[i].Active) {
            Alien[i].Active      = TRUE;
            Alien[i].x           = random(SCREEN_WIDTH);
            Alien[i].x = MAX(MAX_OBJECT_WIDTH / 2, MIN(Alien[i].x,
                SCREEN_WIDTH - (MAX_OBJECT_WIDTH / 2)));
            Alien[i].y           = -(MAX_OBJECT_HEIGHT / 2);
            Alien[i].vx          = random((2 * ALIEN_X_VELOCITY) + 1) -
                ALIEN_X_VELOCITY;
            Alien[i].vy          = ALIEN_Y_VELOCITY;
            Alien[i].Erase[0]    = FALSE;
            Alien[i].Erase[1]    = FALSE;
            Alien[i].Draw        = TRUE;
            Alien[i].ObjectSpec = ALIEN_MOVE_TIME_BASE +
                random(ALIEN_MOVE_TIME_VAR);
            Alien[i].ObjectSpec2 = 0; /* ability to fire immediately */
            /* initialize alien bounding rect */
            ComputeBoundingRect(Alien[i].x, Alien[i].y,
                AlienBitmap->OriginX, AlienBitmap->OriginY,
                AlienWidth, AlienHeight, &(Alien[i].Bounds));
            return;
        }
    }
}


/*
    Function: CreateAlienMissile
    Description:
        Finds a free alien missile in the AlienMissile array and
        initializes it.  The x and y positions of the missile
        are set from the x and y parameters which will place
        them somewhere near an alien gun.
*/
void CreateAlienMissile(int x, int y)
{
    int i;

    for (i = 0; i < MAX_ALIEN_MISSILES; i++) {
        if (!AlienMissile[i].Active) {
            AlienMissile[i].Active      = TRUE;
            AlienMissile[i].x           = x;
            AlienMissile[i].y           = y;
            AlienMissile[i].vx          = 0;
            AlienMissile[i].vy          = ALIEN_MISSILE_VELOCITY;
```

```
                    AlienMissile[i].Erase[0]       = FALSE;
                    AlienMissile[i].Erase[1]       = FALSE;
                    AlienMissile[i].Draw           = TRUE;
                    /* initialize bounding rect */
                    ComputeBoundingRect(AlienMissile[i].x, AlienMissile[i].y,
                    MissileBitmap->OriginX, MissileBitmap->OriginY,
                        MissileWidth, MissileHeight, &(AlienMissile[i].Bounds));
                    return;
                }
        }
}


/*
    Function: MoveSprites
    Description:
        Takes care of moving hero ship and alien sprites, based on
        user input and their behavioral algorithms.  MoveSprites
        is also where missiles are generated and off-screen images
        are removed from play.
*/
void MoveSprites
    (
    BOOL UserInputUp,
    BOOL UserInputDown,
    BOOL UserInputLeft,
    BOOL UserInputRight,
    BOOL UserInputFire
    )
{
    int i;
    static LastFireInput;
    int AlienFireResult;
    int AlienProximity;

    /* first, take care of the hero */
    if (UserInputUp) {
        Hero.y -= HERO_Y_VELOCITY;
    }
    if (UserInputDown) {
        Hero.y += HERO_Y_VELOCITY;
    }
    if (UserInputLeft) {
        Hero.x -= HERO_X_VELOCITY;
    }
    if (UserInputRight) {
        Hero.x += HERO_X_VELOCITY;
    }
    /* limit player movement */
    Hero.y = MAX(HeroYMin, MIN(HeroYMax, Hero.y));
    Hero.x = MAX(HeroXMin, MIN(HeroXMax, Hero.x));
    /* update hero bounding rect */
    ComputeBoundingRect(Hero.x, Hero.y, HeroBitmap->OriginX,
        HeroBitmap->OriginY, HeroWidth, HeroHeight,
        &(Hero.Bounds));
```

```
/* update hero missiles */
for (i = 0; i < MAX_HERO_MISSILES; i++) {
    if (HeroMissile[i].Draw) {
        /* update position */
        HeroMissile[i].y += HeroMissile[i].vy;
        /* stop drawing when it's off screen */
        if (HeroMissile[i].y < - (MAX_OBJECT_HEIGHT / 2)) {
            HeroMissile[i].Draw = FALSE;
        }
        else {
            /* if still onscreen, update bounding rect */
            ComputeBoundingRect(HeroMissile[i].x, HeroMissile[i].y,
                MissileBitmap->OriginX, MissileBitmap->OriginY,
                MissileWidth, MissileHeight, &(HeroMissile[i].Bounds));
        }
    }
}

/* generate hero missiles */
if (UserInputFire && !LastFireInput && Hero.Draw) {
    CreateHeroMissile(Hero.x - HERO_GUN_OFFSET_LEFT,
        Hero.y - HERO_GUN_OFFSET_UP);
    CreateHeroMissile(Hero.x + HERO_GUN_OFFSET_RIGHT,
        Hero.y - HERO_GUN_OFFSET_UP);
}
LastFireInput = UserInputFire;

/* update alien missiles */
for (i = 0; i < MAX_ALIEN_MISSILES; i++) {
    if (AlienMissile[i].Draw) {
        /* update position */
        AlienMissile[i].y += AlienMissile[i].vy;
        /* stop drawing when it's off screen */
        if (AlienMissile[i].y > (REDUCED_SCREEN_HEIGHT +
            (MAX_OBJECT_HEIGHT / 2))) {
            AlienMissile[i].Draw = FALSE;
        }
        else {
            /* if still onscreen, update bounding rect */
            ComputeBoundingRect(AlienMissile[i].x, AlienMissile[i].y,
                MissileBitmap->OriginX, MissileBitmap->OriginY,
                MissileWidth, MissileHeight, &(AlienMissile[i].Bounds));
        }
    }
}

/* move aliens */
for (i = 0; i < MAX_ALIENS; i++) {
    if (Alien[i].Draw) {
        if (Alien[i].ObjectSpec == 0) {
            /* pick a new direction */
            Alien[i].vx = random((2 * ALIEN_X_VELOCITY) + 1) -
                ALIEN_X_VELOCITY;
```

```
            Alien[i].ObjectSpec = ALIEN_MOVE_TIME_BASE +
                random(ALIEN_MOVE_TIME_VAR);
        }
        else {
            Alien[i].ObjectSpec-;
        }
        /* update alien position */
        Alien[i].x += Alien[i].vx;
        Alien[i].y += Alien[i].vy;

        /* clip alien movement horizontally */
        Alien[i].x = MAX(MAX_OBJECT_WIDTH / 2, MIN(Alien[i].x,
            SCREEN_WIDTH · (MAX_OBJECT_WIDTH / 2)));

        /* move alien to top when it gets to bottom */
        if (Alien[i].y > (REDUCED_SCREEN_HEIGHT +
            (MAX_OBJECT_HEIGHT / 2))) {
            Alien[i].y = - (MAX_OBJECT_HEIGHT / 2);
        }

        /* update alien bounding rect */
        ComputeBoundingRect(Alien[i].x, Alien[i].y,
            AlienBitmap->OriginX, AlienBitmap->OriginY,
            AlienWidth, AlienHeight, &(Alien[i].Bounds));

        /* generate alien missiles */
        if (Alien[i].ObjectSpec2 == 0) {
            AlienFireResult = random(100); /* in percent */
            AlienProximity  = Alien[i].x - Hero.x;
            if (AlienProximity < 0) {
                AlienProximity = -AlienProximity;
            }
            if (((AlienProximity < ALIEN_PROX_THRESHOLD) &&
                (AlienFireResult < ALIEN_FIRE_PROB_HERO)) ||
                (AlienFireResult < ALIEN_FIRE_PROB_RANDOM)) {
                CreateAlienMissile(Alien[i].x -
                    ALIEN_GUN_OFFSET_LEFT, Alien[i].y +
                    ALIEN_GUN_OFFSET_DOWN);
                CreateAlienMissile(Alien[i].x +
                    ALIEN_GUN_OFFSET_RIGHT, Alien[i].y +
                    ALIEN_GUN_OFFSET_DOWN);
                Alien[i].ObjectSpec2 = ALIEN_FIRE_LOCKOUT;
            }
        }
        else {
            Alien[i].ObjectSpec2-;
        }
    }
}

/* generate aliens */
if (AlienGenCounter == 0) {
```

```
            /* generate an alien */
            CreateAlien();
            /* reinit generate counter */
            AlienGenCounter = ALIEN_GEN_RATE_BASE +
                random(ALIEN_GEN_RATE_VAR);
        }
        else {
            AlienGenCounter--;
        }

        /* update explosions - note, we don't really "move" them, just */
        /* make the animation go */
        for (i = 0; i < MAX_EXPLOSIONS; i++) {
            if (Explosion[i].Draw) {
                if (Explosion[i].ObjectSpec2 == 0) {
                    Explosion[i].ObjectSpec++;
                    Explosion[i].ObjectSpec2 = EXPLOSION_FRAME_REPEAT_COUNT;
                    if (Explosion[i].ObjectSpec >= MAX_EXPLOSION_BITMAPS) {
                        Explosion[i].Draw = FALSE;
                    }
                }
                else {
                    Explosion[i].ObjectSpec2--;
                }
            }
        }
    }
}


/*
    Function: CreateExplosion
    Description:
        Starts an explosion occurring at the appropriate x and y
        coordinates.
*/
void CreateExplosion(int x, int y)
{
    int i;

    for (i = 0; i < MAX_EXPLOSIONS; i++) {
        if (!Explosion[i].Active) {
            Explosion[i].Active     = TRUE;
            Explosion[i].x          = x;
            Explosion[i].y          = y;
            Explosion[i].Erase[0]   = FALSE;
            Explosion[i].Erase[1]   = FALSE;
            Explosion[i].Draw       = TRUE;
            Explosion[i].ObjectSpec = 0; /* current explosion bitmap */
            Explosion[i].ObjectSpec2 = EXPLOSION_FRAME_REPEAT_COUNT;
            return;
        }
    }
}
```

```
/*
    Function: CheckCollisions
    Description:
        Check for collisions between various objects and start
        explosions if they collide.  Collision detection is
        performed between:
            * aliens and hero
            * aliens and hero missiles
            * hero and alien missiles
        Note that all tests are performed between objects that are
        currently being drawn, not just active objects.
*/
void CheckCollisions(void)
{
    int i, j;

    /* check between hero and aliens */
    for (i = 0; i < MAX_ALIENS; i++) {
        /* Use C short circuit boolean evaluation in a big way. */
        /* Make sure both hero and alien are still being drawn */
        /* (they may still be active but have been removed */
        /* from the screen and are just being erased). */
        /* If they are still onscreen, then perform a rectangle test. */
        /* If the rectangle collision indicates a possible hit, then */
        /* perform a bitmap test. */
        if (Hero.Draw && Alien[i].Draw &&
            CollisionTestRect(&(Hero.Bounds), &(Alien[i].Bounds)) &&
            CollisionTestBitmap(HeroCollisionMap, AlienCollisionMap,
                Hero.Bounds.Left, Hero.Bounds.Top,
                Alien[i].Bounds.Left, Alien[i].Bounds.Top)) {

            Hero.Draw = FALSE;
            CreateExplosion(Hero.x, Hero.y);
            Alien[i].Draw = FALSE;
            CreateExplosion(Alien[i].x, Alien[i].y);
        }
    }

    /* check between aliens and hero missiles */
    for (i = 0; i < MAX_ALIENS; i++) {
        if (!Alien[i].Draw) {
            continue;
        }
        for (j = 0; j < MAX_HERO_MISSILES; j++) {
            /* do similiar short circuit, mondo huge test as above */
            if (HeroMissile[j].Draw &&
                CollisionTestRect(&(Alien[i].Bounds),
                    &(HeroMissile[j].Bounds)) &&
                CollisionTestBitmap(AlienCollisionMap,
                    MissileCollisionMap, Alien[i].Bounds.Left,
                    Alien[i].Bounds.Top, HeroMissile[j].Bounds.Left,
                    HeroMissile[j].Bounds.Top)) {
```

```
                    Alien[i].Draw        = FALSE;
                    HeroMissile[j].Draw = FALSE;
                    CreateExplosion(Alien[i].x, Alien[i].y);
                    Score += POINTS_PER_ALIEN;
                    break; /* alien is destroyed */
                }
            }
        }

    /* check between hero and alien missiles */
    for (i = 0; i < MAX_ALIEN_MISSILES; i++) {
        /* again, rely on short circuiting */
        if (AlienMissile[i].Draw && Hero.Draw &&
            CollisionTestRect(&(AlienMissile[i].Bounds),
                &(Hero.Bounds)) &&
            CollisionTestBitmap(MissileCollisionMap, HeroCollisionMap,
                AlienMissile[i].Bounds.Left, AlienMissile[i].Bounds.Top,
                Hero.Bounds.Left, Hero.Bounds.Top)) {

            AlienMissile[i].Draw    = FALSE; /* destroy missile in any case */
            if (HeroShields == 0) {
                Hero.Draw           = FALSE;
                CreateExplosion(Hero.x, Hero.y);
                break; /* hero is destroyed */
            }
            else {
                /* take away a bit of shields */
                HeroShields--;
            }
        }
    }
}

/*
    Function: EraseSprites
    Description:
        Erase all current bitmaps from the hidden screen.  If the
        erasure marks the last time that the object will be erased
        because it is no longer being drawn, deactivate the object.
*/
BOOL EraseSprites(void)
{
    int i;
    static unsigned DeathCounter;

    /* do player and possibly deactivate */
    if (Hero.Active && Hero.Erase[HiddenPage]) {
        BltPlanarNoTransparent(HeroEraseBitmap, Hero.OldX[HiddenPage],
            Hero.OldY[HiddenPage], PageOffset[HiddenPage]);
        Hero.Erase[HiddenPage] = FALSE;
        if (!(Hero.Draw || Hero.Erase[0] || Hero.Erase[1])) {
            Hero.Active = FALSE;
```

```
                DeathCounter = DEATH_DELAY;
        }
    }


    /* erase and deactivate hero missiles */
    for (i = 0; i < MAX_HERO_MISSILES; i++) {
        if (HeroMissile[i].Active && HeroMissile[i].Erase[HiddenPage]) {
            /* erase missile itself */
            BltPlanarNoTransparent(MissileEraseBitmap,
                HeroMissile[i].OldX[HiddenPage],
                HeroMissile[i].OldY[HiddenPage],
                PageOffset[HiddenPage]);
            /* erase missile trail */
            BltPlanarNoTransparent(MissileTrailUpEraseBitmap,
                HeroMissile[i].OldX[HiddenPage],
                HeroMissile[i].OldY[HiddenPage],
                PageOffset[HiddenPage]);
            HeroMissile[i].Erase[HiddenPage] = FALSE;
        }
        /* deactivate missile if we aren't going to draw or */
        /*   erase it anymore */
        if (!(HeroMissile[i].Draw || HeroMissile[i].Erase[0] ||
            HeroMissile[i].Erase[1])) {
            HeroMissile[i].Active = FALSE;
        }
    }


    /* erase and deactivate aliens */
    for (i = 0; i < MAX_ALIENS; i++) {
        if (Alien[i].Active && Alien[i].Erase[HiddenPage]) {
            BltPlanarNoTransparent(AlienEraseBitmap,
                Alien[i].OldX[HiddenPage],
                Alien[i].OldY[HiddenPage],
                PageOffset[HiddenPage]);
            Alien[i].Erase[HiddenPage] = FALSE;
        }
        /* deactive alien if it's been destroyed */
        if (!(Alien[i].Draw || Alien[i].Erase[0] ||
            Alien[i].Erase[1])) {
            Alien[i].Active = FALSE;
        }
    }


    /* erase and deactivate alien missiles */
    for (i = 0; i < MAX_ALIEN_MISSILES; i++) {
        if (AlienMissile[i].Active && AlienMissile[i].Erase[HiddenPage]) {
            /* erase missile itself */
            BltPlanarNoTransparent(MissileEraseBitmap,
                AlienMissile[i].OldX[HiddenPage],
                AlienMissile[i].OldY[HiddenPage],
                PageOffset[HiddenPage]);
            /* erase missile trail */
```

```
            BltPlanarNoTransparent(MissileTrailDnEraseBitmap,
                AlienMissile[i].OldX[HiddenPage],
                AlienMissile[i].OldY[HiddenPage],
                PageOffset[HiddenPage]);
            AlienMissile[i].Erase[HiddenPage] = FALSE;
        }
        /* deactivate missile if we aren't going to draw or */
        /*    erase it anymore */
        if (!(AlienMissile[i].Draw || AlienMissile[i].Erase[0] ||
            AlienMissile[i].Erase[1])) {
            AlienMissile[i].Active = FALSE;
        }
    }

    /* erase and deactivate explosions */
    for (i = 0; i < MAX_EXPLOSIONS; i++) {
        if (Explosion[i].Active && Explosion[i].Erase[HiddenPage]) {
            BltPlanarNoTransparent(ExplosionEraseBitmap,
                Explosion[i].OldX[HiddenPage],
                Explosion[i].OldY[HiddenPage],
                PageOffset[HiddenPage]);
            Explosion[i].Erase[HiddenPage] = FALSE;
        }
        /* deactivate if explosion has run its course */
        if (!(Explosion[i].Draw || Explosion[i].Erase[0] ||
            Explosion[i].Erase[1])) {
            Explosion[i].Active = FALSE;
        }
    }

    /* hero has died - signal game over after brief delay */
    if (!Hero.Active) {
        if (DeathCounter == 0) {
            return TRUE;
        }
        else {
            DeathCounter--;
        }
    }
    return FALSE;
}

/*
    Function: DrawSprites
    Description:
        Draw all active objects that should be drawn on the
        screen.
*/
void DrawSprites(void)
{
    int i;

    /* do explosions */
    for (i = 0; i < MAX_EXPLOSIONS; i++) {
```

```
        if (Explosion[i].Draw) {
            /* draw explosion */
            BltPlanar(ExplosionBitmap[Explosion[i].ObjectSpec],
                Explosion[i].x, Explosion[i].y, PageOffset[HiddenPage]);
            Explosion[i].Erase[HiddenPage]  = TRUE;
            Explosion[i].OldX[HiddenPage]   = Explosion[i].x;
            Explosion[i].OldY[HiddenPage]   = Explosion[i].y;
        }
    }

    /* draw hero missiles */
    for (i = 0; i < MAX_HERO_MISSILES; i++) {
        if (HeroMissile[i].Draw) {
            /* draw missile itself */
            BltPlanar(MissileBitmap, HeroMissile[i].x, HeroMissile[i].y,
                PageOffset[HiddenPage]);
            /* draw missile trail */
            BltPlanar(MissileTrailUpBitmap, HeroMissile[i].x, HeroMissile[i].y,
                PageOffset[HiddenPage]);
            HeroMissile[i].Erase[HiddenPage]    = TRUE;
            HeroMissile[i].OldX[HiddenPage] = HeroMissile[i].x;
            HeroMissile[i].OldY[HiddenPage] = HeroMissile[i].y;
        }
    }

    /* draw alien missiles */
    for (i = 0; i < MAX_ALIEN_MISSILES; i++) {
        if (AlienMissile[i].Draw) {
            /* draw missile itself */
            BltPlanar(MissileBitmap, AlienMissile[i].x, AlienMissile[i].y,
                PageOffset[HiddenPage]);
            /* draw missile trail */
            BltPlanar(MissileTrailDnBitmap, AlienMissile[i].x,
                AlienMissile[i].y, PageOffset[HiddenPage]);
            AlienMissile[i].Erase[HiddenPage]   = TRUE;
            AlienMissile[i].OldX[HiddenPage]    = AlienMissile[i].x;
            AlienMissile[i].OldY[HiddenPage]    = AlienMissile[i].y;
        }
    }

    /* do aliens */
    for (i = 0; i < MAX_ALIENS; i++) {
        if (Alien[i].Active && Alien[i].Draw) {
            BltPlanar(AlienBitmap, Alien[i].x, Alien[i].y,
                PageOffset[HiddenPage]);
            Alien[i].Erase[HiddenPage]  = TRUE;
            Alien[i].OldX[HiddenPage]   = Alien[i].x;
            Alien[i].OldY[HiddenPage]   = Alien[i].y;
        }
    }

    /* do player */
    if (Hero.Active && Hero.Draw) {
```

```
        BltPlanar(HeroBitmap, Hero.x, Hero.y, PageOffset[HiddenPage]);
        Hero.Erase[HiddenPage]  = TRUE;
        Hero.OldX[HiddenPage]   = Hero.x;
        Hero.OldY[HiddenPage]   = Hero.y;
    }
}

/*
    Function: DrawShieldStatus
    Description:
        Updates the shield status at the bottom of the screen.
*/
void DrawShieldStatus(void)
{
    int i, j;
    UINT8 far * Screen;
    UINT16 LineAdder;

    SetMMR(0xF);
    Screen = MK_FP(VIDEO_MEM_SEGMENT, 0);
    Screen += SHIELD_STATUS_TOP * (GScreenVirtualWidth / 4) +
        (SHIELD_STATUS_LEFT / 4);
    LineAdder = (GScreenVirtualWidth / 4) - (MAX_HERO_SHIELDS *
        SHIELD_STATUS_WIDTH_MULT);

    for (j = 0; j < SHIELD_STATUS_HEIGHT; j++) {
        for (i = 0; i < (MAX_HERO_SHIELDS * SHIELD_STATUS_WIDTH_MULT);
            i++) {
            if (i < (HeroShields * SHIELD_STATUS_WIDTH_MULT)) {
                *Screen++ = SHIELD_STATUS_COLOR;
            }
            else {
                *Screen++ = SHIELD_STATUS_INVERT_COLOR;
            }
        }
        Screen += LineAdder;
    }
}

/*
    Function: DrawScore
    Description:
        Draw the player score at the bottom of the screen.
*/
void DrawScore(void)
{
    char ScoreText[6]; /* five digits plus '\0' */
    int i, j;

    itoa(Score, ScoreText, 10);

    for (i = 0; i < 6; i++) { /* quickly find length */
        if (ScoreText[i] == '\0') {
```

```
            break;
        }
    }

    j = SCORE_NUMBERS_LEFT;
    while (i < 6) { /* draw leading zeros */
        BltPlanarNoTransparent(Numbers[0], j, SCORE_NUMBERS_TOP, 0);
        i++;
        j += 8;
    }

    for (i = 0; ScoreText[i] != '\0'; i++) {
        BltPlanarNoTransparent(Numbers[ScoreText[i] - '0'], j,
            SCORE_NUMBERS_TOP, 0);
        j += 8;
    }
}

/*
    Function: DrawStatus
    Description:
        Draws the status area at the bottom of the screen
        showing the player's current score and shield strength.
*/
void DrawStatus(void)
{
    DrawShieldStatus();
    DrawScore();
}

/*
    Function: InitStatus
    Description:
        Draw the background and "Shield" and "Score" bitmaps.
*/
void InitStatus(void)
{
    LINEAR_BITMAP far * LinearBM;
    PLANAR_BITMAP far * PlanarBM;

    LinearBM = LoadPCX("cpanel.pcx", NULL);
    if (LinearBM == NULL) {
        FatalError("Can't load 'cpanel.pcx'", "InitStatus", __LINE__);
    }
    PlanarBM = LinearToPlanar(LinearBM);
    WaitVerticalRetraceStart();
    BltPlanarNoTransparent(PlanarBM, 0, 0, 0);
    farfree(LinearBM);
    farfree(PlanarBM);
}

/*
    Function: Play
```

```
    Description:
        Play the game!
*/
void Play(int Control)
{
    BOOL      UserInputUp;
    BOOL      UserInputDown;
    BOOL      UserInputLeft;
    BOOL      UserInputRight;
    BOOL      UserInputFire;
    int       GunBlinkCounter;
    int       GunBlinkState;
    RGB_TUPLE Black = {0, 0, 0};
    RGB_TUPLE GunColor;
    BOOL      GameOver;
    BOOL      GameOverInput;
    BOOL      GameOverDeath;
    LINEAR_BITMAP far * Image;

    /* fade screen to remove title page */
    FadeOut(500);

    /* load sprites */
    LoadSprites();

    /* initialize all counters, etc. */
    Score = 0;
    AlienGenCounter = ALIEN_GEN_RATE_BASE;
    HeroShields = MAX_HERO_SHIELDS;

    /* set mode X */
    SetModeX();
    SetUpModeX();

    /* set up palette stuff */
    /* palette.pcx is a single pixel bitmap with the palette */
    /*    this is done because it's easy to load the palette */
    /*    using LoadPCX */
    Image = LoadPCX("palette.pcx", GamePalette);
    if (Image == NULL) {
        FatalError("Can't load 'palette.pcx'", "ProgramInit", __LINE__);
    }
    farfree(Image); /* ignore the single pixel bitmap */
    SetVGAPaletteBlock(GamePalette, 0, 128);
    SetVGAPaletteBlock(GamePalette, 128, 128);

    /* install keyboard or mouse handlers */
    /* do nothing for joystick */
    if (Control == 'm') {
    }
    else if (Control == 'k') {
        SetButtonKeysMode();
    }
```

```
/* set up gun blink stuff */
GetPaletteEntry(GamePalette, GUN_COLOR, &GunColor);
GunBlinkCounter     = GUN_BLINK_RATE;
GunBlinkState       = 1; /* gun blink on */

/* initialize the status screen */
InitStatus();

/* enter main animation loop */
GameOver = FALSE;
while (!GameOver) {
    /* get user input */
    GameOverInput = GetInput(Control, &UserInputUp, &UserInputDown,
        &UserInputLeft, &UserInputRight, &UserInputFire);

    /* move sprites */
    MoveSprites(UserInputUp, UserInputDown, UserInputLeft,
        UserInputRight, UserInputFire);

    /* check for collisions */
    CheckCollisions();

    /* erase */
    GameOverDeath = EraseSprites();

    /* draw */
    DrawSprites();

    /* update status */
    DrawStatus();

    /* wait for page flip */
    PageFlip(PageOffset[HiddenPage]);
    HiddenPage ^= 1; /* flip HiddenPage to other state */

    /* blink the guns */
    if (GunBlinkCounter == 0) {
        if (GunBlinkState == 1) {
            SetVGAPaletteEntry(GUN_COLOR, &Black);
        }
        else {
            SetVGAPaletteEntry(GUN_COLOR, &GunColor);
        }
        GunBlinkState ^= 1; /* flip it to other state */
        GunBlinkCounter = GUN_BLINK_RATE;
    }
    else {
        GunBlinkCounter-;
    }

    /* player either aborts or dies */
    GameOver = GameOverInput || GameOverDeath;
}
```

```
        /* uninstall mouse and/or keyboard handlers */
        if (Control == 'm') {
        }
        else if (Control == 'k') {
            SetNormalKeysMode();
        }

        /* free all memory used to play */
        FreeSprites();

        /* fade to black... */
        FadeOut(250);

        /* return to Mode 13h, as we were */
        SetMode13h();
}

/*
    Function: main
    Description:
        Main program loop.  Init's the program, draws intro screens
        and title pages, and waits for user to hit keystroke
        to indicate what they want to do.
*/
int main()
{
    BOOL    Quit;
    BOOL    DrawTitle;
    char    Key;


    ProgramInit();

    IntroCredits();

    Quit = FALSE;
    DrawTitle = TRUE;

    while (!Quit) {
        if (DrawTitle) {
            TitlePage();
            DrawTitle = FALSE;
        }

        Key = getch();
        Key = tolower(Key);

        randomize(); /* make sure we get a different game */

        switch (Key) {
            case 0: /* extended key (F1, for instance) */
                /* burn next key input which should be */
                /* a scan code corresponding to the key */
```

```
            getch();
            break;
    case 0x1B: /* escape */
    case 'q':
        Quit = TRUE;
        break;
    case 'j':
        if (JoystickPresent) {
            Play(Key);
            NewHighScore(Score);
            DrawTitle = TRUE;
        }
        break;
    case 'm':
        if (MousePresent) {
            Play(Key);
            NewHighScore(Score);
            DrawTitle = TRUE;
        }
      break;
    case ' ': /* space */
        Key = 'k';
        /* fall through */
    case 'k':
        Play(Key);
        NewHighScore(Score);
        DrawTitle = TRUE;
        break;
    case 's':
        DisplayHighScoreScreen();
        DrawTitle = TRUE;
        break;
    default:
        DrawTitle = FALSE;
        break;
    }
}

SaveHighScores();

SetVGAMode(0x3);

return 0;
}
```

ADVANCED TECHNIQUES

Audio Immersion

We were given ears for one purpose: to hear the sound effects in video games. Don't deprive your users of this treat. Read this chapter to see how easily you can add exciting sounds and music to your games.

When I was a little kid, I used to spend the night at my friends' houses every so often. Of course, we'd be up until the wee hours of the morning watching TV. Most of my friends liked to watch the monster movies that ran late-night on Fridays. I wasn't that partial to them myself, but peer pressure being what it is, I'd watch too.

We'd lie on the living room floor, wrapped in sleeping bags with all the lights off. When the scary parts would come, we'd pull the sleeping bags over our heads and close our eyes until the danger had passed. Even still, it was only partially effective. You could always hear the tension build in the music and an "actor" finally scream when something terrible happened. Even with my head covered, it still sent shivers down my spine.

Eventually, however, we found that things were easier to handle if we'd simply turn down the volume on the TV. With the volume all the way down, we could even watch during the scary parts, and it wasn't so bad. In fact, it was often pretty funny. Oh sure, there was still a lot of blood and people jumping out of things, but without the soundtrack to wind your muscles into knots, the whole situation was a lot less tense. Without knowing it, we'd just discovered what every good movie director knows: sound is the other half of the experience. How scary are things that go bump in the night when they don't bump?

And so it is with video games as well: music creates mood and sound effects add the punctuation to an otherwise good, but flat, program. With cheap 8-bit sound cards selling for under $50, there is no reason that every game player shouldn't have at least basic audio capabilities.

In this chapter we'll look at adding the audio half of the sensory experience to *Alien Alley*. We'll provide it with sound effects and a hot soundtrack that will get your adrenalin flowing.

eXPLORER OVERVIEW This chapter will focus on exploring digital sound and the DigPak and MidPak sound driver libraries. We'll examine the changes to *Alien Alley* that will be necessary to support digital sound effects and MIDI music playback. Although we'll develop a short interface module, named DIGMIDIF.C, the real work of generating sounds will be done by DigPak and MidPak themselves.

To start off, let's take a look at what sound is and how it's represented in the computer's digital domain.

SURFING THE SONIC WAVE

Sound is nothing more than a series of compression waves in a medium like air or water. When you play a song from the radio, electronics drive the speaker cone to produce a compression wave that you then hear transmitted to your ear through the air.

A microphone is just like a speaker, but in reverse. In the case of a microphone, waves in the air cause a membrane in the microphone to vibrate. These vibrations are converted to electrical energy and are then converted to radio signals or stored to tape or other electronic media. Our particular concern is with the conversion of sound to the digital domain.

Digital Sampling

Computers are not good at storing true *analog* signals such as a sound wave. Unlike a sound wave, computers are fundamentally digital. They can only represent binary numbers in their storage systems, not continuous functions like the sound wave shown in Figure 12.1.

Computers can, however, store an approximation of a continuous function using a sampling process. When a computer samples a continuous waveform, it takes snapshots of it at distinct points in time, as shown in Figure 12.2. It converts the height of the waveform at the sampling instant to a digital number and stores that in its memory. Unfortunately, this process only approximates the analog waveform; we lose some information about the shape of the wave between our sample points. In short, the sampling process is a *lossy* process.

Although samples can be collected at any time, usually they are evenly spaced, at a fixed sampling rate. The piece of computer hardware that performs digital sampling is called an *analog to digital converter*, or ADC.

After sampling is complete, we'll have a stream of digital numbers that represents the original analog waveform. A stream of digital numbers like this probably isn't foreign to you. If you've ever held an audio CD, you've held a stream of digital samples. An audio CD is created with this same sampling technique.

Now, a stream of digital samples isn't much fun unless you're going to do something with it. In general, the main thing you do with a stream of samples is play back the original waveform. The process of converting a stream of samples back into an analog waveform is handled by a piece of hardware called a *digital to analog converter*, or DAC.

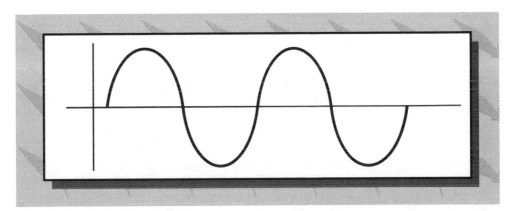

Figure 12.1   *A continuous sound wave.*

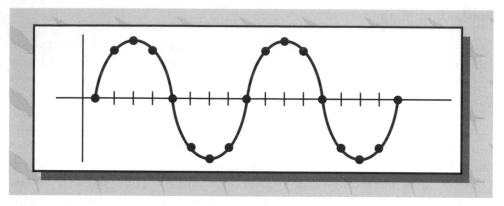

Figure 12.2 *Discrete sampling of an analog waveform.*

A DAC takes a stream of audio samples as input and produces an analog square-wave as output, as shown in Figure 12.3. "How's that?" That square-wave output doesn't look very much like our original waveform. And where do you get off calling a square-wave 'analog'?

Well, I said before that the sampling process is lossy. With just a set of sample points, there is no way for the DAC to know what the waveform looked like between them. Given this, it can only reproduce a square-wave of roughly the same shape as the original waveform. The real question is: does this square-wave sounds very much like the original wave?

The answer is: it depends. Notice that if we sample our original waveform at a higher rate, we'll have a better approximation to it. That is, we'll lose much less information about its shape. Figure 12.4 shows the output of the DAC

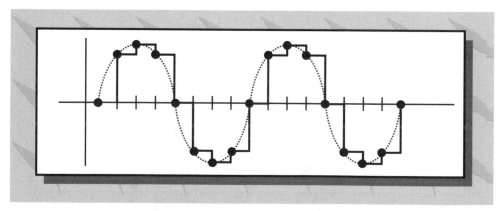

Figure 12.3 *Playing back a digital sample stream.*

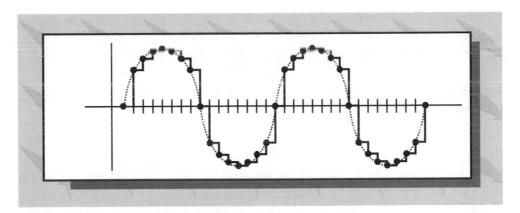

Figure 12.4   *The original waveform played back at twice the sampling rate.*

when our original waveform is sampled at twice the rate shown in Figure 12.3. Notice that the new square-wave is closer to the original waveform.

In theory, we can keep increasing the sampling rate and getting a better and better approximation of our original waveform out of the DAC. In practice, it's difficult, and therefore expensive, to build high-speed ADCs and DACs. Additionally, as the sampling rate goes up, the number of samples necessary to reproduce a waveform of a certain length increases. This process results in an increase in the amount of storage required to hold the sampled data. So how do we know when to increase the sampling rate and when not to? At what point is the sampling rate "good enough?"

Choosing a Sampling Rate

It turns out that to recover a frequency, f, when converting a stream of discrete samples back into an analog waveform, the original waveform must have been sampled at a rate of $2f$ or more. If we want to recover a sound whose highest frequency component is 8 KHz, we must sample the waveform at a rate of 16 KHz or more. Now, this leads us to the next question: What is the highest frequency that we want to reproduce?

Our answer is the result of the limitations of the human ear. The human ear can't hear sounds above approximately 22 KHz. Some people with good ears might be able to hear a little higher, but many of us don't even reach the 22 KHz mark. As a result, it makes no sense to try to reproduce frequencies much above 22 KHz. That says that we should sample our waveforms at no more than 44 KHz. Audio CDs are sampled at 44.1 KHz for just this reason.

Most games don't need nearly the crystal clarity of an audio CD reproducing a philharmonic orchestra, however. In fact, most game sounds—lasers and explosions, for instance—are fundamentally pretty chaotic, and a small amount of distortion is acceptable. We can typically sample game sounds between 11 KHz and 22 KHz and be just fine. These sample rates allow us to reproduce frequencies from 5.5 KHz to 11 KHz.

This rationale is a bit self-serving. In fact, there is another practical reason to use lower sampling rates for game sounds—lower storage requirements. Sampling at 44 KHz for 5 seconds would leave us with 220,000 samples. Lowering the sample rate to 11 KHz results in only 55,000 samples. If you want to distribute your game on anything but a CD-ROM, you'll want to use the lowest sampling rate you can get away with.

Choosing a Sample Resolution

There is another important factor that governs how well things sound as they are converted from digital to analog by the DAC—the resolution of the samples.

Figure 12.5 shows our waveform being sampled with 2-bit resolution. With two bits, we can represent four different wave amplitudes for any sample. We assign 10b to be at the midpoint, 11b to be above the midpoint, and 00b and 01b to be below the midpoint. Using 10b as the mid-point means that these samples are "unsigned." With unsigned samples, the smallest sample value is assigned a numeric value of 0, and the samples increase in value from there. Signed samples place the midpoint value at 0 and use two's-complement values to indicate the magnitude of the sample away from the midpoint. Note

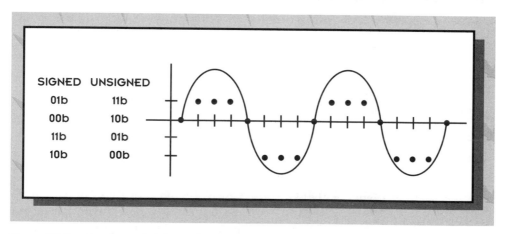

Figure 12.5 *Sampling with 2-bit resolution.*

that you can easily convert signed samples to unsigned samples, and vice-versa, simply by inverting the high-order bit of each sample value. Different pieces of digital audio equipment expect either signed or unsigned samples.

As you can see, at any sample point, there is a lot of error between the actual waveform amplitude and the value of the sample. Even if we sample at a very high rate, there will still be distortion introduced during playback, because the samples don't accurately reflect the original waveform amplitudes.

Figure 12.6 shows the same waveform sampled with 4-bit resolution. We now have 16 different values that can be used to represent the waveform amplitudes. As you can see, the error between the sample value and the actual waveform value is much smaller. These samples will sound much better during playback than the 2-bit samples.

In practice, 2-bit and 4-bit resolution samples are simply too small. At a minimum, you'll want to use 8-bit resolution. This allows 256 different amplitude values to be represented. This is the minimum, however, and professional audio typically uses 16 or more bits of resolution. Audio CDs use 16 bits, for instance.

For game use, 8-bit resolution is just fine. The reasons are the same for why lower sampling rates are acceptable: game sounds can typically put up with some distortion *and* we'll save storage. Cutting the sampling resolution from 16-bits to 8-bits results in a 50 percent reduction in storage requirements. Further, older PC sound cards can only handle 8 bit resolution, and although we could convert 16-bit samples to 8-bit samples for playback on those cards, we won't be storing a lot of extra information that many sound cards aren't capable of using.

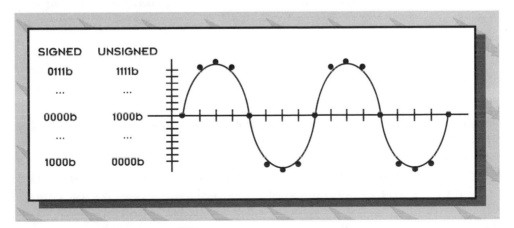

Figure 12.6   *Sampling with 4-bit resolution.*

JUST WHAT IS MIDI?

Although sampling is a good way to store and reproduce sound effects, it's very storage-intensive for musical scores. Even at low sampling rates, say 11 KHz and 8-bit resolution, five minutes of music would take over 3 MB of storage. Fortunately, there is a better way.

If you wanted to send a song to your friend across the country, you could do one two things: you could make a tape of a band playing the song, or you could send him the sheet music. In terms of the amount of storage required to send one or the other digitally, the sheet music requires far less than the digital recording.

MIDI is to a sampled audio waveform as sheet music is to a compact disk recording. MIDI stands for Musical Instrument Digital Interface and is a standard for the digital communication of musical data. MIDI allows you to connect various MIDI-compatible music devices (synthesizers, for instance) together and control them from other MIDI-compatible equipment (a computer, for instance).

MIDI has also defined a file format for the interchange and playback of, effectively, binary sheet music. A MIDI file specifies which notes should be played at what time and by which instruments, in order to create a piece of music. A piece of software on the host computer interprets the commands in the MIDI file and causes hardware to output the correct note of the correct instrument.

Like any piece of sheet music, a MIDI file allows a composer to annotate the raw notes with certain additional pieces of information. For instance, a composer can specify that some notes are to be played more softly than others or that they be played longer or with greater force. Also like any other piece of sheet music, the result of playing back a MIDI file can vary greatly, depending on what sort of hardware and software interpret the file.

For instance, to make sure that your friend hears the exact rendition of a song that you performed, you'll have to send a sampled recording. If you just send a MIDI file, your sound card's version of a piano might differ from your friend's sound card's version. For that matter, you might be playing back the song on your professional synthesizer while your friend might use an old 8-bit sound card. But then, that's just how it would be if you sent a piece of sheet music that you composed. Your friend would get different musicians than the ones you used. They would play back your song, but they might substitute different instruments for the ones you had originally intended. That's the price you pay for a tremendous storage savings.

A LITTLE HELP FROM OUR FRIENDS: DIGPAK AND MIDPAK

The number of sound cards available for the PC platform is tremendous and growing all the time. All these different cards have different capabilities and different programming models. Adding music and sound effects to *Alien Alley* would be a daunting task if we had to support all those different sound cards on our own. Fortunately, there are some other people who have done much of the work for us.

John Ratcliff and John Miles developed the DigPak and MidPak family of audio drivers to help programmers cope with the numerous sound card capabilities and programming models. DigPak and MidPak present a consistent application programming interface (API) to a sound card, no matter what it is. MidPak handles the playback of MIDI music, and DigPak deals with sampled audio waveforms, typically used for sound effects. DigPak and MidPak drivers have been written for most every major sound card in existence, so applications developed inconjunction with them are likely to run on most systems.

Further, since DigPak and MidPak drivers can be loaded dynamically when a program runs, a program isn't limited in what sound cards it can support. A user can add the correct driver for a sound card at a later time, and the program can automatically make use of it without having to be recompiled.

We'll add MIDI and sampled sound support to *Alien Alley* using the MidPak and DigPak APIs.

Installing and Setting Up DigPak/MidPak

Before we can use DigPak and MidPak, we must install the correct drivers for our sound card. When you uncompress the DigPak/MidPak archive, you'll have a directory full of sound card drivers (the .COM files) and a few other executable files.

By convention, the currently installed DigPak and MidPak drivers are named SOUNDRV.COM and MIDPAK.COM. Additional files used by MidPak are named MIDPAK.ADV and MIDPAK.AD. Programs look for these generic names when loading sound drivers, and so you must create files with these names that contain the drivers for your particular sound card.

The SETD and SETM programs included with the DigPak/MidPak archive can be used to select sound drivers appropriate for your sound card, test that they work, and copy the drivers to the SOUNDRV.COM and MIDPAK.COM filenames.

Run SETD and SETM consecutively from the DOS command line. The SETUP.BAT command file can be used to run SETD and SETM quickly in sequence. Both SETD and SETM will allow you to select a driver from a list, will play a short audition to ensure that things are working, and then copy the drivers to the correct filenames.

Once you have run SETD and SETM and the appropriate SOUNDRV.COM, MIDPAK.COM, MIDPAK.ADV, and MIDPAK.AD files have been created, you need to move them to your game programming directory; simply copy the files. If you uncompressed the DigPak/MidPak archive in the same directory as the source code for *Alien Alley*, nothing needs to be moved.

Playing Sound Effects with DigPak

Assuming that the DigPak driver has been loaded into memory (we'll see how in a later section), the DigPak API can be accessed through INT 66h. The file DIGPLAY.ASM contains C-callable wrapper functions that make the API more accessible from C, however. The DIGPLAY.H header file provides interface definitions to the various DigPak API functions.

A summary of some of the DigPak API functions is shown in Table 12.1. See the DIGPKAPI.DOC file in the DigPak/MidPak archive for more detailed information. DigPak contains some other more obscure functions, and descriptions of these functions can also be found in DIGPKAPI.DOC.

In many cases, the DigPak functions take a pointer to a **SNDSTRUC** as a parameter. A **SNDSTRUC** structure is used to store information about a particular digital sample stream, including the location of the digital data, the length of the data, and the correct playback sample frequency. DIGPLAY.H defines **SNDSTRUC** as:

```
typedef struct {
    char far *sound;
    unsigned short sndlen;
    short far *IsPlaying;
    short frequency;
} SNDSTRUC;
```

Playing a sound with DigPak is very simple and requires only four steps, assuming DigPak has been loaded and initialized.

1. Load the sound data into memory.
2. Set up a **SNDSTRUC** structure with all the necessary information.

Table 12.1   *DigPak API Function Summary*

Function Prototype	Description
short DigPlay(SNDSTRUC far *sndplay)	Plays a digital sample
short SoundStatus(void)	Returns the version number of the DigPak driver and whether a sample is currently being played
void MassageAudio(SNDSTRUC far *sndplay)	Preformats digital data to a particular output hardware format; used with DigPlay2
void DigPlay2(SNDSTRUC far *sndplay)	Plays a MassageAudio preformatted digital sample
short AudioCapabilities(void)	Returns the capabilities of the current hardware device
void StopSound(void)	Stops playing the current sound; ignored if no sound is playing.
short PostAudioPending(SNDSTRUC far *sndplay)	Posts a sound to be played when the current sound is completed
short AudioPendingStatus(void)	Indicates whether a sound is currently being played, and if so, if a sound is also pending
short SetStereoPan(short panvalue)	Allows a sound to be panned in stereo on output hardware that supports it
short SetPlayMode(short playmode)	Allows stereo or 16-bit digital data to be played on hardware that supports it
short far * PendingAddress(void)	Returns the address of the pending flag, which can be saved for later and then be used to more efficiently check the pending status, rather than calling AudioPendingStatus
short far * ReportSemaphoreAddress(void)	Returns the address of the DigPak semaphore; when the semaphore is TRUE, DigPak is currently active and shouldn't be invoked from an ISR
short InitDP(short segment)	Initializes DigPak after it has been loaded
void DeInitDP(short segment)	Deinitializes DigPak

3. Preprocess the sound sample data using **MassageAudio**.
4. Play back the sound using **DigPlay2**.

After the first three steps have been performed, a sound can be played back repeatedly by simply calling **DigPlay2**.

In practice, life gets a little more complicated than these four simple steps. DigPak only allows a single sound effect to be played at one time. Because of this limitation, we'll use some of the other functions, such as **StopSound**, to make *Alien Alley's* sound code perform a bit better.

Playing MIDI with MidPak

The MidPak API can also be accessed through INT 66h, similar to DigPak. MidPak will detect the presence of DigPak and route its API function interrupts to it. Because of this, MidPak must be loaded and initialized after DigPak.

MidPak is also accessible through a set of C-callable wrapper functions, which are contained in MIDPAK.ASM. MIDPAK.H declares the various MidPak API functions in MIDPAK.ASM. A summary of some of the functions in the MidPak API is shown in Table 12.2. See the MIDPKAPI.DOC file in the DigPak/MidPak archive for more detailed information about these and other functions.

Table 12.2   *MidPak API Function Summary*

Function Prototype	Description
short CheckMidiIn(void)	Returns 1 if MidPak is installed
short DigPakAvailable(void)	Returns 1 if DigPak is installed
short PlaySequence(short seqnum)	Plays the specified sequence from the currently registered .XMI file
short RegisterXmidi (char far *xmidi, long size)	Registers an .XMI file that has been loaded into memory
short MidiStop(void)	Causes MidPak to stop playing
void ResumePlaying(void)	Resumes playing a stopped sequence
short SequenceStatus(void)	Returns a value that indicates whether the current sequence is playing, stopped, or has completed
short RelativeVolume(short vol)	Returns the current relative volume
void SetRelativeVolume (short vol, short time)	Sets the relative playback volume
short ReportSequenceNumber(void)	Reports the number of the current playing sequence
short InitMP(short midpakseg, short advseg, char far *ad)	Initializes MidPak
void DeInitMP(short midpakseg)	Deinitializes MidPak

MidPak works with .XMI files, not straight .MID files. An .XMI file is a .MID file that has been processed into a format more convenient for MidPak. More than one .MID file can be included in an .XMI file, simplifying the loading, management, and storage of a game's multiple music scores. Each component of an .XMI file is called a *sequence* and is generated from an individual .MID file.

Multiple .MID files are converted to a single .XMI file using the MIDIFORM program that is included in the DigPak/MidPak archive. MIDIFORM takes the name of the output file and the input files as command-line parameters. MIDIFORM's command-line parameters are described when the program is started with no parameters.

Using MIDIFORM with Alien Alley

PROJECT As an example of how to use MIDIFORM, let's create the .XMI file for *Alien Alley*. There are three .MID files used in *Alien Alley*: ALIENINT.MID, ALIENMAI.MID, and ALIENEND.MID. These tunes are played during the title page, main game, and high-score entry page, respectively. These files can be found in the MUSIC subdirectory of the source code archive. Converting these files to an .XMI file is as simple as typing: "midiform alienste.xmi alienint.mid alienmai.mid alienend.mid." The resulting .XMI file, ALIENSTE.XMI ("Alien Suite"), contains three sequences, the first corresponding to ALIENINT.MID, the second to ALIENMAI.MID, and the third to ALIENEND.MID.

Playing an .XMI file with MidPak is very easy. Assuming that MidPak has been loaded and initialized, there are only three steps.

1. Load the .XMI file into memory.
2. Register the .XMI file with MidPak using **RegisterXmidi**.
3. Play a sequence from the .XMI file using **PlaySequence**.

We'll take a more detailed look at how this is done when we examine how MidPak has been integrated into *Alien Alley* in the next section.

ENHANCING ALIEN ALLEY

Now that you've got a little background about digital sound, MIDI, and the DigPak/MidPak sound drivers, it's time to see how all of those concepts are integrated with *Alien Alley*. In this section we'll examine some source code to see how *Alien Alley* plays sound effects and MIDI music at the appropriate places in the game.

Playing Sound and Music with Alien Alley

Alien Alley has been modified with the following changes. The new file and project names are ALIEN2.C and ALIEN2.PRJ. The following section shows only the functions that have changed between ALIEN1.C and ALIEN2.C. You will find the full source code for ALIEN2.C on the companion disk.

Compiling and Linking:

You can compile the ALIEN2 program using the Borland C++ 3.1 IDE by typing "bc alien2.prj" and then selecting Compile | Make from the menu. If you would rather use the command-line compiler, convert the ALIEN2.PRJ file to a makefile using the PRJ2MAK program supplied with Borland C++ 3.1. Simply type "prj2mak alien2.prj" to create the ALIEN2.MAK and ALIEN2.CFG files.

If you're using Borland C++ 4.0, choose Project | Open Project from the IDE menu, and open the ALIEN2.PRJ file. Borland C++ will convert the version 3.1 .PRJ file to a version 4.0 .IDE file. Compile and link the program by choosing Project | Make All from the IDE menu.

Setup

Before a sound effect of MIDI sequence can be played with either DigPak or MidPak, both the audio drivers and the sound data itself must be loaded into memory. **ProgramInit**, shown in Listing 12.1, is modified to call **InitSound** as part of the program-wide initialization. **InitSound** returns a **BOOL**, which indicates whether it was successful in loading and initializing the sound drivers. The global variable **SoundPresent** is set to reflect whether the initialization process was successful. If **SoundPresent** is **FALSE**, then *Alien Alley* will not play sounds or music.

Listing 12.1   The ProgramInit Function

```
BOOL              SoundPresent;
/*
    Function: ProgramInit
    Description:
        Performs all the program-wide initialization at start-up
        time.  This includes sensing the presence of alternate input
        devices and ensuring they are calibrated.
*/
void ProgramInit(void)
{
    UINT16 Xmin, Xmid, Xmax;
```

```
        UINT16 Ymin, Ymid, Ymax;
        RGB_TUPLE Black = {0, 0, 0};

        /* get into graphics */
        SetMode13h();
        /* detect mouse presence */
        if (ResetMouse() != 0) {
            MousePresent = TRUE;
        }
        else {
            MousePresent = FALSE;
        }

        /* detect and calibrate joystick */
        SenseJoysticks(&JsState);
        JsState.JsMask &= 0x3;  /* only enable joystick A */
        if (JsState.JsMask != 0) {
            JoystickPresent = TRUE;
            CalibrateJsMidpoint(&JsState, &Xmin, &Ymin, &Xmid, &Ymid,
                &Xmax, &Ymax);
            JsThresholdUp       = Ymax / 3;
            JsThresholdDown     = (Ymax * 2) / 3;
            JsThresholdLeft     = Xmax / 3;
            JsThresholdRight    = (Xmax * 2) / 3;
        }
        else {
            JoystickPresent = FALSE;
        }

        /* initialize palette */
        FillPaletteBlock(BlackPalette, 0, 256, &Black);
        /* load high-score file */
        LoadHighScores();

        /* init DIGPAK and MIDPAK stuff */
        SoundPresent = InitSound();
}
```

Listing 12.2 shows two functions, **DeInitSound** and **InitSound**. **InitSound**, as we have seen, is called from **ProgramInit**. **DeInitSound** is called to deinitialize and remove the DigPak and MidPak drivers, as well as the sound data, from memory. **DeInitSound** is called just before the program exits.

Listing 12.2   The DeInitSound and InitSound Functions

```
#define SOUND_FX_FREQUENCY      11000

UINT8 far *         MidiAddr;
long                MidiLength;
SNDSTRUC            ExplosionSound;
SNDSTRUC            LaserSound;
```

```
/*
    Function: DeInitSound
    Description:
        Unloads both MidPak and DigPak.
*/
void DeInitSound(void)
{
    DeInitMidPak();
    UnloadMidPak();
    DeInitDigPak();
    UnloadDigPak();
    if (MidiAddr != NULL) farfree(MidiAddr);
    if (ExplosionSound.sound != NULL) farfree(ExplosionSound.sound);
    if (LaserSound.sound != NULL) farfree(LaserSound.sound);
}


/*
    Function: InitSound
    Description:
        Initialize sound stuff.
*/
BOOL InitSound(void)
{
    UINT8 far * Addr;
    long Length;

    /* load the drivers */
    if (!LoadDigPak("SOUNDRV.COM")) {
        return FALSE;
    }
    if (!InitDigPak()) {
        UnloadDigPak();
        return FALSE;
    }
    if (!LoadMidPak("MIDPAK.COM", "MIDPAK.ADV", "MIDPAK.AD")) {
        DeInitDigPak();
        UnloadDigPak();
        return FALSE;
    }
    if (!InitMidPak()) {
        UnloadMidPak();
        DeInitDigPak();
        UnloadDigPak();
        return FALSE;
    }

    /* make these NULL just in case we exit with a fatal error */
    MidiAddr = NULL;
    ExplosionSound.sound = NULL;
    LaserSound.sound = NULL;

    /* load the MIDI file */
```

```
    if (LoadFile("alienste.xmi", &MidiAddr, NULL, &MidiLength)) {
        FatalError("Can't load 'alienste.xmi'", "InitSound", __LINE__);
        return FALSE;
    }
    RegisterXmidi((char far *)MidiAddr, MidiLength);

    /* load the sound effects */
    SetPlayMode(PCM_8_MONO);

    if (LoadFile("explode.8", &Addr, NULL, &Length)) {
        FatalError("Can't load 'explode.8'", "InitSound", __LINE__);
    }
    ExplosionSound.frequency = SOUND_FX_FREQUENCY;
    ExplosionSound.sound = (char far *) Addr;
    ExplosionSound.sndlen = Length;
    MassageAudio(&ExplosionSound);

    if (LoadFile("laser.8", &Addr, NULL, &Length)) {
        FatalError("Can't load 'laser.8'", "InitSound", __LINE__);
    }
    LaserSound.frequency = SOUND_FX_FREQUENCY;
    LaserSound.sound = (char far *) Addr;
    LaserSound.sndlen = Length;
    MassageAudio(&LaserSound);

    return TRUE;
}
```

InitSound calls **LoadDigPak**, **InitDigPak**, **LoadMidPak**, and **InitMidPak** to actually load and initialize DigPak and MidPak. **InitSound** takes care to load DigPak before MidPak and aborts the loading and initialization process if any of the routines returns an error. When one of the routines signals an error, **InitSound** unloads and deinitializes any driver that has successfully loaded and initialized up to that point and returns **FALSE** to **ProgramInit**.

LoadDigPak, **InitDigPak**, **LoadMidPak**, and **InitMidPak** can return an error for a number of reasons. Usually the problem is that DigPak and MidPak have not been configured, and one or more of the SOUNDRV.COM, MIDPAK.COM, MIDPAK.ADV, or MIDPAK.AD files cannot be located. In this case **LoadDigPak** or **LoadMidPak** will return an error. If the wrong driver has been configured (the driver for the Sound Blaster, for instance, when the computer has a Gravis UltraSound installed), **InitDigPak** or **InitMidPak** will signal an error.

LoadDigPak, **InitDigPak**, **LoadMidPak**, and **InitMidPak** are located in DIGMIDIF.C, shown in Listing 12.3.

Once the drivers have been correctly loaded and initialized, **InitSound** loads the actual sound data, an .XMI file named ALIENSTE.XMI and two sample files named EXPLODE.8 and LASER.8.

InitSound uses the **LoadFile** function from DIGMIDIF.C, shown in Listing 12.3, to load the ALIENSTE.XMI file into memory. Once it has been loaded, **InitSound** calls the MidPak API function **RegisterXmidi** to notify MidPak about the .XMI file.

Before loading the digital sound effects files, **InitSound** calls the DigPak API function **SetPlayMode** with **PCM_8_MONO** to let it know that we will be working with 8-bit mono samples. After loading each sample file with **LoadFile**, **InitSound** sets up the **SNDSTRUC** corresponding to each and calls **MassageAudio** to ensure that the sample data has been preprocessed appropriately for the output hardware. Each of the samples is recorded at an 11 KHz sample rate, and the **frequency SNDSTRUC** member is set to reflect this rate.

It's important to note that DigPak expects only raw, 8-bit, unsigned samples. "Raw" means that the file, or at least the buffer passed to DigPak, does not have any file-type-specific headers. The file must contain only digital samples. DigPak cannot play a Microsoft Windows .WAV file, for instance. You'll need to convert your samples to a raw format before you can use them with DigPak. I used my sample editor to export the samples in raw, 8-bit format.

Listing 12.3   DIGMIDIF.C

```
/* File: DIGMIDIF.C
** Description:
**    Interface routines for loading, initializing and unloading
**    Digpak and Midpak drivers.  These routines are based on
**    similar routines provided as example code in the DigPak/MidPak
**    distribution archive.
** Copyright:
**    Copyright 1994, David G. Roberts
*/

#include <alloc.h>
#include <assert.h>
#include <dos.h>
#include <fcntl.h>
#include <io.h>
#include <stdio.h>
#include "gamedefs.h"
#include "digplay.h" /* supplied with DigPak */
#include "midpak.h"  /* supplied with MidPak */

/* private module variables */
static BOOL     DigPakLoaded    = FALSE;
static BOOL     DigPakInit      = FALSE;
static UINT8 far *DigPakAddr;
static UINT16   DigPakParaSeg;
```

```
static BOOL     MidPakLoaded    = FALSE;
static BOOL     MidPakInit      = FALSE;
static BOOL     AdLoaded        = FALSE;
static UINT8 far *MidPakAddr;
static UINT16   MidPakParaSeg;
static UINT8 far *AdvAddr;
static UINT16   AdvParaSeg;
static UINT8 far *AdAddr;

/*
    Function: LoadFile
    Description:
        Loads a file into far memory.  The filename is specified by
        the Filename parameter.  The routine returns the address
        of the file in the Addr parameter.  If the Para parameter
        is non-NULL, the file is loaded aligned to a paragraph and
        the segment portion of the aligned address is returned
        in Para.  Note that the Addr parameter is still set to
        the true start of the address block to which the file
        is loaded and should be used to farfree the block when
        done.  The length is returned in Len.
*/
int LoadFile(char * Filename, UINT8 far *(*Addr), UINT16 *Para, long *Len)
{
    int Handle;
    int Status;
    long Length;
    UINT8 far * Buffer;
    UINT8 far * BufferPara;
    UINT16 BufferSeg;
    UINT16 BufferOff;
    unsigned NumRead;

    assert(Filename != NULL);

    /* figure out file length */
    Handle = open(Filename, O_RDONLY | O_BINARY);
    if (Handle == -1) {
        return 1; /* error */
    }
    Length = filelength(Handle);
    if (Length == -1L) {
        close(Handle);
        return 1; /* error */
    }

    /* allocate buffer */
    if (Para) {
        /* we want this paragraph aligned */
        Buffer = farmalloc(Length + 16);
        if (Buffer == NULL) {
            close(Handle);
            return 1;
        }
```

```
            /* if not paragraph aligned, make it so */
            BufferSeg = FP_SEG(Buffer);
            BufferOff = FP_OFF(Buffer);
            BufferSeg = BufferSeg + (BufferOff >> 4) + 1;
            BufferOff = 0;
            BufferPara = MK_FP(BufferSeg, BufferOff);
        }
        else {
            Buffer = farmalloc(Length);
            if (Buffer == NULL) {
                close(Handle);
                return 1;
            }
            BufferPara = Buffer;
        }

        /* load file into buffer */
        Status = _dos_read(Handle, BufferPara, (unsigned) Length, &NumRead);
        if (Status != 0 || (NumRead != (unsigned) Length)) {
            farfree(Buffer);
            close(Handle);
            return 1;
        }
        close(Handle);

        /* update return values */
        if (Addr != NULL) {
            *Addr = Buffer;
        }
        if (Para != NULL) {
            *Para = BufferSeg;
        }
        if (Len != NULL) {
            *Len = Length;
        }

        return 0;
    }

/*
    Function: LoadDigPak
    Description:
        Loads a DigPak driver into memory.  Returns FALSE if
        something goes wrong.
*/
BOOL LoadDigPak(char *Filename)
{
    int Error;

    /* check to see that we haven't already loaded it */
    assert(!DigPakLoaded && !DigPakInit);

    /* load the driver */
    Error = LoadFile(Filename, &DigPakAddr, &DigPakParaSeg, NULL);
```

```
        if (!Error) { /* everything OK */
            DigPakLoaded = TRUE;
            return TRUE;
        }
        return FALSE; /* something went wrong */
    }


    /*
        Function: InitDigPak
        Description:
            Initializes the DigPak driver already loaded.  Returns
            FALSE if the driver can't be initialized.
    */
    BOOL InitDigPak(void)
    {
        /* make sure we've loaded it */
        assert(DigPakLoaded);

        /* initialize and if everything is okay, return TRUE */
        if (InitDP(DigPakParaSeg)) {
            DigPakInit = TRUE;
            return TRUE;
        }

        /* something went wrong */
        DigPakInit = FALSE;
        return FALSE;
    }


    /*
        Function: DeInitDigPak
        Description:
            Deinitializes the DigPak driver.
    */
    void DeInitDigPak(void)
    {
        /* make sure it's already loaded and initialized */
        assert(DigPakLoaded && DigPakInit);
        DeInitDP(DigPakParaSeg);
        DigPakInit = FALSE;
    }


    /*
        Function: UnloadDigPak
        Description:
            Unloads the DigPakDriver and frees its memory.
    */
    void UnloadDigPak(void)
    {
        assert(DigPakLoaded);

        if (DigPakInit) {
            DeInitDigPak();
        }
```

```
        farfree(DigPakAddr);
        DigPakLoaded = FALSE;
}


/*

    Function: LoadMidPak
    Description:
        Loads the specified MidPak driver files into memory.
        Returns TRUE if all is well, FALSE otherwise.
*/
BOOL LoadMidPak(char * Filename, char *AdvFilename, char *AdFilename)
{
    int Error;

    assert(!MidPakLoaded && !MidPakInit);

    Error = LoadFile(Filename, &MidPakAddr, &MidPakParaSeg, NULL);
    if (!Error) {
        Error = LoadFile(AdvFilename, &AdvAddr, &AdvParaSeg, NULL);
        if (!Error) {
            if (AdFilename) {
                Error = LoadFile(AdFilename, &AdAddr, NULL, NULL);
                if (Error) {
                    /* error loading .AD file */
                    farfree(AdvAddr);
                    farfree(MidPakAddr);
                    return FALSE;
                }
                AdLoaded = TRUE;
            }
            else {
                AdLoaded = FALSE;
            }
            /* everything OK */
            MidPakLoaded = TRUE;
            return TRUE;
        }
        else {
            /* error loading .ADV file */
            farfree(MidPakAddr);
            return FALSE;
        }
    }
    return FALSE;
}


/*

    Function: InitMidPak
    Description:
        Initializes a MidPak driver.  Returns FALSE if the driver
        can't be initialized, TRUE otherwise.
*/
BOOL InitMidPak(void)
```

```
{
    /* make sure it's been loaded first */
    assert(MidPakLoaded);

    /* initialize it */
    /* note that the midpak.h file declares the AdAddr parameter as */
    /*   char far * rather than unsigned char far *, hence the cast */
    if (!InitMP(MidPakParaSeg, AdvParaSeg, (char far *) AdAddr)) {
        MidPakInit = TRUE;
        return TRUE;
    }

    /* something went wrong */
    MidPakInit = FALSE;
    return FALSE;
}


/*
    Function: DeInitMidPak
    Description:
        Deinitializes a MidPak driver.
*/
void DeInitMidPak(void)
{
    /* make sure we're loaded and initialized */
    assert(MidPakLoaded && MidPakInit);

    MidiStop(); /* make sure we don't keep playing */
    DeInitMP(MidPakParaSeg);
    MidPakInit = FALSE;
}


/*
    Function: UnloadMidPak
    Description:
        Unloads a MidPak driver.  Frees the memory associated
        with the main driver, the .ADV file, and the .AD file.
*/
void UnloadMidPak(void)
{
    /* make sure it's loaded */
    assert(MidPakLoaded);

    if (MidPakInit) {
        DeInitMidPak();
    }
    if (AdLoaded) {
        farfree(AdAddr);
    }
    farfree(AdvAddr);
    farfree(MidPakAddr);
}
```

Cranking Up the Music

Once the sound drivers and sound data files have been loaded and initialized, we can use MidPak to play music. There are three MIDI sequences in the .XMI file and they are played at particular points during the program. The first sequence is started when the title page is displayed.

About the Music

The music for *Alien Alley* was composed by Jim Black using algorithmic and live performances. Jim used Cakewalk for Windows for the sequencer, Jammer Pro for the alogrithmic composer, and the MidPak MENU program for tweaking the release. The songs were auditioned for MidPak using a Sound Blaster16. Jim's Kawia K-11 provided sonic inspiration.

The first piece, ALIENINT.MID, comprises live performances recorded with Cakewalk. "Many of the ideas came from old films with Romans and swashbucklers hacking on each other," says Jim. "I thought this source material was appropiate for a theme designed to prepare you for the heroic conquest in *Alien Alley*."

"The main theme, ALIENMAI.MID, was an experiment in style and composition using Jammer Pro. I wrote the musical progressions, then translated them into measures using Jammer Pro. The intention was to build to uncontrollable battle frenzy," Jim says. "Cakewalk was used to edit some of the transitions, but there were no human performances on this piece."

The final piece, ALIENEND.MID, combines both human and algorithmic compositions. "The band is algorithmically generated. Again, I wrote the progressions, then Jammer PRO took over. The solo instrument is a live performance recorded with Cakewalk."

About the Composer

When Jim Black is not lurking the Internet for game music composition jobs, he can be found writing software and designing PC-compatible hardware for a large gaming company. If he is really nice to the game designers, he gets some of his music playing from one-arm bandits once in a while. You might also find him playing bass guitar and singing on the weekends in nightclubs in Denver.

Jim would like to thank The Coriolis Group, Dave Roberts, Miles Design, the Fat Farm, and J. Ratcliff at The Audio Solution for assistance and the opportunity to display his work.

Listing 12.4 shows the **TitlePage** function modified to call **PlaySequence** if the **SoundPresent** flag indicates that the sound drivers have been loaded and initialized correctly. Sequence number 0 is played, which corresponds to the opening title theme.

Listing 12.4   The TitlePage Function

```
/*
    Function: TitlePage
    Description:
        Displays the Alien Alley title page.
*/
void TitlePage(void)
{
    LINEAR_BITMAP far * Image;

    /* start title music */
    if (SoundPresent) {
        PlaySequence(0);
    }

    /* clear screen */
    ClearMode13hScreen();

    /* set everything to black so we can draw without being seen */
    /* use two function calls to avoid snow */
    SetVGAPaletteBlock(BlackPalette, 0, 128);
    SetVGAPaletteBlock(BlackPalette, 128, 128);

    /* first page of stuff */
    Image = LoadPCX("title.pcx", GamePalette);
    if (Image == NULL) {
        FatalError("Can't load 'title.pcx'", "TitlePage", __LINE__);
    }
    BltLinear(Image, 0, 0, MK_FP(VIDEO_MEM_SEGMENT, 0));
    farfree(Image);
    if (kbhit()) {
```

```
        getch();
        SetVGAPaletteBlock(GamePalette, 0, 128);
        SetVGAPaletteBlock(GamePalette, 128, 128);
        return;
    }
    FadeIn(1500);
}
```

The next MIDI sequence is started when the actual game starts. Listing 12.5 shows the function **Play**. As with **TitlePage**, **Play** checks the **SoundPresent** flag, and if it's **TRUE**, it starts a sequence playing. **Play** starts sequence number 1, which is the main game theme. Note that starting a sequence with **PlaySequence** stops the previously playing sequence automatically; we do not have to call **MidiStop** first.

Listing 12.5 The Play Function

```
/*
    Function: Play
    Description:
        Play the game!
*/
void Play(int Control)
{
    BOOL    UserInputUp;
    BOOL    UserInputDown;
    BOOL    UserInputLeft;
    BOOL    UserInputRight;
    BOOL    UserInputFire;
    int     GunBlinkCounter;
    int     GunBlinkState;
    RGB_TUPLE Black = {0, 0, 0};
    RGB_TUPLE GunColor;
    BOOL    GameOver;
    BOOL    GameOverInput;
    BOOL    GameOverDeath;
    LINEAR_BITMAP far * Image;

    /* fade screen to remove title page */
    FadeOut(500);

    /* load sprites */
    LoadSprites();

    /* initialize all counters, etc. */
    Score = 0;
    AlienGenCounter = ALIEN_GEN_RATE_BASE;
    HeroShields = MAX_HERO_SHIELDS;
```

```
/* set mode X */
SetModeX();
SetUpModeX();

/* start game music and get sound effects off disk */
if (SoundPresent) {
    PlaySequence(1);
}

/* set up palette stuff */
/* palette.pcx is a single pixel bitmap with the palette */
/*   this is done because it's easy to load the palette */
/*   using LoadPCX */
Image = LoadPCX("palette.pcx", GamePalette);
if (Image == NULL) {
    FatalError("Can't load 'palette.pcx'", "ProgramInit", __LINE__);
}
farfree(Image); /* ignore the single pixel bitmap */
SetVGAPaletteBlock(GamePalette, 0, 128);
SetVGAPaletteBlock(GamePalette, 128, 128);

/* install keyboard or mouse handlers */
/* do nothing for joystick */
if (Control == 'm') {
}
else if (Control == 'k') {
    SetButtonKeysMode();
}

/* set up gun blink stuff */
GetPaletteEntry(GamePalette, GUN_COLOR, &GunColor);
GunBlinkCounter     = GUN_BLINK_RATE;
GunBlinkState       = 1; /* gun blink on */

/* initialize the status screen */
InitStatus();

/* enter main animation loop */
GameOver = FALSE;
while (!GameOver) {
    /* get user input */
    GameOverInput = GetInput(Control, &UserInputUp, &UserInputDown,
        &UserInputLeft, &UserInputRight, &UserInputFire);

    /* move sprites */
    MoveSprites(UserInputUp, UserInputDown, UserInputLeft,
        UserInputRight, UserInputFire);

    /* check for collisions */
    CheckCollisions();
```

```
        /* erase */
        GameOverDeath = EraseSprites();

        /* draw */
        DrawSprites();

        /* update status */
        DrawStatus();

        /* wait for page flip */
        PageFlip(PageOffset[HiddenPage]);
        HiddenPage ^= 1; /* flip HiddenPage to other state */

        /* blink the guns */
        if (GunBlinkCounter == 0) {
            if (GunBlinkState == 1) {
                SetVGAPaletteEntry(GUN_COLOR, &Black);
            }
            else {
                SetVGAPaletteEntry(GUN_COLOR, &GunColor);
            }
            GunBlinkState ^= 1; /* flip it to other state */
            GunBlinkCounter = GUN_BLINK_RATE;
        }
        else {
            GunBlinkCounter-;
        }

        /* player either aborts or dies */
        GameOver = GameOverInput || GameOverDeath;
    }

    /* uninstall mouse and/or keyboard handlers */
    if (Control == 'm') {
    }
    else if (Control == 'k') {
        SetNormalKeysMode();
    }

    /* free all memory used to play */
    FreeSprites();

    /* fade to black... */
    FadeOut(250);

    /* return to Mode 13h, as we were */
    SetMode13h();
}
```

The final MIDI sequence is played when the player generates enough points to get on the high-score list. **NewHighScore** is called when **Play** exits. **NewHighScore** starts playing sequence number 2 when it has determined that the player has, in fact, generated a high-score. As always, **SoundPresent** is first tested to ensure that the drivers have been loaded.

Listing 12.6   The NewHighScore Function

```
/*
    Function: NewHighScore
    Description:
        Manipulates the HighScore array to make room for the
        user's score and gets the new text.
*/
void NewHighScore(int NewScore)
{
    int i;
    int Row;
    int Column;
    int StrLen;
    int Key;

    /* check to see if it's really a high score */
    if (NewScore <= HighScore[9].Score) {
        return;
    }

    /* start high score music */
    if (SoundPresent) {
        PlaySequence(2);
    }

    /* move other scores down to make room */
    for (i = 8; i >= 0; i--) {
        if (NewScore > HighScore[i].Score) {
            strcpy(HighScore[i + 1].Text, HighScore[i].Text);
            HighScore[i + 1].Score = HighScore[i].Score;
        }
        else {
            break;
        }
    }
    i++;

    /* blank out text of correct slot */
    HighScore[i].Text[0] = '\0';
    HighScore[i].Score = NewScore;

    /* display the text and fade in */
    SetMode13h();
    GetVGAPaletteBlock(GamePalette, 0, 256);
    SetVGAPaletteBlock(BlackPalette, 0, 128);
    SetVGAPaletteBlock(BlackPalette, 128, 128);
    DisplayHighScores();
    FadeIn(500);
```

```
/* get user text string */
Row     = HIGH_SCORE_LINE + i;
Column  = 8;
StrLen  = 0;
do {
    SetCursorPosition(Row, Column);
    DrawChar(127, 9);
    Key = getch();
    if (Key == 0) {
        getch();
    }
    if (' ' <= Key && Key <= 126 && StrLen < HIGH_SCORE_TEXT_LEN) {
        DrawChar(Key, 9);
        HighScore[i].Text[StrLen] = Key;
        StrLen++;
        HighScore[i].Text[StrLen] = '\0';
        Column++;
    }
    else if (Key == '\b' && StrLen > 0) {
        DrawChar(' ', 9);
        StrLen—;
        Column—;
        HighScore[i].Text[StrLen] = '\0';
    }
} while (Key != '\r');

/* erase cursor */
DrawChar(' ', 9);

/* fade to black... */
FadeOut(500);
}
```

Sound Effects

Now that we understand how and when MIDI sequences are played, let's take a look at how and when sound effects are played.

There are two types of sound effects used by *Alien Alley*: a laser sound and an explosion sound. The laser sound is generated whenever the player or an alien fires a laser cannon. Both of these events occur in **MoveSprites**, shown in Listing 12.7. Just after **MoveSprites** calls **CreateHeroMissile** or **CreateAlienMissile** to create a missile object, it also calls **StartLaserSound** to start the audio effect.

Listing 12.7   The MoveSprites Function

```
/*
    Function: MoveSprites
    Description:
```

```
        Takes care of moving hero ship and alien sprites, based on
        user input and their behavioral algorithms.  MoveSprites
        is also where missiles are generated and off-screen images
        are removed from play.
*/
void MoveSprites
    (
    BOOL UserInputUp,
    BOOL UserInputDown,
    BOOL UserInputLeft,
    BOOL UserInputRight,
    BOOL UserInputFire
    )
{
    int i;
    static LastFireInput;
    int AlienFireResult;
    int AlienProximity;

    /* first, take care of the hero */
    if (UserInputUp) {
        Hero.y -= HERO_Y_VELOCITY;
    }
    if (UserInputDown) {
        Hero.y += HERO_Y_VELOCITY;
    }
    if (UserInputLeft) {
        Hero.x -= HERO_X_VELOCITY;
    }
    if (UserInputRight) {
        Hero.x += HERO_X_VELOCITY;
    }
    /* limit player movement */
    Hero.y = MAX(HeroYMin, MIN(HeroYMax, Hero.y));
    Hero.x = MAX(HeroXMin, MIN(HeroXMax, Hero.x));
    /* update hero bounding rect */
    ComputeBoundingRect(Hero.x, Hero.y, HeroBitmap->OriginX,
        HeroBitmap->OriginY, HeroWidth, HeroHeight,
        &(Hero.Bounds));

    /* update hero missiles */
    for (i = 0; i < MAX_HERO_MISSILES; i++) {
        if (HeroMissile[i].Draw) {
            /* update position */
            HeroMissile[i].y += HeroMissile[i].vy;
            /* stop drawing when it's off screen */
            if (HeroMissile[i].y < - (MAX_OBJECT_HEIGHT / 2)) {
                HeroMissile[i].Draw = FALSE;
            }
            else {
                /* if still onscreen, update bounding rect */
                ComputeBoundingRect(HeroMissile[i].x, HeroMissile[i].y,
                    MissileBitmap->OriginX, MissileBitmap->OriginY,
```

```
                            MissileWidth, MissileHeight, &(HeroMissile[i].Bounds));
            }
        }
    }

    /* generate hero missiles */
    if (UserInputFire && !LastFireInput && Hero.Draw) {
        CreateHeroMissile(Hero.x - HERO_GUN_OFFSET_LEFT,
            Hero.y - HERO_GUN_OFFSET_UP);
        CreateHeroMissile(Hero.x + HERO_GUN_OFFSET_RIGHT,
            Hero.y - HERO_GUN_OFFSET_UP);
        StartLaserSound();
    }
    LastFireInput = UserInputFire;

    /* update alien missiles */
    for (i = 0; i < MAX_ALIEN_MISSILES; i++) {
        if (AlienMissile[i].Draw) {
            /* update position */
            AlienMissile[i].y += AlienMissile[i].vy;
            /* stop drawing when it's off screen */
            if (AlienMissile[i].y > (REDUCED_SCREEN_HEIGHT +
                (MAX_OBJECT_HEIGHT / 2))) {
                AlienMissile[i].Draw = FALSE;
            }
            else {
                /* if still onscreen, update bounding rect */
                ComputeBoundingRect(AlienMissile[i].x, AlienMissile[i].y,
                    MissileBitmap->OriginX, MissileBitmap->OriginY,
                    MissileWidth, MissileHeight, &(AlienMissile[i].Bounds));
            }
        }
    }

    /* move aliens */
    for (i = 0; i < MAX_ALIENS; i++) {
        if (Alien[i].Draw) {
            if (Alien[i].ObjectSpec == 0) {
                /* pick a new direction */
                Alien[i].vx = random((2 * ALIEN_X_VELOCITY) + 1) -
                    ALIEN_X_VELOCITY;
                Alien[i].ObjectSpec = ALIEN_MOVE_TIME_BASE +
                    random(ALIEN_MOVE_TIME_VAR);
            }
            else {
                Alien[i].ObjectSpec--;
            }
            /* update alien position */
            Alien[i].x += Alien[i].vx;
            Alien[i].y += Alien[i].vy;

            /* clip alien movement horizontally */
            Alien[i].x = MAX(MAX_OBJECT_WIDTH / 2, MIN(Alien[i].x,
                SCREEN_WIDTH - (MAX_OBJECT_WIDTH / 2)));
```

```
            /* move alien to top when it gets to bottom */
            if (Alien[i].y > (REDUCED_SCREEN_HEIGHT +
                (MAX_OBJECT_HEIGHT / 2))) {
                Alien[i].y = - (MAX_OBJECT_HEIGHT / 2);
            }

            /* update alien bounding rect */
            ComputeBoundingRect(Alien[i].x, Alien[i].y,
                AlienBitmap->OriginX, AlienBitmap->OriginY,
                AlienWidth, AlienHeight, &(Alien[i].Bounds));

            /* generate alien missiles */
            if (Alien[i].ObjectSpec2 == 0) {
                AlienFireResult = random(100); /* in percent */
                AlienProximity  = Alien[i].x - Hero.x;
                if (AlienProximity < 0) {
                    AlienProximity = -AlienProximity;
                }
                if (((AlienProximity < ALIEN_PROX_THRESHOLD) &&
                    (AlienFireResult < ALIEN_FIRE_PROB_HERO)) ||
                    (AlienFireResult < ALIEN_FIRE_PROB_RANDOM)) {
                    CreateAlienMissile(Alien[i].x -
                        ALIEN_GUN_OFFSET_LEFT, Alien[i].y +
                        ALIEN_GUN_OFFSET_DOWN);
                    CreateAlienMissile(Alien[i].x +
                        ALIEN_GUN_OFFSET_RIGHT, Alien[i].y +
                        ALIEN_GUN_OFFSET_DOWN);
                    Alien[i].ObjectSpec2 = ALIEN_FIRE_LOCKOUT;
                    StartLaserSound();
                }
            }
            else {
                Alien[i].ObjectSpec2-;
            }
        }
    }
}

/* generate aliens */
if (AlienGenCounter == 0) {
    /* generate an alien */
    CreateAlien();
    /* reinit generate counter */
    AlienGenCounter = ALIEN_GEN_RATE_BASE +
        random(ALIEN_GEN_RATE_VAR);
}
else {
    AlienGenCounter-;
}

/* update explosions - note, we don't really "move" them, just */
/* make the animation go */
for (i = 0; i < MAX_EXPLOSIONS; i++) {
    if (Explosion[i].Draw) {
        if (Explosion[i].ObjectSpec2 == 0) {
```

```
                    Explosion[i].ObjectSpec++;
                    Explosion[i].ObjectSpec2 = EXPLOSION_FRAME_REPEAT_COUNT;
                    if (Explosion[i].ObjectSpec >= MAX_EXPLOSION_BITMAPS) {
                        Explosion[i].Draw = FALSE;
                    }
                }
                else {
                    Explosion[i].ObjectSpec2-;
                }
            }
        }
    }
}
```

StartLaserSound, shown in Listing 12.8, is used to cause DigPak to play the
laser sound sample. If **SoundPresent** is not **TRUE**, however, **StartLaserSound**
returns immediately. This means the calling routines do not need to include
code to test **SoundPresent** before calling **StartLaserSound**.

Before playing the laser sound sample, **StartLaserSound** calls the DigPak
API function **AudioPendingStatus** to check if another sound effect is currently playing; DigPak is capable of playing only one sound effect at a time. If
AudioPendingStatus indicates that no sound is currently playing, the laser
sound is started using **DigPlay2**.

If another sound is currently playing, **StartLaserSound** would have to cut it
off by calling **StopSound**. Since laser sounds are very common, this would
cause explosions and other laser sounds to be cut off quite frequently. All the
player would commonly end up hearing would be the first portion of the
laser sound, over and over.

Listing 12.8   The StartLaserSound Function

```
/*
    Function: StartLaserSound
    Description:
        Starts a laser sound playing if the sound driver is
        installed.
*/
void StartLaserSound(void)
{
    int Status;

    if (!SoundPresent)
        return;

    Status = AudioPendingStatus();
    if (Status == NOTPLAYING) {
        DigPlay2(&LaserSound);
```

```
        }
        /* else too many sounds, so defer to other stuff */
}
```

The next place that sound effects are generated is when something blows up. When **CheckCollisions**, shown in Listing 12.9, determines that an alien ship or the player has exploded, it first calls **CreateExplosion** and then calls **StartExplosionSound**. **StartExplosionSound** is similar to **StartLaserSound** and is shown in Listing 12.10.

Listing 12.9   The CheckCollisions Function

```
/*
    Function: CheckCollisions
    Description:
        Check for collisions between various objects and start
        explosions if they collide.  Collision detection is
        performed between:
            * aliens and hero
            * aliens and hero missiles
            * hero and alien missiles
        Note that all tests are performed between objects that are
        currently being drawn, not just active objects.
*/
void CheckCollisions(void)
{
    int i, j;

    /* check between hero and aliens */
    for (i = 0; i < MAX_ALIENS; i++) {
        /* Use C short circuit boolean evaluation in a big way. */
        /* Make sure both hero and alien are still being drawn */
        /* (they may still be active but have been removed */
        /* from the screen and are just being erased). */
        /* If they are still onscreen, then perform a rectangle test. */
        /* If the rectangle collision indicates a possible hit, then */
        /* perform a bitmap test. */
        if (Hero.Draw && Alien[i].Draw &&
            CollisionTestRect(&(Hero.Bounds), &(Alien[i].Bounds)) &&
            CollisionTestBitmap(HeroCollisionMap, AlienCollisionMap,
                Hero.Bounds.Left, Hero.Bounds.Top,
                Alien[i].Bounds.Left, Alien[i].Bounds.Top)) {

            Hero.Draw = FALSE;
            CreateExplosion(Hero.x, Hero.y);
            Alien[i].Draw = FALSE;
            CreateExplosion(Alien[i].x, Alien[i].y);
            StartExplosionSound();
        }
    }
```

```
    /* check between aliens and hero missiles */
    for (i = 0; i < MAX_ALIENS; i++) {
        if (!Alien[i].Draw) {
            continue;
        }
        for (j = 0; j < MAX_HERO_MISSILES; j++) {
            /* do similar short circuit, mondo huge test as above */
            if (HeroMissile[j].Draw &&
                CollisionTestRect(&(Alien[i].Bounds),
                    &(HeroMissile[j].Bounds)) &&
                CollisionTestBitmap(AlienCollisionMap,
                    MissileCollisionMap, Alien[i].Bounds.Left,
                    Alien[i].Bounds.Top, HeroMissile[j].Bounds.Left,
                    HeroMissile[j].Bounds.Top)) {

                Alien[i].Draw       = FALSE;
                HeroMissile[j].Draw = FALSE;
                CreateExplosion(Alien[i].x, Alien[i].y);
                Score += POINTS_PER_ALIEN;
                StartExplosionSound();
                break; /* alien is destroyed */
            }
        }
    }

    /* check between hero and alien missiles */
    for (i = 0; i < MAX_ALIEN_MISSILES; i++) {
        /* again, rely on short circuiting */
        if (AlienMissile[i].Draw && Hero.Draw &&
            CollisionTestRect(&(AlienMissile[i].Bounds),
                &(Hero.Bounds)) &&
            CollisionTestBitmap(MissileCollisionMap, HeroCollisionMap,
                AlienMissile[i].Bounds.Left, AlienMissile[i].Bounds.Top,
                Hero.Bounds.Left, Hero.Bounds.Top)) {

            AlienMissile[i].Draw    = FALSE; /* destroy missile in any case */
            if (HeroShields == 0) {
                Hero.Draw           = FALSE;
                CreateExplosion(Hero.x, Hero.y);
                StartExplosionSound();
                break; /* hero is destroyed */
            }
            else {
                /* take away a bit of shields */
                HeroShields--;
            }
        }
    }
}
```

Like **StartLaserSound**, **StartExplosionSound** first checks to see if the sound
drivers have been set up correctly and if not, returns immediately. If the

drivers are up and running, then **StartExplosionSound** stops the currently playing sound and starts an explosion sound using **DigPlay2**.

So why does **StartExplosionSound** stop the currently playing sound while **StartLaserSound** defers when a sound is already playing? Explosion sounds are a lot less common in *Alien Alley* than laser sounds. It's quite often the case that a laser sound is already playing when an explosion is generated. If **StartExplosionSound** didn't play an explosion sound when another sound was already playing, an explosion sound would almost never occur. Since explosions are so infrequent, the player would notice immediately that the sound had not been played.

Calling **StopSound** and then **DigPlay2** ensures that the player hears the explosion for each and every ship that is destroyed. In the case when a laser or explosion sound is already playing, it is truncated in favor of the current explosion sound.

Listing 12.10   The StartExplosionSound Function

```
/*
    Function: StartExplosionSound
    Description:
        Starts an explosion sound playing if the sound driver is
        installed.
*/
void StartExplosionSound(void)
{
    if (!SoundPresent)
        return;


    StopSound();
    DigPlay2(&ExplosionSound);
}
```

CREATING YOUR OWN AUDIO SOUND EFFECTS

Although it's pretty obvious that to create a good sound track you'll need someone with musical ability to compose a song for you, it's often not clear how to go about creating the sound effects you'll need for your game. If you need an explosion sound, should you go out, blow something up, and record it?

No! You'd be surprised what you can find to use instead. Both the laser and explosion sound effect used in *Alien Alley* were created right out of my own mouth. I simply got a microphone, plugged it into my sound card, and used some sampling software to record myself making "explosion" and "laser" sounds. (You should have seen the strange looks my wife gave me after an hour or two of laser sounds.) I used the sampling software to remove extraneous noises before and after the sample I'd made, and applied some special effects filters and such so it wouldn't sound so much like a human voice. Creating both sounds took me only a few hours.

Now, this isn't to say that you'll be able to duplicate all sounds using your voice, but just that you shouldn't necessarily think you'll have to go out and record everything "live." An incredible number of effects can be created using the effects menu of your sampling software on samples created from things around the house.

Look for other sound effects on the Internet, BBSs, and other online services. Even if an effect isn't exactly what you want, you can often apply a bunch of effects processing to it to get something reasonable. Be careful of violating copyright laws by using samples taken from movies or television shows, however. Some of the samples that make their way into BBS and online service archives might be from copyrighted material and so should be avoided, especially if you're going to try to sell your game.

Sampling software is fairly easy to acquire. It is often bundled with sound cards, and many programs are available commercially and even as shareware. For the effects in *Alien Alley*, I used WAVE for Windows, a commercial program from Turtle Beach Systems. WAVE for Windows allows you to record, add digital effects, and save the resulting sample stream in a number of file formats. In particular, WAVE for Windows allows you to export a sample stream in raw 8-bit or 16-bit format, suitable for use with DigPak. Check the resource appendix for a list of other sampling software.

LICENSING DIGPAK AND MIDPAK

Although by buying this book you've been granted permission to use the source code on the disk in your own programs, DigPak and MidPak are commercial products. They require you to adhere to their licensing requirements in order to use them in your own projects. Don't fret, however. The licensing requirements of these products are very favorable to developers. Further, special dispensation has been afforded to authors who release their programs for free or as shareware. *Read the file named README.PRN in the DigPak/MidPak archive for more information about licensing these products for your game.*

SCROLLING ALONG

For our our last adventure, we'll add fast-action scrolling to our *Alien Alley* game.

A few years ago I visited Las Vegas. In the basement of the Excalibur Hotel and Casino is a ride that simulates a roller coaster. After paying your $5 ticket fee, you get ushered into a dark room with several rows of seats. In front of you is a large screen with a first-person view of a roller-coaster track, stretching out into the distance.

When everybody is seated, they start the "ride." The chair you're sitting in tips backwards and the screen shows the track rising up the first hill of the roller coaster. You hear the "clack, clack, clack" of the chain pulling you up. As you crest the hill, the seat tips forward and it appears as if you race down the hill as you would in a real roller coaster. You hear the "whoosh" as the train slides through the air. At the bottom, the track goes into a steeply banked turn and your seat rolls to the side. As long as you keep your eyes on the screen in front of you, it appears as if you are riding a real roller coaster.

Of course, everybody on the ride knew that it was all an illusion, but the effect was so real that people even had their hands up in the air just like on a real coaster. They screamed as the track dipped and rolled. They ducked their heads down as the track raced along under beams and struts. And when it was all over, their legs wobbled as they stood up and left the ride. This was quite an experience.

Well, we'd like to make *Alien Alley* quite an experience, too. Unfortunately, it looks pretty flat right now. It's as if you were on the roller coaster ride but they forgot to bank your chair at the right times. Although you'd get the feeling of what was going on, part of the experience would be missing. Right now, the player of *Alien Alley* is supposed to be flying through space blasting aliens, but although the aliens are there, it doesn't really look like the player is flying through space.

In this chapter, we'll find out how to add a scrolling starfield background to *Alien Alley* to complete the player's sensory experience. As the game progresses, the starfield will move down the screen with the player, alien, missile, and explosion sprites on top of it. The scrolling background will make it appear as if the player's spaceship is travelling through the galaxy as it does battle with the invading aliens. Figure 13.1 shows *Alien Alley* after our scrolling background has been added.

eXPLORER OVERVIEW In this chapter we'll examine the necessary changes to add a scrolling background to *Alien Alley*. Although we won't develop any standalone source code modules, we'll take a look at the techniques that make scrolling possible and the *Alien Alley* functions that implement those techniques. Using these same techniques, you'll be able to add scrolling to your own games.

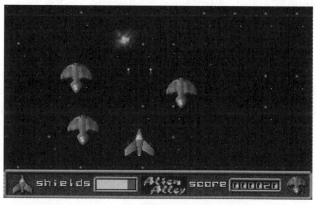

Figure 13.1 *Alien Alley with a scrolling star-field background.*

Save 10% More & Get The Points

Only Waldenbooks
Preferred Readers get...

Extra 10% Discount

On every purchase (except newsstand items and gift certificates)

Earn Points

With every dollar you spend
($1 = 1 Point)

$5 Certificates

Good toward any purchase with every 100 points you earn

Roll Over Points

Renew and roll over any unused points every year

Double Points

When you join or renew

For only a $10 annual membership fee.

Just ask your bookseller to sign you up today or call 1-800-322-2000.

Waldenbooks
Preferred Reader Program

0681473517

SCROLLING ALONG

For our our last adventure, we'll add fast-action scrolling to our *Alien Alley* game.

A few years ago I visited Las Vegas. In the basement of the Excalibur Hotel and Casino is a ride that simulates a roller coaster. After paying your $5 ticket fee, you get ushered into a dark room with several rows of seats. In front of you is a large screen with a first-person view of a roller-coaster track, stretching out into the distance.

When everybody is seated, they start the "ride." The chair you're sitting in tips backwards and the screen shows the track rising up the first hill of the roller coaster. You hear the "clack, clack, clack" of the chain pulling you up. As you crest the hill, the seat tips forward and it appears as if you race down the hill as you would in a real roller coaster. You hear the "whoosh" as the train slides through the air. At the bottom, the track goes into a steeply banked turn and your seat rolls to the side. As long as you keep your eyes on the screen in front of you, it appears as if you are riding a real roller coaster.

Of course, everybody on the ride knew that it was all an illusion, but the effect was so real that people even had their hands up in the air just like on a real coaster. They screamed as the track dipped and rolled. They ducked their heads down as the track raced along under beams and struts. And when it was all over, their legs wobbled as they stood up and left the ride. This was quite an experience.

Well, we'd like to make *Alien Alley* quite an experience, too. Unfortunately, it looks pretty flat right now. It's as if you were on the roller coaster ride but they forgot to bank your chair at the right times. Although you'd get the feeling of what was going on, part of the experience would be missing. Right now, the player of *Alien Alley* is supposed to be flying through space blasting aliens, but although the aliens are there, it doesn't really look like the player is flying through space.

In this chapter, we'll find out how to add a scrolling starfield background to *Alien Alley* to complete the player's sensory experience. As the game progresses, the starfield will move down the screen with the player, alien, missile, and explosion sprites on top of it. The scrolling background will make it appear as if the player's spaceship is travelling through the galaxy as it does battle with the invading aliens. Figure 13.1 shows *Alien Alley* after our scrolling background has been added.

eXPLORER OVERVIEW In this chapter we'll examine the necessary changes to add a scrolling background to *Alien Alley*. Although we won't develop any standalone source code modules, we'll take a look at the techniques that make scrolling possible and the *Alien Alley* functions that implement those techniques. Using these same techniques, you'll be able to add scrolling to your own games.

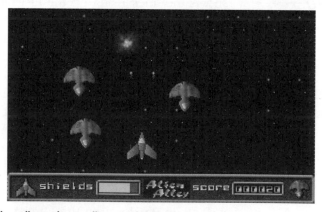

Figure 13.1   *Alien Alley with a scrolling star-field background.*

In particular, we'll learn about using the Start Address register to perform hardware scrolling, how to use tiles to create a large background without using a similarly large amount of memory, and how our drawing and erasing code will interact with the background itself.

INTRODUCTION TO SCROLLING

Before we discuss how *Alien Alley* specifically implements scrolling, let's spend some time talking about various methods that can be used to implement a scrolling background. We'll start by defining the basic problem at hand and then take a look at a naive solution to it. We'll then learn how the VGA Start Address register can provide us with a more efficient and elegant solution. Using the basic Start Address register technique, we'll look at two methods of scrolling: a stop-and-copy solution and an incremental copy solution.

A First Look

Let's examine the basic scrolling problem. For the purposes of this discussion, let's assume that we're scrolling a whole Mode X screen of background graphics, all 240 lines, toward the bottom of the screen at a rate of 2 lines per animation frame. For now, let's ignore any sprites or status areas that may also exist on the screen and just concentrate on scrolling the background graphical data. We'll learn how to deal with the sprites and other associated complications as we go on.

At first look, this doesn't seem like too difficult of a problem. The most obvious solution, shown in Figure 13.2, is simply copy all the screen data down two lines and then fill in the top two lines with new graphics. After all, we

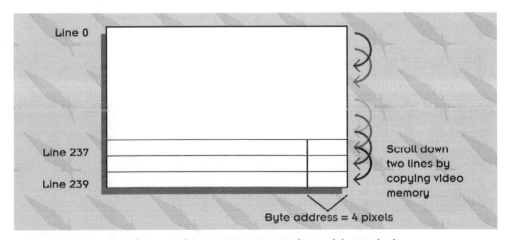

Figure 13.2   *Scrolling the screen down using VGA Write Mode 1 and the VGA latches.*

know how to use VGA Write Mode 1 and the VGA latches to quickly copy data from one region of video memory to another in Modes X and Y. Moving video memory around is pretty easy using this technique, and with the knowledge we've gained in the last few chapters we could write-up a custom routine to do the copying in no time flat. The code might look something like that shown in Listing 13.1.

Listing 13.1   The NaiveScrollLines Function

```
void NaiveScrollLines(UINT16 Offset, int Lines)
{
    UINT8 far * Source;
    UINT8 far * Dest;
    UINT8 ModeRegTemp;
    UINT8 Dummy;
    unsigned NumCopies;

    assert(Lines >= 0);

    Source = MK_FP(VIDEO_MEM_SEGMENT, Offset + (MODEX_HEIGHT - Lines) *
        (MODEX_WIDTH / 4) - 1);
    Dest = MK_FP(VIDEO_MEM_SEGMENT, Offset + MODEX_HEIGHT *
        (MODEX_WIDTH / 4) - 1);
    NumCopies = (MODEX_HEIGHT - Lines) * (MODEX_WIDTH / 4);

    /* set write mode 1 for fast copying using the display latches */
    outportb(GC_INDEX_REG, MODE_INDEX);
    ModeRegTemp = inportb(GC_DATA_REG);
    ModeRegTemp = (ModeRegTemp & 0xFC) | 0x01;
    outportb(GC_DATA_REG, ModeRegTemp);

    SetMMR(0xF);

    while (NumCopies- > 0) {
        Dummy = *Source-;
        *Dest- = Dummy;
    }

    /* reset write mode back to Write Mode 0 */
    ModeRegTemp &= 0xFC;
    outportb(GC_INDEX_REG, MODE_INDEX);
    outportb(GC_DATA_REG, ModeRegTemp);
}
```

Would this solution work? Yes. Can we do better? Certainly.

Hardware Scrolling: The Start Address Register

Although the naive solution presented in Listing 13.1 works, it isn't very efficient. On every frame of animation, virtually all the pixels on the screen must be copied to another location. Now, Write Mode 1 is an efficient method of moving Mode X and Y video memory from place to place, but it's still pretty slow when you have to move a whole screenful of data. If we were to run our program using this technique on a slow VGA card, we'd notice a definite drop in the animation frame rate and a corresponding drop in the number of players interested in our game.

Fortunately, there is a way to scroll the screen using the VGA hardware, rather than a software-based video memory copy. The secret is the VGA's Start Address register. Remember that the Start Address register determines where in video memory the VGA will begin scanning a screen's worth of pixels. In the past, we've used the Start Address register to position our two display pages in video memory when we're using the page-flipping animation technique. Whenever we want to flip display pages, we simply set the Start Address register to the offset of the hidden display page. "Flipping pages" really just amounts to telling the VGA where to get the pixel data for the next video frame.

The Start Address register also can be used to easily implement multiline scrolling, however. For now, let's ignore page flipping and pretend that we're just displaying a background graphic and wish to scroll the Mode X screen by two lines, as before. Let's say the current Start Address register offset is x. We can scroll the display by simply setting the Start Address register to $x - 2*80$. Figure 13.3 shows how this is done.

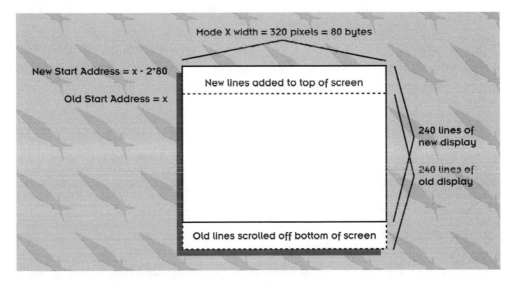

Figure 13.3 *Scrolling the screen using the Start Address register.*

By subtracting an amount equal to two lines worth of pixels from the Start Address register, the VGA begins scanning video memory at a point two lines ahead of its starting point. This makes it appear as if the screen has scrolled. The two lines at the bottom of the old screen aren't scanned by the VGA and so they simply "fall off" the bottom of the display. After scrolling the screen, we'll draw our background graphic on the new top lines of the display.

Note that we can also make the screen appear to scroll down by adding a few lines worth of offset to the Start Address register. Scrolling up or down is equally easy.

Overall, we've done pretty well. To accomplish our scroll, we've simply had to set two 8-bit registers. This operation takes only a small fraction of one time that our naive video memory copying technique would have taken. Because the Start Address register can be manipulated very quickly, it will help us keep our animation frame rate high.

Running Out of Room

In video-game programming, as in life, too much of a good thing can lead to problems, and our scrolling technique using the Start Address register is no exception. Our technique works just fine when the Start Address register points to the middle of video memory. After scrolling the display page for a while through video memory, we'll eventually reach the beginning. At some point, the Start Address register will reach a point where subtracting another two lines worth of video memory from the offset will cause the offset to wrap. For instance, if the Start Address register equals offset 50h (the start of line 1 of video memory), what happens when we subtract 160 bytes from it? Using 16-bit arithmetic, the result wraps around and is FFB0h. Now what happens if we stick this value into the Start Address register? The Start Address register would be pointing at the end of video memory, as Figure 13.4 shows. What does the VGA do?

The answer is that it does one of two things, depending on the particular VGA card. Some cards will wrap around to the beginning of video memory if the Start Address register is placed too close to the end of video memory. As shown in Figure 13.5, these cards will scan our scrolled screen correctly. The original IBM VGA card functioned this way.

Unfortunately, some newer cards don't implement this wrap-around correctly. The failure is associated with the way these cards implement their high-resolution "super VGA" modes. As shown in Figure 13.6, cards that support super VGA resolutions, which includes all the new cards sold today, must have

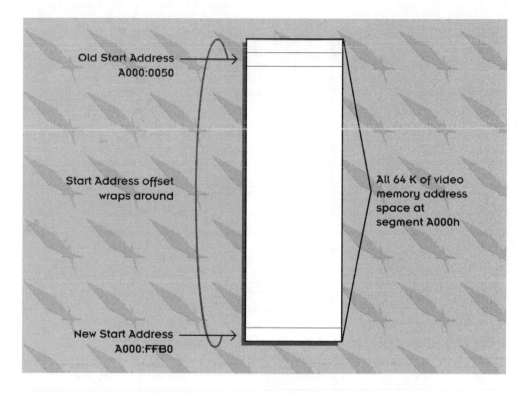

Old Start Address ——→ A000:0050

Start Address offset wraps around

All 64 K of video memory address space at segment A000h

New Start Address ——→ A000:FFB0

Figure 13.4 *Scrolling causes the Start Address register to wrap around.*

more than 256K of video memory to hold all the pixels. Often these cards include 1 Mb to 2 Mb of memory, or more. The first 256K is mapped into the A000h segment, to support the standard VGA modes. There is no standard method of accessing the other memory. It is mapped into the host address space in different ways, depending on the maker of the VGA chipset.

The problem occurs because what appears to be the end of video memory in the host address space is not really the end of video memory as far as the card is concerned. The card still sees more memory following the portion that is mapped into segment A000h in the host address space. When the Start Address register is placed close to the boundary, the card simply continues to scan pixels from the additional memory on the card, without wrapping around. This additional memory contains random video data, (as far as our program is concerned), and so garbage is displayed on the screen.

So what does all this mean? It means that you can't rely on VGA cards to wrap around when they reach the end of video memory during scanning. Although

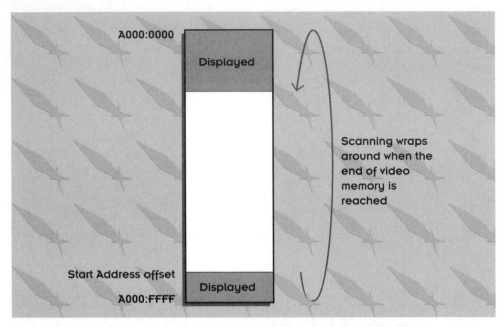

Figure 13.5   *Some cards wrap around when the end of video memory is reached.*

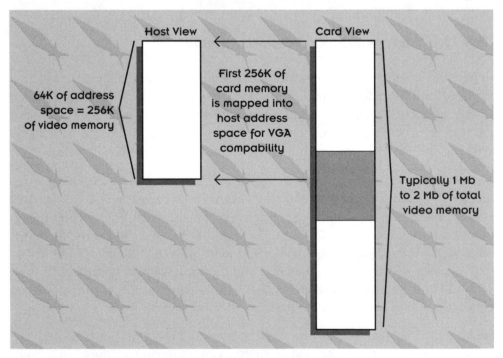

Figure 13.6   *Some super VGA cards don't implement wrap-around correctly.*

some cards will perform the wrap, several popular cards won't. In turn, this means that we can't simply continue scrolling the screen when we reach the top of video memory. We'll have to find a solution that will work on all VGA cards before we can implement our scrolling background for *Alien Alley.*

Before we move on, it's important to note that although our example was to scroll the graphic on the screen down toward the bottom, you can easily implement scrolling in the other direction using the Start Address register. The method is essentially the same, and like our previous example, you'll have to be careful when you get near the end of video memory.

In the coming sections we'll examine a couple of ways to deal with the video memory boundary problem.

Stop and Copy

The first solution to the video memory boundary problem is to detect when the Start Address register wraps around and ensure that it is set to a value that allows the VGA to scan a whole screen of data without wrapping around. Again, let's assume that we're scrolling the screen down, which means moving the Start Address register toward the beginning of video memory. Let's assume that we're very close to the beginning of video memory and one more scroll will take us over the top. Figure 13.7 shows how the Start Address register would need to be reset to point to at least a full screen's worth of video memory before the end of memory.

Of course, none of the video memory at the bottom of segment A000h has been set up with our background graphic. Setting the Start Address register in such a radical manner is basically equivalent to flipping to a different display page that has not had anything drawn on it. Before resetting the Start Address register to its new value, we need to copy most of the video memory corresponding to the current screen location (all but the lines at the bottom of the screen that will scroll off the display) to equivalent locations corresponding to the new screen location.

Using this method, the VGA won't suffer any problems with wrapping around, and the user won't know the difference. The copy of video memory will allow us to get away undetected. Or will it?

Unfortunately, it turns out that the method is suboptimal. The screen will scroll toward the beginning of video memory for quite awhile. During this time, we'll be scrolling by simply subtracting a couple of lines worth of video

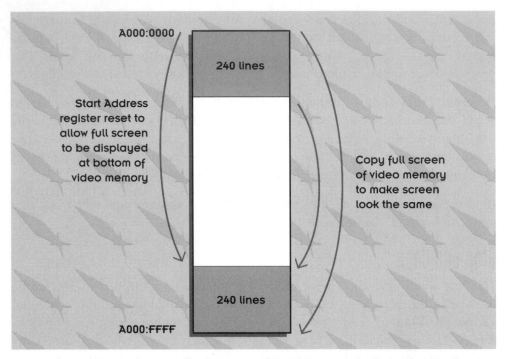

Figure 13.7 *Resetting the Start Address register to allow a full screen to be displayed without wrapping.*

memory addresses of the Start Address register value and things will be moving along quickly.

When we hit the beginning of video memory, the Start Address register will have to be reset back toward the end of video memory, and almost a full screen's worth of video memory will be copied from the beginning of video memory down toward the end. That is, we "stop and copy," which is where this technique gets its name. The problem is that this copy takes too long in comparison to simply setting the Start Address register and redrawing a couple lines at the top of the screen. We'll end up delaying the next animation frame a bit longer than we should, and the user will experience a hiccup in the game play.

Although this hiccup will only happen every so often, it will be noticeable and we should avoid it.

Incremental Copy

The problem with the stop-and-copy technique is that we spend a lot of time copying during one frame of animation. If we could find a way to copy a little

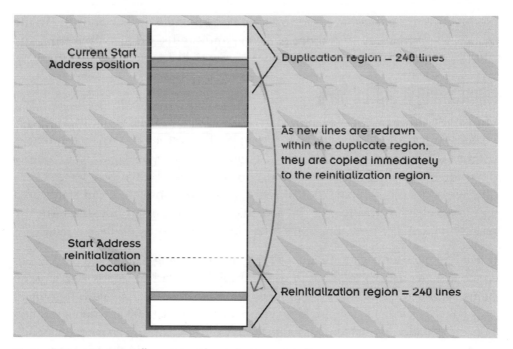

Figure 13.8   *Incrementally copying video memory as we scroll.*

bit of video memory during a few more video frames, the user wouldn't notice such a great delay when the Start Address register was moved toward the bottom of video memory. Making the copy a bit more incremental is pretty easy. Figure 13.8 shows how this is done.

Every time the screen scrolls, the new position of the Start Address register is checked to see if it is within one screen of the beginning of video memory, the "duplication region." If so, the new lines that have just been redrawn at the top of the screen are copied to their corresponding locations in an area at the end of video memory. As the screen scrolls into the duplication region, the new portions of it are automatically copied to the reinitialization region. Since the screen only scrolls a few lines at a time, only a few lines of video memory are copied during each video frame. This means that the copies are fast and don't slow down the overall frame rate.

By the time the Start Address register reaches the beginning of video memory and needs to be reinitialized, a complete copy of the video memory in the duplication region has already been built in the reinitialization region. When we reinitialize the Start Address register to point toward the end of video memory, we don't have to perform a time-consuming copy. Overall, the frame rate of the animation stays more constant, and the user doesn't perceive any change when the Start Address register is reinitialized.

Maintaining a Status Area

One of the things we haven't taken into account in our scrolling discussion is a status area. *Alien Alley* has that region at the bottom of the screen that is used to display the player's shield strength and score. If we were to simply draw the status area at the bottom of the screen we'd have problems. Every time we adjusted the Start Address register to its new position, our status area would scroll with the rest of the screen. We could get around the issue by redrawing it every time, but that's a hassle and also slows things down.

If you'll remember back to Chapter 11, we did something funny with the VGA to create a status area at the bottom of the display. Instead of simply drawing the status area at the bottom of the screen, we used the Line Compare register to cause the VGA to start scanning from video memory offset 0000h when it reached a certain point on the screen. Although there were some immediate benefits, such as being able to avoid clipping aliens as they moved off the bottom of the screen, a big reason for doing this was to make it easy to add scrolling later.

When we use the Line Compare register to create a split screen, the bottom of the screen is *always* refreshed from the same portion of video memory. We can scroll the top portion of the screen by altering the Start Address register and it won't have any effect on bottom of the screen, which contains the status area. We also won't have to redraw the status area background when we scroll. Because the status area is 30 lines worth of video memory, this technique saves us a significant amount of redrawing work on every animation frame.

Of course, we do have to take the status area memory into account when deciding when to reinitialize the Start Address register. The status area is located at the top of video memory, so we have to make sure that we stop scrolling before we move into that area of memory. Figure 13.9 shows the layout of memory.

Because of the lines taken by the status area, the actual height of the screen is reduced to 210 lines. Similarly, the heights of the duplication and reinitialization regions shrink accordingly. The Start Address register will be reset to the top of the reinitialization region when it reaches the bottom of the status area.

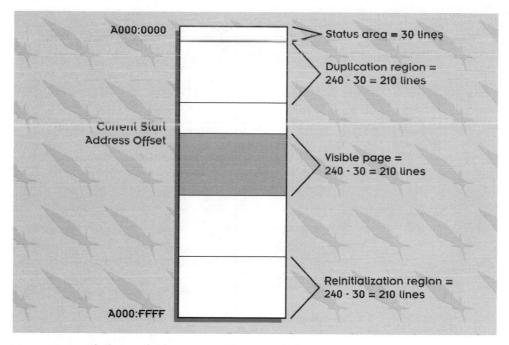

A000:0000 — Status area = 30 lines

Duplication region =
240 - 30 = 210 lines

Current Start
Address Offset

Visible page =
240 - 30 = 210 lines

Reinitialization region =
240 - 30 = 210 lines

A000:FFFF

Figure 13.9 *The layout of video memory with a status display.*

Scrolling while Page Flipping

In the previous sections we've dealt with a single visible screen. We haven't addressed the topic of how we can use our Start Address register scrolling technique together with the page-flipping animation technique used in *Alien Alley*. It turns out that adding page flipping is a natural extension to our scrolling technique.

We simply keep two pages moving through video memory. The offset of each page moves toward the beginning of video memory just as we did in the previous scrolling descriptions. One of the pages is displayed and one is hidden at any point in time. We swap the roles of the pages for each animation frame.

As soon as one of the pages reaches the bottom of the status display, it is moved down toward the end of video memory, to the reinitialization region. As a page moves through the duplication region, screen lines are incrementally copied to the reinitialization region, just as with our single page case. Figure 13.10 shows how this is done.

Note that we must scroll each page twice as far as before, to make the scrolling rate look the same. For instance, if we want it to appear that the screen is

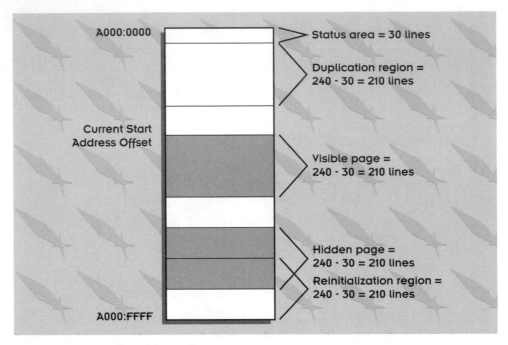

A000:0000 — Status area = 30 lines

Duplication region = 240 - 30 = 210 lines

Current Start Address Offset

Visible page = 240 - 30 = 210 lines

Hidden page = 240 - 30 = 210 lines

Reinitialization region = 240 - 30 = 210 lines

A000:FFFF

Figure 13.10 *Scrolling while page flipping.*

scrolling two lines per animation frame, we must scroll each display page by four lines as it is displayed. Because we alternate animation frames between the two pages, this makes the scrolling rate appear to be two lines per frame.

A BIT OF BACKGROUND: USING TILES

Well, now that we have scrolling figured out, we'll need a background. After all, we need something to move the screen over to give the appearance of motion. In *Alien Alley*, we'll be creating a starfield background to create the illusion that the player is flying through space. As you may have guessed, there are a number of ways that this could be done, some better than others.

The most obvious way to create a starfield background is simply to draw a full-screen PCX graphic with small stars and some planets on it, and scroll the screen over it. We could repeat the graphic over and over as the screen scrolls. Figure 13.11 shows this technique. This would give the player the illusion of flying through an infinite starfield. Unfortunately, this scheme has two problems.

First, it's fairly memory intensive. A full-screen graphic is about 64K in length. That's a lot of memory to burn. Second, it's very repetitive. The whole "world"

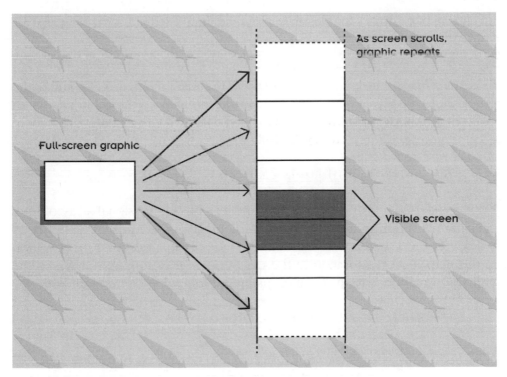

Figure 13.11 *Infinite scrolling over a single full-screen graphic.*

would only be 200 to 240 pixels "long." After 200 pixels or so, the background would repeat. Just as something went off the bottom of the screen, it would reappear at the top.

Now, if the background was *just* a starfield, it probably wouldn't matter. Stars are fairly uniform and the player probably wouldn't notice the repetition. However, as professionals, our background should have a little more pizzazz. Maybe we could add some planets to our universe; unfortunately, those planets, placed strategically every 200 pixels or so, would stick out like a sore thumb. The player would think, "Here comes that planet again."

So the question is, how can we draw a background graphic that is not repetitious and has very low memory requirements? The answer is to use *tiles* to create a much larger background universe from small re-usable pieces.

Tiles are small rectangular bitmaps that are used in much the same way as ceramic tiles in your kitchen or bathroom. They are layed out in a grid to create a much larger pattern, or what will be known as our universe map. We'll only end up storing one copy of the bitmap corresponding to each tile, so as long as most tiles are re-used a few times, we'll see a savings in our memory requirements.

For instance, say we have five different tiles to work with. We can number those tiles from 0 through 4 and store them in separate bitmaps like any of the other sprite bitmaps in our game. We'll store pointers to these bitmaps in an array of **PLANAR_BITMAP** pointers called **Tile**. We can retrieve the bitmap corresponding to tile #2 using the following expression:

```
PLANAR_BITMAP far * TileBitmap = Tile[2];
```

Now, we define our universe background as a two-dimensional array of integers named, appropriately, **Map**. Each element of the **Map** array stores an index into the **Tile** array corresponding to the tile that occupies that position in the map. Given a location in the map (x,y), we can figure out which tile bitmap corresponds to the location using the following expression:

```
PLANAR_BITMAP far * TileBitmap = Tile[Map[x][y]];
```

Figure 13.12 shows how this scheme works.

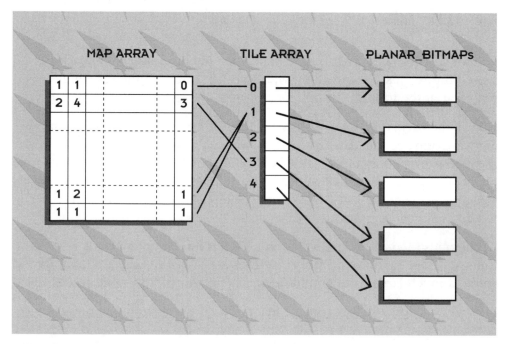

Figure 13.12   *A large universe map created with individual tiles.*

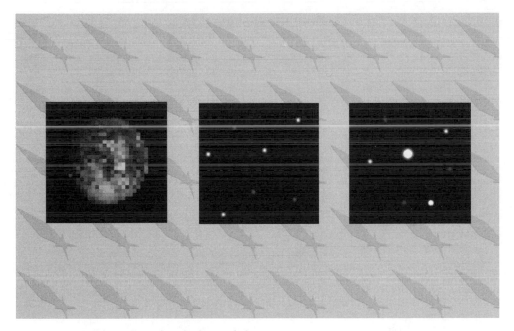

Figure 13.13   *Alien Alley's three background tiles.*

In *Alien Alley*, we'll be using three different 32x32 pixel tiles. Two of the tiles are simple starfield tiles and the third is a planet that looks suspiciously like Earth. Figure 13.13 shows the tiles. These have been clipped out of the TILES.PCX file using the CLIPSPR program discussed in Chapter 11. The individual tile bitmap files are named STARS1.PCX, STARS2.PCX, and EARTH.PCX.

The *Alien Alley* map will be 10 tiles wide and 32 tiles high. With a tile height of 32 lines, the total map height will be 1,024 lines, which is over five screens. Although the map will repeat every so often, it won't happen that quickly, and the user is less likely to notice the same things scrolling by. We could easily make our map larger (say, 64 or 128 tiles in height) if we felt that only five screens worth of background was too little.

MODIFICATIONS TO ALIEN ALLEY

Now that we understand how to scroll the screen using the Start Address register and how to create a large background using tiles, let's get down to the nitty gritty. Let's take a look at how *Alien Alley* implements its background scrolling. The place to start is with the **Play** function, shown in Listing 13.2.

Listing 13.2   The Modified Play Function

```
/*
    Function: Play
    Description:
        Plays the game!
*/
void Play(int Control)
{
    BOOL    UserInputUp;
    BOOL    UserInputDown;
    BOOL    UserInputLeft;
    BOOL    UserInputRight;
    BOOL    UserInputFire;
    int     GunBlinkCounter;
    int     GunBlinkState;
    RGB_TUPLE Black = {0, 0, 0};
    RGB_TUPLE GunColor;
    BOOL    GameOver;
    BOOL    GameOverInput;
    BOOL    GameOverDeath;
    LINEAR_BITMAP far * Image;
    long far * Clock;
    long    OldClock;
    void interrupt (*SavedVector)();

    /* fade screen to remove title page */
    FadeOut(500);

    /* initialize all counters, etc. */
    Score = 0;
    AlienGenCounter = ALIEN_GEN_RATE_BASE;
    HeroShields = MAX_HERO_SHIELDS;
    InitMap();

    /* set mode X */
    SetModeY();

    /* load sprites */
    /* do this after we get into Mode X since we're using */
    /* video mem bitmaps and we don't want them clobbered */
    /* when SetModeX clears video memory */
    LoadSprites();

    /* now up Mode X since we draw the initial screens here */
    SetUpModeY();

    /* start game music and get sound effects off disk */
    if (SoundPresent) {
        PlaySequence(1);
    }
```

```
/* set up palette stuff */
/* palette.pcx is a single pixel bitmap with the palette */
/*   this is done because it's easy to load the palette */
/*   using LoadPCX */
Image = LoadPCX("palette.pcx", GamePalette);
if (Image == NULL) {
    FatalError("Can't load 'palette.pcx'", "ProgramInit", __LINE__);
}
farfree(Image); /* ignore the single pixel bitmap */
SetVGAPaletteBlock(GamePalette, 0, 128);
SetVGAPaletteBlock(GamePalette, 128, 128);

/* install keyboard or mouse handlers */
/* do nothing for joystick */
if (Control == 'm') {
}
else if (Control == 'k') {
    SetButtonKeysMode();
}

/* set up gun blink stuff */
GetPaletteEntry(GamePalette, GUN_COLOR, &GunColor);
GunBlinkCounter    = GUN_BLINK_RATE;
GunBlinkState      = 1; /* gun blink on */

/* initialize the status screen */
InitStatus();

if (SoundPresent) {
    Clock = MidPakClockAddress();
}
else {
    Clock = &TickCount;
    *Clock = 0;
    SavedVector = HookAndProgramSysTimer(ClockInterrupt,
        SELECT_0 | RW_LSB_MSB | MODE_SQUARE_WAVE | TYPE_BINARY,
        COUNTER_FRAME_TIME);
}
OldClock = *Clock;

/* enter main animation loop */
GameOver = FALSE;
while (!GameOver) {
    /* get user input */
    GameOverInput = GetInput(Control, &UserInputUp, &UserInputDown,
        &UserInputLeft, &UserInputRight, &UserInputFire);

    /* move sprites */
    MoveSprites(UserInputUp, UserInputDown, UserInputLeft,
        UserInputRight, UserInputFire);

    /* check for collisions */
    CheckCollisions();
```

```
    /* erase */
    GameOverDeath = EraseSprites();

    /* scroll screen */
    ScrollScreen();

    /* draw */
    DrawSprites();

    /* update status */
    DrawStatus();

    /* wait for page flip */
    PageFlip(PageOffset[HiddenPage]);
    HiddenPage ^= 1; /* flip HiddenPage to other state */

    /* blink the guns */
    if (GunBlinkCounter == 0) {
        if (GunBlinkState == 1) {
            SetVGAPaletteEntry(GUN_COLOR, &Black);
        }
        else {
            SetVGAPaletteEntry(GUN_COLOR, &GunColor);
        }
        GunBlinkState ^= 1; /* flip it to other state */
        GunBlinkCounter = GUN_BLINK_RATE;
    }
    else {
        GunBlinkCounter—;
    }

    /* delay a bit */
    if (SoundPresent) {
        /* make sure each frame takes at least 4/120 = 2/60 of */
        while (*Clock < OldClock + 4);
    }
    else {
        /* No MidPak, so wait 2/70 of a second, minimum */
        while (*Clock < OldClock + 2);
    }
    OldClock = *Clock;

    /* player either aborts or dies */
    GameOver = GameOverInput || GameOverDeath;
}

/* restore timer vector and DOS time */
if (!SoundPresent) {
    UnhookAndRestoreSysTimer(SavedVector);
    RestoreDOSTime();
}
```

```
/* uninstall mouse and/or keyboard handlers */
if (Control == 'm') {
}
else if (Control == 'k') {
    SetNormalKeysMode();
}

/* free all memory used to play */
FreeSprites();

/* fade to black . . . . */
FadeOut(250);

/* return to Mode 013h, as we were */
SetMode13h();
}
```

The first change to **Play** is that it initializes the background map. The **InitMap** function is shown in Listing 13.3. **InitMap** chooses random tiles for each element of the **Map** array. Since planets are more rare in space than stars, the function makes sure that the tile containing the earth bitmap occurs less often.

Listing 13.3   The InitMap Function

```
/*
    Function: InitMap
    Description:
        Initializes the map with random tiles.
*/
void InitMap(void)
{
    int i, j;
    int RandomNum;

    for (i = 0; i < MAP_WIDTH; i++) {
        for (j = 0; j < MAP_HEIGHT; j++) {
            /* seed with mostly stars and a few planets */
            RandomNum = random(100);
            if (RandomNum < 2) {
                Map[i][j] = 2; /* earth */
            }
            else if (RandomNum < 30) {
                Map[i][j] = 1; /* stars2 */
            }
            else {
                Map[i][j] = 0; /* stars1 */
            }
        }
    }
}
```

The Video Memory Map

The next thing **Play** does is set up video memory. It's very important to plan the video memory layout when you create a scrolling background. We gave a rough idea of how video memory would be structured in Figure 13.10, but now we need some more detail. We need to figure out the exact positions of the duplication and reinitialization regions. In defining these, we'll use video lines as our measurement. Figure 13.14 shows how video memory will be layed out.

As you can see, each page display page is going to be 170 lines long. To add the scrolling to our game, we've had to switch from Mode X to Mode Y in order to make everything fit in video memory. Since a Mode Y screen is 200 lines long, subtracting the 30 line status area gives a reduced screen height of 170 lines. If you calculate the total lines needed in Mode X, you'll end up with

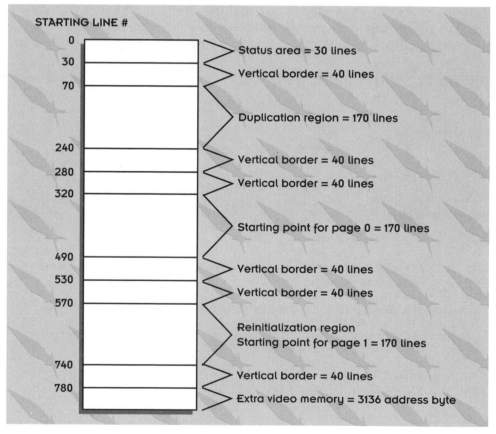

Figure 13.14 *Alien Alley video memory layout.*

900 lines, not 780. Multiplying 900 lines by 80 bytes per line gives us a total of 72,000 address bytes, which is much more than the 65,536 bytes in the video memory segment at A000h. Using Mode Y, everything fits and we still have 3,136 bytes of address space remaining. We'll use this extra memory to store our tiles as video memory bitmaps.

You may notice that we included two vertical borders between the display pages, whereas in Chapter 11 we only included one border. We need this extra border, because we'll be drawing our background as tiles and we may need to draw a tile at the bottom of one page and the top of another. The tiles cannot overlap when they are drawn. In Chapter 11, we simply used the space to allow our alien and missile sprites to move off screen, and we didn't care if the bitmaps from different pages were drawn on top of one another in the off-screen region.

Listing 13.4 shows some constants that define the relevant numbers for our video memory setup.

Listing 13.4   Video Memory Setup Constants

```
#define MAX_OBJECT_HEIGHT    32
#define MAX_MOVE_STEP          8      /* max sprite movement (hero missile) */

/* screen parameters */
#define SCREEN_WIDTH            MODEY_WIDTH
#define SCREEN_HEIGHT           MODEY_HEIGHT
#define SCREEN_WIDTH_BYTES      (SCREEN_WIDTH / 4)
#define VERTICAL_BORDER_LINES   (MAX_OBJECT_HEIGHT + MAX_MOVE_STEP)
#define VERTICAL_BORDER_BYTES   (VERTICAL_BORDER_LINES * SCREEN_WIDTH_BYTES)
#define REDUCED_SCREEN_HEIGHT   (SCREEN_HEIGHT - STATUS_HEIGHT)
#define REDUCED_SCREEN_BYTES    (REDUCED_SCREEN_HEIGHT * SCREEN_WIDTH_BYTES)
#define STATUS_BYTES            (STATUS_HEIGHT * SCREEN_WIDTH_BYTES)

/* scrolling parameters */
#define SCROLL_DISTANCE         2 /* = twice actual scroll per frame */
#define SCREEN_TOP_MIN          (STATUS_HEIGHT + VERTICAL_BORDER_LINES)
#define SCREEN_TOP_REINIT_LINES (STATUS_HEIGHT + \
    (5 * VERTICAL_BORDER_LINES) + \
    (2 * REDUCED_SCREEN_HEIGHT))
#define SCREEN_TOP_REINIT_BYTES (SCREEN_TOP_REINIT_LINES * \
    SCREEN_WIDTH_BYTES)
#define DUPLICATE_REGION_LINE   (STATUS_HEIGHT + VERTICAL_BORDER_LINES + \
    REDUCED_SCREEN_HEIGHT)
#define SCREEN_0_INIT_LINES     (STATUS_HEIGHT + \
    (3 * VERTICAL_BORDER_LINES) + REDUCED_SCREEN_HEIGHT - \
    (SCROLL_DISTANCE / 2))
#define SCREEN_0_INIT_BYTES     (SCREEN_0_INIT_LINES * SCREEN_WIDTH_BYTES)
```

```
#define SCREEN_1_INIT_LINES      SCREEN_TOP_REINIT_LINES
#define SCREEN_1_INIT_BYTES      (SCREEN_1_INIT_LINES * SCREEN_WIDTH_BYTES)
#define FREE_MEM_START_LINES     (SCREEN_TOP_REINIT_LINES + \
    REDUCED_SCREEN_HEIGHT + VERTICAL_BORDER_LINES)
#define FREE_MEM_START_BYTES     (FREE_MEM_START_LINES * SCREEN_WIDTH_BYTES)
```

In order to set up the display pages and get video memory ready, the **Play** functions used to call **SetupModeX**. Now that we're using Mode Y, we've had to rename the **SetupModeX** function to **SetupModeY**. The modified function is shown in Listing 13.5.

Listing 13.5   The SetUpModeY Function

```
/*
    Function: SetUpModeY
    Description:
        Initializes the Mode Y page start variables and sets up the
        status area.
*/
void SetUpModeY(void)
{
    unsigned        LineCompare;
    UINT8           VGARegTemp;
    BOOL            DirtyTiles[MAP_WIDTH][MAP_HEIGHT];
    int i, j;

    /* calculate offsets */
    PageOffset[0]   = SCREEN_0_INIT_BYTES;
    MemLine[0]      = SCREEN_0_INIT_LINES;
    MapLine[0]      = 0;

    PageOffset[1]   = SCREEN_1_INIT_BYTES;
    MemLine[1]      = SCREEN_1_INIT_LINES;
    MapLine[1]      = SCROLL_DISTANCE / 2;

    /* redraw the tiles around each page */
    for (i = 0; i < MAP_WIDTH; i++) {
        for (j = 0; j < MAP_HEIGHT; j++) {
            DirtyTiles[i][j] = TRUE;
        }
    }
    RedrawDirtyTiles(DirtyTiles, MapLine[0], MemLine[0], PageOffset[0]);
    RedrawDirtyTiles(DirtyTiles, MapLine[1], MemLine[1], PageOffset[1]);

    /* set start address to page 0 */
    PageFlip(PageOffset[0]);
    HiddenPage = 1;

    /* set Line Compare register */
```

```
/* Mode X (and Mode Y and Mode 013h) are double scan modes, so */
/*    the number of lines in terms of the VGA is actually */
/*    double the pixel height */
LineCompare = 2 * REDUCED_SCREEN_HEIGHT;
WaitVerticalRetraceStart();
asm cli;
/* write lower eight bits of Line Compare */
outportb(CRTC_INDEX_REG, LINE_COMPARE_INDEX);
outportb(CRTC_DATA_REG, LineCompare & 0xFF);
/* ninth bit is in bit 4 of Overflow register */
outportb(CRTC_INDEX_REG, OVERFLOW_INDEX);
VGARegTemp = inportb(CRTC_DATA_REG);
VGARegTemp = (VGARegTemp & 0xEF) | ((LineCompare >> 4) & 0x10);
outportb(CRTC_DATA_REG, VGARegTemp);
/* tenth bit is in bit 6 of max scan line register */
outportb(CRTC_INDEX_REG, MAX_SCAN_LINE_INDEX);
VGARegTemp = inportb(CRTC_DATA_REG);
VGARegTemp = (VGARegTemp & 0xBF) | ((LineCompare >> 3) & 0x40);
outportb(CRTC_DATA_REG, VGARegTemp);
asm sti;
}
```

SetupModeY initializes a couple of important variables in addition to the **PageOffset** array and the Line Compare register, which **SetupModeX** did before. These variables are the **MemLine** and **MapLine** arrays. These two element arrays keep track of where each display page is within video memory and within the background map. They each indicate the location of the top of each page in lines. Note that **MapLine** doesn't indicate a tile row number, but rather a map line number. If page 0 is positioned at the beginning of tile row 1, **MapLine[0]** would be 32, since a tile is 32 lines high. Figure 13.15 shows how these variables would look after the screen has been scrolled for six animation frames.

In addition to initializing the **MemLine**, **MapLine**, and **PageOffset** variables, **SetupModeY** also draws the initial background on the screen.

Erasing Sprites

As the main animation loop of **Play** shows, the sequence of events in generating an animation frame is to move the sprites, check for collisions, erase the old sprite bitmaps, scroll the screen, and finally draw the sprites at their new locations. One of the most important changes to *Alien Alley* occurs in the **EraseSprites** function, shown in Listing 13.6.

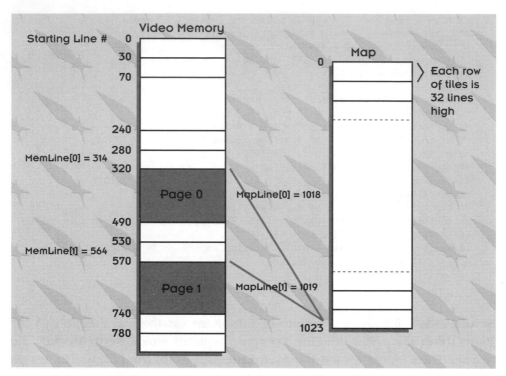

Figure 13.15 *The MemLine and MapLine arrays keep track of the top of each display page within video memory and the background map.*

Listing 13.6 The EraseSprites Function

```
/*
    Function: EraseSprites
    Description:
        Erases all current bitmaps from the hidden screen. If the
        erasure marks the last time that the object will be erased
        because it is no longer being drawn, deactivate the object.
*/
BOOL EraseSprites(void)
{
    int i;
    static unsigned DeathCounter;
    static BOOL DirtyTileMap[MAP_WIDTH][MAP_HEIGHT];


    /* clear out the dirty tile array */
    ClearDirtyTiles(DirtyTileMap);

    /* do player and possibly deactivate */
    if (Hero.Active && Hero.Erase[HiddenPage]) {
        MarkDirtyTiles(DirtyTileMap, MapLine[HiddenPage],
```

```
                Hero.OldX[HiddenPage], Hero.OldY[HiddenPage],
                HeroWidth, HeroHeight,
                HeroBitmap->OriginX, HeroBitmap->OriginY);
            Hero.Erase[HiddenPage] = FALSE;
            if (!(Hero.Draw || Hero.Erase[0] || Hero.Erase[1])) {
                Hero.Active = FALSE;
                DeathCounter = DEATH_DELAY;
            }
        }


        /* erase and deactivate hero missiles */
        for (i = 0; i < MAX_HERO_MISSILES; i++) {
            if (HeroMissile[i].Active && HeroMissile[i].Erase[HiddenPage]) {
                /* erase missile itself */
                MarkDirtyTiles(DirtyTileMap, MapLine[HiddenPage],
                    HeroMissile[i].OldX[HiddenPage],
                    HeroMissile[i].OldY[HiddenPage],
                    MissileWidth, MissileHeight,
                    MissileBitmap->OriginX, MissileBitmap->OriginY);
                /* erase missile trail */
                MarkDirtyTiles(DirtyTileMap, MapLine[HiddenPage],
                    HeroMissile[i].OldX[HiddenPage],
                    HeroMissile[i].OldY[HiddenPage],
                    MissileTrailWidth, MissileTrailHeight,
                    MissileTrailUpBitmap->OriginX,
                    MissileTrailUpBitmap->OriginY);
                HeroMissile[i].Erase[HiddenPage] = FALSE;
            }
            /* deactivate missile if we aren't going to draw or */
            /*   erase it anymore */
            if (!(HeroMissile[i].Draw || HeroMissile[i].Erase[0] ||
                HeroMissile[i].Erase[1])) {
                HeroMissile[i].Active = FALSE;
            }
        }


        /* erase and deactivate aliens */
        for (i = 0; i < MAX_ALIENS; i++) {
            if (Alien[i].Active && Alien[i].Erase[HiddenPage]) {
                MarkDirtyTiles(DirtyTileMap, MapLine[HiddenPage],
                    Alien[i].OldX[HiddenPage],
                    Alien[i].OldY[HiddenPage],
                    AlienWidth, AlienHeight,
                    AlienBitmap->OriginX,
                    AlienBitmap->OriginY);
                Alien[i].Erase[HiddenPage] = FALSE;
            }
            /* deactive alien if it's been destroyed */
            if (!(Alien[i].Draw || Alien[i].Erase[0] ||
                Alien[i].Erase[1])) {
                Alien[i].Active = FALSE;
            }
        }
```

```c
/* erase and deactivate alien missiles */
for (i = 0; i < MAX_ALIEN_MISSILES; i++) {
    if (AlienMissile[i].Active && AlienMissile[i].Erase[HiddenPage]) {
        /* erase missile itself */
        MarkDirtyTiles(DirtyTileMap, MapLine[HiddenPage],
            AlienMissile[i].OldX[HiddenPage],
            AlienMissile[i].OldY[HiddenPage],
            MissileWidth, MissileHeight,
            MissileBitmap->OriginX, MissileBitmap->OriginY);
        /* erase missile trail */
        MarkDirtyTiles(DirtyTileMap, MapLine[HiddenPage],
            AlienMissile[i].OldX[HiddenPage],
            AlienMissile[i].OldY[HiddenPage],
            MissileTrailWidth, MissileTrailHeight,
            MissileTrailDnBitmap->OriginX,
            MissileTrailDnBitmap->OriginY);
        AlienMissile[i].Erase[HiddenPage] = FALSE;
    }
    /* deactivate missile if we aren't going to draw or */
    /*   erase it anymore */
    if (!(AlienMissile[i].Draw || AlienMissile[i].Erase[0] ||
        AlienMissile[i].Erase[1])) {
        AlienMissile[i].Active = FALSE;
    }
}

/* erase and deactivate explosions */
for (i = 0; i < MAX_EXPLOSIONS; i++) {
    if (Explosion[i].Active && Explosion[i].Erase[HiddenPage]) {
        MarkDirtyTiles(DirtyTileMap, MapLine[HiddenPage],
            Explosion[i].OldX[HiddenPage],
            Explosion[i].OldY[HiddenPage],
            ExplosionWidth, ExplosionHeight,
            ExplosionBitmap[0]->OriginX,
            ExplosionBitmap[0]->OriginY);
        Explosion[i].Erase[HiddenPage] = FALSE;
    }
    /* deactivate if explosion has run its course */
    if (!(Explosion[i].Draw || Explosion[i].Erase[0] ||
        Explosion[i].Erase[1])) {
        Explosion[i].Active = FALSE;
    }
}

/* do the actual erase by redrawing dirty tiles */
RedrawDirtyTiles(DirtyTileMap, MapLine[HiddenPage], MemLine[HiddenPage],
    PageOffset[HiddenPage]);

/* hero has died—signal game over after brief delay */
if (!Hero.Active) {
    if (DeathCounter == 0) {
        return TRUE;
    }
```

```
        else {
            DeathCounter-;
        }
    }
    return FALSE;
}
```

In past versions of *Alien Alley*, we've erased sprites by simply drawing an all-black bitmap over them using the **BltPlanarNoTransparent** function. That will no longer work now that we have a scrolling background. If we erased sprites by drawing over them with a black bitmap, we'd also erase a portion of our background. To correctly restore the background, we'd have to redraw a few of the background tiles that got clobbered. So why not just redraw a few of the background tiles without bothering to specifically erase an individual sprite?

Well, that's just what this new version of **EraseSprites** does. **EraseSprites** creates an array named **DirtyTileMap** to keep track of which tiles will have to be redrawn during this frame. For each object on the screen, **EraseSprites** calls **MarkDirtyTiles**, shown in Listing 13.7, to set elements of the **DirtyTileMap** array to TRUE if those tiles have an old sprite drawn over them. These tiles are "dirty" and must be redrawn to restore the background. **MarkDirtyTiles** is shown in Listing 13.7.

Listing 13.7   The MarkDirtyTiles Function

```
/*
    Function: MarkDirtyTiles
    Description:
        Takes the dirty map and sets to TRUE those tiles that
        are under the bitmap specified by the coordinates, width,
        height, and origin.
*/
void MarkDirtyTiles
    (
    BOOL DirtyMap[MAP_WIDTH][MAP_HEIGHT],
    int TopLine,
    int x,
    int y,
    unsigned Width,
    unsigned Height,
    int OriginX,
    int OriginY
    )
{
    int TopRow;
    int BottomRow;
```

```
    int LeftCol;
    int RightCol;

    /* compute tile row and column of each side of the sprite */
    LeftCol = (x - OriginX) / TILE_WIDTH;
    RightCol = (x - OriginX + (int) Width) / TILE_WIDTH;
    TopRow  = (TopLine + y - OriginY) / TILE_HEIGHT;
    BottomRow = (TopLine + y - OriginY + (int) Height) / TILE_HEIGHT;

    /* make sure these are in range on the map */
    /* if out of range, fold them back around */
    LeftCol   = (MAP_WIDTH + LeftCol) % MAP_WIDTH;
    RightCol  = (MAP_WIDTH + RightCol) % MAP_WIDTH;
    TopRow    = (MAP_HEIGHT + TopRow) % MAP_HEIGHT;
    BottomRow = (MAP_HEIGHT + BottomRow) % MAP_HEIGHT;

    /* Mark the tiles corresponding to the four corners as dirty. */
    /* NOTE: This technique assumes that sprites are the same size */
    /* or smaller than the tiles. If the sprites are larger, */
    /* then a sprite could straddle a tile and it would not be */
    /* marked as dirty. */
    DirtyMap[LeftCol][TopRow]      = TRUE;
    DirtyMap[RightCol][TopRow]     = TRUE;
    DirtyMap[LeftCol][BottomRow]   = TRUE;
    DirtyMap[RightCol][BottomRow]  = TRUE;
}
```

After computing which tiles are dirty, **EraseSprites** calls **RedrawDirtyTiles**, shown in Listing 13.8. This function scans the **DirtyTileMap** array passed to it for those tiles that are marked as dirty. For each dirty tile, **DirtyTileMap** calls **DrawTile** to redraw the tile, which ends up erasing all the sprites on the screen.

Listing 13.8   The RedrawDirtyTiles Function

```
/*
    Function: RedrawDirtyTiles
    Description:
        Redraws the tiles that have been marked as dirty in the erase
        routine. This has the effect of erasing all the sprites
        on the hidden page.
*/
void RedrawDirtyTiles
    (
    BOOL DirtyMap[MAP_WIDTH][MAP_HEIGHT],
    int MapTop,
    int MemTop,
    UINT16 Offset
    )
{
    int i, j;
```

```
    for (i = 0; i < MAP_WIDTH; i++) {
        for (j = 0; j < MAP_HEIGHT; j++) {
            if (DirtyMap[i][j]) {
                DrawTile(i, j, MapTop, MemTop, Offset, FALSE);
            }
        }
    }
}
```

Note that **MarkDirtyTiles** doesn't call **DrawTile** for each dirty tile. It could be
the case that more than one sprite lies on top of a given tile. If **MarkDirtyTiles**
called **DrawTile** directly, the same dirty tile could be redrawn more than once.
This inefficiency is eliminated by keeping the **DirtyTileMap** array and using
RedrawDirtyTiles to only redraw each dirty tile once.

SetupModeY also uses **RedrawDirtyTiles** to initialize the background when
video memory is initialized. **SetupModeY** simply marks every tile as dirty,
causing **RedrawDirtyTiles** to try to redraw every tile. As we'll see when we
examine **DrawTile**, those tiles that are outside the screen boundaries are
automatically ignored.

Drawing Tiles

All drawing of tiles to the screen is done using the **DrawTile** function, shown
in Listing 13.9. **DrawTile** computes the location of the specified tile relative to
the current display page. The **MapTop** and **MemTop** parameters are copies
of the **MapLine** and **MemLine** variables corresponding to the given page.

Listing 13.9   The DrawTile Function

```
/*
    Function: DrawTile
    Description:
        Draws the specified tile to the specified page. X and Y are
        the tile location within the map. MapTop specifies where
        the screen is within the map. MemTop specifies where the
        screen is in memory. Offset gives the current offset
        of the page in memory.
*/
void DrawTile(int x, int y, int MapTop, int MemTop, UINT16 Offset, BOOL Dup)
{
    int TileTop;     /* screen coordinates of tile */
    int TileLeft;
    int TileBottom;
    int MapBottom;   /* map line corresponding to bottom of screen */
    int DuplicateTop;
```

```
/* figure out what map line corresponds to the bottom of the screen */
MapBottom = (MapTop + REDUCED_SCREEN_HEIGHT - 1) %
    (MAP_HEIGHT * TILE_HEIGHT);

/* see if the screen is wrapping around on the map */
if (MapTop < MapBottom) {
    /* if not, then compute location of tile relative to screen */
    /* in straight forward manner */
    TileTop    = y * TILE_HEIGHT - MapTop;
}
else {
    /* the screen is wrapping around on the map so do this */
    /* in a little more complicated way */

    /* first determine the map line of the top of the tile */
    TileTop    = y * TILE_HEIGHT;

    /* now compute the location relative to the screen top left */
    /* based on where the screen is in the map and the location */
    /* of the tile */
    if (TileTop <= MapBottom) {
        /* it's in the lower portion of the screen so add in */
        /* the number of lines taken up by the top portion */
        TileTop += (MAP_HEIGHT * TILE_HEIGHT) - MapTop;
    }
    else {
        /* it's in the upper half of the screen so do this */
        /* like the simple case */
        TileTop -= MapTop;
    }
}


/* figure out the other coordinates relative to screen */
TileBottom = TileTop + TILE_HEIGHT - 1;
TileLeft   = x * TILE_WIDTH;

/* if the tile is completely off screen, don't draw it */
if (TileBottom < 0 || TileTop >= REDUCED_SCREEN_HEIGHT)
    return;

/* draw the tile */
BltVideoMemNoTransparent(Tile[Map[x][y]], TileLeft, TileTop,
    Offset);

/* only duplicate tiles when we draw a new row on the screen */
/* as it scrolls, not for dirty tiles */
if (!Dup)
    return;

/* if the tile was drawn in the duplicate region, draw it toward */
/* the end of video memory as well so the screen will be correct */
```

```
    /* when the screen offset is reset */
    DuplicateTop    = MemTop + TileTop;
    if (DuplicateTop < DUPLICATE_REGION_LINE) {
        /* convert DuplicateTop to screen location relative to */
        /* SCREEN_TOP_REINIT_LINES */
        DuplicateTop -= SCREEN_TOP_MIN;
        BltVideoMemNoTransparent(Tile[Map[x][y]], TileLeft, DuplicateTop,
            SCREEN_TOP_REINIT_BYTES);
    }
}
```

If **DrawTile** finds that the given tile is outside the bounds of the current page, it doesn't bother drawing it. It can be the case that a sprite has moved into the vertical border region at the bottom of the screen, for instance; and although a tile is dirty, it is below the bottom of the screen and no longer needs to be redrawn. **DrawTile** skips these tiles in order to save time.

Finally, **DrawTile** takes care of drawing a tile in the reinitialize region if it is also being drawn in the duplication region and the **Dup** parameter is TRUE. This ensures that a copy of the duplication region exists in the reinitialize region, so no copying will have to be done when a display page reaches the top of video memory and the Start Address register must be reinitialized.

Dup is TRUE only when **DrawTile** is called from the **ScrollScreen** function, described in the next section. In this case, scroll screen is exposing another row of tiles, and so we need to make sure that the reinitialization region is updated with those new tiles. **Dup** is always **FALSE** when **DrawTile** is called from **RedrawDirtyTiles**. Dirty tiles have already been drawn on a given display by the **ScrollScreen** function, and so the reinitialization region already has a copy of them. Not copying a dirty tile to the reinitialization region saves time.

Scrolling the Screen

After all the sprites have been erased, the animation loop in **Play** calls **ScrollScreen**, shown in Listing 13.10, to change the variables associated with the hidden page. **ScrollScreen** manipulates the **MemLine**, **MapLine**, and **PageOffset** variables to scroll the screen. **ScrollScreen** does not actually set the Start Address register. The Start Address register is set in the **PageFlip** function to the value stored in the **PageOffset** variable for the hidden page.

Listing 13.10 The ScrollScreen Function

```
/*
    Function: ScrollScreen
    Description:
        Scrolls the hidden page up a few lines and draws the next row
        of tiles above, if necessary. Moves the screen.
*/
void ScrollScreen(void)
{
    int OldMapRow;
    int NewMapRow;

    /* move the page toward the start of video memory */
    MemLine[HiddenPage] -= SCROLL_DISTANCE;
    PageOffset[HiddenPage] -= SCREEN_WIDTH_BYTES * SCROLL_DISTANCE;
    if (MemLine[HiddenPage] < SCREEN_TOP_MIN) {
        /* hidden page is too close to top, so move it */
        /* toward the end of video memory */
        MemLine[HiddenPage] = SCREEN_TOP_REINIT_LINES -
            (SCREEN_TOP_MIN - MemLine[HiddenPage]);
        PageOffset[HiddenPage] = MemLine[HiddenPage] * SCREEN_WIDTH_BYTES;
    }

    /* move the screen up in the map */
    OldMapRow         = MapLine[HiddenPage] / TILE_HEIGHT;
    MapLine[HiddenPage] -= SCROLL_DISTANCE;
    if (MapLine[HiddenPage] < 0) {
        /* we've wrapped on the map */
        MapLine[HiddenPage] = (MAP_HEIGHT * TILE_HEIGHT) +
            MapLine[HiddenPage];
    }
    NewMapRow         = MapLine[HiddenPage] / TILE_HEIGHT;
    if (OldMapRow != NewMapRow) {
        /* the top of the screen is in a new row of tiles, so */
        /* draw it */
        DrawNewMapRow(NewMapRow, MapLine[HiddenPage], MemLine[HiddenPage],
            PageOffset[HiddenPage]);
    }
}
```

After manipulating the **MemLine** variable for the hidden page, **ScrollScreen** checks to see if the display page is too close to the start of video memory. If so, it sets **MemLine** and **PageOffset** to point to the reinitialization region. After manipulating **MapLine**, **ScrollScreen** checks to see if the top of the screen has entered another row of tiles. If so, it calls **DrawNewMapRow**, shown in Listing 13.11.

DrawNewMapRow simply calls **DrawTile** for each tile in the given row. **DrawNewMapRow** sets **DrawTile**'s **Dup** parameter to **TRUE** to cause

DrawTile to copy the tile to the reinitialization region if the current page is positioned in the duplication region.

Listing 13.11   The DrawNewMapRow Function

```
/*
    Function: DrawNewMapRow
    Description:
        Draws a new set of tiles at the top of the map as the
        screen moves up.
*/
void DrawNewMapRow(int Row, int MapTop, int MemTop, UINT16 Offset)
{
    int i;

    for (i = 0; i < MAP_WIDTH; i++) {
        DrawTile(i, Row, MapTop, MemTop, Offset, TRUE);
    }
}
```

Adding Speed Control

After adding the scrolling bitmap to *Alien Alley*, I noticed that the animation frame rate was quite unpredictable. Sometimes it was very snappy and other times it was rather slow. When there was a lot of action on the screen and the music and sound effects were playing, the frame rate would drop considerably. It was clear that I needed to add speed control to even out the frame rate. I decided to use two techniques—one for when sound is enabled and the other for when it is not.

The speed control code is at the end of the animation loop in **Play**, shown in Listing 13.12. Unfortunately, MidPak reprograms the system timer for its MIDI playback, so I couldn't use the vertical retrace synchronization routines we developed in Chapter 10.

Does that mean we have to resort to using a counter loop to slow things down? No. There is an alternative. MidPak reprograms the system timer to a 120 Hz rate. It keeps a count of the number of ticks that have occurred since it was initialized. On each pass through the animation loop, we record the value of this tick count. On the next pass through the loop, after we flip pages, we wait until the tick count indicates a certain time has elapsed. When MidPak has been installed, the delay loop makes sure that each animation frame takes at least 4/120 of a second, which means that about every other vertical retrace is skipped. The specific code from **Play** is shown in Listing 13.12.

Listing 13.12   The Speed Control Code from the Play Function

```
/* delay a bit */
if (SoundPresent) {
    /* make sure each frame takes at least 4/120 = 2/60 of */
    while (*Clock < OldClock + 4);
}
else {
    /* No MidPak, so wait 2/70 of a second, minimum */
    while (*Clock < OldClock + 2);
}
OldClock = *Clock;
```

Even when the sound drivers have not been initialized, the delay code uses a similar technique. The system timer is reprogrammed to generate an interrupt at a rate of 70 Hz, the refresh rate of Mode Y. The code uses a simple timer interrupt service routine, **ClockInterrupt**, shown in Listing 13.13, to increment a global long integer variable. See the **Play** function in Listing 13.2 for more detail about how the timer is reprogrammed and how the interrupt service routine is installed and removed.

Listing 13.13   The ClockInterrupt Function

```
/*
    Function: ClockInterrupt
    Description:
        Simply increments the TickCount variable every 1/70th of
        a second when MidPak is not loaded.
*/
void interrupt ClockInterrupt(void)
{
    TickCount++;
    outportb(PIC, NONSPECIFIC_EOI);
}
```

When MidPak has not been installed, the delay code makes sure that each animation frame takes at least 2/70 of a second. This ensures that at least one vertical retrace is skipped and that the game never runs faster than 35 frames per second.

A FAREWELL

Well, that's it. We're finished! Over the past few hundred pages we've learned a lot about game programming. We've examined the various input devices that the PC supports. We've learned about the VGA and how to draw bitmaps rapidly with bitblt functions. We've learned about animation and explored several different techniques to produce it. We've learned about palette fades and collision testing and speed control. Finally, we've developed a whole game and added music, sound effects, and a scrolling background to it.

Alien Alley may seem like a simple game, and that's because it is. It doesn't have much gameplay to it. It gets repetitive fairly quickly, and it may not even be the sort of game you'd like to develop for yourself. But *Alien Alley* demonstrates all the techniques that we've seen in the previous chapters and should serve as a good reference for you as you develop your own games.

I hope that you've found an appreciation of the art of game programming and, at the same time, found that it isn't as difficult as it first appeared. As I said at the beginning of this book, there is no way I could write down everything about game programming. There are so many different types of games and special techniques that go along with them. Some of them are still secrets of the programmers who wrote them. Game programming is never static, but now you've got the basics and should be able to investigate and learn other techniques without much trouble.

Relax, code well, and by all means have fun. Goodbye and good luck.

GAME PROGRAMMING RESOURCES

Game programming is hard work. Unless you have a lot of time on your hands, you won't be able to develop all the tools you'll need to write your next masterpiece yourself. This section lists a number of libraries, toolkits, editors, and other resources to help you get your game completed.

The programs, tool kits, and libraries listed fall into three categories: freeware, shareware, and commercial. Be sure you know the difference and adhere to all the license terms of each of the products. In particular, if you find a shareware tool useful, *register it!* It's a lot easier to send someone $20 for a simple tool that you find useful than to develop it yourself.

Freeware and shareware programs can be found on the online services listed in this appendix. Files can be found on CompuServe using the CompuServe search facilities. Files can be found on the Internet using the "Archie" service. Consult one of the many Internet books available for more information about using Archie.

Many of the freeware and shareware programs listed here embed revision numbers into their archive filenames. By the time you read this, newer revisions of the programs may be available. Try searching only for the basename of the program. For instance, if the archive was named "ARCADE21.ZIP," this might indicate revision 2.1 of the ARCADE graphics library. Try searching for just "ARCADE" to ensure that you find "ARCADE22.ZIP," revision 2.2, if it's available.

GRAPHICS LIBRARIES
XLIB

XLIB is a freeware Mode X graphics library created by Themie Gouthas and Matthew MacKenzie. XLIB supports both Mode X and Mode Y as well as other higher-resolution, 256-color "tweaked" modes. XLIB is written in 286 assembly language and contains primitives for lines, rectangles, bitblts, and more. All source code is provided and may be used without charge.

Filename: XLIB06.ZIP

YakIcons

YakIcons is a freeware C++ class library for game programming written by Victor Putz. YakIcons uses XLIB (previous page) as its base and layers an object-oriented set of primitives above it. The C++ classes allow you to draw sprites and perform animation while hiding a lot of the details.

Filename: YICONS24.ZIP

Fastgraph

Fastgraph is a commercial graphics library from Ted Gruber Software. Fastgraph has been used by many game programmers to produce commercial products and supports many video modes and graphics primitives. It has routines to draw text and deal with the various input devices including the mouse, joystick, and keyboard. Fastgraph costs $349. Check the BBS for a demo.

Ted Gruber Software
P.O. Box 13408
Las Vegas, NV 89112
(702) 735-1980
BBS: (702) 796-7134

GRAPHICS EDITORS
IMPROCES

IMPROCES is a shareware, 256-color graphics editor written by John Wagner. IMPROCES supports the creation of full-screen artwork in standard Mode 13h resolution (320x200) and many other "tweaked" resolutions, including Mode X (320x240). This is one of the few editors that supports "non-standard" VGA modes. IMPROCES supports many graphics primitives, "fat-bit" editing, and an extensive palette editor. Further, "IMPROCES" stands for "image processor," and IMPROCES includes many graphical digital effects filters that can be used to sharpen, blur, or create other special effects.

Filename: IMPROC42.ZIP

NeoPaint

NeoPaint is a shareware graphics image editor from OSCS Software Development, Inc. NeoPaint supports editing of multiple images at the same time in resolutions as high as 1024x768 but does not support Mode X or other "tweaked" modes. Many graphics primitives are supported including rectangles, elipses, polygons, and Bezier lines. NeoPaint can output images in PCX, GIF, and TIFF format.

Filename: NEOPNT22.ZIP

SOUND LIBRARIES
DigPak/MidPak

DigPak/MidPak is a commercial sound toolkit supporting both digital effects and MIDI music from The Audio Solution. DigPak/MidPak were used to create the sound effects and music in *Alien Alley*. The companion disk contains a stripped down version of the toolkit. DigPak/MidPak is $1,000 for use in commercial products and free for non-commercial use. Call the BBS to retrieve the full archive, named DMKIT.ZIP.

The Audio Solution
747 Napa Lane
St. Charles, MO 63304
BBS: (314) 939-0200

Worx

Worx is a sound toolkit from Mystic Software. Worx costs $79 and is royalty free. Worx+ costs $199 and offers expanded capabilities. Check the BBS for a demo.

Mystic Software Inc.
1504 Encinal Avenue, Suite D
Alameda, CA 94501
(510) 865-9189
BBS: (510) 865-3856

SOUND EDITORS
Cool Edit

A shareware program written by David Johnston. Cool Edit is a Microsoft™ Windows™ program that allows you to edit, record, and playback WAV files.

Cool Edit contains many special effects filters and processing options and can generate various types of waveforms. Cool Edit is very full featured.

Filename: COOL131.ZIP

WAVE for Windows

WAVE for Windows™ is a commercial digital sound editor for Microsoft Windows from Turtle Beach Systems. WAVE for Windows allows you to edit, record, playback, and convert between different sound formats. WAVE for Windows has many types of digital effects such as flanging and echo and can mix multiple waveforms together. Wave for Windows was used to create the sound effects in Alien Alley.

Turtle Beach Systems
52 Grumbacher Road
York, PA 17402
(717) 764-5265

ARTISTS AND COMPOSERS

AIR Design — Kevin Long

Kevin is the graphic artist who created the artwork in *Alien Alley*. Kevin can be reached at:

AIR Design
3354 N.E. 83rd Ave
Portland, OR 97220
Voice Mail:　800-223-3737x594
Email:　air@netcom.com

James Black

Jim Black composed the rousing musical score for *Alien Alley*. Jim can be reached at:

J. Black
PO Box 11740
Denver, CO 80211-0740
Email:　jblack@csn.org

Online Info

"No man is an island entire of itself; every man is a piece of the Continent, a part of the main ..." — John Donne

This is as true today as when John Donne wrote it in 1624, and especially so with game programmers. The key things that game programmers need are access to information and a place to talk over ideas. With the networking capabilities that exist today, there is no reason you should have to work in isolation. The online services below are a great way to get connected to your game programming peers and get access to freeware and shareware tools and libraries.

Internet Newsgroups

The Internet is growing like wildfire. One of the most-used services on the Internet is network news. Network news groups operate like distributed, networked, BBS discussion forums. There are many topics available, each separated into its own group. The whole rec.games.* hierarchy is devoted to discussing games of many categories. Although most of the news groups under this hierarchy are about game playing, rec.games.programmer is specifically about game programming. You can discuss all manner of game development, including programming methods, plot and storyline development, and specific issues and problems you're facing.

Internet FTP Sites

Many freeware and shareware programs and toolkits related to game programming can be found on the Internet, including those programs mentioned previously. To retrieve files on the Internet, use FTP, the File Transfer Protocol. Because the Internet is composed of many, many machines spread all over the earth, sometimes it's a bit hard to find the files you're looking for. To find a specific file, use the Archie catalog service. Details about FTP and Archie can be found in many recent Internet books or from your service provider. To get an idea of some of the great stuff on the Internet, you should pick up a copy of Patrick Vincent's book, *Free $tuff from the Internet*, Coriolis Group Books, ISBN 1-883577-11-X. The following sites are golden nuggets for game programmers, however.

x2ftp.oulu.fi

Directory of interest: /pub/msdos/programming.

X2ftp holds a lot of game-related utilities, toolkits, and example source code. This is one of the primary places to look for freeware and shareware programs, including some of the programs mentioned above.

Note that this site is in Finland! Say "Hi" to Jouni Miettunen, the creator and maintainer of this site, if you see him on rec.games.programmer. You gotta love the 'net!

wuarchive.wustl.edu

Directories of interest: /pub/MSDOS_UPLOADS/ and /systems/ibmpc/simtel.

Wuarchive is one of the largest FTP archive sites on the Internet. Wuarchive allows 250 anonymous FTP users to be logged in at one time and you still may find your connection attempts rejected because of the load. If you find Wuarchive busy, just try back in a minute or so.

SIMTEL (oak.oakland.edu)

Directories of interest: /SimTel/msdos

SIMTEL is another of the larger FTP sites. It is mirrored on many sites (Wuarchive, for instance), and snapshots of its contents can even be found on CD-ROM.

CompuServe

CompuServe has a game programming discussion group in the Gamer's Forum. Use "GO GAMERS" to get there. Many noted game developers and book authors can be found hanging out in this forum.

USEFUL BOOKS

In the introduction of this book, I mentioned that game programming is one of those areas where a lot of knowledge comes together. This bibliography lists some of the books that I have found useful over the years to get some of that knowledge. After each citation, I've included a statement or two about the contents of the book and my thoughts on it.

1. Abrash, Michael, *Zen of Code Optimization*, Coriolis Group Books, Scottsdale, Arizona, 1994, ISBN 1-883577-03-9. A great book about optimizing code for the x86 family of processors—teaches when to optimize as well as how. If you need to go in and hand-craft a critical routine, this is the book to have close by.

2. Abrash, Michael, *Zen of Graphics Programming*, Coriolis Group Books, Scottsdale, Arizona, 1995, ISBN 1-883577-08-X. This book wasn't published by the time my book went to press, but I was fortunate enough to see advance page proofs. If you do any 2-D or 3-D graphics programming, you'll want to have this book by your side.

3. Ferraro, Richard F., *Programmer's Guide to the EGA and VGA Cards*, 2nd ed., Addison-Wesley Publishing Company, Inc., Reading, Massachusetts, 1990, ISBN 0-201-57025-4. This book is about twice as long as it has to be. It covers material that doesn't belong in a VGA reference. It is poorly organized, redundant, and has a considerable number of errors. Still, it's the most complete VGA reference I've seen and even covers many of the popular SVGA chipsets.

4. Gruber, Diana, *Action Arcade Adventure Set*, Coriolis Group Books, Scottsdale, Arizona, 1994, ISBN 1-883577-06-3. This is a new book that gives you a set of tools (visual game editor, game engine, artwork, and so on) for creating your own action arcade-style games. It's a well-written book by one of the leaders in the game development industry.

5. Hummel, Robert L., *PC Magazine Programmer's Technical Reference: The Processor and Coprocessor*, Ziff-Davis Press, Emeryville, California, 1992, ISBN 1-56276-016-5. A great reference book about the x86 family of processors. It details the various instructions, their timing and encodings, and covers both 32-bit protected-mode as well as 16-bit real mode.

6. McConnell, Steve, *Code Complete: A Practical Handbook of Software Construction*, Microsoft Press, Redmond, Washington, 1993, ISBN 1-55615-484-4. A great book about software design, coding practices, and other sorts of issues that you don't usually think about. Even if you've been programming for years, get this book—you'll still learn something.

7. Tennenbaum, Aaron M., *Data Structures Using Pascal*, 2nd ed., Prentice-Hall Inc., Englewood Cliffs, New Jersey, 1981, ISBN 0-13-196668-5. What can I say—everybody's gotta have a book of this type around somewhere. There are others just as good. This happens to be mine.

8. Williams, Al, *DOS 5: A Developer's Guide: Advanced Programming Guide to DOS*, M&T Publishing, Inc., Redwood City, California, 1991, ISBN 1-55851-179-2. A good all-around book for those working with the MS-DOS environment. It introduces DOS and BIOS interrupts, graphics programming, TSRs, and some other more advanced topics.

INDEX

READ THE MAGAZINE OF TECHNICAL EXPERTISE!

Published by The Coriolis Group

For years, Jeff Duntemann has been known for his crystal-clear, slightly-bemused explanations of programming technology. He's one of the few in computer publishing who has never forgotten that English is the one language we all have in common. Now he's teamed up with author Keith Weiskamp and created a magazine that brings you a selection of readable, practical technical articles six times a year, written by himself and a crew of the very best technical writers working today. Michael Abrash, Tom Swan, Jim Mischel, Keith Weiskamp, David Gerrold, Brett Glass, Michael Covington, Peter Aitken, Marty Franz, Jim Kyle, and many others will perform their magic before your eyes, and then explain how *you* can do it too, in language that you can understand.

If you program under DOS or Windows in C, C++, Pascal, Visual Basic, or assembly language, you'll find code you can use in every issue. You'll also find essential debugging and optimization techniques, programming tricks and tips, detailed product reviews, and practical advice on how to get your programming product finished, polished and ready to roll.

Don't miss another issue—subscribe today!

☐ 1 Year $21.95   ☐ 2 Years $37.95

☐ $29.95 Canada; $39.95 Foreign   ☐ $53.95 Canada; $73.95 Foreign

Total for subscription: _____
Arizona orders please add 6% sales tax: _____
Total due, in US funds:_____

Send to:
PC TECHNIQUES
7339 E. AcomaDr., Suite 7
Scottsdale AZ 85260

Name _____
Company _____
Address _____
City/State/Zip _____
Phone _____

Phone
(602) 483-0192
Fax
(602) 483-0193

VISA/MC # _____   Expires: _____

Signature for charge orders: _____

CORIOLIS GROUP BOOKS
Order Form

Name _____

Company _____

Address _____

City/State/Zip _____

Phone _____

VISA/MC # _____ Expires: _____

Signature for charge orders: _____

Quantity	Description	Unit price	Extension
	Free Stuff From the Internet	$19.99 U.S.	
	Action Arcade Adventure Set	$39.95 U.S.	
	Mosaic Explorer (Available 12/94)	$34.99 U.S.	
	FAX, Phone, or send this order form to:	**TOTAL**	

The Coriolis Group
7339 E. Acoma Drive, Suite 7
Scottsdale, AZ 85260

FAX us your order at (602) 483-0193
Phone us your order at (800) 410-0192